AS EASY AS PIE

$4.00

11/15

BOOKS BY SUSAN G. PURDY

AS EASY AS PIE

Susan G. Purdy

DRAWINGS BY SIDONIE CORYN
DIAGRAMS BY THE AUTHOR

COLLIER BOOKS
Macmillan Publishing Company · New York

Collier Macmillan Canada · Toronto

Maxwell Macmillan International
New York · Oxford · Singapore · Sydney

Lines from "Shoo-Fly Pie and Apple Pan Dowdy" by Guy Wood and
Sammy Gallop used by permission of Warock Corp.

Extract from *The Roman Cookery Book* by Apicius, edited and
translated by Barbara Flowers and E. Rosenbaum, used by
permission of the publisher, Harrap Limited.

Collier Books
Macmillan Publishing Company
866 Third Avenue, New York, NY 10022

Collier Macmillan Canada, Inc.
1200 Eglinton Avenue East, Suite 200
Don Mills, Ontario M3C 3N1

Library of Congress Cataloging-in-Publication Data

Purdy, Susan Gold.
    As easy as pie / by Susan G. Purdy ; drawings by Sidonie Coryn ;
diagrams by the author.—1st Collier Books ed.
        p.   cm.
    Reprint. Originally published: From basic apple to four and
twenty blackbirds it's as easy as pie. 1st ed. New York : Atheneum,
1984.
    ISBN 0-02-036080-0
    1. Pies.   I. Title.
TX773.P98   1990
641.8′652—dc20   90-1786   CIP

Designed by Kathleen Carey

First Collier Books Edition 1990

Printed in the United States of America

BOMC offers recordings and compact discs, cassettes
and records. For information and catalog write to
BOMR, Camp Hill, PA 17012.

With Thanks . . .

For encouraging me to write this book in the first place, I want to thank my husband, Geoffrey, who with our daughter Cassandra enthusiastically participated in several years of pie eating and recipe testing. For introducing me in the first place to all the arts—including the art of creative baking—I am grateful to my mother and father, Frances Joslin Gold and Harold A. Gold. For generously sharing family recipes with me, I thank my sister, Nancy G. Lieberman, my aunts Phoebe Vernon, Sesyle Joslin Hine, Bea Joslin, and the latter's mother, the late Bessie Fierstein. For suggesting literary quotations, I thank Alexandra Hine and my mother-in-law, Lucille Purdy. For skillful organizing and editing, I am indebted to Judith Kern. For encouragement and good-natured counsel, I want to thank my literary agent, Jonathan Dolger. For thoughtful advice throughout the development of this project, I particularly thank Nancy Nicholas, friend and editor. For sharing their expertise in the field of fine baking, I am indebted to Nada Gerovac of Nada's Dubrovnik Restaurant, Fort Lauderdale, Florida; Mary Risley and Diane Dexter of Tante Marie's Cooking School, San Francisco, California; Albert Jorant, Chef-Pâtissier of l'École de Cuisine La Varenne, Paris, France; and Leo Silverman, Pastry Chef at the Culinary Institute of America, Hyde Park, New York. I also want to thank Chef Silverman for consulting with me on the technical information contained in the introductory chapters.

Perhaps the biggest thank-you of all goes to all friends, relatives, neighbors, and food professionals who have tasted, tested, and/or shared recipes and pies, given me the benefit of their culinary judgment, and are still willing to visit our home again even though a "test" pie will most probably be on the menu. Most of you I have thanked in person, though a formal "thank you" is gratefully extended to all, including Charley Kanas, Thérèse and Robin Davies, Dick Parks and Jim Garland, Elizabeth MacDonald, Joan Moore, Diana de Vries, Michele Peasley, Barbara W. Cover, E. Barrie Kavash, Kathleen and Howard Bronson, Seth Kincaid Bredbury, Olga and Wilhelm Dichter, Marylois and Carlos Vega, Hugh Bareiss, Amelia and Tim Fritz, Roger Sweatt, Mrs. Ruth Lawrence, David and Delia Lawrence, Andy Schiltz, Sandra Calder Davidson, Frances and Wally Sheper of Franni's, Montreal, Québec, Michael Stern, Michael La Croix of Michael's Restaurant, Derby Line, Vermont, Mr. Phil Gargan, Mrs. Ruth Henderson, owner of the Silo Cooking School in New Milford, Connecticut, and the students in my pastry and pie-making classes at this school (with special thanks to Ruth for allowing publicity photographs to be taken in the school kitchen). Faculty, children, and parents of the Washington, Connecticut, Montessori School, including Mrs. Shelia Secor, and Mrs. Dede Ely-Singer; Dick Gackenback and C. O. Godwin, the late Maria Peterdi, Mrs. Mary Katsiaficas and Mrs. Elpis Kertiles; Yves Atlanti, chef of the Restaurant Muscadin, Azay le Rideau, France; M. Gaudin, Pâtisserie-Confiserie, Fougères, Normandie, France; M. Apolda, Boulangerie-Pâtisserie, Azay le Rideau, France; Chef Harvey Edwards, Café du Bec Fin, Old Greenwich, Connecticut; and Tony and Mina Ferreira, The Portuguese Bakery, Provincetown, Massachusetts. For careful work and ingenious setups in creating the jacket for this book, I thank photographer Bob Rush. For her skillful drawings on pages 39, 42, 44, 45, 46, 47, 48 (curled lattice), 50, 53, 190 (complete Fruit Flower Tart), and 368–371, I thank Sidonie Coryn.

CONTENTS

AS EASY AS PIE

INTRODUCTION

"I love you as New Englanders love pie" wrote Don Marquis in his *Sonnets to a Red-haired Lady.* "Pie in the sky," "as American as apple pie," "apple pie and motherhood"—pie quotations and clichés are as thick as berries in a homemade pie, and with good reason: They ring true. If a vote were taken, pie would be (and in many places has been) chosen hands down as the all-time great national dessert, with apple as the favorite flavor. Yet, oddly enough, when you ask most adults if they bake their own pies or whose pie they prefer, their response is often a nostalgic, even wistful "Grandmother's."

Beloved, but never baked! Homemade pies of all flavors are on their way to becoming a lost art, and for a pleasure that is so close to our hearts (and stomachs), this takes on the proportions of a national disaster. It is my premise that pies are easy and fun to make, and anyone can do it. By "pies," I refer not only to two-crust so-called American-style pies, but also to tarts, strudel, pastry-wrapped hors d'oeuvre—in fact, to nearly any food enveloped in pastry. This book is not meant to be the ultimate pie recipe collection; rather, it is a selection of personal and student-tested favorites presented with the hope of restoring the art of pie and pastry baking to the everyday repertoire of the home baker. And recognizing that the home baker's time is more limited today than ever before, this book offers shortcuts, tips, and freezing aids that make baking a practicable skill.

As Easy As Pie came about in response to the questions and problems raised in the pastry and pie-baking classes I teach at the Silo Cooking School in New Milford, Connecticut. Almost with one voice, my beginner students implore: "I can't [or I hate to] make piecrust." "I'm afraid to handle pastry dough." Those with slightly more experience say, "I need recipes that are quick and easy to prepare but elegant enough to serve at dinner parties." Working men and women with little free time ask, "What can I keep in the freezer for last-minute impromptu desserts?" And *everyone* wants to know: "Why is my piecrust tough?" "Why does my crust shrink when baked?" "Why doesn't my puff pastry rise [or strudel stretch] enough?"

To find the answers to these and other related questions, and to fine-tune my own techniques, I have gone back to school myself—to more classes at the Cordon Bleu in Paris and to intensive study at l'École de Cuisine La Varenne in the same city, where I worked with Chef-Pâtissier Albert Jorant. At the Culinary Institute of America, I sought out Pastry Chef Leo Silverman to answer many technical questions. What I learned from these men, who gave generously of their time and experience, as well as from other chefs, bakers, cookbook writers, and home bakers, reinforced what I already knew—that pastry making is an art form, and like all art forms, it is built on a foundation of techniques that *can* be learned. It is not magic. Sure, there is the added fillip of talent, flair, and creativity—but these come in large measure from experience. The basics are there to be shared, and *you* can enjoy them, too.

In addition to studying, I have traveled in Europe and the United States talking to and collecting recipes from home cooks as well as pastry chefs in restaurants and bakeries. I have visited libraries, read scores of cookbooks, and delved deeper into my own recipe collection, gathered over some twenty years of baking, teaching, and writing books (including five cookbooks) and food and travel articles. At the present time I am the food writer for *Suburbia Today*, a Sunday magazine published by Gannett Publications for nine newspapers in Westchester and Rockland counties, New York. For this weekly column of food lore and recipes, I research all manner of edibles. Drawing on this background, I have tried to introduce in *As Easy As Pie* a wide variety of recipes and to give the practical reasons behind the techniques used.

These kitchen-tested recipes include both sweet and savory pastries, and range from old-fashioned country kitchen favorites to chic classical confections, the whole leavened by a measure of original and unusual treats for family fare as well as easy entertaining. Each recipe is introduced by notes explaining whether it is quick and easy or requires more skill and time. Advance preparation and timing notes will help you plan ahead for carefree serving. I suggest that you read through a recipe entirely before beginning, in order to plan intelligently your use of pantry supplies, time, and energy.

I have attempted to maintain in my writing the informal yet informative tone of my baking classes. Rather than assume my reader has advanced skills, I have broken down the recipes into step-by-step procedures that will guide the beginner yet produce professional results for the experienced baker as well. I hope you will not be put off by the length of some of the recipes, such as those for

Puff Pastry or Strudel. Length of recipe is not a measure of difficulty, but rather an indication that in some cases, for the sake of clarity, I have provided a more thorough explanation.

Following the pattern of my classes, I have addressed piecrust and pastry dough as the first order of business. I have explained the function and interaction of ingredients so one can understand the *whys* of baking as well as the *hows*. I suggest that the beginner master these introductory chapters and techniques before experimenting with the other pastry recipes that are included in the Pastry Recipe Collection. These recipes are referred to by title in the main recipe sections that follow. The recipe chapters are divided by types of pastry—that is, fruit and berry pies, chiffon pies, custard and cream pies, cobblers, etc. Blackberries, for example, may appear in several chapters, used in pies and tarts as well as cobblers. To find a complete list of recipes using a particular ingredient (such as blackberries) look in the index.

I hope you will dip into this collection, taste here and there, and find to your delight that you *really can* make a light, flaky piecrust, a high-rising puff pastry, and a sturdy Cornish Pasty—and that sharing these skills with those you love to bake for gives you as much pleasure as it gives me.

Whenever possible, I have tried to give credit for recipes where credit is due. Although it was sometimes impossible to determine the exact origin of pies contributed by friends or handed down through my family, I have done my best to research sources and have never knowingly used another baker's recipe without acknowledging the fact. Some pies that are in the traditional pastry repertoire I have made my own by adding personal touches. Nevertheless there are limits; there are only so many changes you can make to an apple pie before you have a pizza.

The History of Pies

As long as men have gathered grains and herbs, they have satisfied their hunger with various forms of flat baked dough—the ancestor of our modern pies. Stone Age men pounded nuts and wild grains with rocks, mixed a paste with water, and made a type of porridge. Later, this crude batter was baked into flat cakes on hot stones over fire. At first, seeds, oils, nuts, and dried fruits were used to flavor this dough. There exist many Biblical descriptions of such flavored flat breads or cakes. Later, as advances in milling techniques produced finer qualities of flour, more elaborate doughs became possible and a wider variety of fillings and flavorings were added. To trace the history of pies, we must follow the evolution of grains and flour from their use in crude peasant breads to the infinite variety of sophisticated pastries we have today.

We know from grain storage bins, bread molds, and bread ovens unearthed at sites in the rich river valley of Mesopotamia, that the baker's craft was an early and essential one. About 7000 B.C., nomads in this area began to form communities, because they had discovered they could cultivate grain. Prior to this, men roamed the land seeking wild wheat grass and barley, the earliest grains, which they reaped and crushed between two flat-faced stones.

Like the peoples of Mesopotamia, Egyptians cultivated grain in their river delta. The Nile's annual flooding left soil rich enough for growing the grain crops that formed the basis of the Egyptian economy. The stock of grain represented the country's national wealth, and workers' wages were paid in bread and beer. In fact, historians date the first strike on record as occurring in Egypt about 1100 B.C. when bread rations were withheld from farm laborers. The Egyptians' bread was a flat loaf called *ta,* made from a barley sourdough that the baker kneaded with his feet. Occasionally, flat loaves of *ta* were mixed with sesame seeds or honey for flavoring, and large cone-shaped loaves were placed in tombs for the final journey of the dead. *Ta* is the direct ancestor of our piecrust, as well as the Mexican tortilla, the Scottish oatcake, the Middle Eastern pita, and the Italian pizza.

From one civilization to the next, advances in milling technology produced refinements in flours, changing the staple supplies available and thus influencing the types of bread and pastry man could bake. After the crude rock pounding of wild grains by Stone Age man and the rubbing together of two flat-faced stones, the Egyptians' saddle-stone mill was a great improvement. It was a grooved flat rock that held grain while a stone rolling pin was pushed over it by hand. This is the type of mill still used in Mexico for grinding corn flour for tortillas. The Greeks improved on this with a device of two flat stones worked by the movement of a lever. The Greek miller using this fairly sophisticated device even had a flutist to provide a musical accompaniment. With this new type of mill, it was possible to produce a much more refined flour; its nearly white, light texture and the pastry it produced were accomplishments for which the Greeks were justly famous.

Barley was the most popular grain in early Greece, with barley porridge and bread for staples, barley cakes as luxuries, and barley grains scattered as offerings to the gods. Wheat was also used, however, and by Alexander's time it surpassed barley in popularity, as fine delicate pastries, sweets, and breads became a specialized art, and bakers became clearly distinguished from the cookers of meat and poultry. Greek banquets in later periods were lavish entertainments during which perfumed guests wearing wreaths reclined on cushioned beds and watched dancing girls and musicians while they dined on an incredible variety of fish, birds, soups, nuts, fruits, wines, hot rolls (made with finely milled Phoenician flour), sweet cakes, and even a type of cheesecake. Athens was famous for her pastries; at a banquet in this city, one would be offered a selection of molded or layered, baked or fried sweet cakes made with fine dough and seasoned with a variety of seeds, nuts, or wine. The fried cakes were often soaked in honey syrup—the ancestor of today's baklava.

From their political contacts with, and conquests over, the Greeks, the Romans learned of their cooking techniques, among other skills. Everything the Greeks did the Romans did bigger and, sometimes, even better. The Roman aristocracy preferred leavened white bread to the coarse dark breads of the peasants. To this end, they improved upon the Greek grain mills, inventing the rotary mill in the first century B.C., and for the first time, produced refined flour in large quantities. Surviving mills from Pompeii indicate that flour was ground here on an enormous scale, enabling the twenty public bakeries to serve the 20,000 inhabitants of the city with ease.

Roman chefs were highly specialized. A sweetmeat maker or tart baker was not to be confused with the bread baker. Chefs in rich and/or royal homes had virtual armies of slaves at their service, as well as fully equipped kitchens, fruit and vegetable gardens, and larders stuffed with produce from every corner of the Roman Empire. Roman pastry doughs were made of a variety of ingredients, including, for example, one with oat flour, cheese, and honey, and another flavored with wine, milk, olive oil and spices. Though peasants still ate their humble bread, emperors and their countless guests gorged themselves in banquets that lasted for days. The author of history's earliest surviving cookbook, named for Marcus Gavius Apicius, legendary Roman gourmet, describes such events and details some of the pastries, including huge two- and three-crust pies filled with filets of fish, chicken, songbirds, and meat, seasoned with eggs, herbs, wine sauce, and spices. He also lauds whole hams stuffed with honey and figs and baked in pastry crusts. The author himself admits to a weakness for such treats as camels' heels and flamingo tongues, while the Emperor Heliogabalus, two centuries later, preferred cockscombs from live birds and ostrich tongues.

As the Roman Empire spread toward Western Europe, Roman food, drink, plants, edibles, and culinary customs spread as well. Thus, medieval French, Italian, and English cuisines derived directly from the Roman before they began to influence one another. In pastry making especially, the Italians influenced the French, who became so expert in and enamored of the art that by 1270 in Paris, they had established the first trade union of pastry chefs. The French, in turn, influenced the English, both in cooking techniques and cooking vocabulary.

We owe the start of this tradition largely to William the Conqueror, who brought along his French-Norman kitchen staff when he crossed the English Channel in 1066. The rich pastries of the Romans had intrigued the French, as well as the English, and the latter developed them into their own versions of meat pasties, meat and game pies, stews, forcemeats, *herbelades* (minced herb tarts), as well as custards, cakes, and *doucettes* (sweet pies and tartlets). Besides refinements in cooking, the Normans brought to the English their specialized kitchen staffs, including the position of pastry chef. In the great manor houses, he was a most important member of the cooking staff, a creative specialist. In less imposing establishments, however, the pastry chef also had to master general skills, as noted by Chaucer in the Prologue to the *Canterbury Tales*:

> A cook they hadde with hem for the nones [occasion] . . .
> He koude rooste, and sethe, and broille and frye,
> Maken mortreux [stew], and wel bake a pye.

The Normans were great pie bakers and introduced the custom of sending a pie to the king for Christmas (see Fresh Plum Pie, page 139). The favorite court pie of the Normans was made of lamprey, an elongated eel-like fish, and lamprey pie became an honored tradition. It was a favorite of Queen Elizabeth; Queen Victoria so admired it she was given a twenty-pound version. The custom of court pies continued through the centuries, though the contents varied, until 1930 when King George V received one of the last offerings of record, "twenty-four woodcocks baked in a pie," from the Governor-General of the Irish Free State.

Piers Plowman in the fourteenth century describes eating "hote pies" made of chopped meat in rough pastry, and England is often credited as the birthplace of pie as we know it, though in truth the Greeks and Romans preceded them in this art.

Throughout the Middle Ages, as ever, the vast majority of the people were poor and ate grains, crude breads, vegetables, roots, nuts, and whatever meat they could poach. But for the aristocracy, life was a far easier and somewhat more elegant matter. The great halls of feudal manor houses set the stage for banquets that rivaled the Romans'. Typically, cloth-covered groaning boards were spread with all manner of food, served upon relatives of piecrust known as trenchers: slabs or "plates" of coarse bread. (The word comes from Old French *trenchier*, to cut, and our word "trencherman," signifying a hearty eater, stems from this root.) Round or square-cut, trenchers were often colored with herbal paints for decoration, and their purpose was to hold food and absorb gravy; afterward they were tossed to the dogs or fed to servants or the poor. The custom remained popular until the time of Elizabeth I, when earthenware or metal plates were introduced.

Elaborate musical entertainments accompanied these banquets, which were attended by many servants, including butler and carver, cupbearer, and pantler. The pantler was, in fact, one of the primary servants, as he was keeper of the lord's salt and bread. (His title derives from the French word *pain*, bread.) The pantler used special knives to cut the various types of breads, including one reserved for cutting only the upper crust off rolls and breads to be served exclusively to the master. Hence, the origin of the expression denoting those in power: "the upper crust."

As foods were eaten chiefly with the fingers in the Middle Ages, the most popular dishes were those most easily handled, "finger foods" such as bite-sized meat or fruit-filled pastries, dough-wrapped pâtés, breads, individually sized *doucettes* or tartlets, and *coffyns,* or two-crust pies.

With the introduction of household ovens, pastry chefs dreamed up ever more outrageous pastries. Holidays were their showcases. A Christmas banquet, for example, would not fail to provide a swan pie as well as a Grete Pye, consisting of a pastry shell encasing chicken, capon, peacock, game, and small songbirds all roasted, then inserted one into the other like Chinese boxes. Other pies contained stews or cooked mixtures of meats and fruits combined, such as beef with pears, dates, and nuts, or fruit, wine, eggs, and herbs. Some combinations were more imaginative, such as beef, mutton, mallards, woodcocks, marrow, eggs, raisins, prunes, cloves, cinnamon, and saffron.

In addition to creative variety, medieval banquets stressed appearance and illusion in foods. Not only were trenchers painted, but all sorts of edibles were gilded and decorated to create picturesque "subtleties" for the guests' amusement. Unlikely combinations of creatures such as baked pigs and chickens had their carcasses stitched together to create mythological animals. Peacocks were carefully plucked, roasted, boned, then reassembled and refeathered to look as if they were alive when presented at table. In addition, illusion foods were created for spectacles between courses. Pastry chefs strained their ingenuity to devise outrageous pies for this purpose. From the fifteenth through the seventeenth centuries, "animated pyes" were the most popular banquet entertainments. The nursery rhyme "Sing a Song of Sixpence . . . four and twenty blackbirds baked in a pie," refers to such a pie. According to the poem, "When the pie was opened, the birds began to sing/ Wasn't that a dainty dish to set before the King?" In all likelihood, those birds not only sang, but flew briskly out at the assembled guests, as they were live birds tethered inside a prebaked pastry shell. Rabbits, frogs, turtles, other small animals, and even small people were also set into pies, either alone or with birds, to be released when the crust was cut.

At the coronation banquet of Henry VII in 1485, a "goodlie Custard Pye" was served. Four strong men costumed in red and gold liveries carried this enormous pie to the king, who cut the first slice as fifteen pigeons and one hunchbacked dwarf flew out. This event gave rise to what was said to be a favorite joke of Queen Elizabeth's court: that a man too close enmeshed in a woman's charms was like "the dwarf in the pie."

The Elizabethans prepared pork and mutton pies, of the type Piers Plowman earlier described. These were herb-seasoned chopped meats baked in shells of molded hot water paste, sold by street hawkers throughout the countryside. The filling was supposed to be sealed with an aspic or clarified butter to prevent air from spoiling the contents. Disreputable or lazy piemen who neglected this sealer often poisoned their customers. Travelers were warned to be cautious about tasting pies. This led to the implied admonishment in the eighteenth century poem we know as "Simple Simon met a pieman/ Going to the Fair;/ Says Simple Simon to the Pieman,/ 'Let me taste your ware.' "

While the English were perfecting their pies, the Romans were working wonders on flat round pieces of dough, shaping it into plain flat cakes topped by a few seeds and herbs and typically eaten at breakfast. This simple fare is the direct ancestor of pizza as we know it. Pizza, according to Waverley Root in *The Food of Italy,* was invented by the Neapolitans, who ate dough topped with lard, oil, herbs, and cheese long before explorers brought the tomato to Italy from its native Peru. By the seventeenth century, pizza was so popular that the King of Naples, Ferdinand IV, instructed his cook to bake it for him at his summer palace; and in 1889, a Neapolitan chef baked a pizza in honor of Margherita, consort of the first King of All Italy. It featured the colors of the Italian flag: red (tomatoes), white (mozzarella cheese), and green (basil), and became Naples' most famous export to America: pizza Margherita.

Immigrants from other countries brought their own native specialties to our shores. The earliest of these were the Pilgrims, who brought family pie recipes among their meager possessions. The colonists and their pies adapted simultaneously to the ingredients and techniques available to them in the New World. At first, they baked pies with berries and fruits pointed out to them by the Indians. Besides baking fruit pies and tarts as they had in their homelands, sparse new foods were stretched by being encased in pastry shells; sometimes foods were stretched even further by placing them between *two* crusts of dough or topping them with mashed potatoes.

As settlers moved and frontiers pushed westward, American regional pies developed. Molasses-sweetened pies were favored in southern homes near the eastern coastal ports frequented by molasses and rum traders coming from the Caribbean Islands. Northeasterners sweetened their pies with maple syrup, a trick of flavoring they learned from the Indians. Midwestern dairy farmers developed cream-based pies.

While early homemakers baked with the ingredients available on their farms and in their gardens, we have access today to an ever-changing variety of ingredients from around the world. But like our ancestors, we continue to adapt and invent new recipes to suit available ingredients and the changing fashions of food and diet.

The Language of Pies

Just exactly what is a pie? And when is a pie a tart or a croustade? What is the difference between a cottage pie and a cake pie? When is a pie a flan? The answers can be as confusing as the questions, but as all types are mentioned in this book, some attempt at definition must be made.

An American-style *pie* generally is any pastry crust with a sweet or savory filling baked in a shallow round dish with slanted sides. Pies are served from their baking dishes. Open-face pies have no top crust; deep-dish pies have similar fillings to other pies but are baked in deeper plates, lack a bottom crust, and always have an upper crust.

A *tart* is the European cousin of the pie. It generally contains sweetened fruit or preserves or custard filling, though there are savory tart recipes as well; a tart looks like an open-face pie: a filled pastry shell. Sometimes, tarts as well as open-face pies have pastry-strip lattice crusts. European-style tarts are baked in straight-sided rather than slope-sided pans, often with fluted edges. Before serving, tarts are separated from their baking pans, which are formed with removable bottoms to facilitate this procedure. In England and France, the words *tart* and *flan* are used interchangeably, while in America, the *tart* and *flan* are usually called open-face pies. The *flan* is actually named for the round metal disk in which it is baked. It is basically a pastry case containing any one of a variety of fillings, like the tart. However, in Spain and parts of France, a flan also signifies a pudding or molded egg-cream mixture.

The *cake flan* is yet another creature, a cousin of the tart baked with a sponge or Génoise batter instead of pastry. This cake is baked with a depression on top that is filled with glazed fresh fruits. A smooth-sided American-made cake flan pan is called a Mary Ann; the German cake flan pan has fluted sides and is known as an *Obsttortenform* ("fruit tart pan").

A *galette* is literally a round flat French cake. The most widely known galettes in France are made for Twelfth Night celebrations and contain a good luck charm or tiny porcelain statue of Jesus. In the north of France, Twelfth Night galettes are made of puff pastry, while in the south they are baked with yeast dough. However, as long as it is flat, a free-form (as opposed to pan-shaped) fruit tart can also be called a galette.

The term *timbale,* according to *Larousse Gastronomique,* comes from the Arab *thabal* meaning drum, and refers to a receptacle. Originally, timbales were metal or earthenware vessels for food. Today, they may refer to any hot, savory preparation served in a prebaked pie shell with a decorated, glazed pastry top crust molded over a metal form and shaped like a dome.

A *croustade* is like an English pie: a filling baked in a pie plate topped by rolled-out pastry. However, pastry shells made with short or puff pastry can also be known as croustades when topped by savory sauces or stews. A *shepherd's pie* originally was an entrée pie made with lamb, though now it can contain any type of leftover meat or poultry and is usually topped by mashed potatoes rather than a pastry crust. *Cottage pie* is similar to a shepherd's pie. Both, by the way, are similar to the English *hasty pie,* made with leftover meat, potatoes, perhaps a vegetable, bound with gravy, and topped with mashed potatoes.

Pâte is the French word for "paste," meaning dough. *Pâté* refers to a totally enclosed pastry case containing a forcemeat of meat, vegetables, or (less commonly) fruit. A pâté to be strictly correct in daily usage should refer only to a pastry-enclosed meat or fish mixture baked in the oven and served either hot or cold. By contrast, a *terrine* is a similar forcemeat baked *without* a pastry case (usually in an earthenware vessel, also called a terrine), with strips of fat or bacon on top; terrines are served cold only. And while we are in the family, a *galantine* is also forcemeat, a terrine in fact, but baked inside boned poultry.

A Note About the Recipes in This Book

1. All measurements are level.

2. All eggs are U.S. Grade A large (2 ounces).

3. All flour is unbleached all-purpose or regular cake flour, unless otherwise stated.

4. Grated "zest" of orange or lemon refers to the most brightly colored part of the peel; the white pith under the zest can have a bitter flavor and is best not used.

5. All butter is unsalted unless otherwise noted. Do not substitute margarine unless noted in the recipe.

6. In the ingredients list for the recipes, the pastry recipe suggested first is the one I think the most suitable. However, other ideas are also suggested, or you may prefer to select your own recipe from the Pastry Recipe Collection (see page 59).

Measurements and Equivalents

Note that all measurements used in this book are level. All eggs used in recipes in this book are U.S. Grade A large.

1 U.S. grade A large egg	= 2 ounces = 3 tablespoons
1 large egg yolk	= 1 generous tablespoon

1 large egg white	= 2 tablespoons = ⅛ cup
2 large eggs	= scant ½ cup = 3 medium eggs
6 to 7 large yolks	= ½ cup
4 large whites	= ½ cup
3 large whites beaten stiff	= 3 cups meringue, enough to top a 9-inch pie
4 large whites beaten stiff	= 4 cups meringue, enough to top a 9- or 10-inch pie
1 cup heavy (36 to 40 percent butterfat) cream	= 2 cups whipped cream

(*Note:* Store-bought nondairy whipped topping can be substituted for whipped cream.)

1 pound butter	= 2 cups
¼ pound butter	= 1 stick = 8 tablespoons
1 pound unbleached all-purpose flour	= 4 cups, sifted
5 pounds unbleached all-purpose flour	= 20 cups
1 pound cake flour or pastry flour	= 4½ cups plus 2 tablespoons

(*Note:* For flour substitutions, see page 26.)

1 pound granulated sugar	= 2 cups
5 pounds granulated sugar	= 10 cups
1 pound brown sugar	= 2¼ cups, packed
1 pound confectioners' sugar	= 4 to 4½ cups, unsifted
1 pound whole almonds, shelled	= 3 to 3¼ cups
1 cup whole almonds	= 5 ounces
6-ounce package sliced almonds	= 1½ cups
1 pound almonds, ground	= 2⅔ cups
1 pound whole walnuts	= 4 cups
10-ounce package walnuts, shelled, broken	= 2½ cups
1 pound whole pecans, shelled	= 4½ cups
1 pound whole hazelnuts, shelled	= 3¼ cups
1 pound seedless raisins	= 3½ cups
6 ounces semisweet chocolate morsels	= 1 cup
1 ounce regular-sized chocolate morsels	= ⅛ cup = 2 tablespoons
1 ounce chocolate	= 1 square Baker's (premeasured)
12 ounces dried apricots	= 2 cups, packed
1 average size coconut (4-inch diameter)	= 3½ cups grated coconut

4 ounces coconut, dried and flaked or shredded	= 1 scant cup
1 premeasured envelope unflavored gelatin	= 2 teaspoons; to hard-set 2 cups liquid
1 whole lemon	= 2 to 3 tablespoons juice plus 2 to 3 teaspoons grated zest
1 whole orange	= 6 to 8 tablespoons juice plus 2 to 3 tablespoons grated zest
1 large peeled apple (6 ounces whole) or 1 large unpeeled pear (5 ounces)	= 1 generous cup when cored, and sliced = 4 ounces
3 large apples or 3 large pears	= 1 pound = 3 cups sliced ⅛-inch thick = enough to top one 11-inch tart with overlapping slices
5 to 6 medium-large apples or pears	= 5 cups sliced = enough to fill one 9-inch pie
1 medium-sized peach, nectarine, apricot, or plum (3 to 4 ounces)	= ½ cup, pitted and sliced
4 to 5 peaches, nectarines, and plums, or 6 apricots	= 1 pound = 2 to 2½ cups fruit, pitted and sliced ¼-inch thick
6 to 7 peaches, nectarines, and plums or 7 to 8 apricots	= 1½ pounds = 3 to 3½ cups sliced ¼-inch thick = enough to top one 11-inch tart with overlapping slices
2¼ pounds peaches or nectarines	= 5 cups sliced = enough to fill one 9-inch pie
1¾ pounds plums	= 4 to 5 cups = enough to fill one 9-inch pie
1½ to 2 pounds apricots	= 4 cups = enough to fill one 9-inch pie
5 to 6 kiwis (about 3 ounces each)	= 1 pound = 2½ to 3 cups peeled and sliced ⅛-inch thick; you need 6 to 7 kiwis, peeled and sliced, to top one 11-inch tart with overlapping slices
1 quart berries	= 4 cups
4 to 5 cups small fresh berries (blueberries, raspberries, etc.) or 4 cups large fresh berries (strawberries, etc.)	= enough to top one 11-inch tart or fill one 9-inch pie

PASTRY QUANTITY GUIDELINES

Pastry made with 1½ cups flour will make one 2-crust 9-inch pie or one 9-, 10-, or 11-inch pie or tart shell, or eight 2- to 3-inch tartlets or four 4- to 4½-inch tartlets.

Pastry made with 2 cups flour will make one 2-crust 9-inch pie or two 9-inch single crusts or one 10-, 11-, or 12-inch tart shell, or twelve 2- to 3-inch tartlets or six to eight 4- to 4½-inch tartlets.

Pastry made with 3 cups flour will make one 2-crust 10-inch pie, or three 9-inch pie or tart shells, or sixteen 2- to 3-inch tartlets or eight to ten 4- to 4½-inch tartlets.

PIE AND TART SERVING GUIDELINES

8-inch pie	= 4 to 6 slices
9-inch pie	= 6 slices
10-inch pie	= 8 slices
11-inch tart	= 8 to 10 slices

Pastry-Making Critique: Hints and Tips

In general, tips on all phases of pastry making will be found within the chapter describing each process. However, here are a few miscellaneous pointers that will prove very helpful.

1. To keep bottom piecrusts from becoming soggy: Be sure the oven is preheated and the temperature is hot enough (check with an auxiliary oven thermometer hanging inside the oven). Begin baking pies in the lower third of the oven so the greater heat in this area can quickly set the lower crust. Do not underbake pie crust.

Do not add moist filling to piecrust until just before baking, except where directed otherwise in the individual recipe. Do not set the filled pie plate on a cold baking sheet in the oven; if you are using a baking sheet underneath the pie plate, preheat it in the oven.

With moist pie fillings, partially prebake the pie shell before filling or glaze the lower crust with moisture-proofing such as beaten egg glaze or brushed-on fruit preserves; for moist fruit fillings, sprinkle cracker or cereal crumbs over the lower crust before filling.

Cool all pies on a wire rack to prevent moisture condensation on the lower crust as the pie cools.

Butter pie pans; it helps the lower crust to brown.

Use pie plates of Pyrex glass or sturdy anodized aluminum with a dull finish; shiny metal deflects heat and extra-thick pans take longer to absorb heat, causing slow baking.

2. *To prevent shrinking of piecrusts:* Roll dough large enough in the first place so it fits comfortably into its pan. Never pull or stretch dough to fit or it will shrink back during baking.

Chill formed dough until firm before setting into a preheated hot oven. Use auxiliary oven thermometer to monitor temperature.

Do not use excess liquid in mixing dough; this can contribute to shrinking during baking.

Do not bake in too cool an oven; slow baking contributes to shrinking.

3. *To prevent too-fast browning of pastries or top pie crusts:* Cover pastry edges or tops with foil (shiny side up to deflect heat) after the pie has begun to brown; for oddly shaped pastries, make a foil tent (page 25) to set atop the browned area, or use strips of foil.

The more sugar in the dough, the quicker it will tend to darken and burn. Therefore, roll very sweet dough slightly thicker than normal and protect it from overbrowning with a foil edging.

4. *To prevent smoking of pie juices spilled on oven floor:* Sprinkle salt on spilled juice. Or spread a sheet of foil (with edges folded up) on the oven floor before baking. Do not place foil on shelf under pie or it will deflect heat and prevent proper baking.

5. *For ease in handling a removable-bottom tart pan:* Bake on a flat cookie sheet. However, preheat sheet before placing tart upon it; a cold sheet will retard browning of lower crust.

6. *Always use pan size called for in recipe.* Measure pans across top inside diameter.

7. *To form a piecrust that is either too sticky or too crumbly to roll out:* Simply pat it into the pie plate with your fingers. Keep thickness even and avoid overdense corners. Pinch or pat up a lip around the edge. Chill dough before baking. Bake as directed.

8. *To have a handy supply of quickly made pie dough:* Make your own dry mix (page 69) and just add water and flavoring when needed.

9. *To have a handy supply of ready-made piecrusts and fillings:* Make a double or triple batch of pastry while you are at it. Roll out this extra dough into rounds that fit your pie plates, then stack the rounds between layers of *lightly* floured foil and set over a piece of stiff cardboard. Wrap the package airtight with foil, put into a thick plastic bag, label it, and freeze. It only takes a few minutes to defrost one of these sheets of rolled dough and slip it into a pie plate to fill and bake. Or prebake pie shells, wrap, and freeze until needed. Fruit

fillings can also be prepared and formed into appropriate pie-plate shapes, wrapped, and frozen (page 56). When ready to use, simply unwrap a pack of filling and bake it in a premade pie shell.

10. To cut meringue-topped pies with ease: Butter or oil your knife blade.

11. If your pastries are not baking in the stated times or are giving uneven results: Check oven temperature. Put an auxiliary oven thermometer inside the oven and adjust thermostatic setting until the *inner* reading is accurate.

12. To prevent fruit pie juices from leaking out: On a single-crust pie, be sure fluting is high enough to contain all the filling; on a 2-crust pie, be sure top crust edge is sealed over bottom crust edge and that both are sealed together and fluted.

Do not overfill a pie, then stretch crust over it; the stretched crust will surely shrink during baking, and juices will escape. Remember to cut steam vents in the tops of 2-crust pies.

13. To prevent toughening of piecrust: Do not overhandle pastry dough.

Do not use too much flour or too little fat or too much liquid; follow recipe proportions carefully.

14. To patch tears or holes in piecrust: For torn unbaked crusts, brush water or beaten egg over the edges of the tear and press on scraps of rolled dough before baking.

For partially prebaked shells, brush beaten egg or egg white over the cracked area and press on scraps of rolled raw dough; complete baking after the filling is added.

For completely prebaked shells, remove from oven as soon as a crack is visible, brush the crack with beaten egg and patch with some rolled dough scraps. Return shell to oven to complete baking.

15. To measure molasses or honey with ease, first oil the measuring cup.

Equipment

Stripped back to basics, pastry making requires little special equipment other than your hands, a countertop, a rolling pin, a baking sheet or pie plate, and an oven. However, thirty seconds in any cookware shop may convince you that you cannot blend flour and water without an astonishing array of sophisticated gadgetry. Not so. But to be fair, you may want to add a few helpful tools to your list of essentials.

As in all things, your tools can vary from the modest to the lavish. For the art of pastry making, consider function rather than fashion; the oldest materials and methods are often still the best.

WORK SURFACES

Marble, for example, is the oldest, most luxurious, and best work surface for pastry because it retains and transmits cold, chilling the dough and preventing the fat from melting. If you do not have a marble counter, a portable marble slab is handy and can even rest on your refrigerator shelf until needed. Stainless steel and Formica are widely used; both work well and clean easily. Care should be taken, however, as they can easily be scored by a knife. In warm weather, chill these countertops by setting upon them a roasting pan filled with ice water. Wood shares many of the properties of Formica, but is slightly more difficult to clean because of its porosity. Still, the warmth of wood's color lends beauty to any kitchen, and it is a fine surface for the rolling out of dough. A looped plastic scrubbing ball is helpful for lifting off dough bits stuck to wood.

If you plan to do a lot of pastry making, you will save yourself countless backaches if you take pains to adjust your countertop height to your own stature. Extend your arms full length, then lower the palms to the height at which you are most comfortable.

DOUGH-WORKING TOOLS

For general handling of dough, I recommend the one tool I could not work without: a dough scraper, also called a *coupe-pâte,* or dough knife. This is simply a rectangular metal scraper with a wooden handle along one edge. Similar tools are also made in both stiff and flexible plastic, good for scraping dough out of bowls. In general, this is the tool for cutting, kneading, lifting, and scraping dough as well as for cleaning dough off countertops. If need be, substitute a broad pancake turner or a 3- or 4-inch wide putty knife purchased in the hardware store.

Your cool fingertips, as opposed to your warm palms, are the perfect tools for combining flour and fat to make dough. Fingertips are much more sensitive to the nuances of dough than, say, a food processor (although that device has its own advantages). Using your fingertips, you can mix dough in a large mixing bowl, or directly on a countertop, eliminating the need for any bowl at all.

If you prefer a slightly more elaborate scenario, you can keep your hands clean and combine flour and shortening with 2 cross-cutting table knives or a pastry blender made of several wire loops fastened to a handle. Or you can use the electric mixer or food processor. Procedures for each of these devices are given following the basic recipe for Basic All-Purpose Flaky Pastry (page 34). The food processor, used correctly, gets my vote for being the best pastry-making *machine.* It consistently produces a fine product quickly and effortlessly. The speed of the machine not only keeps the dough so cold it can be rolled out without chilling, but forms the dough so quickly that toughening gluten has no time to develop to any significant extent.

SIFTERS

In this book, it is necessary to sift flour only when specified in a particular recipe. You should be aware that pastry and cake flour are milled finer than all-purpose and tend to clump more. Thus, it is best to sift these flours, to aerate and lighten them; I prefer to use a single-layer sifter; the 3-tiered box sifters are impossible to clean and unnecessarily complex. Although many types of flour are labeled presifted, you should sift or not as directed by your recipe. For further details on flour, see pages 26–29.

DOUGH-ROLLING TOOLS

While you can certainly roll out dough with the handle of a broom or the side of a wine bottle, there is a definite ease, elegance, and efficiency to be found in a good rolling pin. It should have a smooth, hardwood, nonabsorbent finish, be well-balanced, and heavy enough to contribute its weight to the rolling and flattening of the dough. At home I use an 18-inch hardwood pin 3½-inch diameter with ball bearing handles. It is heavy and efficient. I do not recommend either porcelain pins, which are too fragile, or glass pins, which hold ice cubes and condense moisture on the outside, making dough damp. American rolling pins have a central wooden cylinder with handles. I prefer handles that turn on ball bearings, a feature that helps in rolling dough to an even thickness. Ordinary French or Italian rolling pins are longer than American pins and have either straight or tapered ends, without handles. Some people feel they have more control with these pins than when holding the handles of the American type. For the special purpose of rolling out puff pastry, the French have designed the Tutove, a pin whose wooden cylinder is grooved with narrow ribs, running handle to handle, to distribute butter evenly between the layers of dough. The Tutove works, looks chic hanging on the wall, and is a conversation piece, but you can do the same job perfectly well with any all-purpose pin. In short, I agree with the Parisian pastry chef who dismissed this device as "nothing but cinema!"

If you are feeling creative, or have been taken aback by the prices of fancy imported rolling pins, take a tip from the students at the Culinary Institute of America and cut 1½-inch smooth-grained hardwood dowels into any length you prefer. (Dowels this size are available in building supply stores.) Sand the dowel ends, and you have a homemade rolling pin. Whatever style pin you prefer, never soak it in water to clean it. Simply wipe it with a damp cloth and dry it immediately.

Dough can be rolled out directly onto a lightly floured countertop (page 38) or between two sheets of floured wax paper or between a rolling pin covered with a tubular cotton sock and a pastry cloth or canvas. Some cloths are marked with circles to help in measuring diameters of piecrusts. The cloth method has class and certainly results in exceptional ease in handling even the oiliest dough. Pastry cloths and pin socks (or stockings as they are sometimes called) should be rubbed with flour, then shaken free of the excess, before using. After use, cloths can be shaken out, stored in a plastic bag, and reused without washing. Occasionally, they should be rinsed in mild soapy water.

MEASURING DEVICES

When cutting rolled-out pastries to measure, I use a seamstress' tape measure, which I hang around my neck for convenience. A stiff ruler 12-inch long is handy for measuring the thickness of rolled dough, and a yardstick is useful for measuring strudel, but neither is essential. A neat trick for measuring the thickness of rolled dough is to mark the desired thickness on the sides of a wooden toothpick. Then stick the toothpick into the dough to gauge the depth.

DOUGH-CUTTING DEVICES

Tools for cutting dough can be plain or fancy. To cut strips of rolled dough for a lattice-topped pie, a sharp paring knife held against a ruler will do a fine, straight-edged job, but a wavy-edged stainless steel pie jagger or pastry wheel, will do the same job effortlessly *and* decoratively. Furthermore, it will not pull the dough, as a knife is apt to. A plain-edged pizza wheel is also good for this purpose. To crimp or flute the edges of a pie, you can use your fingers or a fork. Or you can indulge your fantasy and fortune with any number of elaborate crimpers on the market; all are basically grooved wheels rotating on a handle. Professional bakers use stainless steel crimpers to guarantee the dough seal of turnovers and filled pastries.

PIE WEIGHTS

When a pastry shell is baked empty before the filling is added, this is called baking blind (page 42). When this is done, the oven heat often causes steam in the dough to push up large bubbles in the crust. To prevent this, and also to help prevent shrinking, you can cover the dough with foil and weight it down during baking. A variety of pie weights are sold for the purpose, from a 9-inch heavy unglazed pottery disk to bean-shaped pieces of metal. Raw rice or dry beans do the same job and cost much less. If you use them, keep them in a jar and reuse them only for this purpose; do not cook and eat them. Marble chips sold in nursery or garden supply stores work well as pie weights; their weight is greater than rice or beans and thus they are more effective in pressing the dough down firmly. In France, some pastry chefs use cherry pits for this purpose.

PASTRY BRUSHES

A pastry brush is nearly essential for applying egg washes and jelly glazes to piecrusts and fruit tarts. Although you can do the job with your fingertips, a good brush greatly simplifies the task. To select a brush, note that the finer the bristles, the more delicate the job it can do. A flat, square-ended 1- or 2-inch wide brush made of sterilized hog's hair or nylon bristles is a useful all-purpose tool. Nylon, however, tends to be too coarse for glazing the tops of delicate pastries. Hog's hair is the better of the two. Select a brush with dark hairs so they will be visible and can be extricated if they fall into the batter or stick to the dough. Finding such a hair is never a wonderful experience and always brings to my mind a cartoon I once saw of a fat rabbit sitting atop a small bowl on a dining room table. Before him sits an apoplectic gentleman shouting: "There's a hare in my soup!"

For the very lightest touch when applying an egg glaze to delicate pastries, I recommend an imported European goosefeather brush with its pretty handle of braided quills. It is lovely to look at as well as to use, is inexpensive, and available in gourmet or specialty cookware shops and catalogues. This brush washes easily in mild soap and warm water and lasts for years.

DECORATING TUBES AND PASTRY BAGS

For piping whipped cream or meringue topping onto tarts or pies, or for

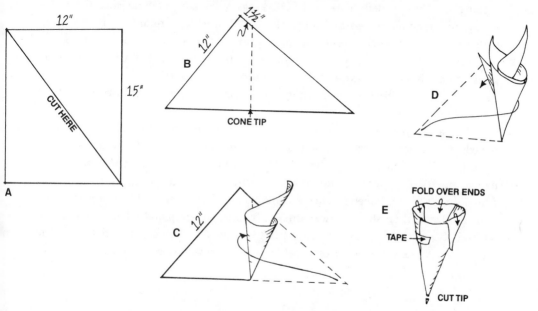

squeezing fillings into éclairs, a pastry bag with removable assorted tips is the answer. Select a bag lined with plastic or made of nylon, as both types are flexible and neither absorbs fat. Wash bags in hot water and dry after each use. Bags are available in a range of sizes from 7 or 8 inches to nearly 24 inches in length; choose one larger than you think you need as small bags are harder to handle.

As a substitute, you can make your own disposable bag out of waxed or parchment paper folded into a cone with a hole cut out of the tip (see diagrams). Cookware shops also sell precut paper triangles for folding into disposable cones. Metal tips can be dropped into these paper cones to pipe decorative designs.

PIE PLATES AND BAKING PANS

Pie plates are available in an infinite variety, but some clearly produce superior results. For old-fashioned American pies, you can choose either heat-proof Pyrex glass or metal pans with sloping sides in 8-, 9-, and 10-inch sizes. For quiches, you can use pie plates or fluted quiche pans made of china, pottery, or metal. For deep-dish pies, use pans at least 2 inches in depth. Avoid certain earthenware pie plates which must be placed in a *cold* oven because extreme heat causes cracks in the clay. Never lose sight of the fact that you are baking a pie, not a pie plate; the pot should *not* be telling you how to cook it! To avoid disappointment, read utensil directions and cautionary notes with care before buying.

Be aware that glass pans absorb heat quickly and thus bake slightly faster than pottery or *heavy* metal pans. Pies baked in heavy pottery or metal pans with a textured or dull dark finish may take slightly longer than glass, but these pans absorb heat well, causing pastry to brown nicely. By contrast, highly polished metal pans tend to deflect heat, thus baking slower and endangering the quick setting of your piecrust—a bad idea. My first choice for regular pies is the Pyrex glass pie plate. Another excellent choice, preferred by professional bakers, is the medium-heavy aluminum pan (*not* the foil type) with a dull finish. Aluminum pans absorb heat and transmit it very quickly, thus setting the crust quickly. For tarts, I use either French tinned or American black steel tart pans with removable bottoms.

Pies and quiches are generally served from the pans in which they were baked. Tarts, however, are presented free-standing, removed from the straight-sided pans in which they were baked. There are many varieties of tart pans. The flan form is a bottomless band of metal bent into a ring or rectangular shape which simply creates an edge when set upon a flat baking sheet. The dough is fitted onto the form, then shrinks away during baking, so the metal edge can be lifted off and the tart slid onto a serving platter. You may prefer instead to use the fluted French tart pan with removable bottom, that comes in a wide range of sizes. Identical tartlet pans are available in various very small sizes, as well. To unmold a tart from this type of pan, see page 43. As a substitute for this French tart pan, you can use a false-bottomed straight-sided American cake pan, widely available in 8-, 9-, and 10-inch sizes.

Pie plates and small tartlet pans made of inexpensive pressed aluminum, are available in supermarkets. The pan surfaces are shiny, deflecting heat, and they are extremely thin. To compensate, you can double the plates beneath your pie for ease in handling after pies are baked. The chief virtue of these plates is that they are disposable and thus perfect for donating pies to the school bake sale and the church bazaar. (*Note:* Tartlet pans of pressed aluminum are slightly *larger* than the heavy metal imported varieties, while *pie plates* of pressed aluminum are slightly *smaller* than equivalent sized pans of other types.)

Be sure to butter all tart and tartlet pans before lining them with pastry; if the sides of the pans are fluted, press a buttered finger or brush into each indentation, to be sure the job is done thoroughly.

The cake flan is a cousin of the French fruit tart. Made with a sponge, or Génoise, batter, it is baked in a specially designed, round pressed metal pan with a raised circular platform on the bottom. This shape creates a depression on top of the baked and inverted cake, which is filled with glazed fresh fruits. When the pan is made in the United States, it generally has smooth sides, and is called a Mary Ann. In Germany, where this tart is most at home, the pan is made with fluted sides and is called an *Obsttortenform*. Both styles are available in specialty cookware shops and catalogues in the United States.

Baking sheets, like pie plates, are best when made of heavy metal with a dull finish that absorbs heat instead of deflecting it. Cookie sheets generally have only one narrow edge, while so-called jelly roll pans have an edge approximately $\frac{1}{2}$ to 1 inch high all around. The latter are best for baking puff pastry which may drip melted butter into the oven. If you have only thin sheets, or they tend to bake too quickly, try using two pans, one beneath the other, during baking. At l'École de Cuisine La Varenne in Paris, this practice of double-plaquing was common in the pastry classes, even though heavy, professional-quality pans were used. The purpose was to slow down the baking slightly because oven heat was very high.

To allow for even circulation of your oven heat, be sure your baking sheets are of a size that permits between 1 and 2 inches of clear air space between it and the oven wall.

OVENS

Ovens vary beyond belief, and often beyond endurance, in their ability to hold heat calibration. For example, one of the several ovens in my home is

100°F hotter than its thermostatic setting. While I have periodically had it adjusted, it always returns to this state. I am finally resigned and accommodate to it by always having *two* oven thermometers hanging inside the oven: one in front, the other in the rear, to check variations within the oven itself. Mercury-type glass thermometers mounted on metal stands are the most accurate for this purpose. However, I often use modestly priced hardware store thermometers (replaced every year, for accuracy) to carry to cooking school or department store ovens when I do demonstration baking. More recipes are spoiled by inaccurate oven temperatures than any other cause. In fact, this is probably the most important tip in this book: *Get an oven thermometer at once and learn to use it, adjusting your oven thermostat on the outside so the internal oven temperature is correct at all times.* I guarantee your baking results will improve and be consistent. Remember: You cannot blame a cookbook for poor results until you are sure the fault doesn't lie within your oven.

TIMERS

A good timer is absolutely necessary if you expect predictable results in baking. Many good ones are on the market, available in hardware or cookware shops. No need to invest in a digital or computerlike timing device, a simple ticker with a bell is adequate. A timer that hangs on a cord around your neck is great if you are either absentminded or often called to the telephone or both, as I am.

GADGETS

Baking gadgets can be fun, and some will even provide dinner party conversation, though your pastry will surely steal the show on that count. Take the pie bird, for instance: an English invention whereby a small hollow pottery bird sits in the center of your pie. He not only helps support the top crust, but the steam escapes through his wide-opened beak, replacing the steam vent normally cut into the crust. This is the modern replacement for the "four and twenty blackbirds baked in a pie" (page 373). The most widely available pie bird is, in fact, a ceramic blackbird. Pie birds are available in mail-order cookware catalogs and in specialty gourmet shops.

If you have ever struggled to retain your dignity while removing the first piece of a crumbling pie in front of your dinner guests, you will appreciate the pie lifter, a stainless steel wedge with a lip that fits the rim of a pie plate. (Be aware, however, that not all varieties of lifters fit all pie plates; test for fit before using.) This gadget is baked right into the pie and after slicing along its sides, the first piece is simply lifted out upon the baked-in metal wedge . . . *voilà!* These are available from the same sources as pie birds.

A pastry pincher, sometimes called a crimper, is a handy device used by professional bakers to give a finished edging to tarts. It is a small, hinged pair of arms with grooves or teeth on the opened edges. When these teeth are applied to the top edge of a pastry shell at regular intervals, they produce a decorative marking.

FOIL

Aluminum foil has many uses in pastry making. To prevent pastry from overbrowning in the oven, foil can be molded over the crust to deflect the heat. For 1- or 2-crust pies, strips of foil can be cut about 3 inches wide and used for this purpose, or you can easily make the handy device called a foil frame: For a 9-inch pie, cut roughly a 10-inch square piece of foil, fold it in quarters, and tear out the center, leaving about a 2-inch edging. Unfold and set the opened frame over the pie or tart. Gently crimp the edges to the pan rim. When baking small dough decorations on top of pies, timbales, or puff pastry cases, you can make small foil tents to set over the highest pastry pieces which may brown too quickly.

Foil may be cut into a 12-inch square and used as a liner for pie weights when baking an empty shell. (*Note:* The shiny surface of foil deflects heat; therefore, turn foil *shiny side down* before filling with weights so heat will reach the pastry.)

FOLD

UNFOLDED FOIL FRAME

STAINLESS STEEL KNIVES AND NONREACTING SAUCEPANS

Because certain types of metal utensils (particularly aluminum and iron) react chemically to darken or discolor egg or wine preparations such as custards and sauces, I recommend that these items be cooked in an enamel, ceramic, or stainless steel pan. Custards should be tested for doneness with a stainless steel knife or the more elegant and old-fashioned silver knife.

Ingredients

A well-made pie pastry should be tender and flaky, and have a delicious flavor appropriate to its sweet or savory filling. To define our terms, a "flaky" crust will, when broken, have clearly visible layers or flakes; it may cut unevenly. The term "short" applied to a crust can refer to one that is flaky or one that is of finer crumb, more sandy than layered but still tender; this type will easily cut in a neat line. A "crumb" crust, by the way, is not really a pastry in the literal sense, since is is made from crumbs rather than a flour paste. While any one of several pastry recipes will produce good results, an understanding of what ingredients do and why will guarantee you fear-free, care-free pastry making with consistently professional results.

FLOUR

The singular point to remember about wheat flour is that it contains gluten, stretchy elastic cell walls that develop as soon as wheat proteins are mixed with liquid. Gluten is actually made up of two of the several proteins present: gliadin (located inside the endosperm, or core of the wheat kernel) and glutenin (located in the outer layer of the kernel). Gliadin provides elasticity and glutenin provides strength; both are needed to give flour the characteristics we require for baking. The proportions of these two elements in flour are affected by the method of milling as well as by the type of wheat—whether hard or soft—and where, geographically, it was grown. Thus, some flours are more elastic, others more delicate and tender, and each has a specific purpose.

For a tender, flaky, or short piecrust, low gluten flour is most desirable. The development of existing gluten must be kept to a minimum. By contrast, the rich development of a large quantity of gluten is desirable for kneaded yeast breads, which require a strong elastic structure to support the gases given off by the expanding yeast. This quality is also desirable for unleavened kneaded strudel or phyllo dough, which must be elastic enough to stretch from a small ball to a tissue-thin sheet.

Several factors inhibit the development of gluten and contribute to keeping dough flaky. You will recognize them as familiar admonishments in pastry recipes: cold (ice water, touching with cool fingertips rather than warm palms, chilling dough); acid (lemon juice, vinegar, sour cream or yogurt); minimal handling (overworking toughens dough); limited liquid (liquid activates gluten).

In pastry making, the baker is confronted with a wide variety of flours. It is important to select the type suited to your needs. All-purpose unbleached flour is milled from a blend of hard and soft wheats and contains roughly 10 to 13 percent gluten; pastry flour is milled from soft wheats only and has a slightly lower gluten content, roughly 8 to 12 percent. Pastry flour is milled to hold a lot of fat without becoming tough, a quality which produces a flaky product. Cake flour, also milled from soft wheat, has somewhat less gluten, about 6½ to 10 percent, and is specifically designed to produce a tender grain in cakes. It is also used to soften other types of flour, such as when combined with all-purpose flour for puff pastry dough. Used by itself, its low-gluten characteristic produces an excellent piecrust, and it can be substituted for pastry flour. *Self-rising* cake flour is another item altogether and should *not* be substituted for pastry flour; it contains added calcium acid phosphate or monocalcium phosphate, bicarbonate of soda, and salt. Bread flour, also called high-protein flour, is milled exclusively from hard wheat, has a high gluten content, 12 to 15 percent, and is perfect for products that must be kneaded or stretched.

Many commercially available brands of all-purpose flour are actually prepared blends of all-purpose flour (80 percent) and cake flour (20 percent) and thus are ideal for piecrusts. For this reason, I recommend all-purpose flour for many recipes in this book. To aid in your flour selection, read the flour package labels carefully, or write to the flour companies if you wish more details. Labels are helpful in determining gluten (protein) content. Under "nutritional information" on the labels of most widely available commercial brands, you will find that per 1 cup flour, all-purpose flour has between 11 and 12 grams protein, while bread flour or high protein flour has 14 grams. Pastry flour contains about 8 grams and cake flour 7. Protein content, as noted, varies depending upon brand and where in the country the flour was grown. Therefore, midwestern brands may differ from southern or northern varieties. Just remember (if you move and can't figure out why your baking results have changed) that the flour with the *lower* amount of protein is best for short or flaky pastries; the higher amount best for elastic dough to be kneaded or stretched.

If you cannot find the type of flour suited to your needs, you can make your own combinations. You may enjoy experimenting to blend your own pastry flour by combining 80 percent unbleached all-purpose flour with 20 percent cake flour, or use two thirds unbleached all-purpose flour to one third cake flour. Or, to transform all-purpose flour into pastry flour, substitute 1 tablespoon cornstarch for 1 tablespoon flour in every cup; to make your own cake flour from all-purpose flour, substitute 2 tablespoons cornstarch for 2 tablespoons flour in every cup. To make pastry flour from bread flour, measure 1 cup less 2 tablespoons bread flour and add 1½ tablespoons cornstarch.

The recipes in this book are tested and specific; for good results, use the recommended type of flour. The bottom line is that for pastries and piecrusts, pastry flour is theoretically best but hard to find outside commercial sources. The readily available unbleached all-purpose flour produces excellent results for most purposes, and I use it in my home and cooking classes. Occasionally, for its softer quality, I substitute cake flour or make my own pastry flour from a blend of the two types.

Among white flours, it is widely believed that "unbleached" flour has slightly more nutritional value than "bleached," because some of the wheat bran is retained during the milling and refining processes. I admit I am a believer and use unbleached flour in my home. Nevertheless, when you analyze and compare most commercially milled American flours, you find that both bleached and unbleached are in fact bleached and highly refined, though to differing extents depending upon brand. Some are chemically bleached, others bleached by aging. The commercially avowed purpose is to mature the wheat and thus increase storage time of the flour. This is a dubious virtue as far as performance and taste are concerned; flour in France, for example, is not bleached, is baked daily, and has incomparable taste and texture.

Whole wheat flour provides more nutritional value than white flour since it does retain more of the germ and bran of the wheat. It is good for pastry if finely enough milled. Look in health food stores for whole wheat pastry flour, milled specifically for this purpose. For whole wheat piecrusts, my own preference is to combine whole wheat pastry flour half and half with white all-purpose or pastry flour.

Theoretically, for pastries to have a fine texture, the flour should always be sifted before being measured. The reason is that too much flour can toughen pastry. However, unless it is measured by weight, a practice unfortunately uncommon in this country, flour quantities can vary. To get the most accurate measure by volume, either sift first or simply pour a lot of flour into a bowl, then lightly spoon or scoop it into *dry* measuring cups and level across the top with a knife blade; don't use cups designed for measuring liquids.

I should confess here that in actual practice, I seldom sift flour for piecrusts; I use the pour-scoop-level method and get excellent results. Where sifting is essential in the recipes, it is so noted. One exception to sifting, as noted in some recipes, is when using the food processor to make dough. In specific instances, you can use a few quick pulses of the machine to swirl and lighten the dry ingredients as if they had been sifted.

Flour should be stored in a cool, dry place, raised off the floor, and well ventilated. It will absorb odors if stored next to a strongly-scented product such as animal food or kept in a damp cellar. Flour stored for a length of time in warm weather can develop insects even when chemically bleached. The best solution is to store flour in the refrigerator or freezer. At 0°F, it keeps at least a year. Using cold flour only enhances the desired effect of keeping all ingredients well chilled. Another way to keep the bugs literally at bay is to place whole bay leaves in your flour canister. It's admittedly old-fashioned, but still works (most of the time) in my kitchen. The bay, by the way, does not impart any flavor to the flour. However, my guests have been known to discover the odd leaf in their piecrusts, so you may prefer to sift your flour and do as I say, not as I do!

FATS

Fat is the generic term for butter, margarine, lard, or vegetable shortening used in pastry dough. The richness and tenderness of pastry depends upon the type of fat used and the manner in which it is combined with the flour. For a flaky or short crust, chilled solid fat is ideally cut in to the flour by one of several methods, creating small separate particles that retain their own individuality. The colder and harder the fat, the less it is absorbed by the starch in the flour. The more separate the fat remains, the more it layers with the flour, creating dough flakes in the oven. The size of the flake—whether long or short—depends upon the size of the particle of fat worked into the flour.

When fat is melted, or when oil is used in place of solid fat, the liquid is absorbed into the flour starch, producing a firmer crust with a fine, slightly sandy crumb. This type of crust is good for pies with moist fillings, as it tends to be less absorbent than flaky crusts.

Of all fats, butter gives the best flavor by far. One reason it tastes so delicious is because of its lower-than-body temperature melting point, which enables it literally to melt in the mouth. I always recommend unsalted butter, both because it is usually fresher (salt prolongs shelf life) and because the salt content of butter varies and I prefer to control the amount of salt in my recipes. Although butter imparts excellent flavor, an all-butter crust can be somewhat firm of texture and not sufficiently flaky.

Note that when fat is combined with flour, it coats the solid and elastic strands of gluten, making them slippery, separated, and softened or tenderized. This contributes to the tenderness and flakiness of the pastry. As a guideline, butter has about 80 percent fat, while margarine (a solid vegetable shortening), Crisco (partially hydrogenated vegetable or "white" shortening), and lard (an animal fat) contain approximately 100 percent fat. The combination of butter (for good taste) plus a high fat shortening (for flakiness) produces the ideal pastry.

By comparison, high fat shortenings used alone produce flaky pastry that is nearly tasteless. This will be the result with any Criscolike product used as the sole fat. Crisco, on the other hand, has the advantage of being stable and can be stored at room temperature rather than refrigerated. So-called white shortenings like Crisco, as well as margarine, are actually hydrogenated or solid vegetable or animal fats, artificially created by forcing pressurized hydrogen gas through oils. In addition to hydrogenated oils, some brands of margarine also contain skim milk or whey, flavorings, and salt. Margarine was invented to simulate butter; however, its taste varies but never duplicates the real thing. It also has a much higher melting point (110°F), so it never melts as quickly in the mouth. Because it is created from oils, margarine has a softer consistency than butter and should always be well chilled or partly frozen before being added to pastry dough. Margarine will produce a slightly oily crust, one that is best rolled out between layers of wax paper. Be sure not to use margarine spreads as a substitute for solid margarine in baking; the results are not satisfactory. Although margarine has neither taste nor texture to recommend it for baking, it is frequently preferred to butter because it contains less (or in some cases nonexistent amounts of) cholesterol. To satisfy kosher dietary laws, select a brand of margarine made without milk solids or animal fats.

Lard is almost 100 percent animal fat, plus a certain percentage of water. It has the best shortening power and produces the most tender crust of all fats. The best type is leaf lard, rendered from pork kidney fat. Some lard is rendered from fat of other parts of the pig and may have a stronger pork flavor than leaf lard. Though high in cholesterol and bland in flavor, lard makes a marvelously flaky crust. To improve the taste, I prefer to add a little butter. All-lard crusts are perfect for pâté cases and savory pies. Before the great American cholesterol consciousness-raising, lard pastry was the farm wife's standby. For storage, lard must be refrigerated (unless it is a hydrogenated lard—check the label carefully). Regular lard stored at room temperature can turn rancid; never use lard that has an off scent or off flavor.

To measure butter, lard, or shortening most easily, purchase it in quarter-pound sticks with tablespoon markings. As an alternative, you can use the water-displacement method: for example, to measure ¼ cup butter, fill a measuring cup ¾ full with cold water. Add pieces of butter until water reaches the 1-cup mark. Pour off water, and you are left with ¼ cup measured butter. Or simply pack the butter or other shortening down very firmly into a measuring cup, but be sure there are no air spaces trapped in the bottom.

LIQUID

Liquid is added to dough to dissolve the salt and sugar, to work the flour, and—along with the moisture in the melting shortening—to create the steam that pushes apart the dough flakes in the oven's heat. Liquid should be used sparingly, as too much overactivates the gluten, toughening the pastry. When added to dough, liquid should be ice cold. You can use water, eggs, milk, fruit juice, even alcohol for the liquid in pastry dough. (*Note:* Alcohol adds flavor but evaporates fast in the oven and can create a rather tough crust.)

Lemon juice or vinegar can be added as part of the measured liquid without noticeably altering the pastry's flavor. The addition of acid softens the gluten, tenderizing the crust. This explains why our grandmother's piecrusts were so light and flaky—in her day, vinegar crust recipes were most common. Yogurt and sour cream used in place of liquid, as is the practice in Eastern European baking, similarly contributes the benefits of acidity in addition to adding flavor.

EGGS

Eggs add richness, color, and flavor to dough, as well as leavening power. However, the protein of egg white also adds toughness. This can be desirable when you want to strengthen or moisture-proof a crust for a pâté or pie with a moist filling. To add richness without toughening, use only the egg yolk, and save the white to brush over the crust for a glaze. Eggs can also be beaten with a small amount of water and brushed over pastries before baking (page 121) to produce a deep golden glaze, called a *dorure,* or gilding, in French. Note that for the greatest volume, eggs should be at least 2 days old. All eggs used in these recipes are U.S. Grade A large (2 ounces). One large yolk is approximately one generous tablespoon and one large white equals 2 tablespoons.

Eggs separate most easily as soon as they come from the refrigerator. To separate eggs, you have your choice of methods. There is on the market an egg separating gadget more clever than useful, which is basically a disk with a ring-shaped slot cut out just inside the edge. When an egg is broken onto the disk, the yolk is retained in the center of the disk and the white slides through the slot into a cup below. The most commonly used separating procedure is to break the egg in half, then hold the half-shell containing the yolk upright in one hand while you pour the egg white from the other half-shell into a cup. Then tip the yolk out into the empty shell while the white that surrounds it falls into the cup below. Place yolk in another cup. The third method is fun and infallible if you don't mind getting your hands messy. Crack the egg by tapping it sharply against the side of a bowl. As you pull the halves of the shell apart, simultaneously turn one half-shell upright, so it will contain all the egg. Holding this full half-shell upright with one hand, discard the empty half-shell. Then turn your empty hand palm up, and dump the egg into it. Spread your fingers slightly to let the white slip through them into a bowl below. The yolk will remain in your palm and can be turned into another container.

FLAVORING

Salt and sugar are added to pastry for flavoring, as well as for caramelization or browning. A small amount of salt and/or sugar can be added without changing the texture of the crust. However, be aware that the more sugar you add, the more breakable and crumbly the dough becomes. Pastry with as much as ½ cup sugar in it tastes like a sugar cookie and, when made with butter, is perfect for a rich tart crust. When you get more than ½ cup sugar in the dough, you may prefer to pat the dough into the pie plate with your fingers because it is so crumbly and hard to handle when rolled out. In France, it is common to use confectioners' sugar interchangeably with granulated sugar in pastry dough; in fact, confectioners' sugar is often preferred because of its softer quality.

You can experiment and create your own flavorings. Try adding an interesting combination of herbs or grated cheese to the dough for a savory tart, or add ground nuts or grated orange rind to complement a sweet filling.

NUTS

Many pie fillings and toppings require toasted nuts. Toasting dries out the moisture of the nuts somewhat, making them easier to grate or grind. It also darkens their color slightly and intensifies their flavor. To toast, spread nuts on a shallow pan and set in a preheated 300°F oven for 5 to 6 minutes (8 minutes for hazelnuts) or until the nuts are aromatic and a light golden color. Toss or stir once or twice for even coloring. Or toast nuts until golden in a frying pan set over low heat.

To remove brown skins from hazelnuts, wrap toasted nuts in a textured towel for several minutes to steam, then rub off the skins.

To blanch almonds, cover the nuts with water and boil 2 or 3 minutes. Drain. Cool nuts in cold water. Pinch off skins.

THE BASICS
OF PASTRY-MAKING

Promises and pie-crust are made to be broken.
Jonathan Swift, *Polite Conversation*

Her hand was as light with her pastry as with her husband,
and the results as happy.

LvUP

All-Purpose Flaky Pastry

Unlike a broken promise, the breaking of this crust is a cause for celebration; it is delicious, tender, and flaky. Moreover, it is much easier to handle than a husband, though a light touch certainly helps! This recipe is foolproof; the equivalent of the French *pâte brisée,* or short paste, it is the best recipe for beginning bakers, but also satisfies the experienced pastry chef. When sugar is added, it becomes *pâte brisée sucrée.* With the addition of sugar and egg yolk, it is known as *pâte sablée,* sandy paste, or *Mürbeteig* in German.

This recipe and its variations are followed by instructions for the Basic Preparation Technique. After these you will find the procedures for preparation by the Classic French Hands-on Method, the Electric Mixer, and the Food Processor.

(*Note:* The quantity of water needed will vary with the type of flour used and the weather; moisture in the air dampens flour somewhat and changes the amount of liquid it can absorb. Be flexible and watch the dough rather than the recipe.)

Your pastry will be flaky with or without the use of the egg yolk; its presence adds richness to the dough. However, I find the yolk also makes the dough somewhat easier to handle and recommend that beginners use it.

For best flavor, use recipes as written, combining butter and vegetable shortening or lard. However, if you are concerned about limiting your butter intake, you can increase the amount of other fats and omit the butter (see Fats, page 29), or make Oil Pastry (page 60).

BASIC ALL-PURPOSE FLAKY PASTRY RECIPE

I use one egg yolk plus lemon juice or vinegar as part of the measured liquid to guarantee a tender, easy-to-handle pastry. This is especially important if you have a tendency to overhandle the dough.

Quantity: For one 2-crust 8- or 9-inch pie (with some dough left over for trimming), or one 11- or 12-inch pie or tart shell, or nine 4-inch tartlets. For one single 8- or 9-inch shell, divide recipe in half (1 cup flour).

> *2 cups all-purpose flour, sifted*
> *¾ teaspoon salt*
> *½ cup unsalted butter, chilled*
> *3 tablespoons shortening (lard, Crisco, or*
>   *margarine), chilled*
> *5 to 6 tablespoons ice water, or use 1*
>   *tablespoon lemon juice or*
>   *unflavored vinegar as part of the*
>   *measured liquid*
> Optional: *1 large egg yolk (1 tablespoon),*
>   *included as part of measured liquid*
>   (Note: *To strengthen pastry for use*
>   *with moist fillings, use 1 whole large*
>   *egg [3 tablespoons] instead of the*
>   *yolk alone.*)
> Optional sweetener: *2 to 4 tablespoons*
>   *granulated or confectioners' sugar.*

Quantity: For one single 9-, 10-, or 11-inch pie or tart shell, or eight 3-inch tartlets. Double recipe for one 2-crust 10-inch pie or three 9-inch pie shells (3 cups flour).

> *1½ cups all-purpose flour, sifted*
> *½ teaspoon salt*

6 tablespoons unsalted butter, chilled

*3 tablespoons shortening (lard, Crisco, or
     margarine), chilled*

*3 to 4 tablespoons ice water, or use 2
     teaspoons lemon juice or
     unflavored vinegar as part of the
     measured liquid*

Optional: *1 large egg yolk (1 tablespoon)
     included as part of the measured
     liquid. (*Note: *To strengthen pastry
     for use with moist fillings, use half
     of one whole large egg, beaten [1½
     tablespoons] instead of the yolk
     alone.)*

Optional sweetener: *1 or 2 tablespoons
     granulated or confectioners' sugar.*

BASIC FLAKY PASTRY VARIATIONS:

The quantities given below are for Basic All-Purpose Flaky Pastry Recipe made with 2 cups flour. If you are changing the amount of flour in your recipe, change these variations proportionately: i.e., halve the amounts for 1 cup flour, reduce them only slightly for 1½ cups.

Nut Pastry. Add ½ cup fine-chopped or ground nuts (almonds, peanuts, hazel-nuts, pecans, brazil nuts) as part of the dry ingredients in the basic recipe.

Sesame Seed Pastry. Toast ⅓ cup hulled sesame seeds in a frying pan, stirring constantly over medium heat *just* until seeds are fragrant and golden. Add as part of the dry ingredients.

Coconut Pastry. Add ½ cup sweetened flaked coconut along with the dry ingredients.

Orange or Lemon Pastry. Use 2 tablespoons orange or lemon juice as part of the liquid and add 2 teaspoons grated zest of orange or lemon along with the dry ingredients.

Chocolate Pastry. Add 4 tablespoons unsweetened Baker's cocoa, sifted, plus ¼ cup light brown sugar, packed, along with the dry ingredients.

Cheddar Cheese Pastry. Add ½ cup grated sharp natural cheddar cheese, combining just after the shortening is cut into dough.

Herb Pastry. Add 2 teaspoons celery seed or 1 tablespoon mixed dried herbs (thyme, marjoram, dill, parsley, celery seed).

Sherry Pastry. Substitute dry cocktail sherry for all the liquid in the recipe.

Wheat Germ Pastry. Add 3 tablespoons toasted wheat germ to the dry ingredients.
Old-Fashioned Vinegar Pastry. Make All-Purpose Flaky Pastry (page 33). For
each 1½ cups flour in the recipe, use 1 tablespoon unflavored vinegar as
part of the measured liquid.

BASIC PREPARATION TECHNIQUE

(*Note:* Specific instructions follow for using the Classic French Hands-on
Method, the Food Processor, and the Electric Mixer.)

1. Combine the dry ingredients (flour, salt, sugar) with the cut-up, chilled fat
(butter, lard, Crisco, or margarine) in a large bowl. Working quickly and lightly,
pinch and slide the lumps of dough between your fingertips until the mixture resembles dry rice. This process layers the shortening and flour together, creating
"leaves" that will form flakes when baked. Fingertips are used instead of the
warmer palm of your hand because warmth melts shortening, which can then be
absorbed by the flour, causing the dough to toughen. The rule: Keep everything
as cold as possible. Instead of using fingertips to mix dough, you can also use a
pastry blender (wire loops attached to a handle), a fork, or two cross-cutting
table knives.

2. At this point, add liquid of your choice (ice water, lemon juice or vinegar,
eggs) plus flavorings. Take care not to overwork the dough lest you develop its
elasticity. Lightly combine the dough until it *just* begins to cling together in
clumps, but before it forms a ball. Sprinkle on a tiny bit more water if the dough
looks too dry. Dough should feel pliable like clay, but not sticky. If you catch the
dough at this point, even if you are using a machine, you will not overwork the
pastry.

3. Turn the dough out onto a sheet of wax paper. Lift the paper's opposite
corners and press them together, squeezing the dough into a cohesive ball. Wrap
the dough and refrigerate 20 to 30 minutes at least, but the longer the better, up
to several hours or overnight. Chilling allows the glutenous, or elastic, properties
of the flour to relax and helps prevent the dough from shrinking during baking.
Wrapped dough can be refrigerated 3 to 4 days, or frozen for up to 6 months.
(*Note:* Allow chilled dough to sit out at room temperature a few minutes to lose
its extreme hardness before rolling it out.) To roll out, form, and bake the dough,
see page 38.

Classic French Hands-on Method

1. Read Basic Preparation Technique, above. Measure sifted flour onto the
counter and form a well, or hollow, in the center. Into the well, measure about 1
tablespoon of the liquid, the salt and sugar, and all the fat, cut up in small pieces.

2. With your fingertips, working from the center of the well out, slowly add

in more flour as you pinch these ingredients together to form small flakes or lumps about the size of dry peas or rice. This step is known as *sabler* ("to reduce to sand").

3. Finally, add egg and any other flavoring, if using it, plus most of remaining liquid. Work the dough lightly just until it will clump together. Sprinkle on a tiny bit more water if the dough feels too dry. Do not overhandle. Form the dough into a ball.

4. At this stage, the fat and flour are further layered together by a technique known as the *fraisage,* from the word *fraiser,* meaning to break off a small lump of dough, put it under the heel of your hand on the counter, and push on the dough as you slide it forward about 4 inches. Scrape up and set aside that piece of dough and repeat with the remaining dough. Re-form the dough ball, wrap it in wax paper, and refrigerate at least 20 to 30 minutes, or several hours. To roll out, form, and make dough, see page 38.

Electric Mixer Method

1. Read Basic Preparation Technique, above. If your mixer is so equipped, fit it with the paddle attachment, otherwise you can use regular beaters. To the mixing bowl, add sifted flour, salt, sugar if you are using it, and cut up fat. Beat on low speed until mixture forms rice-sized bits.

2. A little at a time, add liquid (including eggs and flavoring if you are using them) and beat on low-medium speed only until the dough *begins* to pull away from the bowl sides and clumps together. Sprinkle on a tiny bit more water if the dough looks too dry. Do not allow a dough ball to form. Turn the dough out onto a piece of wax paper, wrap it into a ball, and refrigerate at least 20 to 30 minutes, or several hours. To roll out, form, and bake dough, see page 38.

Food Processor Method

1. Read Basic Preparation Technique, above. Freeze or hard-chill the butter and shortening (Crisco does not have to be chilled), then cut it up into small pieces. Measure flour and salt (and sugar if you are using it) into the work bowl fitted with the steel blade. Cover the bowl and pulse quickly (short on-off spurts) 2 or 3 times, to lighten, or sift, the dry ingredients.

2. Uncover the bowl and add cut-up butter and shortening. Process 5 to 10 seconds until the dough has the texture of rough cornmeal.

3. Through the feed tube, add egg and lemon juice or vinegar, if you are using it. Also add *part* of the water. Pulse 2 to 3 times. Add other flavorings (ground nuts, grated cheese, etc.) now. Add more liquid as needed, following each addition by 2 quick pulses. Watch the dough carefully at this stage, and stop the machine the instant the dough starts to clump together. It will still look rough and lumpy, and you may see specks of yolk and butter. This is normal. If it looks

too dry and crumbly, sprinkle on a little more water and pulse once more. Turn off the machine. Lift the cover and pinch the dough between your fingers. If the dough holds together, it is done. Do not allow a dough ball to form on the machine blades, or pastry will be overworked and tough.

4. Turn the dough out onto a piece of wax paper. Lift the opposite corners of the paper and press on the dough, forming it into a ball. Wrap the dough and refrigerate 20 to 30 minutes, or several hours. To roll out, form, and bake dough, see below.

Rolling, Fitting, Shaping, and Baking Pie and Tart Crusts

PREPARATION

After the dough is made and chilled, it is ready to be rolled out. Pat the prepared dough into a ball, then flatten the ball into a thick disk with smooth sides. Set the dough in the center of a lightly floured work surface. Sprinkle the top of the dough with a little flour, and rub some flour into the rolling pin. Remember that too much flour toughens dough; use only enough to prevent sticking.

ROLLING OUT DOUGH

Roll out dough with short even strokes from the center of the dough ball to the edges. Lift rolling pin as you approach the dough edge; rolling over edges thins dough too much. To keep dough from sticking and to make an even circle, lift and turn the dough after every few strokes; at this time, toss a fine dusting of flour beneath dough if it is needed. If dough sticks to the work surface, use a dough scraper or spatula to ease it up. Roll dough to a ⅛-inch thickness, or as specified in recipe, and 2 to 3 inches larger around than the pie or tart baking pan, which you can set upside-down over the dough to measure. For example, a 9-inch pie plate needs a circle of dough roughly 12 inches in diameter to fit into the pan easily.

ROLLING DOUGH BETWEEN SHEETS OF WAX PAPER OR ON PASTRY CLOTH

Oily or very soft or crumbly doughs roll most easily between 2 lightly floured sheets of wax paper. If the paper wrinkles badly, lift and reposition it occasionally. To keep paper from slipping, dampen the work surface beneath it. Dough of any consistency, but particularly soft or problem doughs, can easily be rolled out on a floured pastry cloth with a flour-rubbed cloth sock on the rolling pin.

(*Note:* If dough feels too soft to roll, chill it an extra 30 minutes. Or simply press dough into baking pan with your floured fingertips. Nut or suger crusts are sometimes especially crumbly and best shaped in this way. No shame in that.)

A NOTE ABOUT BUTTERING BAKING PANS

Tarts are served free-standing, out of their pans, and must be easily un-molded. Thus, tart pans and flan rings set on flat baking sheets must be well buttered before they are lined with pastry. Pie plates do not have to be buttered; however, buttering aids in the quick browning of pastry, so buttering is optional. Dome-shaped timbale molds must always be well buttered.

FITTING DOUGH INTO PIE PLATES OR TART PANS

If you have rolled the dough between sheets of wax paper, peel off the top paper, lift the dough on its backing paper, and center it, upside-down, over the baking pan. Lower the dough into place and peel off the backing paper, which is now on top.

If you have rolled dough out on a floured countertop, use a dough scraper or spatula to help lift the edges of rolled dough. Once dough is released, fold it in half onto itself, then fold in quarters. Pick up this folded dough triangle and position it over the baking pan so the center point of the folded dough triangle is in the center of the pan. Unfold dough, allowing it to drape evenly across the pan. Alternatively, you can roll dough up onto the rolling pin, lift it into place, and unroll it over the pan.

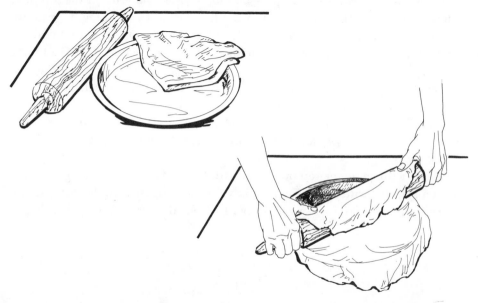

Once positioned over the pan, pick up one edge of the dough and ease it down so it fits flat along the bottom and up the sides of the pan. Go all around the pan, easing in the dough. Press out air pockets with your fingertips or small dough ball dipped in flour. *Never* stretch dough to fit or it will shrink during baking. If there are any holes or tears in the dough, dab water on the edges, then press on a scrap of rolled dough.

TRIMMING DOUGH

With a sharp knife or kitchen shears, cut off excess dough around the rim *after leaving* about a ¾ inch to 1 inch overhang all around. Refrigerate or freeze dough scraps for tartlets, or save for trimming.

TO SHAPE AND BAKE DOUGH
FOR A TWO-CRUST PIE

Prepare dough, following the recipe of your choice. Divide the total amount of dough in half. Wrap and refrigerate one half while lining the pan with the other. Following directions (page 38), roll out dough ⅛-inch thick on a floured surface, fold dough into quarters, lift and position it on the pie plate. Or roll dough onto the rolling pin, lift, and unroll it in place. Ease dough into pan without stretching. Press dough to pan to remove air pockets. Trim ¾-inch overhang.

Following the directions in your specific recipe, moisture-proof the lower crust with egg glaze if required, then add pie filling. For the top crust, combine any dough scraps with the remaining chilled dough and roll it out into a circle as you did previously. For a fruit pie, you should cut steam vents in the top piece of dough (page 49). Moisten the rim of the lower crust by brushing on water or egg beaten with 1 tablespoon water. Add the rolled-out top crust by folding it in half or quarters, lifting it, and positioning it over the filled pie. Or use a rolling pin to lift and position the crust. Trim ¾-inch overhang on top crust. Fold top crust edge under bottom crust edge and press them together to seal. Pinch edges up into a raised rim all around. Crimp or flute as desired (page 44). Cut steam vents now if you haven't already done so. (*Note:* If you are freezing the pie before baking, do not cut any steam vents at this time.) To freeze pie before or after baking, see page 55.

If you wish, glaze the top of the pie with brushed-on milk or egg glaze (page 121) and sprinkle with sugar, for a slightly darker, crisper crust. To bake, follow specific baking directions in your recipe. In general, however, 2-crust fruit pies are set into the lower third of a preheated 425°F oven for 10 to 12 minutes; then the heat is lowered to 350°F, the pie is raised to a center shelf, and the baking is continued for about 40 to 45 minutes, or until the filling is done. Be sure to check the pie when it is about half-baked and add a foil edging or frame (page 25) to protect the crust if overbrowning. Cool the pie on a wire rack.

TO SHAPE AND BAKE DOUGH FOR SINGLE-CRUST PIE, TART, OR QUICHE SHELL

Prepare dough for a single-crust pie or tart, according to the recipe of your choice. Following the directions (page 38), roll out the dough ⅛-inch thick on a floured surface, fold the dough into quarters, lift, and position it on the pan. Or roll dough onto the rolling pin, lift, and unroll it in place. Ease dough into the pan without stretching. Press dough into pan bottom and sides to remove air pockets. Take care when lowering dough over a fluted metal tart pan as the edges are sharp and can cut the dough. Repair any tears by pressing the dough back into place. Or, dab a little water on torn dough edges and press on a dough patch. Trim ¾-inch overhang.

For a Single-Crust Pie Shell. Line pan with dough as explained above. Fold under the overhang, making a double-layered edging even with the rim of the pie plate. Then pinch the edge up into a raised rim all around and crimp or flute as desired (page 44). At this point, the pastry-lined pan can be wrapped and frozen (page 53) or baked as explained below.

For a Tart or Quiche Shell. Use a removable-bottom tart pan or a flan ring set on a baking sheet or a quiche pan. Be sure to butter the bottom and sides of the pan well. Line the pan with dough as explained above; trim a ¾-inch over-hang, and fold it inward toward the center of the pan. Press the double edge gently to the pan sides to compress and seal. The double-thick edge gives the strength needed by a tart or flan because it is to be removed from the supporting pan before serving; since the filling presses outward, the pastry edging will be under stress and may crack if very thin. To cut off excess dough and to com-press the edging, roll a rolling pin over the top of the pan. Lift off any dough bits caught on the pan's outer edge. If you want to be fancy, you can now pinch up the dough edge into a straight-sided lip about ¼-inch high. Do not let this lip bend over. Crimp the top of the lip with a pastry pincher or score with slanted lines pressed in at ¼-inch intervals with the back of a floured knife. At this point, the pastry-lined pan can be wrapped and frozen (page 53) or baked as follows.

GENERAL BAKING NOTES

At this point, depending upon your specific recipe, the pastry shell can either be baked raw along with its filling, or partially or completely baked in advance. To prevent lower crusts from becoming soggy when filling is moist, it is always best to partially prebake shells.

Before prebaking for a tart or quiche, the prepared pastry should be pricked all over the bottom with the tines of a fork. (Pie shells are not pricked unless they are to be prebaked.) All types of prepared shells also benefit from being chilled at least 30 minutes to firm the dough before baking. This relaxes the gluten, thereby helping to make the pastry tender, and also reduces shrinkage. Pricking holes permits steam to escape from unfilled baking dough and thus reduces its tendency to puff up.

TO BAKE EMPTY PASTRY SHELLS, ALSO CALLED BLIND-BAKING

After being lined, pricked (in most cases), and chilled, pastry is ready to be baked. This is always done at first in the hottest part of the oven, the lower third, in order to set the pastry quickly and help make it flaky. However, the steam produced during the hot baking sometimes causes the dough to puff up in spite of the pricked fork holes. To remedy this, you have several choices. The first is simply to peek in the oven from time to time and pierce any dough bubbles with a fork and press down the dough with a potholder.

The second and most common method of preventing dough from puffing is also the most reliable: to weight it down. To do this, cut a square of wax paper, parchment, or foil slightly larger than the baking pan and set it over the pricked or unpricked pastry. Always use foil *shiny side down* so as not to deflect heat away from the pastry. Fill the liner half full with pie weights (rice or beans or other weights used exclusively for this purpose, see page 20).

Professional pastry chefs have another method: they mold the rolled dough over the back side of a buttered pie plate. Then they fit another pie plate, buttered on the inside, over the dough so that it is sandwiched. After excess dough is trimmed off around the rim, the pastry sandwich is set upside-down on the center shelf of a preheated 425°F oven and baked until the dough edging appears to be slightly golden. At this point, the sandwich is removed from the oven, inverted, and the inner, or top, plate removed. Finally, the pastry, resting on the other plate, is returned to the oven to complete baking, from 3 to 15 minutes, depending upon whether it is to be partially or completely baked.

For a Partially Prebaked Shell. Bake the pricked and/or weighted shell in preheated 425°F oven for 10 to 12 minutes. Remove liner and weights if any. Brush the shell with moisture-proofing glaze if called for in recipe. Replace shell in oven and continue baking an additional 3 to 5 minutes, or until the dough is no longer translucent but not yet golden brown. Cool on a wire rack. This shell will be filled and baked again.

For a Completely Prebaked Shell. Bake the pricked and/or weighted shell in preheated 425°F oven for 10 to 12 minutes. Remove liner and weights if used. Brush shell with moisture-proofing glaze if called for in recipe. Lower heat to 350°F and continue baking an additional 10 to 15 minutes, or until the pastry looks golden brown. Look in oven to observe color; do not overbake. Cool on a wire rack. This shell will not be baked again.

To Moisture-proof Partially or Completely Baked Pastry Shells. When shells are to be filled with particularly juicy fruits or liquid mixtures, you can prevent a lower crust from becoming soggy by giving it a moisture-proof coating. According to specific recipes, you will be instructed to brush the shell, before filling, with warm apricot preserves, Plain Fruit Glaze (page 120), or egg glaze (an egg beaten with 1 tablespoon water). Or you can lightly caramelize the inside of the shell by sprinkling it with a little granulated sugar mixed with grated lemon or orange zest and heating it in the oven just until sugar begins to melt. As another alternative, certain chiffon pies are complemented by a thin undercoating layer of melted semisweet chocolate brushed over the shell.

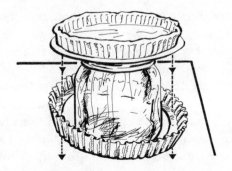

TO UNMOLD TART AND FLAN PANS

To remove a flan ring after baking and cooling the tart, simply lift it directly up off the tart. The pastry will shrink during baking, separating it from the ring. Finally, use a broad spatula to ease the tart off the baking sheet onto a flat serving platter. (*Note:* Single-crust pies and certain quiches, depending on the recipe, are served directly from their baking pans.)

After baking and cooling a tart made in a removable-bottom pan, center the bottom over a wide-topped jar. The tart will remain on the meal disk sitting on the jar, while the outer ring will fall down. Use a broad spatula to ease the tart off the bottom disk onto a flat serving platter, or simply serve the tart from the disk.

TO CRIMP OR FLUTE THE PASTRY EDGES

This procedure produces a decorative edging around a pie or tart. For 2-crust pies, it also helps seal the layers of pastry together to prevent juices from escaping. There are a variety of styles:

Plain Fork Tines. This is the easiest edging to make. Dip the tines of a table fork into flour, then press the tines into the dough at right angles to the pan edge. Repeat all around.

Herringbone Fork Tines. Press floured fork tines into the dough rim on a diagonal. Then turn the fork 90 degrees and make the next depression beside the first, so the lines alternate directions all around the rim.

Simple Flute. Form an even, raised dough edge around the rim. Place your left forefinger inside the pie rim and your right thumb and forefinger outside the rim. Press your fingers toward each other, forming the raised dough edge into a V. Repeat, making side-by-side V's all around the rim. Move the pie plate around after a series of V's to get a better angle; it's easier than moving yourself. To make more pointed shapes, you can pinch together the tip of each V.

Deep Flutes. Make a 1-inch wide U shape with the thumb and forefinger of one hand, pointing downward. Place this upside-down U against the inside edge of the pastry-lined pie plate. Reach inside the U with the forefinger of the other hand and pull inward on the raised dough edge. Simultaneously, press the sides of the U to the outside, away from the pie center. Repeat, making another flute alongside the first. Continue around the plate. It may feel more comfortable to you to move the plate around after a few flutes, rather than reach across it to work.

Scallops. Make simple or deep flutes as above. Then press the floured tines of a fork on the flutes that rest on the plate rim. This is a good method for sealing juicy 2-crust pies.

Rope. Make a neat, high-standing dough edge. Press your right thumb into the dough edge at an angle. Grip and squeeze the dough between your thumb and the knuckle of your forefinger. Repeat, keeping your thumb at an angle and making a ropelike edging all around.

Leaf Edging. With tiny hors d'oeuvre cutters or a sharp paring knife, cut out ¾- to 1-inch long oval leaves from rolled dough scraps. Press veins on the leaves with the back edge of a floured table knife. Moisten the dough on the rim of the pie with brushed-on beaten egg or water. Position the leaves in an overlapping pattern around the edge. Glaze the tops of the leaves with egg wash before baking.

LATTICE TOPPING

Dough strips crisscrossed or woven into a lattice make a decorative topping for fruit pies or tarts. This is a fancy alternative to the plain 2-crust pie. (*Note:* Lattice tops require the same amount of dough as a plain 2-crust pie.)

Prepare pastry for 2-crust pie. Roll out, fit the bottom crust into the pan, and add the filling. Trim lower dough edge to ¾-inch overhang. Roll out the second crust to the same size as the first (2 to 3 inches bigger than pan). If you are using paper, peel off the top layer. (*Note:* Roll this dough slightly thicker than usual, a generous ⅛ inch, for ease in handling.) With plain or fluted pie jagger, by eye or against a ruler, cut ½-inch-wide strips of dough. Following instructions below, form the lattice. The longest strips, cut from the center, go in the center of the pie, the shorter strips go on the edges. After forming the lattice, glaze it as you would a regular crust by brushing with milk or egg glaze.

Simple Lattice. This is a shortcut method where strips are crisscrossed instead of being woven. Dampen the edge of the lower crust by brushing on a coating of beaten egg or water. Press on a row of cut dough strips about ¾ inch apart across the baking pan. Press the strip ends in place on the dough rim and pinch off the excess. Place the remaining strips at similar intervals in the *opposite* direction, so they cross the first strips at right angles. Fasten and cut off the strip ends as before. Or make a diamond lattice by positioning strips at angles to each other to make diamond-shaped holes.

To complete, lift up the overhang of bottom crust and press it onto the lattice strip ends to seal. Pinch the dough edge up into a raised rim and flute as desired (page 44).

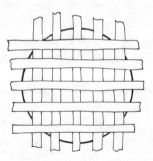

Curled Lattice. Cut dough strips slightly longer than for plain lattice. Twist the strips 4 or 5 times as they are set in place on the pie.

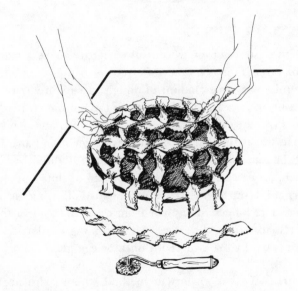

True Woven Lattice. The easiest method is to make this on a piece of lightly floured wax paper or foil, then position the woven strips directly over the pie and invert, setting the lattice in place and peeling off the backing paper. Alternatively, strips can be woven directly on the pie as follows.

Position 5 dough strips evenly spaced across the top of the pie. Leave the strip ends overhanging all around; these are called the side strips. Fold back in half side strips 2 and 4. To start the weave, select a long center strip from those still on the counter; place it across the center of the pie at right angles to the side strips. Unfold the two side strips so they now overlap the central cross strip.

Fold back side strips 1, 3, and 5, and add a second cross strip about ¾ inch from the first. Unfold strips. Continue, folding back alternate side strips as you weave in the cross strips. Work from the center of the pie out to each side. Trim the lattice ends to the edge of the pan.

Brush water or beaten egg on the rim of the lower crust under the lattice ends, then fold the lower crust edge over the lattice ends and press to seal. Pinch the dough edge up into a raised rim and flute (page 44). Make a high fluted edge if needed to hold in the juices of a fruit pie.

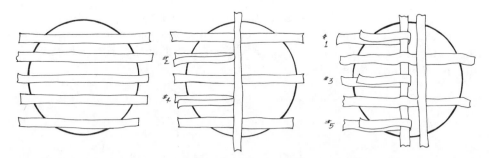

Free-Form Lattice. Cut dough strips and arrange them in any pattern you like atop the pie. Try spelling out a name or initials, or make a spiral from the center out to the edge. Or make a series of wedges or V's inside each other, pointing to the center of the pie.

STEAM VENTS AND SLITS

To allow steam to escape from juicy 2-crust pies or any moist filling wrapped in crust, steam vents or slits are cut into the top crust. The vents can be plain or fancy.

Chimney. For the top of a *pâté en croûte,* you can make a steam vent chimney by rolling a strip of folded foil into a tube about ½ inch in diameter and about 1 inch tall. Or a wide tube of raw macaroni can be used instead. This chimney is simply inserted into a round hole of the same diameter cut into the top crust before baking.

Snowflake Cut. This is a decorative cut for vents in a juicy 2-crust fruit pie. After rolling out the top crust, fold it into quarters. With kitchen shears or a sharp knife, cut 2 parallel slits 1 inch apart and 1 inch long into each folded side. Unfold the crust and position it over the filling. The cut slits will make symmetrical double V lines in a square pattern. (See next page.)

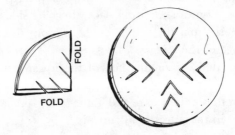

Free-Form Cuts. After rolling out the top crust but before positioning it, use the tip of a sharp paring knife to cut a freehand heart, flower, or letter shape from the center of the dough. Or cut a shape with an hors d'oeuvre cutter. Then position the dough over the filling.

Direct Cuts. After rolling out and positioning the top crust over filling, a round ¾-inch diameter hole can be cut into the center of the top crust with the tip of a sharp paring knife. Then you can make diagonal slashes around the pie, halfway out from the center. Or cut fruit or other free-form shapes from the dough before positioning.

TO SHAPE AND BAKE TARTLETS OR
FREE-STANDING PASTRY SHELLS

Tartlet shells are almost always prebaked before filling. Any pastry recipe can be used, but traditionally the preferred ones are *pâte brisée sucrée* (All-Purpose Flaky Pastry made with one egg yolk and 3 to 4 tablespoons confectioners' sugar, page 33). Cream Cheese Pastry (page 65), or Rich Tart Pastry (page 64). Try adding grated zest of a lemon or orange to tartlet dough for a delicious flavor.

Preparation. Tartlet molds come in all sizes and shapes, from fluted round cups to oval boats. Any type can be used. Tartlets can also be made by shaping dough over the cups of an upside-down muffin pan.

Make and chill the dough (page 36). Set out the molds and butter them well. Be sure to run a buttered finger into each groove of a fluted tin.

Rolling. Pat the dough into a flattened ball, set it on a floured surface, and roll out with a floured rolling pin. Or roll between 2 sheets of lightly floured wax paper, or a flour-rubbed pastry canvas and cloth-covered pin. (*Note:* Too much flour makes dough tough; use only enough to prevent sticking.) The more sugar in the dough, the quicker it tends to darken and burn. To avoid this, roll very sweet dough slightly thicker than normal. If dough feels too crumbly, it can always be molded into pans with your fingers.

Fitting. Place six small buttered molds side by side. Lift up dough on rolling pin and drape it over the tops of the molds. With a small dough ball dipped in flour, press the dough down into each mold, fitting it to the sides. Roll your pin over the mold tops to cut off excess dough. Use your fingertips to press the dough firmly into each mold, raising the top edge slightly above the rim of the mold. Chill until the dough is firm before baking.

To fit dough into medium-sized or large buttered tartlet molds, cut rounds about 2 inches larger than the diameter of the mold with a cookie cutter or the floured rim of a glass. While the dough is flat, prick it all over with a fork. Then lift the dough round and fit it into the mold. Press out the air with a small floured ball of dough or your fingertips. Use your fingertips to press the dough firmly into each mold, raising the top edge slightly above the mold rim. Chill the dough until firm before baking.

To fit dough over the back sides of muffin cups, use a cookie cutter or the floured rim of a glass to cut dough rounds about 2 inches greater in diameter than the muffin cups. For a 3-inch cup use a 5-inch dough round. While the dough is flat, prick it all over with a fork. Then lift the dough round and fit it over the buttered back and sides of a muffin cup. Press the dough firmly and pleat the edges to fit. Chill until the dough is firm before baking.

Weighting Tartlets for Blind or Empty Baking. To keep the dough from puffing up in the heat of the oven, you can line each tartlet pan with a square of foil (shiny side down) and fill it with some dry rice or beans used only for this purpose. Or you can press on a second mold of the same shape, with its bottom buttered, sandwiching the dough in the middle.

Or instead of weighting the dough, you can simply prick any bubbles that appear during baking with a fork, then press the dough down with a potholder. If you do this, check progress in the oven regularly.

Baking Tartlets. For ease in handling, set groups of small, pastry-lined tartlet molds upon a flat baking sheet. Set them in a preheated 400°F oven and bake about 5 to 6 minutes. After this time, remove the foil and weights from the tartlets. For *completely* baked tartlet shells, continue baking an additional 5 to 8 minutes, or *just* until the pastry looks golden brown and is completely baked through. Timing depends upon the type and thickness of the dough; larger tartlets can take 20 minutes. To *partially* bake tartlets, bake *only* until the pastry loses translucence. Check the oven from time to time and bake by color, not by recipe. Cool the molds slightly, then remove the pastry shells and cool them on a wire rack. Do not unmold partially baked shells since they will be baked again.

For dough molded over upside-down muffin cups, bake at 400°F for 5 to 8 minutes altogether. With this method, gravity helps prevent the dough from puffing up, eliminating the need for weights. However, if you notice a bubble in the baking dough, prick and deflate it with a fork. Cool these cups, right side up, on a wire rack.

To Shape and Bake Free-Standing Pastry Shells. You can make your own free-standing pastry shells by molding the dough (rolled out a generous 1/8-inch thick) over the back side of any buttered pan whose shape appeals to you—a ring mold or oval baking dish, for example. Or model your own "pan" from a triple-thickness of heavy-duty foil. Turn the pan upside down, butter the bottom of the pan, and press the dough over it. Trim the rough edges, but leave them fairly high since they tend to shrink. Prick the dough all over (bottom and sides) with a fork; if you are using foil for a "pan," be careful not to puncture it. Before baking, chill the dough on the pan until firm.

To bake, set the pastry-covered pan directly on a shelf in the lower third of a preheated 425°F oven and bake about 4 to 5 minutes. Gravity usually prevents the dough from puffing up; however, occasionally it happens. Look in the oven; if the dough is beginning to bubble up in places, pierce the bubbles with a fork very gently to release steam and deflate. Or press the bubbles down gently with a potholder. If the bubbles still persist—and this only works on real rather than foil "pans"—you can weight the baking pastry with another plate of the same size, buttered on the bottom and filled with beans to make it heavy. Remove the weight dish a few minutes before the end of baking time.

Bake a total of 6 to 8 minutes for a partially baked shell to be filled and baked again later. Bake a total of 12 to 15 minutes or until golden—time depending upon the thickness and type of dough—for a completely baked shell that will not be baked again. (*Note:* These free-standing shells bake slightly faster than bean-weighted pastry-lined shells.) Finally, lift the pastry shells off their molds and cool them upright on a wire rack. To moisture-proof these shells, brush with egg glaze (page 121) or Plain Fruit Glaze (page 120) after baking but before filling.

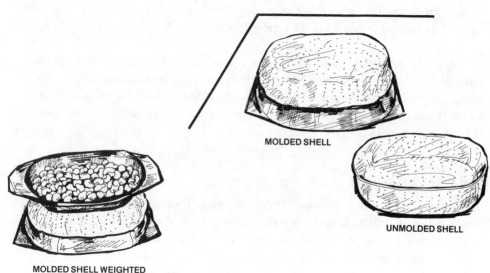

MOLDED SHELL

UNMOLDED SHELL

MOLDED SHELL WEIGHTED

About Freezing Pastry

Absolutely no pastry tastes as good after freezing as it does freshly baked. After this disclaimer, I must also add that freezing baked goods can be a great time-saver as well as a convenience when you are entertaining. You *can* freeze baked and unbaked pies, pie fillings, and piecrusts. Fruit, berry, and mince pies and tarts are the most successful candidates, along with most individually shaped, pastry-wrapped hors d'oeuvre. Pumpkin, squash, and certain types of chiffon pies will freeze successfully, as well. Opinion is divided about cream and custard pies, since their fillings can separate on freezing; I prefer not to freeze them. Be sure, when freezing pies to be baked or reheated in the oven, that you use a metal pie plate or one that you are sure can go from freezer to oven.

Your Freezer. To protect your health as well as the quality of your frozen products, it is important to use an auxiliary freezer thermometer to monitor temperature levels. Check the manufacturer's directions as to temperatures. For a guideline, note that a fast-freeze shelf or section may be as low as 10°F to 20°F below zero, while the main section should be a constant 0°F to no higher than 5°F.

Packaging for the Freezer. Pies and pie shells should be wrapped airtight in heavy-duty aluminum foil or freezer-weight plastic or coated paper. Check package labels to be sure the material you are using is freezer-weight. You can also use heavy-duty polyethylene bags, but not the type supermarket fruit is packaged in; these are too thin. To protect pies, pie shells, and individual pastries or bite-sized hors d'oeuvre from being poked or dented on a freezer shelf, wrap them airtight in foil or a plastic bag, then store in a protective plastic or cardboard box (waxed is best), appropriately labeled.

Labeling for the Freezer. Every item placed in the freezer should be labeled, with date and quantity noted. Oil-base felt-tipped pens will mark easily on foil or plastic or paper. Freezer tape is a special product that will adhere at cold temperatures. If you use ordinary masking tape, mark labels on the package itself, not on the tape, which may fall off.

FREEZING DO'S AND DON'TS

- Do not top pies with meringue before freezing; do not freeze meringue at all *unless* baked stiff, because freezing toughens whipped egg whites.
- Do not cut steam vents in top crusts or fruit pies to be frozen before baking.
- Do not glaze tops of fruit pies to be frozen before baking.
- Do not freeze custard or cream pies unless so specified in the recipe.
- Do not freeze cream cheese unless it is to be used in combination with other ingredients; freezing makes it grainy.
- Do not freeze sour cream; it separates.
- Do freeze: mousses
    - spices (fresh or dried)
    - eggs (separate and freeze yolks and whites; or beat whole eggs with pinch of salt or sugar and freeze in ice cube trays; 1 cube = 1 egg)
    - milk
    - butter or margarine
    - cream

flour

sugar

brown sugar (to prevent lumps)

nuts, whole or chopped

crumbs (cookie, cake, cracker, etc.)

hard cheeses

piecrusts, baked or partially baked or raw (in lumps of dough or
   rolled into rounds or shaped into pie plates)

fruit pies and tarts, baked or unbaked

deep-dish pie or cobbler fruit mixtures

savory pot pie mixtures (in freezer-to-oven containers; to use, thaw
   or not as you wish, add top crust, bake)

• You can refreeze empty baked or partially baked pie shells

FREEZER STORAGE TIMETABLE

(To be used only as a guideline)

Baked and unbaked empty pie shells . . . . .3 months

Baked fruit and berry pies . . . . .6 to 8 months

Unbaked pies . . . . .4 months

Baked chiffon pies (if recipe contains egg whites or whipped
   cream) and Lemon Meringue Pie *without* meringue topping . . .1 month

Savory pot pie mixtures . . . . .6 months

Frozen fruit pie filling . . . . .6 months

THE QUESTION: TO FREEZE BEFORE OR AFTER BAKING

There are two schools of thought on the question of whether to freeze pies
before or after baking. Personally, I prefer to freeze before and bake the pie
frozen. I find that the hot oven will quickly set the pastry, keep it flaky, and prevent juices from penetrating the lower crust. Some bakers increase the quantity
of their pie thickener when freezing raw pies, but I do not; for especially juicy
fruits I may use slightly more thickener (and I generally prefer tapioca to flour
except for apple pie), but I never find this a problem. You should note, however,
that pies frozen before baking can be stored a shorter time (4 months) than those
baked first (6 to 8 months). The latter, after thawing and reheating, seem to me
to have a less crisp pastry and less fresh flavor. My advice: Make 2 pies, perform
your own test, and judge the results for yourself.

FREEZING TWO-CRUST FRUIT PIE

(*Note:* For especially juicy fruits or for any type of berries, use 3½ table-spoons quick-cooking tapioca or cornstarch for the thickener.)

Method I: Freezing Before Baking. Follow any specific recipe for making 2-crust fruit pie. Flute the edges decoratively (page 44). Do not cut steam vents; do not glaze the pie top. Wrap the pie airtight in freezer-weight material and label. Freeze pie.

To bake the frozen, unthawed pie, set it in the lower third of a preheated 450°F oven for 20 minutes. After the first 10 minutes, you can open the oven and cut steam vents in the top crust. Then lower the heat to 350°F, raise the pie to oven center, and cover the pastry edges with foil (page 25) if they seem to be browning too fast. Continue baking an additional 40 to 45 minutes, or until the pastry is golden brown. (*Note:* If you want to glaze the pie top, apply egg glaze and a sprinkling of sugar *before* setting the pie in the oven.) Cool on a wire rack.

Method II: Baking Before Freezing. Follow any specific recipe for making a 2-crust fruit pie. Flute the edges decoratively (page 44). Cut steam vents and glaze the pie top with egg glaze and sugar if desired. Bake according to recipe instructions or at 425°F for 15 minutes, then reduce heat to 350°F and bake an additional 40 to 45 minutes. Cool on a wire rack. When the pie is completely cold, wrap it in freezer-weight material, label it, and freeze. To serve, unwrap and thaw the pie, then warm it for 15 minutes in a 350°F oven.

FROZEN FRUIT PIE FILLING

To avoid the possibility of fruit juices penetrating and softening the lower crust before a frozen 2-crust pie is baked, simply freeze the filling and the crust separately and combine them immediately before baking. I prefer to roll out rounds of piecrust and freeze them flat between layers of foil to save freezer room. Pie-sized batches of seasonal fruits can be prepared quickly and easily, and stored in foil packets molded to the shape of the pie plate. Fruits that freeze especially well are apples (cooking type), fresh apricots, peaches, and nectarines, plums, rhubarb, berries (strawberries, blueberries, blackberries, raspberries).

(*Note:* Use this recipe as well for deep-dish and cobbler fillings.)

Special equipment: Heavy-duty aluminum foil, cut into one 12 × 24-inch square for each pie.
Freezing time: Up to 6 months without loss of flavor.
Quantity: One 9-inch pie.

4 to 6 cups fresh fruit, washed, peeled if
necessary, hulled or cored, and
sliced if necessary
¼ to 1 cup granulated or brown sugar
(amount and type depends upon
type and sweetness of fruit)
Optional: ½ teaspoon each cinnamon
and nutmeg
1 to 3 teaspoons fresh lemon juice
(depending upon type and flavor
of fruit)
3 to 3½ tablespoons tapioca, quick-
cooking type, or same quantity
cornstarch (amount depends on
juiciness of fruit)

Toss the prepared fruit with all remaining ingredients. Let stand a few minutes to soften the tapioca slightly. Center a foil sheet over pie plate. Mound the prepared fruit on the foil and pat gently to compress. Fold up the long foil flaps and make a wide double fold, pushing out the excess air. Fold over the side edges and pinch to seal. Label and date the package. Leaving the filling on the pie plate, set it on the fast-freeze shelf of your freezer until the fruit is hard. Remove the pie plate and return the fruit package to freezer.

To bake, line a pie plate with a layer of frozen and thawed pastry and brush with egg glaze (1 egg or egg white beaten with 1 tablespoon water) or fruit preserves. Unwrap the frozen fruit packet (do not thaw) and set it on the pastry. Cut steam vents in the rolled-out top crust. Moisten the edges of the lower crust, then cover the pie with its top crust. Fold the edges of the top crust over the lower one and pinch to seal. Mold the edge into a raised rim and flute (page 44). If you wish, glaze the pie top with brushed-on beaten egg and a light sprinkling of granulated sugar. Bake in the lower third of a preheated 425°F oven for 25 minutes. Reduce heat to 350°F, raise pie to center of oven, and cover pastry edges with foil (page 25) if they seem to be browning too fast. Continue baking another 35 minutes, or until the pastry is golden brown and the fruit tender and bubbly. Serve warm for best texture and flavor.

(*Note:* Tapioca sometimes presents a problem when used in fruit pies topped by lattice pastry and *frozen before baking.* Occasionally, the tapioca does not soften sufficiently and remains hard after baking. To remedy, use cornstarch thickener for frozen lattice pies.)

SHORTCUT FROZEN PIE AND TART CRUSTS

Prepare the pastry of your choice and roll it out (page 38) 2 or 3 inches larger than the diameter of the baking pan to be used. Sandwich the pastry round between 2 layers of wax paper or regular-weight foil set on a cardboard backing. Repeat with as many layers as you like; it's handy to make a double or triple batch of dough one day and have a ready supply of pie or tart crusts on hand. Enclose airtight, in heavy-duty foil, then set into a large plastic bag. Label; if more than one type of pastry is included, label each round by simply writing its type (with pencil) on a slip of clean white paper set atop that piece of dough. To use, remove a dough round and set it flat to thaw about 10 minutes, fit it into the pie or tart pan, shape, and bake (page 39).

As an alternative, crusts can, of course, be fitted and shaped in freezer-to-oven pie plates before being frozen raw or baked.

PASTRY RECIPE COLLECTION

The following collection includes a wide variety of recipes, from quick and easy to prepare basic short crusts and cobbler toppings, to the more elaborate strudel and puff pastry. Each recipe in the main section of the book will refer you back to this collection, or to the All-Purpose Flaky Pastry recipe (and variations) that precedes it, see pages 33–36. Feel free to use my suggestions or select your own choices from this collection.

WHOLE WHEAT PASTRY

Quantity: One 2-crust 9-inch pie.

> *1 cup all-purpose flour*
> *1 cup whole wheat pastry or all-*
>   *purpose flour*
> *¾ teaspoon salt*
> *½ cup unsalted butter, chilled*
> *3 tablespoons vegetable shortening,*
>   *chilled*
> *1 egg yolk*
> *5 to 6 tablespoons ice water, as needed*
> **Optional sweetener:** *2 tablespoons*
>   *granulated sugar*

Read Basic Preparation Technique (page 36). Measure flour, salt, and sugar, if you are using it, into a bowl. Cut up the butter and shortening and work them into the dry ingredients until the mixture is crumbly, with bits the size of rice. Add the yolks or whole egg. Mix lightly, just until the dough begins to cling together in clumps. Add a little ice water, one tablespoon at a time, if dough is too dry. Turn the dough out onto wax paper, form a ball, wrap, and chill at least 30 minutes before rolling out.

VARIATION:

Whole Wheat-Wheat Germ Pastry. Add 3 tablespoons toasted or raw wheat germ to the whole wheat flour.

OIL PASTRY

If you use polyunsaturated oil, this recipe is good for those who want to limit their cholesterol intake. The dough will be tender, with a somewhat sandy texture. For ease in handling, you can simply press it into the pie plate with your fingers. Or roll it out between two sheets of lightly floured wax paper or on a canvas pastry cloth. Chill dough at least 30 minutes before rolling out. If the dough feels too soft, chill for an additional 30 minutes.

Quantity: One 8- or 9-inch shell; for a 2-crust pie, double the recipe.

> *1⅓ cups all-purpose flour*
> *½ teaspoon salt*
> *½ teaspoon sugar*
> *⅓ cup polyunsaturated vegetable oil*
> *1 tablespoon lemon juice plus 3 or more*
> *tablespoons cold water, as needed*
> Optional sweetener: *2 tablespoons*
> *granulated sugar*

Read Basic Preparation Technique (page 36). Sift into a bowl the flour, salt, and ½ teaspoon sugar. (Add optional sugar for a sweet-tasting crust.) Add the oil and lemon juice, and mix. Add in one or two tablespoons cold water and stir. If the mixture is too dry, add a little more water, until the dough will form a ball. Wrap and refrigerate the dough ball for at least 30 minutes. Or roll out dough between 2 sheets of lightly floured wax paper and refrigerate just that way for at least 30 minutes or until you are ready to peel off the paper and line the pie plate.

FLOUR PASTE PASTRY

Years ago, this method of making dough was the one beginning bakers were taught first. The reason: There is no guesswork or "feel" required in the recipe, and it produces a very pliable and easy-to-handle dough that bakes into a light, tender pastry layered with long flakes. The texture is slightly less fragile than All-Purpose Flaky Pastry prepared in the traditional manner.

Quantity: One 2-crust 9-inch pie.

> *2 cups all-purpose flour*
> *¾ teaspoon salt*
> *¼ cup water*
> *½ cup unsalted butter*
> *3 tablespoons margarine or Crisco*

Sift the flour and salt into a large bowl. Measure out ⅓ cup of this mixture and place it in a second, smaller bowl. Stir the water into the ⅓ cup flour, making a paste. In the large bowl, cut all the shortening into the remaining dry ingredients until the mixture is crumbly, with bits the size of rice. Finally, stir in the paste, blending it well. When the dough forms a ball, wrap it and chill 30 minutes or until needed. Or roll out on a floured board and use immediately.

HOT WATER PASTRY

Rules, like piecrusts, were made to be broken! That is the only explanation I can think of for the invention of this recipe, which breaks every rule there is for pastry crusts. But never mind. This is an old, tried and true English recipe. It is especially easy to handle (I recommend it for beginning bakers) and perfect as a *pâte à croûstade*—that is, for covering pies, pot pies, and pâtés that have moist or juicy fillings. The baked pastry has a texture halfway between a butter crust flakiness and the crumble of an oil crust.

Although boiling water is used to melt the shortening for the dough, note that it is cooled before mixing in the flour. As you would expect, the dough appears to be slightly stretchy; this is because the warmth has activated the gluten. However, chilling relaxes the gluten. To this end, the dough is chilled at least 30 minutes, or for as long as overnight, before being rolled out. (*Note:* The fat for this dough can be all lard, all solid vegetable shortening [margarine], or all butter. For best flavor and texture, I prefer a mixture of the last two, as the recipe is written.)

Quantity: One 2-crust 8- or 9-inch pie.

> *½ cup unsalted butter, cut in ½-inch*
> *cubes*
> *4 tablespoons margarine, cut in ½-inch*
> *cubes*
> *⅓ cup boiling water*
> *2 cups all-purpose flour*
> *1 teaspoon salt*
> *½ teaspoon baking powder*

Hand Mixing or Electric Mixer Method

Measure butter and margarine in a small bowl, add boiling water, and stir until the fat melts. Cool to lukewarm. Sift the dry ingredients into a large mixing bowl. Slowly add the cooled liquid mixture, beating gently after each addition, until the dough forms a ball. If the dough is too sticky, sprinkle on about 1 more tablespoon flour. The dough will feel soft and slightly warm. Wrap the dough ball and chill at least 30 minutes, or overnight.

Food Processor Method

Measure the butter and margarine into a pitcher or a 2-cup measuring cup. Pour on boiling water and stir until the fat is melted. Cool to lukewarm. In the work bowl of the processor fitted with its steel blade, combine the dry ingredients and pulse 2 or 3 times to lighten. Pour the melted and cooled liquid mixture slowly through the feed tube while pulsing the processor in short on/off spurts. Just as soon as the liquid has been absorbed, stop the machine and examine the dough. If it is too moist and sticky, add 1 more tablespoon flour and pulse once or twice again, but not more. Do not overwork the dough. The dough will feel soft and warm. Wrap the dough in a ball, and chill at least 30 minutes or overnight.

LARD PASTRY

This is Grandmother's old-fashioned farm favorite. It produces a very flaky crust and can be used for sweet fruit or savory pies.

Quantity: One 2-crust 9-inch pie.

> *2 cups all-purpose flour*
> *¾ teaspoon salt*
> *⅔ cup lard, cut up*
> *5 to 7 tablespoons ice water*

Read Basic Preparation Technique (page 36). Sift the flour and salt into a bowl. Work in the cut-up lard until the mixture is crumbly, with bits the size of rice. Sprinkle on 5 tablespoons water and mix very lightly, just until the dough begins to clump together. Turn the dough out onto wax paper, form a ball, wrap, and chill at least 30 minutes, or until needed.

BUTTER-LARD PASTRY

This pastry is as flaky as the all-lard recipe, but has more flavor because of the addition of butter. The dough is very easy to handle and can be used for any sweet or savory pie.

Quantity: One 2-crust 9-inch pie.

> *2 cups all-purpose flour*
> *¾ teaspoon salt*
> *⅓ cup lard, cut up*
> *⅓ cup unsalted butter, cut up*
> *5 to 6 tablespoons ice water*

Read Basic Preparation Technique (page 36). Sift the flour and salt into a bowl. Add the lard and butter and work them into the dry ingredients until the mixture is crumbly, with bits the size of rice. Sprinkle on 5 tablespoons water and mix lightly, just until the dough holds together in clumps. Add extra water only if the dough looks too dry. Turn out onto wax paper, form a ball, wrap, and chill at least 30 minutes, or until needed.

PORTUGUESE LARD PASTRY

This recipe has a higher proportion of flour to fat than plain lard pastry. It is the traditional recipe used to line tartlet pans for Portuguese Bean-Custard Tartlets (*Pasteis de Feijão*, page 273).

Quantity: Twenty-one tartlets, 2 inches in diameter.

> *4 cups unbleached all-purpose flour,*
> *   sifted*
> *1 teaspoon salt*
> *⅔ cup lard*
> *¾ cup plus 2 tablespoons ice water*

Read Basic Preparation Technique (page 36). Sift flour and salt together into a mixing bowl. Cut in lard until the mixture is crumbly, with bits the size of peas. Sprinkle on ¾ cup ice water a little at a time, tossing the mixture with a fork until it will clean the sides of the bowl. Add an extra 2 tablespoons ice water, if necessary, to make the mixture cling together. Turn the dough out onto wax paper, form a ball, wrap, and chill at least 30 minutes, or until needed.

RICH TART PASTRY

Because of the quantity of sugar and egg, this pastry tastes rather like a sugar cookie. It is perfect for sweet tarts or tartlets, and you can vary the flavoring to complement the filling.

Quantity: One 2-crust 9-inch pie or one 10-, 11- or 12-inch tart shell, or seven 4½-inch tartlets.

> *2 cups all-purpose flour*
> *¾ teaspoon salt*
> *⅓ to ½ cup confectioners' sugar, to taste*
> *½ cup unsalted butter, cut up*
> *3 tablespoons margarine or Crisco, cut up*
> *½ teaspoon vanilla extract*
> *3 large egg yolks*
> *Ice water, only if needed*
> Optional flavoring: *Grated zest of one*
> *lemon or orange (2 teaspoons) or*
> *½ teaspoon almond extract*

Read Basic Preparation Technique (page 36). Sift flour, salt, and sugar into a bowl. (*Note:* The more sugar you use, the sweeter and more crumbly the dough.) Work the cut-up shortening into the dry ingredients until the mixture is crumbly, with bits the size of rice. Add the vanilla, yolks, and optional flavoring, and mix lightly just until the dough begins to cling together. If it feels dry and crumbly, add a tablespoon of ice water. Turn the dough out onto wax paper, form a dough ball, wrap, and chill at least 30 minutes. If the dough feels sticky when rolled, sprinkle on a little more flour or try rolling it between 2 sheets of floured wax paper. Or simply press the dough into the pan with your fingers.

EGG YOLK PASTRY

This is a rich pastry, lightly lemon scented, with a texture slightly more compact and substantial than the All-Purpose Flaky Pastry. It is good for quiches or sweet tarts with moist custard or pudding fillings.

Quantity: One 2-crust 9-inch pie.

> *2 cups all-purpose flour*
> *½ teaspoon salt*
> *¾ cup unsalted butter, cut up, or 9*
> *tablespoons butter plus 3 tablespoons*
> *margarine*
> *3 large hard-boiled egg yolks, sieved*
> *2 teaspoons grated lemon zest*
> *5 to 7 tablespoons milk, as needed*
> Optional sweetener (omit for quiches):
> *3 tablespoons confectioners' sugar*

Read Basic Preparation Technique (page 36). Sift the dry ingredients into a bowl, along with the sieved yolks, grated lemon zest, and optional sweetener. Work in the cut-up shortening until mixture is crumbly, with bits the size of rice. Add milk, 1 tablespoon at a time, until the dough begins to clump together. Form a dough ball, wrap in foil, and chill at least 30 minutes or until needed.

CREAM CHEESE PASTRY

This delectable pastry is sometimes called Viennese or quiche pastry. It is perfect for sweet or savory pies and tarts as well as for bite-sized jam-filled pastries, tartlets, and turnovers, and when chilled, it is an extremely easy dough to handle.

Quantity: One 2-crust 8- or 9-inch pie, or one 10-, 11- or 12-inch tart or quiche shell, or forty-eight 4-inch crescents.

> *8 ounces cream cheese (not whipped*
> *type), at room temperature*
> *1 cup lightly salted butter at room*
> *temperature. (Note: Do not*
> *substitute margarine.)*
> *2 cups all-purpose flour*

Read Basic Preparation Technique (page 36). Cut up cream cheese and butter in a mixing bowl. With a fork or an electric mixer, blend them together until creamy. Sift the flour directly into the bowl. Blend in flour just until the dough holds together. If it feels too sticky to handle, add a little more flour. Wrap the dough ball in wax paper and chill at least 30 minutes or until needed.

SOUR CREAM PASTRY

This traditional Hungarian recipe is especially good with fruit tarts, small jam tartlets, and envelopes. The sour cream contributes to the flavor as well as to the tenderness of the pastry.

Quantity: One 2-crust 9-inch pie or one 10- or 11-inch tart shell or eight 4-inch tartlets.

> *2 cups all-purpose flour*
> *¾ teaspoon salt*
> *10 tablespoons lightly salted butter*
>   *cut up*
> *4 to 5 tablespoons dairy sour cream (or*
>   *plain yogurt)*
> Optional sweetener: *3 tablespoons*
>   *confectioners' or granulated sugar*

Read Basic Preparation Technique (page 36). Sift the flour, salt, and optional sweetener into a bowl. Cut in the butter and pinch it into the dry ingredients until the mixture is crumbly, with bits the size of rice. Add the sour cream 1 tablespoon at a time and mix lightly until the dough just begins to cling together in clumps. Form a dough ball, wrap in foil, and refrigerate at least 30 minutes or until needed.

HAMANTASCHEN PASTRY

This is the pastry traditionally used to make triangular turnovers filled with poppyseeds or prunes for the Jewish holiday of Purim. It has a distinct lemon flavor that complements the sweet filling (page 277), and can also be used for tartlets or small jam-filled pastries or turnovers.

Quantity: About 24 hamantaschen (turnovers).

2 eggs
½ cup granulated sugar
½ cup butter or margarine,
    melted
2 tablespoons water
1 teaspoon vanilla extract
Grated zest and juice of 1 lemon
½ teaspoon baking soda
½ teaspoon baking powder
A pinch of salt
3 cups all-purpose flour

Read Basic Preparation Technique (page 36). In a mixing bowl, beat together the eggs, sugar, melted butter or margarine, water, and vanilla. Add the grated zest and juice of lemon. Sift in the baking soda, baking powder, salt, and flour. Stir the dough until it forms a ball, feels stiff, and is no longer sticky. Add a little more flour if necessary. Wrap the dough ball in wax paper and refrigerate at least 30 minutes or while preparing the filling.

LINZER PASTRY

This pastry comes from the town of Linz, Austria, where it was created by a pastry chef in the early 1800's. Traditionally it is flavored with a generous amount of cinnamon and cloves and used as the shell for Linzertorte (page 179). The dough itself can also be formed into clove-studded ball cookies and rolled in confectioner's sugar (page 181).

Quantity: One 11-inch tart plus thirty 1-inch round cookies or two 9-inch tarts or one 11-inch and one 8-inch tart.

3 cups all-purpose flour, sifted
1 cup granulated sugar
¼ teaspoon salt
⅛ teaspoon ground cloves
¾ teaspoon cinnamon
1¼ cups unsalted butter
1 cup ground almonds (or walnuts)
2 teaspoons grated lemon zest
1 egg plus 1 yolk
Optional cookie garnish: *whole cloves*

Read Basic Preparation Technique (page 36). In a large mixing bowl, or a large model food processor (with a capacity of 5 cups dry ingredients), combine flour, sugar, salt, cloves, and cinnamon. Cut in the butter until the mixture is crumbly, with bits the size of rice. Stir in the ground nuts and lemon zest. Finally, add the egg and yolk and mix lightly just until the dough begins to cling together in clumps. Turn out onto wax paper, form a ball, wrap, and chill at least 30 minutes. For one 11-inch tart use ⅔ of the dough and save the rest for cookies.

POTATO PASTRY

This recipe comes from Finland, where boiled potatoes are a staple and pastry is often made out of the leftovers. Whether or not you use leftovers, the mashed potatoes added to this dough give it a special texture and flavor that go well with all savory tarts and pies as well as meat pastries and tartlets. Try it for a top crust over a Shepherd's Pie or Hasty Pie instead of plain mashed potatoes. The dough is very easy to handle.

Quantity: Two 9-inch crusts.

> *1½ cups all-purpose flour*
> *1 teaspoon baking powder*
> *½ teaspoon salt*
> *½ cup butter, or use half butter plus*
> *   half margarine, cut up*
> *1 cup mashed potatoes, made from ½*
> *   pound raw potatoes, boiled, peeled,*
> *   and mashed*
> *3 to 4 tablespoons milk, as needed*

Read Basic Preparation Technique (page 36). Sift the dry ingredients together in a bowl. Work in cut-up butter. When the mixture is crumbly, with bits the size of rice, mix in the mashed potatoes, then add only enough milk to allow the dough to cling together in clumps. Turn out onto wax paper, form dough ball, wrap, and chill at least 30 minutes. Or, according to the instructions in your recipe, roll the dough out on a floured surface immediately.

HOMEMADE PIECRUST MIX

To save time, you may want to prepare this mix ahead and store it in a cool pantry; hydrogenated vegetable shortening does not have to be refrigerated. At the last minute, you just add water, mix, and roll out the dough.

> *6 cups all-purpose flour, sifted*
> *1 tablespoon salt*
> *1 (1 pound) can (2⅓ cups) hydrogenated*
>   *vegetable shortening such as Crisco*

Mix flour and salt together, then cut in shortening until mixture is crumbly, with bits the size of rice. Store in a covered container for up to a month in a cool place. Makes about 9 cups mix, or six 9-inch pie shells.

Crust Size:	Add mix for *one* crust:	Or mix for *two* crusts:	Plus ice water:
8-inch	1¼ cups	2 to 2¼ cups	2 to 4 tablespoons
9-inch	1½ cups	2¼ to 2½ cups	2 to 4 tablespoons
10-inch	1¾ cups	2⅓ to 2¾ cups	3 to 5 tablespoons

To use, measure required mount of mix into a bowl. Sprinkle on ice water and work lightly with a fork just until the mixture holds together. The quantity of water will vary with dampness of weather and quality of flour; use as little water as possible. Form a dough ball, wrap in wax paper, and refrigerate 30 minutes. To roll out, form, and bake dough, see page 38.

PIZZA DOUGH

This is a good all-purpose pizza dough. It makes a fine crisp crust and can be topped with a variety of ingredients. For specific recipes, see index. Note that the dough requires about one hour to rise, so plan your time accordingly.

Advance preparation: After rising, the dough can be punched down, set in a covered bowl, and refrigerated for several hours or overnight. To use, bring to room temperature, punch down if risen again, and shape.

Special equipment: A rectangular baking sheet 14 × 17 inches or a large round pizza pan; optional: pizza cutting wheel.

Quantity: One 13 × 16-inch rectangle or one 14- to 15-inch diameter circle; to serve 4 (with 8 slices).

> *2 packages granular dry yeast*
> *1 cup warm water*
> *1 tablespoon granulated sugar*
> *1 teaspoon salt*
> *1 tablespoon oil*
> *2¾ to 3 cups unbleached all-purpose flour*

In a small bowl, combine the yeast with ½ cup warm water 105–110°F, and the sugar. Set aside until the mixure looks bubbly—about 4 to 5 minutes. In a large mixing bowl, combine salt, oil, and the remaining ½ cup warm water. When the yeast mixture is bubbly, add it to the other ingredients and stir. Add about 2¾ cups flour, mixing well until the dough looks elastic and forms a ball. Turn it out onto a floured surface and knead about 10 minutes; add extra flour if necessary, working until the dough is no longer sticky and feels smooth to the touch. Rinse out the large bowl, dry it, and add about 1 tablespoon oil. Turn the dough ball in the oil, then cover it with a piece of wax paper, and set it in a warm place (such as an *unlighted* oven with a pan of hot water on bottom shelf) to rise about one hour or until doubled in bulk. Prepare the sauce while the dough rises. Complete shaping and topping according to specific recipe instructions.

DEEP-DISH PIE TOPPING

Using only a top layer of crust eliminates the problem of soggy bottoms for very moist pie fillings and also eliminates half the pastry calories.

Prepare Basic All-Purpose Flaky Pastry (page 34), using 1½ cups flour. Roll out one single crust, 1 inch larger than the diameter of your baking dish. Prepare the fruit filling according to recipe instructions. Fill the pie plate, then cover with rolled pastry. Crimp the edges to the plate rim by pinching with your fingers and pressing with floured fork tines. For a tighter seal, you can brush the plate rim with egg glaze (page 121) before crimping the dough. Cut a hole in the center of the pastry to vent the steam. Brush with egg glaze or milk and sprinkle with granulated sugar; bake according to specific recipe instructions. Decorative vine and leaf shapes, or initials, can be cut from dough scraps and applied to egg-glazed pastry. Be sure to glaze the tops of the decorative cutouts before baking.

(*Note:* Scraps of Classic Puff Pastry [page 85] or Quick Puff Pastry [page 82] can be used for topping sweet or savory deep-dish pies. The high-rise of the dough is particularly attractive on these pies.)

For another alternative, top sweet deep-dish pies with Oat-Wheat Germ or Nut-Crumb Streusel Topping (page 112).

COBBLER TOPPING AND DUMPLINGS

This recipe can be spooned over hot sweet or savory stews and cooked in a covered pot on a stove top or baked in the oven. Use the sugar for fruit cobblers but omit it for savory fillings.

Special equipment: Mixing bowl or food processor fitted with the steel blade; for cooking: 2- to 3-quart stove-top oven-proof casserole or 9-, 10- or 11-inch deep-dish baking pan or oven-proof skillet. (*Note:* For stove-top cooking, be sure skillet has a tightly fitting lid.)

Quantity: Serves 6.

> *1½ cups all-purpose flour*
> *1½ teaspoons baking powder*
> *¼ teaspoon salt*
> Optional sweetener: *2 tablespoons*
> *granulated sugar*
> *4 tablespoons butter or margarine, at*
> *room temperature*
> *⅔ cup milk*
> *1 large egg*

Sift the dry ingredients into a mixing bowl or the work bowl of the food processor, fitted with the steel blade. Cut in the fat until the mixture is crumbly (only a few pulses in the processor). Add the milk and egg, stirring only a little, until the mixture is moistened completely. Set the batter aside until the fruit or savory filling is prepared. While the filling is still *hot,* spoon on batter.

For dumplings, place separate tablespoonfuls of batter slightly apart all over filling; for a single-layer crust, spoon out batter in even-sized dabs, then gently spread it into a single layer. Bake in a 425°F oven, uncovered, for 20 to 25 minutes, or until the topping is golden. Or cover the pan tightly and place on the stove top over medium-high heat. Bring the filling mixture to a boil, then reduce heat and simmer 12 minutes without lifting the lid. Then peek. The topping should be puffed up and dry inside. Cook longer if necessary.

Crumb and Nut Crusts

Crumb crusts are most often used with unbaked fillings such as chiffon or ice cream. They are best for freezer pies because frozen crumbs are not quite as brittle—or hard to cut—as frozen pastry. Crumb crusts are quick and easy to prepare using cereals, ground cookies or cracker crumbs, or nuts. When mixed with melted shortening and chilled, the crumbs hold their shape. To enhance the flavor and add a little more rigidity to the crust, you may bake it for a few minutes, though this is not essential. Some crusts are best chilled, others best baked slightly. Notice the variations in the recipes below. (*Note:* It takes about 30 minutes to chill a crumb crust until firm in the refrigerator.) To speed this process, you can freeze the crust.

A variety of cookie and cereal crumbs are available commercially. To prepare your own crumbs, break cookies or crackers into small pieces and place them in a plastic bag. Tie the bag, then tap and roll it with a rolling pin until the crumbs are finely and evenly crushed. Or process the crumbs in the blender or in the food processor fitted with the steel blade. (*Note:* When you are grinding nuts for a nut crust, you may find that some type of nuts get too oily too fast in the blender; the food processor can handle oily nuts with ease. To prevent this problem in the blender, dry nuts on a baking sheet in a 200°F oven for 5 to 7 minutes. Blend only ½ cup nuts at one time.)

PROCEDURE

Preheat the oven, if it will be used. Combine crumbs and sugar, if used, in a mixing bowl (or use the pie plate itself). Pour on melted shortening and gently toss crumbs to coat. Press the crumbs evenly over the bottom and sides of the pie plate. Take care not to build up too thick a layer in the corners. Use the back of a spoon or your fingers to press the crumbs. To make a rim, hold the thumb or forefinger of your left hand horizontally on top of plate rim, while fingers of the other hand press the crumbs up to it, making a firm lip. Bake as directed, setting the pie in the center of the oven. Or chill as directed and do not bake.

CRUMB AND NUT CRUSTS

For one 9-inch crust (for other sizes see below):	Quantity of crumbs needed:	Granulated sugar:	Melted butter or margarine:	Chill until:	Baking temperature:	Baking time:
Graham Cracker (*Note:* Four 2½-inch square crackers = ¼ cup crumbs.)	1¼ cups crumbs made from 20 2½-inch squares	2 tablespoons to ¼ cup, to taste	5⅓ tablespoons	firm	or 350°F	for 8 minutes
Graham-Nut	1 cup graham cracker crumbs plus ½ cup ground nuts	¼ cup	5⅓ tablespoons	firm	or 350°F	for 8 minutes
Zwieback	1½ cup zwieback crumbs	2 tablespoons	4 tablespoons	firm	—	—
Vanilla Cookie	1½ cups vanilla cookie crumbs	3 to 4 tablespoons	5⅓ tablespoons	firm	or 350°F	for 7 minutes
Almond Cookie-Nut	1¼ cups crushed Italian amaretti cookies plus ½ cup ground toasted almonds	¼ cup	5⅓ tablespoons	—	375°F (in *buttered* pie plate)	for 5 minutes
Gingersnap	1⅓ cups gingersnap crumbs made from 25 cookies 2 inches diameter	none to 2 tablespoons	5⅓ tablespoons	firm	or 375°F	for 6 minutes

CRUMB AND NUT CRUSTS—Continued

For one 9-inch crust (for other sizes see below):	Quantity of crumbs needed:	Granulated sugar:	Melted butter or margarine:	Chill until:	Baking temperature:	Baking time:
Chocolate Wafer	1½ cups chocolate wafer cookie crumbs made from 8 ounces of cookies	none to 2 tablespoons	5⅓ tablespoons	firm	—	—
Oreo Crumb	1½ cups cookie crumbs made from 18 Oreo cookies	none	2 tablespoons	firm	—	—
Chocolate-Almond (or Chocolate-Pecan, Hazelnut, Peanut, or Walnut)	¾ cups chocolate wafer crumbs made from 4 ounces of wafers plus ¾ cup ground nuts of your choice	none to 2 tablespoons	5⅓ tablespoons	firm	—	—
Nut (Almond, Hazelnut, Brazil Nut, Walnut, Pecan, Peanut, or a blend of the above)	1¾ to 2 cups ground nuts made from 1 pound shelled whole nuts	¼ cup	See Note.	—	375°F	for 8 minutes

(*Note:* Instead of added fat, you can process the nuts in the food processor until a paste forms. Pat the dough into the pie plate.)

Corn Flakes or Rice Cereal (Use as wheat substitute)	1⅓ cups crumbs made from 3 cups whole flakes plus a pinch each cinnamon and nutmeg	none to 2 tablespoons	4 tablespoons	firm	*or* 375°F	for 8 minutes
Granola-Nut	1 cup crushed toasted style granola cereal plus ½ cup ground walnuts	3 tablespoons dark brown sugar	5⅓ tablespoons	firm	—	—
Coconut	2 cups finely flaked or shredded sweetened coconut	none	4 tablespoons	—	325°F	for 15–20 minutes or until light golden color

Quantity of crumbs required for a variety of shell sizes:

for 8-inch shell: 1 cup crumbs, as per recipe

for 9-inch shell: 1⅓ to 1½ cups crumbs, as per recipe

for 10-inch shell: 1½ to 1¾ cups crumbs plus 1 tablespoon extra sugar and 7 tablespoons melted shortening instead of quantity indicated in recipe for 9-inch shell; for 10-inch Graham-Nut Crust, use 1 cup graham cracker crumbs plus ¾ cup ground nuts.

for one 3½-inch to 4-inch tartlet: ⅓ cup crumbs

for one 4½-inch tartlet: ⅓ cup plus 1 tablespoon crumbs

CHOCOLATE SHELLS

Of course, these chocolate candy shells are not pastry, but they make a very easy and elegant substitute for piecrust when used with special fillings. Double the recipe and keep the extra batch in your freezer for instant party tartlets (page 270). Fill them with a scoop of ice cream or a dollop of vanilla pastry cream topped with fresh berries and a rosette of whipped cream. For a deluxe dinner party finale that is made and frozen ahead, serve chocolate shells with Frozen Praline Mocha Pie filling (page 266), topped by a Chocolate Leaf. Read About Chocolate (page 115).

Advance preparation: Chocolate shells can be prepared well in advance and frozen until needed. Chocolate takes only 5 to 10 minutes to harden in the refrigerator. If you are storing them in the freezer, keep the cups in an airtight box, as they are fragile.

Special equipment: Muffin trays and paper or foil liners of matching size (use double liners in each cup for ease of handling). (*Note:* Other cup-shaped objects like seashells can be coated with chocolate as well. Try Coquille St. Jacques-style scallop shells, coated on the *outer* surface with pressed-on foil before adding chocolate.)

Quantity: 6 chocolate cups 3 inches in diameter.

> *1 cup semisweet chocolate morsels*
> *1 tablespoon butter or margarine*

Melt the chocolate and butter or margarine over medium heat in the top of a double boiler over hot (not boiling) water. While the chocolate is melting, set 2 paper or foil liners inside each muffin cup. Or press foil firmly to outside surface of cup-shaped shells. When the chocolate is soft, stir well, then remove from heat and set aside to cool about 3 minutes; do not let it harden. Working with one muffin cup at a time, spoon about 1½ tablespoons melted chocolate into the liner. Hold the paper at its top edge while spreading chocolate over the inside surface with the back of the spoon. Draw the chocolate up from the bottom. The coating should be fairly thick. If chocolate is too warm, it may run to cup bottom; if this happens simply refrigerate chocolate-lined cups a few minutes, then respread chocolate. (If coating seashells, set them foil side up on a paper-covered tray. Spread the melted chocolate over the shells in a generous layer.) Set muffin tins or tray of shells in the refrigerator or freezer until the chocolate is very hard—5 minutes in freezer, slightly longer in refrigerator. When hard, remove the chocolate-lined muffin cups or shells and set them on the counter to warm up for about 2 to 3 minutes. Then peel off the paper liners; for shells, first remove shell, then peel off foil. If the paper or foil sticks to the chocolate, it is still too cold. Fill the cups and serve, or refreeze in plastic bags set into a protective box until needed.

About Meringue Pie Shells

Tales of the origin of meringue are nearly as numerous as the confections it creates. *Larousse Gastronomique* credits a pastry chef, Gasparini, with producing the first crisply baked egg-white pastry in 1720 in the Swiss town of Meiringen, for which he named his invention. Though the tale may be apocryphal, the popularity of meringue spread from Switzerland to France, where it became a great court success, and Marie Antoinette herself (so it is said) delighted in making her own *vacherins,* or meringue nests.

Meringue is always dramatic when used on top of a pie (page 110), but it is just as special on the bottom, baked into a light, crisp shell, filled with fruit, whipped cream or ice cream, or precooked custard. However you use it, there are some important things to remember when working with meringue: Select a cool, dry day if possible since rainy, humid weather may soften the meringue. Keep all utensils scrupulously clean; a speck of fat (such as yolk) in the egg whites prevents them from beating to full volume because fat becomes suspended in the natural moisture of the whites, softens the protein, and thus weighs them down. Beware of plastic bowls, which are hard to get grease-free. A wet mixing bowl or beaters likewise will prevent whites from foaming properly. (*Note:* Eggs separate most easily when cold, but whites beat to fullest volume when at room temperature, 70°F.) Therefore, separate eggs as soon as they come from the refrigerator, then let them sit awhile; or set bowl of whites inside another bowl of warm water until they warm up. To separate eggs, see page 31. Frozen egg whites can be used, but should be defrosted at room temperature. Acidity stabilizes egg white foam; salt helps egg white proteins to remain firm. Therefore, the trick with meringue is to add acid (cream of tartar) and salt to the whites just before you begin beating them. To this end, you can also wipe your bowl and beater— before adding whites—with a paper towel dampened with white vinegar (be sure to dry them carefully), or use a copper bowl, which imparts its own acidity.

To hold its shape, meringue must be properly beaten. For the best effect with the least personal effort, use an electric mixer with the largest balloon beater available and a bowl that fits it most closely. The object is to keep the entire mass of whites in constant movement. Length of beating time will vary, depending upon your method, from 10 to 30 minutes or more. If you have a strong arm and are a traditionalist, by all means use a large balloon whisk with a copper bowl. To avoid fatigue, try to let your arm, from the elbow down, do most of the work; otherwise you expend most of your energy developing your pectorals. Hand beating will usually result in a greater volume of whites, and, of course, you get all the glory as well. Beat whites until they have a shiny satin appearance and can hold very stiff peaks. My grandmother's test for doneness is still effective: Set a whole raw egg—in its shell!—atop the beaten whites. The egg should sink in just a tiny bit (¼ inch). If it sinks in further, beat longer; if it doesn't sink at all, the whites are overbeaten. Occasionally, overbeaten whites become grainy. To save them, lighly beat in about ¾ of one fresh egg white.

The sugar added to meringue can be either the regular granulated type or superfine. The latter is best because the smaller grains dissolve faster. You can make your own superfine by grinding granulated sugar in the food processor fitted with the steel blade. Sugar (and vanilla or other flavor) should be added to the whites gradually and *only after* they begin to look fluffy; adding sugar too soon may prevent expansion. Beat the sugar into the whites until it is entirely dissolved, or the baked meringue may later "weep" when the sugar granules melt and ooze out. To be sure the sugar is completely melted, pinch some of the meringue between your thumb and forefinger. If it feels grainy, the sugar granules are still whole; if smooth, the sugar is dissolved. Old timers claim weeping is prevented by sifting a little cornstarch into beaten whites along with the sugar.

> *Note:*
> One large egg white = 2 generous tablespoons = ⅛ cup
> 4 large egg whites = 8 tablespoons = ½ cup
> 3 whites beaten stiff = 3 cups meringue = one 9-inch pie shell = eight
> 3-inch tartlets
> 4 whites beaten stiff = a generous 9-inch or regular 10-inch pie shell =
> ten or eleven 3-inch tartlets

MERINGUE SHELL RECIPE

Meringue crusts or shells are used for fresh fruit tarts, whipped cream or ice cream pies, or with cooked custard fillings (Angel Pies). Meringues can be baked in a buttered pie plate or in tartlet pans, or hand-formed on a prepared baking sheet into large and small nests: *vacherin* and *petit vacherin* in French. Before making meringue shells, read About Meringue on page 77.

Special equipment: 9-inch pie plate; electric mixer with balloon whisk; rubber spatula; for tartlets: baking sheet lined with brown paper cut from paper bag or baking sheet well buttered and dusted with flour; soup spoon; optional: pastry decorating bag fitted with large star tip.

Quantity: One 9-inch pie shell or eight 3-inch tartlets free-formed on a baking sheet.

> *3 large egg whites, at room temperature*
> (Note: *For a 10-inch meringue shell*
> *use 4 egg whites, but the same*
> *quantities of other ingredients.*)
> ¼ *teaspoon cream of tartar*
> ⅛ *teaspoon salt*
> ¾ *cup superfine sugar*
> Optional: ½ *teaspoon vanilla extract*

1. If you are using a pie plate, butter it generously. If you are using a baking sheet, butter it well and dust with flour, or line it with brown paper cut from a paper bag. Preheat the oven to 275°F. Combine the egg whites, cream of tartar, and salt in a mixing bowl. Beat until fluffy. Add ¼ cup sugar and beat again. Gradually add remaining sugar, beating after each addition. Add the vanilla with the last of the sugar. While beating, use a rubber spatula to stir down the whites from the side of the bowl from time to time. Beat 10 to 12 minutes on medium-high speed, or until all the sugar is dissolved (pinch the meringue to feel if it is still grainy) and the meringue is shiny satin in appearance.

2. If you are making a meringue piecrust, spread the meringue onto the bottom and sides of the well-buttered pie plate. Use the back of a spoon to pull up swirls around the rim, or fill a decorating bag fitted with a large star tip and pipe meringue rosettes around rim for a fancy edging. To form tartlet nests (*petits vacherins*), drop large spoonfuls of meringue, evenly spaced, onto the prepared sheet, and mold them with the back of the spoon into 3-inch diameter bowls with raised sides. Alternatively, you can pipe meringue from a decorating tube into 3-inch round disks, piping a second layer around the edge of each disk to create a rim.

3. Bake the meringue pie shell or individual tartlet shells 60 to 65 minutes at 275°F, or until they feel firm and crisp. If they are not hard after this time, turn off your oven, leave the door ajar slightly, and leave the meringues inside another 30 to 45 minutes, or overnight, to dry out. Theoretically, the baked shells should remain white, but don't worry if the color turns a light beige. However, do not brown as for a meringue *topping*.

4. When done, cool the meringue pie shell on a wire rack. As soon as meringue *tartlet* shells are done and while *still warm*, remove them from the baking sheet with a spatula and set them on a wire rack to cool. If the meringues stick to the brown paper, simply dampen the *underside* of the paper with a wet sponge, then lift off the meringues. They shouldn't stick, but occasionally it happens.

(*Note:* The edges of a meringue pie shell rise somewhat during baking but sink slightly when cool. Shells may crack when cold. Never mind; the filling and topping will hide everything, and I'll never tell.)

VARIATIONS:

Nut-Meringue Shell. Just before molding the meringue into the pie shell or tartlets, fold in ⅓ cup fine-chopped toasted almonds or pecans or other nuts. Or you can sprinkle fine-chopped nuts over the molded meringues just before baking.

Brown Sugar-Pecan Meringue. Add ⅓ cup fine-chopped pecans and substitute brown sugar for white.

PUFF SHELL DOUGH (*PÂTE À CHOUX*)

Cabbages (*choux*) are what the French call the round puffed pastries baked from this dough; the Germans name is "windbags" (*Windbeuteln*). Both terms are accurate descriptions, for this light eggy batter literally blows up in the heat of the oven, creating shells of light, crisp pastry with nothing inside but air. They are perfect for filling with all sorts of sweet or savory mixtures. Pastry cream-filled Cream Puffs, ice cream-filled Profiteroles, Éclairs, small cheese-filled hors d'oeuvre, or large ring-shaped cakes filled with Pastry Cream St. Honoré (Gâteau Paris-Brest) are but a few of the dramatic and flavorful creations made with this dough.

Puff shell dough is very quick and easy to make once you get the idea, but it does require attention to detail. Measure ingredients accurately and follow instructions with care.

Advance preparation: You can make these shells ahead and store them in airtight containers for a day or two. However, they always have the best texture and flavor the day they are baked. Shells can also be baked, wrapped airtight, and frozen. Unbaked dough can be covered and refrigerated up to 12 hours before being used if you must; but again, dough is best used right after mixing.

Special equipment: 3-quart heavy-bottom enamel or stainless steel saucepan; baking sheets; optional: electric mixer or food processor fitted with steel blade; wax paper; plastic wrap.

Baking time: 400°F for 25 to 35 minutes.

Quantity: 12 Cream Puffs about 3 inches diameter or 24 Profiteroles 1½ inches diameter or two 8-inch diameter ring cakes (Gâteau Paris-Brest) or 12 Éclairs 4 inches long.

1 cup all-purpose flour
½ teaspoon salt
1 cup water
½ cup unsalted butter, cut up
Optional sweetener for dessert pastry:
    1 tablespoon granulated sugar
4 to 5 large eggs, at room temperature
Egg glaze: *1 egg beaten with 1 tablespoon*
    water

1. Sift flour and salt together onto a piece of wax paper and set it aside.

2. In a large heavy-bottomed saucepan, combine the water and butter with the sugar, if you are using it. Place over medium heat until the butter melts, then raise the heat and bring to a fast boil. Immediately remove the pan from the heat before any liquid has time to evaporate and thus change the proportions of the ingredients. At once, pour in all the flour mixture and beat vigorously with a wooden spoon until the mixture forms a smooth ball that pulls away from the sides of the pan. Return the pan to the stove over low heat and beat hard with a wooden spoon for one minute longer to evaporate some of the excess water. This evaporation enables the dough to absorb more eggs, making a lighter pastry that puffs more. Set the pan aside, off the heat, to cool slightly.

3. Break 1 egg into a cup, beat it with a fork, and set it aside to be added to the batter later if needed.

At this point the remaining eggs are beaten into the batter as follows. You can be traditional and do this with a wooden spoon, or you can transfer the batter to the electric mixer or food processor fitted with steel blade. In any case, beat the dough after *each* egg has been added. Add the eggs one at a time, then beat well until the dough looks smooth. Don't skimp on beating here since this is what makes the dough light. After adding the fourth egg, test the consistency of the dough. It should be smooth and shiny and thick, but you should still be able to drop it from a spoon. It should slide from the spoon slowly; if the mixture is too thick to slide off the spoon, you need a *little* more egg. Add only *half* the reserved egg, beat the mixture, then test again. You should use only as much of this last egg as you require to make a shiny smooth dough. Too much egg makes a soft dough that will not hold its shape when baked. Finally, before using the dough, beat it vigorously for about one full minute by hand or in the electric mixer, or about 6 seconds in the processor.

4. If you are not planning to use the dough immediately, dab some butter over the top of it to prevent a film from forming. The dough can wait about 1 hour in a warm place, or up to 12 hours, covered with wax paper or plastic

wrap in the refrigerator. If the dough has been chilled, bring it to room temperature and beat it well before shaping and baking. (*Note:* You will get the best textured and highest-puffed shapes when the dough is used immediately after mixing.)

To shape pastries from puff shell dough, see specific recipes. In general, the pastry is brushed with egg glaze, then baked at 400°F for about 25 to 35 minutes, or until well-puffed and golden brown. Cool on a wire rack. Be sure to prick the baked shapes with a fork as soon as they come from the oven to allow steam to escape, keeping the shapes crisp.

(*Note:* The inside of baked shapes will always have some soft layers of dough clinging to the crisper edges. This is okay, but if you wish, the soft layers may be removed with a fork before you fill the pastry.)

QUICK PUFF PASTRY

This is a speeded up, easy-to-make version of Classic Puff Pastry (page 85) in which a Basic All-Purpose Flaky Pastry (page 34) has additional butter rolled and layered into it. The baked result is startlingly successful, rises well though not quite as high as the classic recipe, and tastes very buttery. Try this dough with all the classic puff pastry shapes and shells (see specific recipes in index).

Advance preparation: The dough can be prepared and frozen, or shaped as directed in a specific recipe, then frozen (up to 6 months) and baked unthawed. Dough leftovers can be wrapped airtight and frozen. Baked shapes can also be wrapped airtight, set in a protective box, and frozen up to 6 months, though after 6 weeks they lose some flavor.

Special equipment: Mixing bowl or food processor fitted with steel blade; dough scraper; rolling pin; tape measure or ruler; pastry brush; plastic bag or foil.

Baking time: 425°F for about 20 minutes, depending on specific recipe.

Quantity: Two 8-inch piecrusts.

> *2 cups all-purpose flour*
> *½ teaspoon salt*
> *11 tablespoons unsalted butter, cut up,*
> *   plus 5 more tablespoons butter for*
> *   rolling into dough*
> *5 to 6 tablespoons ice water, as needed*

1. Read Basic Preparation Technique (page 36) and prepare dough as you would for All-Purpose Flaky Pastry: sift flour and salt into a bowl, then pinch in butter until mixture is crumbly, with bits the size of rice. Add only enough water to enable mixture to hold together in clumps. Add a tiny bit more water if the dough feels too dry. Turn it out onto wax paper and form into a ball.

2. On a lightly floured surface, roll the dough out to a rectangle about 6 × 12 inches × ½ inch thick. Soften the remaining 5 tablespoons butter by pinching it with your fingers or tapping it with a rolling pin until it is pliable but not sticky or soft. The butter should be the same firmness as the dough; chill one or the other if it feels too soft.

3. On the upper half of the rolled-out dough, spread the softened butter into an even layer coming within ½ inch of the edge. Fold the bottom half of the dough up, covering the butter, and turn the dough crosswise so that the open edge faces to the right. Brush excess flour off the dough with a pastry brush.

Fold dough in thirds, as you would a letter. Again turn dough so the long open edge faces right. Roll out to about 6 × 12 inches. This is called the first *turn*. Fold the dough into thirds again, as for a letter, turn it open-edge-right, and roll out 6 × 12 inches to make the second turn. Fold dough into thirds another time, wrap, and chill at least 15 minutes.

4. After chilling, roll dough to about 6 × 12 inches, and this time make a *book fold* by bringing the top edge of the rolled dough down to the center line and the bottom edge up to the center line. Brush off excess flour, then fold top and bottom edges together. Dough will appear to be closing like a book when you turn it so the open edge faces to the right.

5. Wrap and chill the dough until ready to use, or roll out and cut as needed now. (*Note:* Dough should be chilled as long as possible whenever you have the time.)

To bake, follow directions in specific recipes. In general, this dough should be set on a baking sheet lightly sprinkled with cold water to give added moisture and baked in a 425°F oven for 20 to 25 minutes, depending on the individual recipe.

About Classic Puff Pastry

Eating a piece of well-made puff pastry is a supremely sensual experience: Its golden color delights the eye, it smells and tastes buttery, and it has an ethereal flakiness that defies gravity and intrigues the tongue. In short, it sounds too good to be true and too exotic to be home-baked. Wrong! You may be frightened off by the legend of this classic recipe, or by the length of the directions, but I urge you to reconsider and try it just once. It takes much longer to describe than to make; the hardest part is waiting out all the chilling periods when neither you nor the dough have anything to do but rest. If you are the impatient type, or just very busy, make Quick Puff Pastry (page 82) instead—it is remarkably fast to prepare and rises effectively, though not quite as high as the traditional puff pastry.

The magic of the puffed layers is actually a matter of chemistry and mathematics. When layers of butter are rolled between layers of dough in a carefully prescribed pattern and set into a very hot oven, the moisture in the dough and the butter boils and creates steam. The steam rises, pushing apart the layers of dough as the heat bakes them into separate leaves. The oven heat must be high to accomplish this lifting and setting of leaves before the fat melts and is absorbed by the flour starch. The layers must be rolled out evenly and chilled thoroughly in order to rise evenly.

A successful puff pastry will rise in the oven to at least four times its original height, and it will be made up of over 1,000 layers of dough, hence the name of the dough in French: *pâte feuilletée*, "leafy paste (pastry)." Anywhere from 1,245 to 2,380 layers will produce a fine rise (don't try to count the layers or figure it out, the instructions do it for you), though if you get carried away and give too many folds and turns you can conceivably make too many weak layers that will not be able to rise properly. It is, therefore, important to follow these instructions carefully and consider the following general notes before you begin:

In order to keep the butter from melting and being absorbed by the flour, the dough must be kept chilled. In fact, everything that comes in contact with the dough must be cold, to protect and separate the butter layers. Use a marble counter if possible; in very hot weather, chill your work surface by setting upon it roasting pans full of ice water (and remember to dry the surface well before setting down the dough). Chill your rolling pin in the refrigerator as well, if you like, as pastry chefs do in France. Be sure to chill the dough at least the minimum time noted in the recipe. This cold rest relaxes the gluten in the flour and firms up the butter and dough layers. If the weather is extremely hot and moist and you are making puff pastry for the first time, consider waiting for a cooler day. Or pay strict attention to dough chilling instructions. (*Note:* Do *not* chill dough in the freezer during the folding and turning process; the dough will harden unevenly when placed in extreme cold for a short period.)

If the butter breaks out of a dough layer during the rolling, pinch the dough closed over the tear and sprinkle it with a little flour.

When rolling dough, work from the center out to the ends. To maintain the even thickness of the dough layers, do not run the rolling pin over the edges of the dough or they will get thinned out. Instead, roll just up to, but not over, the dough edges.

To avoid toughening dough by adding extra flour, use a pastry brush to remove any excess flour on the dough before folding it.

Follow the directions in specific recipes for cutting out, shaping, and baking Puff Pastry. (Note, however, that dough cut within ½ inch of the edge of a rolled out sheet will never rise evenly; for this reason, cut large important shapes from the central area and save the edges and scraps for hors d'oeuvre and other pastries that do not require maximum rising.

Always roll dough between ⅛ inch and 3/16 inch thick before cutting shapes. Always cut with a sharp knife, never one that compresses, squeezes, or pulls the dough; this impedes the rising.

Leftover dough scraps, called *rognures* in French, will never rise as high as the original dough once they are combined and rerolled; for this reason, they are known as *demifeuilletage*. To reuse scraps, set them alongside one another, or make 2 layers, keeping the layers as nearly horizontal as possible. The object is to retain the layering. Roll out, chill the sheet of dough until firm, then cut and shape pieces. As they will rise unevenly, scraps should not be used for large presentation pieces; use instead for cocktail savories (page 391) or piecrusts or meat pie toppings, wherever Quick Puff Pastry is recommended.

Before or after rolling, scraps can be wrapped airtight and frozen.

Just before baking, puff pastry pieces are glazed with an egg wash made by beating together 1 egg and 1 tablespoon water. Do not let this glaze drip down the sides of the pastry, or it will glue the edges together, and they will not rise.

Sprinkle water on the baking sheet before setting the pastries upon it to bake. The water holds the bottom layer of dough in place, letting the dough lift and rise, and the extra moisture aids the rising.

Always bake puff pastry in a thoroughly preheated, 425°F to 450°F oven. Baking time is generally 20 to 30 minutes for medium-sized pieces, longer for large cases, depending on the specific recipe. You need the hot oven in order to separate and set the pastry layers quickly. (*Note:* In some large thick shells, like the vol-au-vent, the dough center will not bake through entirely in the time it takes the outer layers to brown. You can leave the pastry in a 300°F oven for a slightly longer time, to dry out inside, or simply scoop out the doughy center layers and discard them. You will still have a fine pastry base of cooked layers on the bottom.) To prevent pastry from rising in the central area when you wish a raised pastry border, pierce the dough with the tines of a fork to allow steam to escape. This impedes rising somewhat. If the area rises in spite of your efforts, you can prick it again during baking, or flatten it gently with a potholder.

CLASSIC PUFF PASTRY (*PÂTE FEUILLETÉE*)

This recipe is based upon the technique taught at l'École de Cuisine La Varenne in Paris, wherein a small amount of flour is worked into the butter to make it more stable and easier to handle before it is layered into the dough. This procedure eliminates many of the hazards associated with the making of puff pastry, such as sticky butter that melts or breaks out from between the dough layers. The combination of flours used (cake plus all-purpose) gives a dough with the proper elasticity and rising ability, and the acidity of the lemon juice or vinegar cuts down the gluten and makes the dough tender.

Advance preparation: Puff pastry can be prepared up to step 6 (4 turns), then wrapped and refrigerated or frozen. Refrigerate dough up to a week; freeze it, wrapped airtight, up to 6 months. Or bake pastry shapes, then store them up to a week in a cool place in an airtight container, or freeze them wrapped and packed in a protective box. (*Note:* Baked dough, frozen, keeps only about 6 weeks before losing its delicate flavor.) Leftover dough scraps can be wrapped and frozen for later use. (*Note:* Freezing is actually good for the un-baked dough, since the cold relaxes the gluten.) Frozen precut dough shapes can be baked unthawed; simply leave them in the oven a longer time to bake thoroughly and watch carefully to be sure they do not overbrown before bak-ing completely inside. For large frozen pieces, reduce the oven heat to 300°F or 350°F *after* the outside has risen well and browned; bake 10 to 15 minutes longer to dry out the interior.

Special equipment: Large mixing bowl; optional: food processor fitted with the steel blade; dough scraper; tape measure or ruler; pastry brush; timer; sharp knife or pizza-cutting wheel for cutting dough.

Baking time: 425°F for 20 to 30 minutes, depending on specific recipe.

Quantity: 2 pounds dough; enough for one 10- or 11-inch vol-au-vent (patty shell, page 366) or two 9-inch square cases or twenty-one 3-inch square cases or ten 4-inch square cases (page 186).

> *3 cups all-purpose flour*
> *1 cup cake flour*
> *2 cups unsalted butter (do not substitute*
>   *margarine), left at room temperature*
>   *about 10 minutes*
> *2 teaspoons salt*
> *2 teaspoons lemon juice or white vinegar*
> *¾ to 1¼ cups ice water, as needed*

1. Combine the flours in a large mixing bowl. Stir them together, then remove one fourth of the flour (1 cup) and set it aside to be mixed with the butter in a later step. Divide the butter into quarters. If weather is *hot,* return

¾ of the butter to the refrigerator. To the flour in the large bowl, add 1 teaspoon salt and one quarter of the butter, cut up.

With your fingertips or a pastry blender (or in the food processor fitted with the steel blade, pulsed for only 6 to 10 seconds), lightly and quickly work the flour into the butter as you would for a flaky piecrust. When the mixture is crumbly, add all the lemon juice and a few tablespoons of the water at a time, using *only* enough water to hold the dough together. Do not add excess liquid and do not overhandle the dough. If using the processor, pulse only a couple of times as the liquid is added; stop entirely as soon as the dough begins to clump. When dough clumps together, form it into a ball by hand, then flatten it into a square shape on your floured work surface. With a sharp knife, cut a cross into the surface of the dough, about halfway through its thickness; this speeds the chilling of the interior of the dough. Wrap in a plastic bag and refrigerate 15 to 25 minutes, until firm but not hard. This coarse-looking dough packet is called in French the *détrempe,* meaning flour and water tempered or blended into a paste. While this dough chills, prepare the remainder of the butter.

2. To prepare the butter for incorporation into the dough, it must be softened, then blended with the reserved 1 cup flour to make it easy to handle. Place the remaining three fourths of the butter on the floured counter. If too cold to work, let it stand at room temperature a few minutes. Then, with your floured fist or a floured rolling pin, pound the butter until it is pliable but not sticky or soft. The idea is to get it to the same degree of firmness as the dough now chilling in the refrigerator. When the butter is workable, cut into it the remaining 1 cup of flour and 1 teaspoon salt. Working in a bowl or on the floured counter, use the dough scraper to help lift, turn, toss, and cut the butter and flour until it is fairly well blended. Your hands are warm; touch the buttery dough as little as possible.

Now form this buttery mixture into a ball and set it between 2 floured sheets of wax paper. Roll it out into approximately a 7-inch square, then wrap and refrigerate it until firm but not hard (15 to 25 minutes).

3. Now you are ready to combine the first batch of dough with the square of butter, making what the French call a *pâton.* On a lightly floured surface, using a floured rolling pin, roll out the dough into an 11-inch square. Set the 7-inch butter square diagonally in the center of the dough. Fold over each of the four visible dough corners so they meet and form a cross, enclosing the butter completely inside a dough envelope. Pinch the edges of the dough to seal, then pat gently with the rolling pin to compress it slightly. With a pastry brush, brush off the excess flour from dough. Wrap and refrigerate 15 to 25 minutes, so butter and dough will become the same temperature before being rolled out.

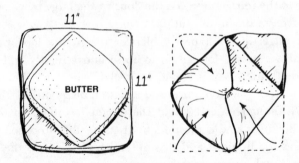

4. On a lightly floured surface, place the dough seam side down and roll it out about 6 × 15 inches × ½ inch (a). Whenever rolling dough, go almost up to but not over the dough edge. Keep all edges square; if they waver, tap alongside them with the side of the rolling pin to bring them into line. Use a pastry brush to remove the excess film of flour from the dough after rolling.

Each time the dough is rolled and folded up, it is called a turn. To make the first turn, fold the dough in thirds as you would a letter, bringing the bottom third of the dough up, and folding the top third down over the bottom (b). Press across the dough 3 or 4 times with the rolling pin to compress it slightly. Then turn the dough "letter" over, face down and swiveled 90 degrees around, so the seam is underneath facing toward the right side and the opened ends are at the top and bottom (c). This takes much longer to describe than to do, so don't be put off! Press your fingertip into the dough to mark the number of turns it has so far received (one). This mark will tell you where you left off in case the phone rings or you have to refrigerate the dough for some reason before continuing.

5. Now roll out the dough again into a rectangle about 6 × 15 inches, keeping the thickness even and the edges straight as you roll. Brush off excess flour, fold dough into thirds as before, and turn. This is the second turn; mark 2 fingertips in the dough. Place the dough in a plastic bag and refrigerate 15 to 25 minutes to chill.

6. Give dough 2 more turns as above, and make four marks with your fingertips to indicate the total number of turns (d; four). Wrap and refrigerate 15 to 25 minutes. At this point, the dough can be wrapped airtight and refrigerated up to a week or frozen up to 6 months. The final 2 turns (for a total of 6) must be given just before rolling and shaping.

7. Before using, the dough needs 2 more turns. After giving these, as described above, mark with your fingertips to indicate that dough now has had 6 turns in all.

After 6 turns, you should wrap and refrigerate the dough at least 25 minutes.

It *can* be rolled out, cut, and baked after that, but if possible it is best to chill it up to 2 hours or overnight to relax the dough thoroughly before baking.

(*Note:* After rolling out and cutting the dough shapes, they should be chilled one final time on their baking sheets just before being set into a very hot oven.) For shaping and baking, see specific recipe instructions. In general, however, puff pastry pieces are baked on dampened baking sheets at 425 to 450°F for 20 to 30 minutes, depending on the individual recipe. Finished pieces should be well puffed and a rich golden brown. Cool on a wire rack.

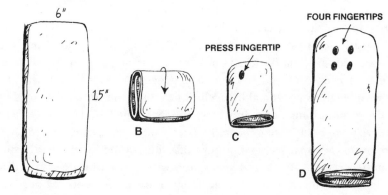

About Strudel

Strudel and its close relative phyllo (*filo*) (page 96) are among the most fascinating of all pastry doughs—translucent sheets of ethereal lightness wrapped around sweet or savory fillings to produce pastries of indescribable delicacy. This special dough was first introduced to the Mediterranean region by the Saracens, who brought it with them when they invaded the area in the eighth century. According to Waverly Root in his *Food of Italy,* their flaky pastry was the direct ancestor of the French *millefeuille,* the Adriatic's phyllo, and even Central Europe's strudel.

The superb lightness of this finely stretched pastry seems to most of us to be the magical product of old Hungarian or Bavarian or Greek grandmothers, or at least of clandestine commercial bakeries delivering to supermarkets frozen packets of dough under cover of darkness. While it may be true that the legend of skillful, rosy-cheeked grandmothers contributes to the magic of strudel-from-scratch, it is equally true that it is a technique that can be taught. How else could it have been handed down from mother to daughter over so many generations? Sure there are tricks, but I will put on my babushka and share them with you. And if you will try it just once, I guarantee you will find it surprisingly easy and fun.

A little practice will give you enough assurance and feel for the dough to have confidence, and from that point on you will take pleasure in creating imaginative strudel fillings and watching your culinary reputation soar.

It was the fabulous strudel-making reputation of Nada Gerovac that brought me, one spring day, to the kitchen of Nada's Dubrovnik Restaurant in Fort Lauderdale, Florida. A delightful and energetic woman, Nada was born in Banja Luka, Yugoslavia, and came to southern Florida in 1951. Her restaurant specializes in Yugoslavian and Hungarian cuisine, but her fame comes deservedly from her apple, cheese, spinach, and cherry strudel, which for a while she sold commercially for supermarket distribution. Today, she limits herself to making small quantities of freshly baked strudel, which she serves hot from the oven to the eager and appreciative diners in her small establishment. Despite her busy schedule as master chef and baker, Nada generously spent an entire morning sharing with me her strudel-making technique. Under her direction, my daughter, then eight years old, my aunt, and I carefully stretched Nada's dough across the cloth-covered work table. She assured us we could do it, and we did. Then we watched entranced by her casual, almost offhand manner as she deftly sprinkled on the butter, crumbs, fruit, and sugar, and with a few quick gestures lifted the cloth and rolled up the strudel. It seemed only moments before we were exclaiming over the taste and texture of the crisp, light-as-air flakes of warm, sugared pastry washed down with steaming cups of strong tea and lemon. "You must slice the strudel the moment it comes from the oven," warned Nada, "to keep it crisp. Otherwise, the steam makes the dough soggy as the strudel cools." Nada reminded us that, like most pastry making, the secrets of strudel have to do with a combination of chemistry and technique. Once you understand the basics of both, "getting the feel of it" will make sense to you.

The most important thing to remember is that in order to transform a ball of kneaded unleavened dough into a large translucent tissue, you must have an elastic dough, one that will willingly stretch, not a short, flaky dough such as you would use for piecrust. For strudel, you must use a flour with a high enough gluten content to permit the handling necessary (see Flour, page 26). In my kitchen tests, I consistently found that high gluten bread flour gave the best results and always stretched with ease. All-purpose flour, on the other hand, was unpredictable and sometimes difficult to stretch thin enough (though this flour works well for Nada). If you cannot find high gluten bread flour, try to locate hard-wheat flour in a health food store and mix it half and half with all-purpose flour.

The second element to remember is the importance of "resting" the dough. Kneading dough develops the elasticity of the protein strands, or gluten, in the flour. Resting gives strands time to lose their tautness, like a stretched elastic band returning to its original shape. Once relaxed, the dough can be stretched again, just like the rubber band. As you follow the recipe, pay attention to the resting times. If your phone rings, answer it and let the dough rest longer. In this case, longer is better, but skimping can be disastrous. If your dough fights you and keeps retracting as you stretch it, it is asking for more time to rest. Well rested dough gives in graciously; unrested dough, like a tired baker, resists all attempts to cajole and coax.

The third secret is in oiling the dough. When you let the dough rest the first time after kneading, put it in a bowl with several tablespoons of oil over and around it. When you are ready to stretch the dough, shake off most but not all the oil. An oil coating will remain on the dough, helping to keep the skin from drying out too quickly. If, as you stretch, the edges or center of the dough dry out and become brittle, brush on a little more oil to moisten the surface.

Another tip involves the table covering, which can be anything from a clean old sheet to a worn tablecloth. It is used both to prevent the dough from sticking to the table and to act as a convenient "pusher," enabling you to lift one edge of the strudel and roll it over onto itself without ever touching it with your hands. You may find it a help to use a cloth with a printed design, the more delicate the design the better. For once you can see this pattern clearly through the dough, you will know it is stretched sufficiently thin. Or you may prefer to slide a magazine page beneath the dough to test visibility and thinness; the clearer the type, the more delicately stretched and tender the dough.

The final trick is in handling the stretching of the dough. Many bakers lift the dough up on the backs of their hands, then stretch it by spreading the hands apart, working from the underside of the dough. Nada, on the other hand, showed us how she works, pulling and stretching the dough by placing her hands palms-up under the dough. Go slowly, experiment, and find the method that feels comfortable for *you*. The end result is what counts.

STRUDEL

Advance preparation: Early in the day, or the evening before you use it, you can prepare the basic strudel dough, setting it to rest until needed. The completely filled and rolled strudel can be placed on a buttered baking sheet and refrigerated for up to 2 days before baking. Or, the completed, unbaked strudel may be wrapped airtight in buttered heavy duty foil and frozen until ready to bake without thawing. Baked strudel can also be foil-wrapped and frozen, then unwrapped and warmed before serving (see step 12).

Special equipment: Stretching table—a flat surface *at least* 3 × 4 feet or larger. If you do not have a table roughly this size, plan to work with half the dough at one time, keeping the rest oiled and covered.

Cover the table with a clean sheet, preferably patterned, or an old table-cloth. If the cloth slides as you work the dough, tape the corners underneath the table. Rub about ¼ to ⅓ cup flour into the cloth all over.

Mixing bowl and spoon or electric mixer or food processor fitted with the plastic dough blade; pastry brush; small saucepan for melting butter; sifter; thin sharp serrated knife for slicing strudel; baking sheet, 12 × 16 inches, buttered; heavy-duty foil for freezing strudel.

Timing: From start to finish, you can make this in about 2½ hours. For a first attempt, allow yourself a whole morning, or about 3 hours.

Quantity: The amount of strudel dough produced by this recipe will stretch to a sheet of dough roughly 4 feet square. When filled and rolled, this makes a 30- to 32-inch long roll that serves 15 to 16; one serving is a slice about 2 inches wide. The final size of your strudel will vary with your skill in stretching the dough and the type of filling used.

> *2¼ cups high-gluten bread flour, or half*
> *all-purpose and half bread flour*
> *¼ teaspoon salt*
> *1 large egg*
> *2 tablespoons unsalted butter, at room*
> *temperature*
> *½ to ¾ cup lukewarm water*
> Coating for dough: *¼ cup vegetable oil*
> Fillings, see page 307

1. Mix the dough using one of the following methods:

Hand Mixing Method

In a large bowl, combine flour and salt. Make a well in the center and add egg, butter, and ½ cup water. Combine, stirring at first with a spoon, then flour your hands and work all ingredients together with your fingers, adding in more and more flour as you go. Add more water, 1 tablespoon at a time, until the dough forms a ball. Turn it out on a lightly floured board and knead 10 minutes, adding more flour if necessary, until the dough is smooth, elastic, and without stickiness. Measure ¼ cup oil into a small bowl, add the dough, and turn it over in the oil. Cover with plastic wrap and set it aside to rest at least 30 minutes.

Electric Mixer Method

Use regular beaters or attach dough hook if your machine has one. In the mixing bowl, combine flour and salt. Add egg, butter, and ½ cup water. Mix on low speed (Kitchenaid #1 or #2) until the dough blends together. If your machine cannot work the dough once it is blended, remove it and complete by hand as above. Add more water to the mixing bowl, 1 tablespoon at a time, until the dough forms a ball and all flour leaves the sides of the bowl. The dough should be soft and pliable but not sticky. In a Kitchenaid, knead on low speed for 8 to 10 minutes; if you do not have a dough hook, knead by hand. Well-kneaded dough should be smooth, elastic, and without stickiness. Measure ¼ cup oil into a bowl, add the dough, and turn it over in the oil. Cover with plastic wrap and set aside to rest at least 30 minutes.

Food Processor Method

In the work bowl of your machine fitted with the plastic dough blade, combine flour and salt. Pulse 3 times to lighten flour. Add egg, softened butter, and ½ cup water. Process until the dough forms a ball. Turn off the machine and stir down the mixture if necessary. If it is too dry, add more water, 1 tablespoon at a time, until a ball forms and all dough leaves the sides of the bowl. Process continuously for 2 minutes, to knead dough. Stop once for a few seconds during this time to rest the machine and turn over the dough ball. Kneaded dough should be smooth, elastic, and without stickiness. Measure ¼ cup oil into a bowl, add the dough, and turn it over in the oil. Cover with plastic wrap and set aside to rest at least 30 minutes.

2. While the dough is resting, prepare filling ingredients (page 307) and set them out on a tray. After the dough has rested 30 minutes, remove it from the oiled bowl, drain off most of the oil, and place the dough in the center of the floured cloth. With a rolling pin at room temperature (not chilled), roll the dough into a rectangle roughly 10 by 15 inches. Allow the rolled dough to rest flat on the table for 5 minutes.

3. Remove your watch and rings and roll up your sleeves. Flour your hands. To begin, pick up the dough and place both your closed fists palms down under its center. The dough is now draped over the backs of your fists like a large floppy napkin. Slowly and gently, move your fists apart. The motion is as if you were talking with your hands, describing an expanding dome or a rainbow that is growing ever larger. After a couple of stretches in this manner, open your fists, but keep your hands back up and continue this motion. You can also move your hands gently up and down as you stretch the dough. Gravity is your partner here, since the dough's own weight pulls it down and helps the stretch as your hands move apart. You are, in fact, opening up the central area of the dough in the same way and for the same reason a pizza maker opens and spins his dough in the air. You, too, can spin the dough. Give it a twirl in the air, if you are feeling brave—the worst that can happen is that it will fall onto the covered table (hopefully not on the floor). Actually, the dough will surprise you with its

obedience, opening with ease to a circle about 24 inches in diameter. You will soon see that the central area begins to look slightly translucent.

At this point, toss the dough onto the table so the stretched portion traps air and forms a bubble. Let the dough rest in this position about 5 minutes. The air bubble will gradually deflate.

4. Start the stretching process now. With the backs of your hands, or palms up if that feels more comfortable, reach under the dough and spread your hands slowly apart as you raise them up a little, allowing the dough to lift and stretch. If you are working alone, hold one hand flat down on top of the dough and gently pull the dough in the opposite direction. It helps to have a partner working on the opposite side of the table to create a two-way stretch, but this is not essential. Remember to work very slowly, giving yourself and the dough plenty of rest. If the dough begins to look dried out or cracked in any place, brush on a little more oil. Work on the thicker, less transparent areas with attention; stay away from already thin and transparent areas.

Holes will occur in patches that are especially thin. Do not panic; don't even worry. Ignore holes, period. If they bother you more than you can bear, you can patch them by moistening the edges with a little water and sticking on a stretched bit of dough cut from one edge. However, when your dough is finally filled and rolled up, the holes will never show, since they will be buried between layers. The more experience you have, and the more slowly and evenly you stretch the dough, the fewer holes you will have and the less they will bother you. To stretch dough alongside a hole, hold down the torn edge with one hand, while the other hand stretches the nearby dough.

Gradually, the dough edges will become evenly translucent, with fewer and fewer thick areas. The edges of the dough may drape over your tabletop. It may take you anywhere from 15 to 35 minutes or more to stretch the dough completely. You have succeeded when you can read newsprint easily through it. Test this by sliding a sheet of newspaper or a magazine beneath the dough. Or, if you are using a printed tablecloth, check to see that the design is easily visible through the dough. With scissors or a sharp knife, cut away—without pulling—the thick outer edge all around the dough. This thick edge is too rubbery to reuse and should be discarded. Surprisingly, it will weigh nearly 8 ounces, almost a third of the dough's total weight. After the thick edges are trimmed, the dough will be more or less in the shape of a rectangle. We will call one end, preferably a short end, the head or top of the strudel, and will refer to this when giving filling instructions.

5. Preheat the oven to 450°F. Let the stretched dough dry out for 5 minutes before filling, unless, of course, the stretching has taken so long that the dough is beginning to look dry and brittle. In that case, fill immediately.

(*Note:* You should work more quickly in hot dry weather or when a warm stove or heater is nearby to dry out the dough.) Next to your dough-covered table, set out the tray with the filling ingredients, including the pan of melted butter with the pastry brush.

6. The first step in filling a strudel is to sprinkle, or lightly brush, melted butter all over the dough. If you are using a brush, set on the butter with light, one-way strokes to avoid tears. Next, sprinkle on a layer of bread or graham cracker crumbs, then the other ingredients, following the recipe directions.

7. According to the specific recipe instructions, the filling is spread over the dough in a particular area rather than all over: Beginning about one inch away from the top or head edge of the strudel, spread the filling ingredients evenly over ⅔ to ¾ of the dough, leaving roughly a 1- to 2-inch clean border along the side edges, and leaving the remaining ⅓ to ¼ of the stretched dough covered *only* by the melted butter and crumbs. The unfilled area has a purpose: When the strudel is rolled up, its final 2 or 3 layers will be made up of this "clean" area, and because the dough is not weighted down with filling, these outer layers will puff up to be crisp and light, creating a picturesque and toothsome exterior.

8. Fold the "clean" side edges over onto the filling. Fold the "clean" 1-inch top border over the filling. To roll up the strudel, stand at the head edge and gather up the cloth. With your hands spread apart—one near each end of the strudel—lift the cloth high enough to allow the dough to roll over onto itself. It should just gently flip over, making a strip about 3½ to 4 inches wide. Continue to lift the cloth, pulling it slightly toward yourself as you lift and the strudel rolls up. After each rollover, you can, if you like, brush more melted butter over the top of the strudel. *Roll loosely,* so the strudel will have room to expand in the heat of the oven. Brush melted butter generously over the top of the completely rolled strudel. The roll should be approximately 4 inches wide,

about 1½ inches thick, and between 26 and 32 inches long, or longer if you were extremely skillful in stretching the dough. Dimensions vary, depending not only upon the thinness of the dough but also upon the type of filling.

9. To bake the strudel, either cut it in half, or into whatever length fits comfortably on a buttered baking sheet (a 12 × 16-inch sheet will hold 2 halves of one whole strudel); or ease the entire roll onto the buttered sheet and curve it into a horseshoe shape. (*Note:* If you have cut the strudel into short sections, be aware that a little soft filling may run out the ends during baking. This can be ignored—it is not serious. However, to prevent this, you can seal the cut edges by brushing them with melted butter and pressing on stretched scraps of dough.)

10. Before baking, it is best (but not absolutely critical if you are in a hurry) to refrigerate the strudel on its buttered baking sheet for 20 to 30 minutes. This allows the butter to firm up and the dough to relax, making for a more flaky product.

11. To bake the strudel, set it in the lower third of a preheated 425°F oven. Bake 20 minutes, then lower heat and bake at 350°F for an additional 20 minutes, or until the pastry is a rich golden brown. Ease the strudel onto a wire rack. To prevent the cooling dough from becoming soggy as the steam escapes, immediately cut strudel into 2-inch sections with a thin, sharp, serrated knife. Sift on a light sprinkling of confectioners' sugar and serve warm.

12. If you do not intend to bake the strudel immediately, wrap it in buttered foil and refrigerate on trays for up to 2 days. Or wrap it in buttered foil, set on a flat surface, and freeze. To bake, place *frozen* strudel on a buttered baking sheet in the center of a preheated 350°F oven for 30 minutes; raise heat to 425°F and bake 15 to 20 minutes longer, or until the pastry is a rich golden brown.

Previously baked strudel may also be foil-wrapped and frozen. Before serving, reheat unwrapped, *thawed* strudel on a buttered baking sheet in a preheated 350°F oven for 15 to 20 minutes, until the inside is warm and the outer layers of pastry are crisp. Sift on a fresh sprinkling of confectioners' sugar.

(*Note:* For savory Strudels, see index for fillings used in *Spanakopitta, Empanadas,* or Seafood Timbale [thicken this with 8 tablespoons bread crumbs]).

About Phyllo

Like strudel, phyllo (also spelled filo) is a finely stretched paper-thin sheet of dough. Strudel, however, is kept in one sheet and rolled for baking, while phyllo is traditionally cut into smaller leaves, hence the word *phyllo,* meaning "leaf" in Greek. These are brushed with butter and stacked into layers over or around a variety of fillings before being baked into delectable golden puffs. As the Strudel recipe (page 91) contains similar ingredients and will attain an acceptable translucence, it can be substituted for phyllo in the recipes in this book. Simply cut the strudel into leaves of appropriate size and keep them covered until used so they will not dry out.

There is no stubstitute for the large sheets of homemade strudel dough, but I prefer not to make my own phyllo because a perfectly satisfactory substitute is widely available frozen in most supermarkets or oriental specialty shops. I admit I am influenced by another factor as well: I had always suspected I could not produce at home a phyllo as thin as the commercial product, but after a visit to a phyllo bakery in Crete, I was convinced.

The day I had this revelation was magical in every way. As I wandered the sunny streets of Heraklion, my eye was caught by the simplicity of a white stucco building punctuated on its upper level by aquamarine and olive-colored shutters and a row of pink geranium pots edging the roof. At street level, a dark, open archway led to a descending flight of stairs. As I peered down, I saw an old man beckoning. "*Ela, ela . . .* come," he said. I entered, along with my daughter Cassandra and a Greek-speaking American friend, Susan Kanas. Like Alice falling down the rabbit hole, we stumbled into a cavernous basement. It was lighted only by a couple of bare ceiling bulbs; the floor space was filled with enormous square tables. With floury welcoming hugs and handshakes, Kyriós (Mister) Sideris introduced himself to us as the patron and papa, who ran this bakery with his two sons and a daughter-in-law. Adonis, the appropriately named younger son, joined us, curious to see "tourists" for the first time in their establishment. With thick dark hair, dark black eyes flashing in his tan face, and a wide white smile, Adonis helped his father explain to us the technique of phyllo making. They preferred a mixture of Canadian and French flour, he said almost apologetically, because it produced a higher gluten content than their native Greek flour. This they blended with water and salt before mixing in the archaic electric dough machine that quietly groaned and rumbled in the corner. The last stage of production, he announced with a flourish, was the most dramatic. He was right. To demonstrate, the father rolled out a disk of dough flattened like a pizza. After resting it to relax the gluten, he lifted the disk and spun it in the air to Adonis, who caught it midair and, spacing his hands farther and farther apart, stretched the dough to a silken sheet whirling over his head. Suddenly, he tossed the sheet onto the center of a large table, where, trapping a huge bubble of air, it sat to rest like a beached white turtle. After a few minutes, the second brother entered the act, doing a sort of primitive folk dance as he walked rhythmically around the table with slow short steps, reaching out at even intervals to give a gentle tug to the edge of the dough bubble. Gradually, the air pocket deflated. As the boy continued to tug the edge, the dough began to stretch, and after some six or seven minutes, the dough had opened into a flawless, translucent skin covering the entire ten-foot square surface. The ragged dough edges overhanging the table were cut off unceremoniously with several quick slashes of a razor blade wielded with definite ferocity by the daughter-in-law. Finally, Adonis flipped a linen cloth over the sheet of dough and the process began again. "From one batch of dough," he explained, "we can make about 240 large sheets, which we stack in layers of up to fifty on these tables." After the linens equalize the moisture and the layers dry sufficiently, they are cut up and refrigerated in one-kilo packets to await the arrival of the local housewives, who purchase it several times a week.

"Do you have phyllo in America?" asked Adonis.

"Well . . . I use a frozen type," I started to reply.

He beckoned me closer to the work table and with a grin spread the day's newspaper flat on the counter. This he covered with a sheet of phyllo he had just removed from the refrigerator. "See that!" he laughed, pointing to the newsprint clearly visible beneath the dough. "And that?" He cavalierly added a second sheet of dough over the first and pointed to the smallest print, still clear. As he positioned the third layer of dough, he explained apologetically: "Now we can read only the headlines because today is Monday." I, of course, thought we were having a translation problem until he explained that the phyllo we were "reading" was made the previous Saturday and, as they did not bake Sundays, the dough was 3 days old and already beginning to cloud and dry out. "If only this were fresh," he sighed, "then we would *really* have something to show you—reading the smallest print through *five* layers!"

TO USE FROZEN PHYLLO DOUGH

Frozen phyllo dough is available in Greek, Middle Eastern, or Oriental specialty shops, gourmet stores, and most supermarkets. In Greek or Armenian food stores, you may also find fresh phyllo. The frozen type is packed in 1 or 1½ pound packages containing about 25 sheets, rolled up together.

Frozen phyllo must be allowed to defrost several hours or overnight in its own package in the refrigerator. If defrosted at room temperature, the outer layers may become moist and unusable from condensation inside the package. After use, the dough can be rewrapped in a plastic bag and stored several days in the refrigerator, or about 3 months if returned to the freezer.

When defrosted, phyllo appears to be very fragile, but is actually quite pliable and strong enough to withstand gentle handling *if not allowed to dry out*. To this end, the defrosted phyllo should always be set on a tray and covered immediately with a sheet of wax paper or plastic wrap topped by a dampened tea towel. Keep it this way until brushed with butter and formed into pastries according to your recipe. When uncovered and exposed to the air too long, phyllo will crack and become impossible to handle. Small tears and cracks, however, should be ignored. These always occur; simply brush butter over the edges and press on a patching piece of dough.

To use, cut, fill, shape, and bake phyllo according to individual recipes. For a list of all phyllo recipes in this book, see the "phyllo" entry in the index. Individual recipes are grouped according to type (pie, hors d'oeuvre, etc.).

(*Note:* Since leaves of phyllo are brushed with butter as pastries are formed, it is best to bake individually formed hors d'oeuvre or pastries on a jelly roll pan with a lip to catch the excess fat as it melts in the oven.)

PASTRY FILLINGS
AND TOPPINGS

VANILLA PASTRY CREAM (*CRÈME PÂTISSIÈRE*)

Traditionally, this vanilla cream is used as a filling beneath glazed fresh fruits in tarts, or inside éclairs, cream puffs, napoleons, or cakes such as Gâteau Paris-Brest (page 302). The classic version uses as many as 6 egg yolks for 2 cups milk; I usually use 4 yolks, but if you worry about cholesterol, you can cut that down to only 2 or 3 yolks or 2 whole eggs, and the recipe will still work. (*Note:* The vanilla bean imparts an excellent flavor to the cream, but vanilla extract, added at the end of the recipe, is a good substitute.) In fruit tarts, this cream is most often flavored with vanilla or almond. However, for pastry fillings, you may wish to try some of the other flavor variations that follow.

Advance preparation: Pastry cream can be made ahead and refrigerated, tightly covered, for a week.

Special equipment: 2½-quart heavy-bottom enamel or stainless steel saucepan; whisk; mixing bowl; plastic wrap.

Cooking time: 12 to 15 minutes.

Quantity: About 2⅓ cups, enough for a 9-, 10-, or 11-inch fruit tart or two 9-inch fruit tarts or 12 to 14 cream puffs or éclairs, or one large or 2 small ring cakes.

⅔ cup granulated sugar
2 tablespoons cornstarch plus 2
    tablespoons all-purpose flour
A scant pinch of salt
4 egg yolks (or 2 to 3 yolks, or 2 whole
    eggs)
2 cups milk
1 vanilla bean, slit lengthwise; or 2
    teaspoons vanilla extract
2 tablespoons butter

(*Note:* The classic technique for preparing this recipe infuses the vanilla bean in hot milk, then removes the bean and whisks the hot milk into the egg-sugar-starch mixture before cooking them together. My technique, which I find easier and just as dependable, combines cold milk with the egg-sugar-starch mixture and cooks them together with the vanilla bean until the cream thickens. The longer the vanilla bean is left in, the more flavor it imparts. Try this method. Even if it seems unorthodox, it works.)

1. Stir together sugar, cornstarch and flour, and salt in a heavy-bottom saucepan.

Separate the eggs (page 31), putting the yolks in a mixing bowl and the whites in container to freeze for another use. Whisk the milk into the yolks (or whole eggs if you are using them), then whisk them into sugar-starch mixture. Whisk well to be sure all cornstarch and flour are picked up off the pan bottom and dissolved. Add the vanilla bean if you are using it; if you are using vanilla extract, do not add it until the end of the recipe or the cooking will dissipate its flavor.

2. Set the pan over medium heat and cook the custard mixture about 12 minutes, until thickened and brought to a boil. To do this, stir on and off for the first 5 minutes, then stir constantly about 7 minutes longer, until the mixture really thickens and reaches a boil, when you will see fat heavy bubbles work up to the surface and burst between stirs. Occasionally, use a whisk instead of a spoon, to break up and remove any lumps. Boil 1 full minute while stirring constantly, covering the entire bottom of the pan with the spoon. Remove the pan from the heat. The cream is sufficiently cooked if smooth and thick and if it will generously coat the spoon; it should hold a clearly defined line when you draw your fingertip through the cream clinging to the back of a coated spoon.

Remove the vanilla bean; wash and dry it for reuse. Stir in the butter and vanilla extract if you are using it. Spoon the cream into a bowl. To prevent a skin from forming, press a piece of plastic wrap into the surface or dab it with butter or sift on a light coating of confectioners' sugar. Cool. Cover and refrigerate.

VARIATIONS:

Praline Pastry Cream. Prepare Vanilla Pastry Cream. Fold into the finished, warm cream ⅓ to ½ cup powdered peanut or almond brittle. (Powder the broken pieces of brittle in a food processor or blender or a plastic bag pounded with a hammer.)

Coffee Pastry Cream. Prepare Vanilla Pastry Cream but dissolve 2 tablespoons powdered instant coffee into the milk before whisking it into the egg yolk mixture.

Chocolate Pastry Cream. Prepare Vanilla Pastry Cream. Melt 3 or 4 ounces finest quality semisweet or unsweetened chocolate in a double boiler, then stir into the finished, warm cream. The amount of chocolate depends on the amount of flavor you desire; I prefer the maximum.

Mocha Pastry Cream. Prepare Vanilla Pastry Cream. Melt 3 ounces semisweet chocolate in a double boiler. Stir in 4 teaspoons powdered instant coffee dissolved in 1 tablespoon hot water. Stir this into the finished, still warm cream.

Almond Pastry Cream. Prepare Vanilla Pastry Cream but stir 1 teaspoon almond extract into the cream along with the butter. You can also add ½ cup ground blanched almonds to make this Frangipane, a suitable filling for fruit tarts.

Orange Pastry Cream. Prepare Vanilla Pastry Cream but add 1 tablespoon grated orange zest to the milk-yolk mixture before cooking. Stir 2 or 3 tablespoons orange-flavored liqueur into the completely finished, warm cream.

Pastry Cream St. Honoré. (Saint Honoré is the patron saint of bakers.) Prepare Vanilla Pastry Cream. Beat 4 egg whites with a pinch of salt until fluffy. Add 2 tablespoons sifted confectioners' sugar; beat until stiff. Fold the whites into the hot pastry cream as soon as the butter has been added. The heat of the cream must poach the whites to create the correct consistency. Chill. Use to fill cream puffs or Gâteau Paris-Brest (page 302).

Butterscotch Pastry Cream. Prepare Vanilla Pastry Cream. Substitute ½ cup dark brown sugar for the granulated sugar.

Liqueur-Flavored Pastry Cream. Prepare Vanilla Pastry Cream but add 2 tablespoons rum, kirsch, or other liqueur of your choice, stirred into the cream along with the butter.

Whipped-Cream Pastry Cream. Prepare Vanilla Pastry Cream and set it aside to cool, then chill while you whip ½ cup heavy cream. Fold creams together.

Instant Pastry Cream. For desperate moments when time is precious, prepare one small package French vanilla pudding, *instant type,* using 1 cup milk. Whip ½ cup heavy cream until stiff and fold it into the pudding along with 1 teaspoon vanilla or almond extract. Or for even better (though packaged) flavor, use *cooked-style* vanilla pudding prepared as directed on the box and mixed with whipped cream and vanilla or almond extract.

ALMOND PASTRY CREAM (*FRANGIPANE*)

This almond-flavored cream is used as a filling beneath fruit in tarts and tartlets. It can be baked as a separate layer in the pastry shell, then topped by glazed fresh fruit, or it can be baked along with its fruit topping. In the latter case, the cream puffs up around the fruit, making a decorative presentation. Frangipane cream can also be used uncooked, spread over a prebaked pastry shell, and topped by glazed fresh fruit. For another version, see page 102.

Advance preparation: If it is to be used right away, keep frangipane at room temperature. To store, keep it covered in the refrigerator for 2 to 3 days, or frozen. If it is too stiff to stir easily after chilling, blend in a few tablespoons cream.

Special equipment: Food processor or blender or nut mill to grind nuts; mixing bowl; baking sheet for drying out nuts.

Quantity: 1 cup; enough to fill one 10- or 11-inch tart or 12 to 15 tartlets.

> *5 tablespoons butter, at room*
> *temperature, cut up*
> *5 tablespoons granulated sugar*
> *1 large egg*
> *4 ounces blanched almonds (⅔ cup,*
> *ground)* (Note: *To be sure the nuts*
> *are ground rather than turned to*
> *paste, you can first dry them on a*
> *baking pan in a 200°F oven for*
> *about 5 minutes. If you grind nuts*
> *in the food processor, be careful that*
> *the machine is turned off as soon as*
> *a fine powder is formed;*
> *overprocessing can make paste*
> *unless the nuts are very dry.)*
> *1½ tablespoons all-purpose flour*
> Flavoring: *½ teaspoon almond extract or*
> *1 tablespoon rum*

Hand Method: In mixing bowl, cream butter and sugar together until soft and smooth. Beat in the egg and flavoring. When these are well blended, stir in the ground nuts and the flour.

Food Processor Method: After grinding the almonds, add the cut up butter and pulse 2 or 3 times. Add sugar and pulse twice. Add egg, flavoring, and flour and blend smooth.

LEMON DOUBLE CREAM TART FILLING

This uncooked filling is quickly and easily made. The tangy lemon-cream cheese flavor is mellowed slightly by the addition of whipped cream. Spread the filling in completely prebaked tart or tartlet shells and top with any combination of fresh glazed fruits. Refrigerate.

Advance preparation: The filling can be made a day or 2 ahead *without* the whipped cream. Refrigerate. If it is too stiff to stir when chilled, add a table-spoon or 2 of milk or whipped cream to soften before folding in the remaining whipped cream. *With* whipped cream, the mixture will hold refrigerated for one day.

Special equipment: Food processor fitted with steel blade or electric mixer or blender; chilled electric mixer bowl and beater for whipping cream.

Quantity: 1½ to 1⅔ cups; enough to coat generously one 11-inch tart shell or 8 to 10 small tartlets.

> *8 ounces cream cheese (not whipped type)*
> *1 cup sifted confectioners' sugar*
> *2 tablespoons fresh lemon juice*
> *1 tablespoon grated lemon zest*
> *Optional flavoring: 2 tablespoons dark*
>   *rum or Grand Marnier or other*
>   *fruit-flavored liqueur*
> *¾ cup heavy cream*

Beat together the cream cheese, sugar, lemon juice, grated zest, and optional flavoring until the mixture is light and smooth. In a separate chilled bowl with chilled beater, whip the cream until just stiff (but do not overbeat). Fold in the cream cheese mixture. Follow specific recipe to spread into pastry and top with fruit. Chill.

ORANGE CREAM CHEESE TART FILLING

This uncooked filling is quickly and easily made. It is refreshingly flavorful and can be spread onto a completely prebaked pastry shell and topped with any combination of glazed fresh fruits. Or omit the fresh fruit and simply chill to set the filling, then spread with your favorite bottled fruit preserves before serving.

Advance preparation: This can be made a day or 2 ahead and refrigerated, although it is so easy to prepare that it really is not necessary to do in advance. If the mixture is too stiff to spread after chilling, beat well to soften, or stir in a tablespoon of cream.

Special equipment: Food processor fitted with steel blade or blender or electric mixer.

Quantity: 1½ cups filling; enough to coat generously one 11-inch tart shell.

> *12 ounces cream cheese (not whipped*
> *type)*
> *6 tablespoons granulated sugar*
> *2 tablespoons cream or orange-flavored*
> *liqueur or rum*
> *1 tablespoon grated orange zest*
> *4 teaspoons frozen orange juice*
> *concentrate, undiluted*

Cream all ingredients together in processor, blender, or electric mixer until the mixture is light and smooth. Follow specific recipe to spread into completely prebaked pastry shell and cover with glazed fresh fruit, or top with fruit preserves. Chill.

About Cream and Whipping Cream

I decided to solve the whipping cream question for myself once and for all after an embarrassing moment in one of my pastry classes some time ago. Sixteen university club women, who had watched me demonstrate the process of preparing five elaborate pies and tarts, were eagerly awaiting the finishing touches. I picked up my star-tipped pastry bag filled with whipped cream and attempted to pipe a rosette edging on a chocolate crème de menthe pie. Right before *all* our eyes, the crisply edged rosettes melted into soft blobs, and I was obliged to spread the cream with a spatula and conceal it under a shaving of chocolate. Not bad tasting, but not the presentation I had in mind. The cream, I realized too late, was the wrong type. Of course, professional chefs add gelatin or cornstarch to stabilize garnishing cream, but that was not the problem. Butterfat content was.

Mistakenly, I had purchased plain whipping cream. This whips up but not stiffly enough because it contains only about 30 percent butterfat. The trick is to whip *only* cream with 36 to 40 percent butterfat, generally labeled "heavy" or "heavy whipping" cream. The butterfat content is usually marked on the carton; if it is not and you must choose, select "heavy" or "heavy whipping" instead of "whipping cream." Light cream has a butterfat content of between 18 and 20 percent, while half-and-half has only 10½ to 12 percent; neither will whip properly.

To whip cream by hand, use a large balloon whisk or a rotary beater, and a large bowl, preferably metal which holds cold once chilled. To do the job more easily, use an electric mixer with the largest balloon-type beater available and a metal bowl, if you have one. In addition to using well-chilled cream, prechill the beaters and bowl, a job most quickly accomplished in the freezer. The colder the cream and utensils, the firmer the butterfat in the cream and the quicker and stiffer the whipped result. In extra-hot weather, beat cream in a bowl set over a pan of ice water.

(*Note:* Cream doubles in volume when whipped; 1 cup heavy cream = 2 cups, whipped.)

Along the way, it passes through several stages:

Chantilly Stage. This is when soft mounds appear, before the cream is really firm. Chantilly cream is best for adding to mousses and Bavarian creams or for stirring into puréed fruits for pudding-type desserts or tartlet fillings. This is the point at which flavoring and/or sugar should be added to cream that will be whipped more stiffly. Sugar added to liquid cream may impede the whipping process somewhat.

Stiffly Beaten Cream. At this stage, swirl lines from the beating are clearly visible in the cream; they do not melt away. Firm peaks hold on the beater. Be careful about this stage; it occurs quickly, and beating should be halted at once. Otherwise, you may have butter, which tastes delicious but may not be what you had in mind at the time. To try to save slightly overbeaten cream, *gently* whisk in 2 tablespoons cold milk or cream; it sometimes works.

Sugar, as noted above, is added to cream after it is partially whipped. You can use superfine, granulated, or sifted confectioners' sugar. Confectioners' sugar contains cornstarch (to prevent caking) and thus tends to stabilize the whipped cream; use it if you will be holding the whipped cream awhile before serving. To hold unstabilized whipped cream several hours before using, you can put it in a cheesecloth-lined strainer set in a bowl in the refrigerator. Straining will separate the whipped cream from any liquid that drains out.

Honey can be substituted for sugar in whipped cream. Be sure the honey is liquefied and strained. Stir it gently into stiffly whipped cream.

Stabilized Whipped Cream. To decorate pies and tarts with a firmer textured cream that can be piped through a decorating bag and will hold shape for a long time, add some gelatin. For every 1 cup of heavy cream to be whipped, dissolve 1 teaspoon unflavored gelatin in 2 tablespoons cold water. Heat the gelatin until melted, then cool it but keep it liquid. Whip the cream until soft peaks form, then slowly add the gelatin while beating until stiff.

WHIPPED CREAM TOPPINGS FOR PIES AND TARTS

Review About Cream and Whipping Cream, page 105. Unless otherwise noted in recipes below, follow this procedure: Whip the cream *just* to soft peaks, add the flavoring extract or liqueur and the granulated or sifted confectioners' sugar. Whip to firm peaks, then chill or use immediately.

VARIATIONS:

Lattice Cream. Using cream whipped to firm peaks, pipe a latticework pattern over the top of a 1-crust pie, using a pastry bag fitted with a star tip. To finish, pipe rosettes or a ring around the rim to cover the ends of the lattice strips.

"Diet" Cream. To lessen the butterfat content of your pie topping, use half whipped cream and half stiffly beaten egg whites, folded together.

Rum Cream
> *1 cup heavy cream*
> *2 tablespoons rum or 1 teaspoon rum extract*
> *3 tablespoons confectioners' sugar, sifted*

Amaretto Cream
> *1 cup heavy cream*
> *2 tablespoons amaretto liqueur plus ¼ teaspoon almond extract*
> *2 tablespoons confectioners' sugar, sifted*

Cassis Cream
> *1 cup heavy cream*
> *3 tablespoons double crème de cassis liqueur (black currant flavor; tints cream pink)*
> *2 tablespoons confectioners' sugar, sifted*

Mint Cream

1 cup heavy cream

2 tablespoons white crème de menthe liqueur (green type will tint cream) plus 1/4 teaspoon peppermint extract

4 tablespoons confectioners' sugar, sifted

Orange Cream

1 cup heavy cream

Grated zest of 1 orange plus 1/2 teaspoon orange extract

2 tablespoons orange-flavored liqueur (curaçao, Grand Marnier, etc.)

2 tablespoons confectioners' sugar

Apricot Cream

1 cup heavy cream

2 to 3 tablespoons apricot liqueur

3 tablespoons confectioners' sugar, sifted

Ginger Cream

1 cup heavy cream

1/2 teaspoon ground ginger, sifted

2 tablespoons confectioners' sugar, sifted

1 to 2 tablespoons candied ginger, minced fine, to taste

Whip the cream to soft peaks, add the ground ginger and sugar. Whip stiff, then fold in the minced candied ginger.

Coffee Cream

1 tablespoon instant coffee (or instant espresso)

1 cup heavy cream

3 to 4 tablespoons confectioners' sugar, sifted, to taste

Dissolve instant coffee in chilled cream before whipping. Whip to soft peaks, add sugar, whip stiff.

Chocolate Cream

1 cup heavy cream

1 ounce semisweet chocolate

2 tablespoons confectioners' sugar, sifted

In small pan, combine 1/2 cup cream and the chocolate. Stir over low heat until the chocolate melts. Stir to blend smooth. Whisk in the remaining cream and chill in refrigerator at least 1 hour; when cold, whip to soft peaks, add sugar, whip stiff.

Mocha Cream. Same as Chocolate Cream plus 1 1/2 teaspoons instant coffee, dissolved into melting cream and chocolate on the stove.

Mocha-Praline Cream. Same as Mocha Cream plus 1/2 cup powdered praline powder (broken almond or peanut brittle powdered in the blender or food processor) folded into the stiffly whipped cream.

Butterscotch Cream.

    1 cup heavy cream

    6 tablespoons dark brown sugar, packed

    ½ teaspoon vanilla extract

Combine all ingredients in a bowl. Stir well to soften and partly dissolve the sugar. Whip stiff. To complement the delicate flavor of this cream, it is best to use a plain butter-flavored pastry with a fairly bland filling.

Maple Cream.

    1 cup heavy cream

    5 tablespoons pure maple syrup

Whip the cream to soft peaks. Fold in the syrup. Whip stiff.

About Meringue Topping

It is hard to beat the appeal of a pie topped with waves of golden-tinged meringue. To some, the magic of beaten egg whites reaches its apogee in meringue topping, although, in my opinion, baked Meringue Shells (page 78) turn the same ingredients into an equally delightful creation. Light, frothy meringue toppings are especially good, and traditionally used, on custard and cream pies, but they go equally well with baked fruit or berry pies; just leave off the top crust and replace it with meringue.

Albert Jorant, pastry chef of l'École de Cuisine La Varenne in Paris, likes to remind his students that cooking is like music: Millions have laughed or cried over the sounds made from only eight notes. Similarly, he says, ten basic cooking techniques can produce many things, and cooking can also make you laugh or cry. Many a beginning baker has, indeed, cried over trying to make a successful meringue topping. Yet frustration is unnecessary if the technique is understood and the basic rules are followed. For complete instructions on how to beat the egg whites, see About Meringue Pie Shells (page 77).

Preheat your oven when you begin beating egg whites, so the meringue can be applied to the pie and baked as soon as it is completely whipped. For best results, the entire process should be done as close to serving time as possible. To apply meringue to the pie, note first whether your recipe requires that the filling be hot. Many recipes do, and the reason is that the heat of the filling poaches the underside of the meringue layer, thereby preventing it from liquefying. Avoid stirring a hot pie filling; stirring may release steam, which may then condense into a watery layer beneath the meringue. Mound your meringue onto the center of your pie with a rubber spatula, then spread it outward with a broad spatula or the back of a spoon, distributing it evenly to the edges all around in order to seal the whites to the rim of the crust. This prevents the meringue from shrinking during baking. Use the back of the spoon to swirl the meringue or swoop it up into peaks all over. Don't make the peaks too high, though, or the highest tips will overbrown too soon. Alternatively, meringue topping can be piped over the pie in a lattice, rosette, or other pattern using a pastry bag fitted with a star tip.

Set the pie into a preheated 325°F to 350°F oven and bake for 12 to 15 minutes, or just until the meringue is golden. Watch carefully and peek often, as meringue will burn easily. Cool away from drafts. To prevent the knife from sticking when you cut the meringue, dip the blade into hot water or spread it with a little vegetable oil.

Health note: Be sure your egg whites come from pure, fresh eggs with unbroken shells. Bacteria causing a common food poisoning, salmonellosis, can be present in unsanitary egg whites and cannot be destroyed by the quick cooking given the whites in meringue topping. For this reason, be sure also to refrigerate leftover meringue-topped pie.

MERINGUE TOPPING RECIPE

Advance preparation: Theoretically, none; meringue should be made and applied to the pie as close to serving time as possible. However, to be practical, pie *can* be topped with meringue, baked, and successfully held at room temperature for several hours or even frozen. For health reasons, meringue pies should be refrigerated if left overnight.

Special equipment: Copper, glass, glazed ceramic, or stainless steel round-bottom bowl; large balloon whisk, or electric mixer with largest balloon whisk available and narrow-sided bowl; rubber scraper; spoon or spatula.

Quantities:
For one 8-inch pie:

> *2 large egg whites, at room temperature*
> *¼ teaspoon cream of tartar*
> *A pinch of salt*
> *4 tablespoons superfine or granulated*
> *sugar*

For one 9- or 10-inch pie:

> *4 large egg whites, at room temperature*
> *¼ teaspoon cream of tartar*
> *A pinch of salt*
> *6 to 8 tablespoons superfine or granulated*
> *sugar*

(*Note:* For a slightly less generous meringue on a 9-inch pie, you can use 3 whites with ¼ teaspoon cream of tartar, a pinch of salt, and 6 tablespoons sugar.)

Review About Meringue Topping (page 109). Preheat the oven to 350°F. Combine the egg whites, cream of tartar, and salt in bowl. Beat with a whisk or electric mixer on medium speed, until soft peaks form. Add sugar, 2 tablespoons at a time, beating a little after each addition. Beat 3 to 5 minutes longer (total beating time can be 4 to 6 minutes or more, depending on the machine and the number of whites), until the whites are shiny, satiny, and hold stiff peaks on the beater when it is removed and inverted. Be sure the sugar is completely dissolved. Apply meringue to pie, seal by smoothing to the edges of the crust, and make peaks with the back of a spoon. Or pipe meringue onto the pie with a pastry tube.

Bake the meringue-topped pie in the preheated oven for 12 to 15 minutes, or until top is golden brown. (*Note:* Meringue toppings for small tartlets can be shaped on buttered and floured foil and baked as above. Simply slide them off the foil onto the tartlets just before serving.)

VARIATIONS:

Coconut Meringue Topping. Sprinkle ¼ cup sweetened shredded coconut over the meringue just before baking. (*Note:* Some recipes call for coconut folded into the meringue; I find this weights the whites down and flattens the meringue.)

Almond Meringue Topping. Sprinkle ¼ cup slivered, sliced, or fine-chopped almonds (or other nuts) over the meringue before baking.

MERINGUE TOPPING CRITIQUE: WHAT WENT WRONG AND WHY?

Meringue too flat? Too much sugar used (best proportions are 2 tablespoons sugar per 1 large egg white); no acid used (cream of tartar, lemon juice, copper bowl, or white vinegar) to stabilize whites; meringue cooled in a cold draft.

Meringue tough? Too much sugar used; oven heat too high (overheating causes egg protein to shrivel and toughen).

Meringue "weeps" or beads after baking? Too much sugar used, or sugar undissolved because meringue not beaten long enough. Add a little cornstarch.

Meringue shrinks? Meringue not spread sufficiently onto edges of crust all around pie; meringue baked in too cool an oven (under 325°F) or too hot an oven; meringue-topped pie cooled too quickly because it was set in a cold draft.

OAT-WHEAT GERM STREUSEL TOPPING

Use this crunchy topping over fruit crisps, deep-dish pies, or to replace the top pastry crust of a regular fruit pie.

Advanced preparation: Topping can be prepared ahead and stored in a covered jar in the refrigerator or freezer for several days.

Quantity: 1⅔ cups; enough for a 9- or 10-inch pie or 1½- to 2-quart baking dish.

> ¼ *cup granulated sugar*
> ¼ *cup dark brown sugar, packed*
> ½ *cup old-fashioned rolled oats, or*
>   *quick-cooking type*
> ¼ *cup toasted wheat germ*
> 5 *tablespoons all-purpose flour*
> *A pinch of salt*
> ⅓ *cup butter or margarine, at room*
>   *temperature, cut up*
> ¼ *teaspoon each cinnamon and nutmeg*

Combine all ingredients in large bowl and crumble them together with your fingertips. Spread the mixture over the prepared fruit in a buttered baking dish or pie plate and bake as directed in the specific recipe.

NUT-CRUMB STREUSEL TOPPING

This recipe makes a somewhat less crunchy topping than the one above.

Advance preparation: Topping can be prepared ahead and frozen or stored in a covered jar in refrigerator for several days.

Quantity: About 2½ cups; enough for one 9- or 10-inch pie or 1½ to 2½-quart baking dish. Use 1½ to 1¾ cups topping for 9-inch pie; use all for 10-inch pie.

> ⅔ *cup granulated sugar*
> 7 *tablespoons butter or margarine, at*
>   *room temperature, cut up*
> ½ *cup plus 2 tablespoons all-purpose*
>   *flour*
> 1 *cup walnuts, pecans, or almonds, fine*
>   *chopped*
> ¼ *teaspoon each cinnamon and nutmeg*

Combine all ingredients and crumble them together with your fingertips. Spread mixture over prepared fruit in buttered baking dish or pie plate and bake as directed in the specific recipe.

TOASTED COCONUT TOPPING

Use this topping to sprinkle over a vanilla or coconut cream pie, or over vanilla ice cream or yogurt.

Quantity: 1 cup, to top one 9-inch pie.

> *1 cup sweetened shredded or flaked*
> *coconut, or grated fresh*

Spread coconut on a sheet of foil with edges turned up. Bake in a preheated 375°F oven for 6 to 8 minutes, tossing the coconut occasionally to color it evenly, until golden brown. Cool and sprinkle over the pie.

CUSTARD SAUCE (*CRÈME ANGLAISE*)

This rich custard sauce is traditionally flavored with vanilla, but may also contain orange, rum, or other liqueur. Serve it warm over Apple or Peach Dumplings in Pastry (pages 286–88) for a delightful dessert. Or serve it over any 2-crust berry pie.

Advance preparation: Sauce may be made early on the day it is to be served, or up to two days ahead, and refrigerated, covered. To serve warm, reheat in a double boiler, stirring over *warm* water.
Special equipment: 2-quart heavy-bottom enamel or stainless steel saucepan; whisk or electric mixer; double boiler; strainer.
Quantity: 2 cups sauce, to accompany a 9- or 10-inch pie.

> *1 vanilla bean (or 2 teaspoons vanilla*
> *extract)*
> *2 cups milk*
> *4 large egg yolks*
> *1 teaspoon cornstarch*
> *4 tablespoons granulated sugar*

If you are using a vanilla bean, slit it lengthwise, place it in a saucepan with the milk and bring slowly to a boil. During this time, beat together the yolks, cornstarch, and sugar in a bowl until very thick and light. When the milk boils, remove it from the heat. Pour about half the hot milk onto the yolk mixture in a slow stream while whisking constantly. Then pour the warm yolk mixture back into the saucepan with the remaining milk. To be safe, you can now set the pan over a double boiler. Or watch it very closely and set over low heat, stirring constantly with a wooden spoon, until thick enough to coat the spoon and leave a clearly defined line when you draw your finger through the cream on the back of the spoon. Remove the custard from the heat and strain it into a bowl. Do not overcook, or it will tend to curdle, though cornstarch helps prevent this. Remove vanilla bean, wash, and set aside to reuse. Or stir in the vanilla extract. To store, cool completely, then cover and chill.

VARIATION:

> 1 tablespoon orange-flavored liqueur or dark rum stirred in with the vanilla extract after the custard has cooked.

HARD SAUCE

This sauce is traditionally served with old English plum pudding or warm Mince Pie (page 147). But is equally good with tart peach or apple pie.

Advance preparation: Hard Sauce can be made up to a week ahead and refrigerated in a covered container. Before serving, bring to room temperature and stir to soften slightly.
Special equipment: Electric mixer or food processor fitted with steel blade.
Quantity: 2 cups, 16 servings of 2 tablespoons each, for two 9-inch pies.

> *1 cup lightly salted butter*
> *4½ cups confectioners' sugar, sifted*
> *4 tablespoons brandy or 2 teaspoons*
>   *brandy extract plus enough milk or*
>   *cream (about 3 tablespoons) to*
>   *soften sauce*

In a mixer or food processor, beat the butter until soft. Add the sifted confectioners' sugar a little at a time, blending until combined. Add flavoring and milk as needed until the sauce is creamy. Serve at room tempertaure.

YOGURT-RUM SAUCE

This is one of those inventions of which necessity is the mother. I ran out of cream and discovered by happy accident that the flavor of vanilla yogurt goes well with rum to make a sauce for spiced pies such as pumpkin, mince, or ginger-scented peach.

Advance preparation: Yogurt-Rum Sauce can be made a day or two in advance and refrigerated in a covered container.

Quantity: 1 cup, enough for one 9-inch pie.

> *1 cup vanilla-flavored yogurt*
> *1 to 2 tablespoons dark rum, to taste*
> *2 teaspoons confectioners' or*
> *granulated sugar, sifted*

Beat all ingredients together well. Store in a covered jar in the refrigerator. Serve at room temperature.

VANILLA ICING GLAZE

Use this as a glaze for éclairs or small cakes.

Quantity: ⅓ cup, enough for one recipe of éclairs or one 9-inch pie or cake.

> *1 cup confectioners' sugar, sifted*
> *3 to 4 tablespoons warm milk*
> *¼ teaspoon vanilla extract or lemon*
> *juice*

Blend all ingredients until smooth. Spread over pastry. The glaze hardens somewhat as it dries.

About Chocolate

For the chocolate garnishes in this book, I have used only pure semisweet or unsweetened chocolate, available either in 1-ounce squares or blocks of various weights. Unless you are using premeasured 1-ounce squares of chocolate, it is handy to have a kitchen scale available. However, as a guide, ⅛ cup regular-sized chocolate morsels = 1 ounce = 2 tablespoons. Hershey's, Nestlé's, Maillard Eagle, Baker's and Baker's German Sweet are widely available brands that I like. The excellent imported chocolates I use include Lindt Extra-Bittersweet and Tobler Bittersweet made in Switzerland and Callebaut Semi-Sweet or Bittersweet from Belgium. I also commonly use Hershey's or Nestlé's pure chocolate semisweet morsels (chips) with good results.

To Melt Chocolate. Chocolate is an emulsion; unless handled carefully, the fat will separate out. For this reason, chocolate must be melted very slowly, preferably in a double boiler over hot (not boiling) water. If you are in a rush, you can set the pan of chocolate directly over a very low heat, but watch it carefully. Chocolate burns easily; therefore, it is best to remove it from the heat *before* it is thoroughly melted and stir it, or just let it sit while its internal heat completes the melting process. Also, beware of liquid getting into pure chocolate as it melts—a drop of water added by mistake, or present in a damp pan, can cause the chocolate to seize and harden. This is not always salvageable, but you can try smoothing it out by stirring in 1 teaspoon partially hydrogenated white shortening (Crisco) for each ounce of chocolate.

CHOCOLATE LEAVES

Chocolate leaves are made by coating real leaves (see Note) with melted chocolate. When the chocolate is hard, the real leaf is peeled away, leaving an edible garnish for chiffon or whipped cream-topped pies and tarts or tartlets. As a bonus, you can also flavor melted chocolate with peppermint extract (or other liqueur or extract) and prepare a whole tray of chocolate leaves, to be passed as elegant after-dinner mints.

Advance preparation: Chocolate leaves can be prepared well in advance and frozen for several months in a protective airtight container.

Special equipment: Double boiler; leaves (see Note); wax paper; tray; pastry brush or small spatula for applying chocolate (though I prefer to use my finger). (*Note:* For the prettiest effect, use gracefully shaped leaves with a waxy surface and a pronounced pattern of veins on one side. Lemon, magnolia, camellia, gardenia, ivy, even rose leaves work well. However, you should be aware that certain types of leaves meet all other criteria but can be poisonous! If you are uncertain, check with a nursery or a botanist. I use lemon or camellia leaves from a local florist, who also supplies them to neighboring restaurants. Lemon leaves work well because they are strong enough to be reused without tearing. If you have a misshapen or extra-large leaf, simply cut it to size with scissors before coating it with chocolate.)

Quantity: As a rough guideline, 1 ounce of melted chocolate will coat about 6 leaves, depending upon their size; 8 ounces, then, will make roughly 50 leaves. Make as many as you wish; 5 or 6 leaves are enough to top a 9- to 11-inch pie or tart, but you should always make several extras in case some break (or get eaten). Excess melted chocolate can be poured into a paper muffin cup liner and chilled, to be stored and reused for another purpose.

> *8 ounces semisweet chocolate, or milk*
> *chocolate*
> *2 teaspoons Crisco or margarine*

Melt the chocolate and shortening together in the top of a double boiler over hot (not boiling) water. Set aside to cool until the chocolate is comfortable to the touch. Set clean, dry leaves, vein-patterned sides up, on a wax paper-covered tray. (*Note:* The most pronounced vein pattern is generally on the underside.) With a pastry brush, small spatula, or your fingertip, spread a generous ⅛-inch layer of chocolate on the leaves, one at a time. Remember that you should be covering the side of the leaf where the vein markings are most visible. Brush the chocolate up to, but not over, the leaf edges, and try to avoid thinning the edges too much. Set the coated leaves, chocolate side up, on a wax paper-covered tray and place in the refrigerator or freezer for a few minutes, until the chocolate is hard-set.

To make curled leaves, allow the chocolate leaves to cool partially, then set them into the curved surface of a French-bread pan or tube-shaped baking pan and chill to set. (If curved too soon, the melted chocolate will all run to the middle of the leaf.)

When chocolate is completely set, remove the firm chocolate leaves from the refrigerator or freezer. Carefully break off any uneven chocolate edges that wrap over onto the front of the real leaves. Allow the chocolate to warm about 30 seconds at room temperature; then, starting at the stem end, peel the real leaves away from the chocolate. Take care to handle the chocolate leaf as little as possible to avoid leaving fingerprints. Set the chocolate leaves back on the tray or in a protective container and refreeze until needed. Reuse real leaves, coating them with more chocolate as long as they hold their shape, but get fresh ones for each new batch of chocolate leaves.

(*Note:* If this is your first time, it is best to make a few test leaves at the start to determine the quality of the chocolate coating. Chocolate leaves should have a delicate appearance; ease up if you made the chocolate too thick. If, on the other hand, the chocolate shatters when the leaf is peeled away, apply more chocolate the next time and warm the leaf a few more seconds in your hand before peeling it off.)

CHOCOLATE CURLS

Professional pastry chefs make chocolate curls, or long fat chocolate cigarettes, by spreading a coating of melted chocolate over a marble slab. When the chocolate (usually a coating chocolate commercially available only in bulk) is nearly set, they draw a wide-bladed sharp knife across the surface, causing a thin sheet of chocolate to roll up on itself in a long curl. It takes practice to perfect this technique.

An easier method, producing smaller but acceptable chocolate curls, is to draw a swivel-type vegetable peeler across the surface of a thick candy bar or piece of block chocolate. Be sure you work over a sheet of wax paper and lift completed curls with a toothpick poked into their sides. The trick is to have the chocolate at the correct temperature: If it is too cold and hard, the curls will crumble or shave; if too soft, they will collapse. The easiest thing to do is to set the chocolate in a *barely* heated oven for 10 to 15 minutes; some ovens are warmed sufficiently by their pilot lights. In warm weather, use the sun. If the chocolate feels too soft, chill it slightly; experiment until it works. Chocolate curls can be stored in a protective airtight box in the freezer or in the refrigerator for several days until needed.

GRATED CHOCOLATE

To grate or shave chocolate as a decorative topping for pies, simply take a piece of block chocolate, a chocolate bar, or a 1-ounce square of chocolate and pass it across the medium-sized holes of a box grater. This can be done over a piece of wax paper or directly over the pie top. The wax paper method gives you more control in positioning the shavings. Unused grated chocolate can be stored in the freezer in an airtight container; it requires no thawing before use.

RICH CHOCOLATE SAUCE

Advance preparation: Can be made up to a week ahead and stored, refrigerated, in a covered container. Warm over low heat before serving.
Special equipment: Saucepan and whisk; storing jar with lid.
Quantity: 1 cup, 8 to 10 servings or enough for 2 dozen Profiteroles (page 275).

1 cup (8 ounces) semisweet chocolate (or
use 4 ounces unsweetened plus 4
ounces semisweet)

½ cup heavy cream
Optional flavoring: *1 to 2 tablespoons*
  rum or orange-flavored liqueur or
  amaretto liqueur, to taste

Measure the chocolate into the top of a double boiler and melt over hot (not boiling) water. Remove the chocolate from the heat just before completely melted. Whisk to melt completely, then very slowly whisk in the cream a little at a time, blending until smooth and thick. Stir in the flavoring liqueur if you are using it. Serve warm.

CHOCOLATE ICING

Use this easily made icing to top éclairs or cream puffs.

Quantity: ½ cup, to frost 1 dozen éclairs or cream puffs.

2 ounces semisweet chocolate (or ¼ cup
  semisweet chocolate morsels)
1 tablespoon butter
½ cup confectioners' sugar, sifted
2 tablespoons hot water
¼ teaspoon vanilla extract

In a double boiler, melt the chocolate with the butter over hot (not boiling) water. Whisk in the sifted sugar, hot water, and vanilla. Cool. Spread over pastries as directed in the individual recipe.

About Fruit Glazes

A fruit glaze has several purposes: It can be brushed over the top of a fresh fruit tart to prevent oxidation of the fruit and to impart a brilliant sheen, or it can be brushed inside a pastry shell to provide a light, flavorful moisture proofing before the filling is added. The finest quality apricot preserves and red currant jelly are most commonly used for glazing because they contain a sufficient amount of pectin to stiffen somewhat when cooled after boiling.

The apricot preserves should be warmed and strained to remove any pieces of fruit. You can select either type of jelly, but it is preferable to use the one whose color complements the color of your fruit. Apricot gives a golden-orange hue to white, yellow, or orange fruits such as bananas, pineapples, or peaches, while red currant gives a reddish hue, best for strawberries, cherries, and red grapes.

Either apricot preserves or red currant jelly can be flavored with some kirsch or other liqueur before using. Note particularly that the Plain Fruit Glaze (below) contains nothing but jelly and liqueur; it will remain intact as a coating on fresh fruit no more than a couple of hours before it starts to soften and melt. For a glaze that must hold longer than 2 or 3 hours before serving, use Firm Fruit Glaze (page 120), which is stiffened with a little gelatin.

(*Note:* Be sure fruit to be glazed is dry; do not sprinkle it with sugar, as sugar will melt and dissolve the glaze.)

PLAIN FRUIT GLAZE

Quantity: ½ cup glaze, to coat one 9- to 12-inch pie or tart.

> ½ *cup apricot preserves or red currant*
> *jelly*
> Optional flavoring: 2 *tablespoons*
> *kirsch or other fruit-flavored*
> *liqueur*

If you are using apricot preserves, stir over medium heat in a small saucepan until melted. Strain through a sieve (return strained fruit pieces to the preserves jar). Return the strained preserves to the saucepan; or, instead, measure red currant jelly directly into the saucepan. In either case, add liqueur if you are using it and bring the jelly to a boil over medium heat. It should cook about 2 minutes, or until thick enough to coat a spoon. Remove from the heat and cool until the glaze begins to thicken slightly but is still lukewarm. Use a pastry brush to coat *dry* fruit on top of a pie or tart, or brush glaze over the unfilled pie shell as directed by your recipe. Chill to set the glaze. Store leftover glaze in a covered jar in the refrigerator; reheat to use.

FIRM FRUIT GLAZE

This is the recipe to use when a fruit pie or tart must be glazed, then held several hours or longer before serving. The addition of gelatin to the recipe keeps the glaze from melting, yet does not make it noticeably rubbery.

Quantity: ½ cup glaze, to coat one 9- to 12-inch pie or tart.

> ½ *cup apricot preserves or red currant*
> *jelly*
> *1½ teaspoons unflavored gelatin*
> *2 tablespoons kirsch, or other fruit-*
> *flavored liqueur, or fruit juice*

If you are using apricot preserves, stir over medium heat in a small saucepan until melted. Strain the preserves through a sieve (return strained fruit pieces to the preserves jar). Place strained preserves in the saucepan; or instead, measure red currant jelly directly into the saucepan. Add gelatin and liqueur or fruit juice. Stir over medium heat until the mixture is smooth and clear and the gelatin completely dissolves. Bring to a boil for about 30 seconds, then cool to lukewarm. Use a pastry brush to apply glaze over dry fruit on top of a pie or tart. Chill to set the glaze. Store leftover glaze in a covered jar in the refrigerator; reheat to use.

Egg, Milk, and All-Purpose Pastry Glazes

Egg glazes have two purposes in pastry making: They are used to give a moisture-proof coating to pastry shells before a liquid filling is added, and they are brushed over the tops of pastries to impart a rich golden luster to the finished product. The protein in the egg coagulates and darkens in the heat of the oven to produce the color. Because of its golden tone, the French call the egg glaze a *dorure,* or gilding, from *or,* meaning "gold."

BASIC EGG GLAZE

This contains the egg yolk and gives the best color to pastry tops.

> *1 whole egg beaten with 1 or 2*
> *tablespoons water*

Egg Yolk Glaze (French *dorure*).

> *1 large egg yolk beaten with 2 tablespoons*
> *milk or water*

Egg White Glaze. This is most often used for moisture-proofing crusts, rather than for adding color to pastry tops. (*Note:* Water softens the protein of the egg white, so it will not produce a rubbery layer.)

> *1 egg white beaten with 1 or 2*
> *tablespoons water*

MILK OR BUTTER GLAZE

For a rustic or farm-kitchen glaze atop your fruit pie, brush milk (or melted butter or margarine) over the crust before baking. This gives a dull finish rather than the high gloss achieved with egg.

ALL-PURPOSE GLAZE

Use this glaze for topping pastries or breads. It produces a fine glaze on baked piecrusts and will not toughen as an egg white glaze sometimes does.

> *1 whole egg*
> *3 tablespoons melted butter*
> *3 tablespoons warm milk*

Beat all ingredients together and brush over pastry. Be sure the milk is warm so that it mixes with the melted butter; cold milk will harden the butter instead.

SWEET PIES AND TARTS

FRUIT AND BERRY PIES

But I, when I undress me
Each night, upon my knees
Will ask the Lord to bless me
With apple-pie and cheese.

Eugene Field, "Apple Pie and Cheese"

It is true that almost nothing can make you feel as good as a freshly baked apple pie. And nothing so clearly symbolizes the country kitchen as an old-fashioned pie with sweet steam wafting from the vents in its sugar-glazed, golden brown crust. In the countryside, you can tell the time of year by the fruit you see: bushels of red-blushed apples beside the orchard, or cherries, plums, pears—each fruit in season and each in a pie!

As a basic rule of thumb, the procedure for making an all-American 2-crust classic is to line a 9-inch pie plate with flaky pastry, fill it with 4 to 8 cups of sliced fresh fruit mixed with spices and sugar, and thicken it with 2 to 3 tablespoons flour, cornstarch, or tapioca. Cover with the top crust, glaze if you wish, and bake.

There are several tricks to insuring flaky pastry with a crisp, rather than soggy, lower crust. First, use Basic All-Purpose Flaky Pastry (page 34) or either of the Lard Crusts (page 62), and brush a moisture-proofing egg glaze (page 121) on the lower crust before adding the filling. Or sprinkle the lower crust with a handful of dry bread or cereal crumbs to absorb excess moisture. Then, set the prepared pie in the lower third of a preheated hot oven for about 15 minutes to set the pastry quickly. If it browns too much, cover the edges of the crust with foil (page 25). Finally, raise the pie to oven center, lower the heat to moderate, and bake until the fruit filling is tender. To protect the oven from dripping juices, set a sheet of foil with edging turned up directly on oven floor.

My mother's technique for pies that look as good as they taste is to use an extra cup of fruit, piled high in the center so the top crust is dome-shaped rather than flat. For special occasions, the top crust can also be made of crisscrossed pastry strips (page 47) and the pie served with a variety of toppings (pages 100–122). To roll out, fit, and shape pastry for 2-crust pies, see page 40. Bakers concerned with saving time will want to freeze pie fillings ahead of time when fruits are in season (page 56) in addition to freezing pastry (page 54) or completely made pies (page 55).

This chapter contains a selection of classic 2-crust fruit pies as well as single-crust and lattice-topped pies and other variations on the theme. For a change, try Apple-Custard Pie baked with Phyllo Pastry, or Apple-Cranberry-Walnut Pie, or Plum-Good Pie with a custard-fruit filling. Deep-dish pies use the same fillings as fruit or berry pies, but contain more of them (at least 6 cups). They save you a few calories by using only one crust, a top layer made with a short Basic All-Purpose Flaky Pastry or a streusel (crumb) topping. A cobbler (page 71), which is also deep-dish, is topped with a biscuit-type dough.

Note that for variation you may wish to bake open-faced pies in tart pans or vice versa. Also, some open-face pies or tarts can benefit from the addition of a lattice pastry top.

FRUIT PIE THICKENERS

2 tablespoons flour will thicken 1 cup liquid for a medium-thick sauce; 2½ to 3 tablespoons flour thickens 1 cup liquid for a thick sauce. Instead of flour you can use 2 to 3 tablespoons quick-cooking tapioca to set the filling for a 9- or 10-inch pie. Tapioca produces a clear sauce. Use the larger amount for very juicy fruit. As other alternatives to flour, you can use arrowroot, cornstarch, or potato starch, all of which are good thickeners with about *twice* the thickening power of flour. All will cook to a clear sauce.

FRUIT MEASURING GUIDE

As a basic guide to fruit quantities, note that 3 large apples = one pound = 3 generous cups when peeled, cored, and sliced ⅛ inch thick; 4 to 5 peaches, nectarines, or plums = one pound = 2½ cups, pitted and sliced ¼ inch thick. For additional measurements, see Measurements and Equivalents, page 12.

OLD-FASHIONED APPLE PIE

This is IT!—what our country and flag are as American as. Since the earliest colonial days, apple pies have been enjoyed in America for breakfast, for an entrée, and for dessert. Colonists wrote home about them and foreign visitors noted apple pie as one of our first culinary specialties. According to the *American Heritage Cookbook* (Penguin Books, 1967), a Swedish parson named Dr. Acrelius wrote back to his family in 1758: " 'Apple-pie is used through the whole year, and when fresh apples are no longer to be had, dried ones are used. It is the evening meal of children. House-pie, in country places, is made of apples neither peeled nor freed from their cores, and its crust is not broken if a wagon wheel goes over it.' " In 1851, a Norwegian immigrant living in Wisconsin wrote to friends back home, " 'Strawberries, raspberries, and blackberries thrive here. From these they make a wonderful dish combined with syrup and sugar, which is called *pai*. I can tell you that is something that glides easily down your throat; they also make the same sort of *pai* out of apples . . . and that is really the most superb.' "

For pies, select apples that are firm and tart such as Greenings, Jonathans, Cortlands, or Granny Smiths. Eating apples such as Delicious or McIntosh soften too much when baked. Serve apple pie warm, topped with a slice of sharp cheddar cheese or a dollop of heavy cream.

Advance preparation: Apples may be sliced, seasoned as described below, and frozen in individual pie-sized packets in advance (page 56) and pastry can be prepared ahead and frozen (page 53). Complete pies can also be frozen before or after baking (page 56).

Special equipment: 9-inch pie plate; rolling pin; pastry brush; aluminum foil strips or frame (page 25).

Baking time: 425°F for 15 minutes; 350°F for 40 to 45 minutes.

Quantity: One 9-inch pie.

> Unbaked pastry for a 2-crust, 9-inch
> (unsweetened) pie: *Basic All-Purpose*
> *Flaky Pastry (page 34) or with*
> *Cheddar Cheese Pastry Variation*
> *(page 35) or Old Fashioned*
> *Vinegar Pastry (page 36) or*
> *Whole Wheat Pastry (page 59) or*
> *Lard Pastry (page 62)*
> Egg glaze: *1 egg beaten with 1 tablespoon water*
> *6 to 8 medium-large Granny Smith or*
> *Greening apples, peeled and sliced*

(6 to 8 cups; quantity determines height
of pie)
⅓ to ½ cup brown sugar, packed
(amount depends upon tartness of apples)
Juice of 1 large lemon
2 to 3 tablespoons flour
½ teaspoon each nutmeg and cinnamon
2 tablespoons butter, cut up

Optional: *4 tablespoons plain cracker or*
cornflake crumbs
Granulated sugar or milk for glaze

1. Prepare the pastry, roll it out, and line the pie plate (page 38). Trim ½-inch pastry overhang. To moisture-proof the lower crust, brush with egg glaze and/or sprinkle with crumbs. Preheat the oven to 425°F.

2. In large bowl, toss the sliced apples with the sugar, lemon juice, flour, and spices. Add fruit to pastry-lined pan and dot with butter. Brush egg glaze over edge of lower crust.

3. Roll out top crust (page 40) and fit it over the fruit. Trim ¾ inch overhang. Fold the edge under the bottom crust and pinch together to seal, making a raised rim all around. Flute the edge as desired (page 44). Cut vent holes in the top (page 49). Brush the top of the pie with egg glaze and sprinkle with sugar, or simply brush with milk or leave plain.

4. Set the pie in the lower third of the preheated oven and bake 10 to 12 minutes. Reduce the heat to 350°F, raise pie to center of oven, and bake an additional 40 to 45 minutes, or until the pastry is golden brown and the fruit is tender when pierced with a fork through a vent hole. Check the pie halfway through the baking time and add a foil edging if necessary to prevent the crust from overbrowning. Cool the pie on a wire rack. Serve warm as is or topped by slices of sharp cheddar cheese, vanilla ice cream, or other toppings (page 100).

VARIATIONS:

Bourbon Apple Pie. Prepare Old-Fashioned Apple Pie, but sprinkle 2 to 3 tablespoons bourbon over the sliced apple filling before baking pie.

Apple-Walnut Pie. Prepare Old-Fashioned Apple Pie using ¾ cup brown sugar and adding ½ cup coarsely chopped walnuts to the apple filling. You can also add ½ cup seedless raisins if you like.

Apple-Cranberry-Walnut Pie. Prepare Old-Fashioned Apple Pie with ¾ cup brown sugar and add along with the apples: 1 cup whole fresh or frozen cranberries plus ½ cup coarsely chopped walnuts. Top with egg-glazed lattice topping (page 107). The pie can also be baked in a tart pan and served free-standing, garnished with Orange-flavored Whipped Cream, (page 108).

Dutch Apple Pie. Prepare Old-Fashioned Apple Pie, cutting a 1¼-inch round steam vent in the top crust. Glaze the top and bake as directed, but 5 minutes before the end of the baking time, pour ½ cup heavy cream into the vent hole. Bake 5 minutes more and serve warm.

Apple-Custard Cream Pie. This pie has a creamy custard filling blended with the apples. Use medium or soft (eating type) apples such as McIntosh or Golden Delicious, as harder cooking apples may take a little longer to bake.

Prepare Old-Fashioned Apple Pie using ½ cup granulated sugar instead of the brown sugar. Omit the lemon juice but use all other ingredients. Just before baking, pour over the fruit in the pastry-lined pan a custard made by whisking together 1 egg plus ¾ cup heavy cream. (*Note:* You can substitute pears, cored and sliced, for half the apples in this recipe.)

Deep-Dish Apple Pie. Prepare Old-Fashioned Apple Pie or the Apple-Cranberry-Walnut Variation, but use 6 to 7 cups sliced apple filling. Prepare only half the pastry recipe; omit the bottom crust. Place the fruit in a 7- to 8-cup (1½ to 2 quarts) oven-proof baking dish at least 2 inches deep. Cover the fruit with pastry rolled out and fitted to the edges of the pan, and cut steam vents as for a regular crust. Glaze the top if you wish.

Deep-dish pie can also be topped with a lattice crust (page 47) or with Oat-Wheat Germ Streusel or Nut-Crumb Streusel Topping (page 112). Follow baking time for a regular 2-crust pie.

(*Note:* For an even greater amount of fruit, double the filling in the original recipe and use a larger pan.)

APPLE AND CUSTARD PIE IN PHYLLO PASTRY

The rich custard filling in this pie is complemented by the flavor of the tart apples and the texture of the crisp flaky pastry. It is best served warm, directly from the oven.

Advance preparation: Use frozen phyllo pastry, thawed overnight in the refrigerator. The pie is best made fresh; leftovers can be stored in the refrigerator and reheated before serving.

Special equipment: Flat tray about 14 × 18 inches; pastry brush; 9-inch Pyrex or metal pie plate; plastic wrap or wax paper and dampened tea towel for covering phyllo; small saucepan.

Baking time: 450°F for 12 minutes, 350°F for 30 to 40 minutes.

Quantity: One 9-inch pie.

½ pound frozen phyllo dough, thawed
as directed on package, or ½ recipe
strudel dough (page 91), cut in
leaves about 12 inches square
1 cup unsalted butter, melted
5 medium large Granny Smith or
Greening apples, peeled, sliced, and
sprinkled with the juice of ¼
lemon and ¼ teaspoon ground
nutmeg
½ cup blanched almonds, toasted and
ground (page 32)
Granulated sugar

Custard
1 egg plus 1 yolk
½ cup heavy cream
1½ tablespoons calvados, dark rum, or
brandy
⅓ cup granulated sugar
¼ teaspoon cinnamon

1. Read To Use Frozen Phyllo Dough (page 98). Thaw the phyllo as directed, then set it out on a tray covered with wax paper topped with a dampened towel. Set out the melted butter and the pastry brush. Cut the phyllo sheets, all at once, to 12-inch-square size for a 9-inch plate, or equivalent size to fit your pie plate. Cover the phyllo sheets. Preheat the oven to 450°F.

One at a time, remove a sheet of phyllo, brush it with a layer of melted butter, and set it in the pie plate. Repeat, building up 6 buttered layers. Allow the pastry edges to overhang the pie plate all around.

2. Set out the prepared apples and nuts. Spread the apples on the phyllo layers in the plate. Sprinkle with the nuts. Butter the edges of the overhanging phyllo sheets, then fold them over the top of the filling. Butter and add 6 more sheets of phyllo to make the top crust. Tuck the overhanging top edges between the bottom crust and the inside rim of the plate. Butter the top layer. With the tip of a sharp paring knife, cut a 1¼-inch hole in the center of the top crust for a steam vent and custard-pouring hole. Sprinkle the top crust with a little granulated sugar.

3. Set the pie in the lower third of the preheated oven for 12 minutes. To prepare the custard while the pie is baking, whisk together the egg plus yolk, the cream, calvados, sugar, and cinnamon in a mixing bowl. Transfer the custard to a

container with a pouring spout. After 12 minutes, remove the pie from the oven and reduce the heat to 350°F. Raise the shelf to the center of the oven. Slowly pour the custard into the hole in the top crust. Return the pie to the center shelf of the oven and bake an additional 25 to 30 minutes, or until the pastry is puffed up and golden brown. Serve warm or at room temperature. The pie will flatten as it cools.

FRESH APRICOT PIE

Unless you are lucky enough to live in an apricot-producing region such as southern California, it is not easy to find fresh apricots that ripen with full sweet flavor before they spoil. If you are blessed, take advantage of it and make this pie. If not, sad to say, you are better off using dried or canned apricots for other types of apricot pie (see index).

Advance preparation: Apricots may be halved, pitted, seasoned as described below and frozen in individual pie-sized packets (page 56); the pastry can also be prepared ahead and frozen (page 53). The complete pie can also be frozen *before* baking (page 56).

Special equipment: 9- or 10-inch pie plate; rolling pin; pastry brush; aluminum foil strips or frame (page 25).

Baking time: 425°F for 10 minutes; 350°F for 30 to 40 minutes.

Quantity: One 9- or 10-inch pie.

> *Unbaked pastry for 2-crust 9- or 10-inch*
> *pie (see Note) made with Basic All-*
> *Purpose Flaky Pastry (page 34) or*
> *with other pastry of your choice*
>
> Egg Glaze: *1 egg beaten with 1*
> *tablespoon water*
>
> *1½ to 2 pounds fresh ripe apricots,*
> *pitted and quartered (about 4 cups)*
>
> *1 to 1¼ cups granulated sugar, or to*
> *taste depending on sweetness of*
> *fruit*
>
> *3 tablespoons quick-cooking tapioca*
>
> *1 tablespoon lemon juice, only for very*
> *sweet fruit*
>
> *¼ teaspoon nutmeg*
>
> *2 tablespoons butter*

(*Note:* For late-summer apricots, use the 10-inch pie plate. Late-summer fruit, available in the northeast, is very tart and requires the maximum amount of sugar. This combines with the soft-baked texture to produce extra pan juices— hence the larger sized pan is preferable.)

1. Prepare the pastry, roll it out, and line the pie plate (page 40). Trim ½-inch pastry overhang. Preheat the oven to 425°F.

2. In large bowl, toss the apricots with sugar, tapioca, lemon juice, and nutmeg. Add the fruit to the pastry-lined pan and dot with butter. Brush egg glaze on edge of the lower crust.

3. For a covered pie, roll out top crust (page 38) and fit over fruit. Trim ¾-inch overhang. Fold the edge under the bottom crust overhang and pinch together to seal, making a raised rim all around. Flute the edge as desired (page 44). Cut vent holes (page 49). Or cut rolled crust into ½-inch strips and arrange in a lattice pattern (page 47) over the fruit. Brush the top crust or lattice with egg glaze and sprinkle lightly with granulated sugar.

4. Set the pie in the lower third of the preheated oven and bake 10 minutes. Reduce the heat to 350°F, raise the pie to the center of the oven, and bake an additional 30 to 40 minutes, or until the pastry is golden brown. Check the pie when about half-baked and, if it's overbrowning, add foil strips or a frame to protect the crust. Cool on a wire rack. Serve warm, with Butterscotch or Maple Whipped Cream (page 109).

APRICOT-WALNUT PIE

This open-face pie has a tart apricot filling covered with a crunchy layer of caramelized custard and chopped nuts.

Advanced preparation: The apricots may be prepared ahead and refrigerated for a day or two; the pastry may be prepared ahead and frozen (page 53).
Special equipment: 9-inch pie plate; 3 medium-sized bowls; 2-quart saucepan; strainer.
Baking time: 375°F for 20 minutes; 325°F for 40 to 50 minutes.
Quantity: One 9-inch pie.

> *Unbaked pastry for a single crust 9-inch*
> *pie made with Basic All-Purpose Flaky*
> *Pastry (page 34), or Whole Wheat*
> *Pastry (page 59), or another recipe*
> *of your choice*

1 box (8 ounces) dried apricot halves
   (2 cups)
2 cups water
2 large eggs
1 cup granulated sugar, divided in half
1 teaspoon vanilla extract
⅛ teaspoon cinnamon
4 tablespoons heavy cream or milk
½ cup walnuts, chopped fine

1. Prepare the pastry, roll it out, and line the pie plate (page 38). Crimp the edge in flutes or scallops (page 44). Be sure the edging stands up slightly to hold in the filling. Chill the pastry-lined pan in the refrigerator while perparing the filling. To prepare the apricots, measure them into a saucepan and cover with water. Cover the pan and bring to a boil over high heat. Lower the heat slightly and boil gently about 15 minutes, or until the fruit is fork-tender. When soft, remove the apricots from the heat and drain well through a strainer set over a bowl. Save juice to drink if you wish; set aside the fruit to cool in another bowl. Preheat oven to 375°F.

2. To prepare the custard, beat together the eggs, ½ cup of the sugar, the vanilla, cinnamon, and cream or milk. Set aside.

3. Stir the remaining ½ cup sugar into the apricots. Add a little more sugar, if necessary, to your taste. Spread the apricots in an even layer over the prepared pastry shell. Sprinkle on the chopped nuts, then pour the custard mixture over the top.

4. Carefully set the pie in the lower third of the preheated oven and bake for 20 minutes. Then raise the pie to the center of the oven, reduce the heat to 325°F, and continue baking 35 to 40 minutes longer. Check the pie after half the baking time and add a foil edging if necessary to prevent the crust from over-browning. You may wish to increase the heat to 350°F for the last 10 minutes to brown the pastry, if necessary. Cool on a wire rack.

APRICOT-ORANGE SOUFFLE PIE

This baked soufflé combines meringue with orange-scented apricot purée to create a texture slightly more dense than a traditional soufflé, but much lighter than a fresh fruit pie. The flavor is tart and intensely apricot-y, a must for those who love this fruit. If you prefer a sweeter pie, add another ¼ cup sugar to the recipe.

Advance preparation: The completely prebaked pie shell can be prepared ahead and frozen (page 54). Apricot purée can be prepared as much as several days in advance and refrigerated; bring to room temperature before using. The texture of this pie is best if baked not more than several hours before serving; however, it *can* stand before serving, unlike a regular baked soufflé.

Special equipment: 9-inch pie plate; 1½-quart stainless steel or enamel saucepan with lid; blender or food processor; grater (for zests); electric mixer; rubber spatula.

Baking time: Completely baked pie shell: 425°F for 10 minutes with pie weights, then 10 to 12 minutes empty; Soufflé Filling: 325°F for 25 minutes.

Quantity: One 9-inch pie.

> *Completely prebaked 9-inch pie shell*
> *made with Basic All-Purpose Flaky*
> *Pastry (page 34) prepared with*
> *egg yolk and 2 tablespoons sugar or*
> *Cream Cheese Pastry (page 65)*
> *1 box (8 ounces) apricot halves dried*
> *(2 cups)*
> *⅔ cup orange juice or water*
> *1 teaspoon grated orange zest*
> *½ cup plus 3 tablespoons granulated*
> *sugar*
> *3 egg whites*
> *A pinch of salt*
> *Orange-flavored Whipped Cream (page*
> *108) for garnish*

1. Preheat the oven to 425°F. Prepare the pastry, roll it out, and line the pie plate (page 38). Trim a ¾-inch overhang, fold the pastry edge inward, and flute as desired (page 44). Prick the pastry bottom with a fork, then chill 30 minutes, until the dough is firm. Blind-bake the shell (page 42) by lining it with foil and pie weights and baking in the lower third of preheated 425°F oven for 10 minutes. Remove the liner and weights and continue baking 10 to 12 minutes longer, or until golden. Cool on a wire rack. Reduce oven heat to 325°F.

2. In a saucepan, combine the apricots, juice or water, orange zest, and ½ cup of the sugar. Cover and bring to a boil. Reduce the heat and simmer, covered, for 10 minutes. Remove the cover and cook 5 minutes longer, or until the fruit is fork-tender. Remove 6 nicely shaped apricot halves and set them aside on a

plate for garnishing the pie. Purée the remaining apricot halves with the cooking liquid in a processor or blender until quite smooth. You should have one generous cup of purée.

3. In the bowl of an electric mixer, combine the egg whites and salt. Beat until fluffy, add the remaining 3 tablespoons of sugar, and beat until stiff but not dry. Check the apricot purée; it should be a soft, spreadable consistency. If the purée feels too stiff, warm it slightly and/or stir in 2 or 3 tablespoons orange juice, water, or cream. Stir about 4 tablespoons of the beaten whites into the purée to lighten it, then fold in the rest. Spoon the filling into the prepared pastry shell and bake at 325°F for 25 minutes or until set and delicately browned.

4. To garnish after baking, set one reserved apricot half (cut side down) in the pie center, then arrange the other five halves as petals around the center, making a flower. Serve warm or cold, with Orange-flavored Whipped Cream (page 108) alongside.

CHERRY PIE

There are many varieties of cherries, but basically, they are either sweet or sour. Some are pale, some deep ruby red, others mottled or somewhere in between. If you have fresh cherries, use whatever type you have but be sure they are unbruised and still holding on to their stems (which indicates firm flesh). Wash cherries before using to remove possible sprays. To pit, use the marvelous mechanical cherry stoner, a sharp paring knife and pointy fingertip, or a bent hairpin. Or best of all, employ a willing child. If you are using canned cherries, try varying the flavor by combining half dark sweet cherries and half tart cherries.

Picture-book cherry pies have ruby-red fruit, as I am sure you have noticed. This unnaturally bright color is often added artificially with food coloring. I prefer—and recommend if the choice must be made—paler cherries and healthier pies. Note that Cherry-Berry Pie, listed as a variation, includes blueberries and strawberries, which enhance the color of the pie naturally.

Advance preparation: Use canned cherries for quick preparation. Pastry can be prepared ahead and frozen (page 53).
Special equipment: Cherry-pitting gear (see introduction above) if you are using fresh cherries; 9-inch pie plate; pastry brush; aluminum foil strips or frame (page 25).
Baking time: 425°F for 40 minutes.
Quantity: One 9-inch pie.

Unbaked pastry for 2-crust pie made with
Basic All-Purpose Flaky Pastry (page
34) or other pastry of your choice
Egg glaze: 1 whole egg beaten with 1
tablespoon water
4 cups fresh pitted sour cherries or 4 cups
(two 1-pound cans) tart cherries,
drained, with ⅓ cup juice reserved
2¾ tablespoons quick-cooking tapioca
A pinch of salt
¾ cup granulated sugar, or to taste,
depending on sweetness of fruit
2 teaspoons lemon juice
¼ teaspoon almond extract or kirsch
2 tablespoons butter

1. Prepare the pastry and line the pie plate (page 38). To moisture-proof the lower crust, brush it with egg glaze, then place pastry-lined pan in the refrigerator while the fruit is prepared. Preheat oven to 425°F.

2. In a large bowl, combine the fruit, tapioca, salt, sugar, and flavorings. If you are using canned, drained fruit, add in ⅓ cup fruit juice. Stir, and let the fruit mixture sit about 5 minutes.

3. Spoon the fruit into the pastry-lined pan and dot with butter.

4. Roll out top crust a generous ⅛-inch thick and cut into ½-inch strips with a knife or fluted pastry jagger. Moisten the rim of the lower crust with egg glaze, then arrange the pastry strips in a twisted or plain woven lattice (page 47). Fold overhanging lower crust over the ends of the lattice, pinch to make a raised rim, and flute to seal (page 44). Brush the lattice strips with egg glaze.

5. Set the pie in the lower third of the preheated oven and bake 40 minutes. Check the pie when half-baked and add foil strips or frame to protect crust if it is overbrowning.

Cool on a wire rack. Serve with vanilla ice cream or plain sweetened or flavored whipped cream (page 107).

VARIATIONS:

Cherry-Berry Pie. The combination of fruits in this pie produces a brilliant color and delicious flavor. Prepare Cherry Pie above, but for fruit, use only 2 cups fresh cherries or 1 can (1 pound) tart cherries drained, with ⅓ cup juice reserved. Add 1 cup blueberries (fresh or frozen) and 1 cup strawberries (fresh, hulled and halved, or frozen). Do not thaw frozen berries, just knock off any clinging frost or ice.

Cherry-Cranberry Pie. Prepare Cherry Pie above, but use 2 cups fresh or 1 can (1 pound) tart cherries, drained, plus 2 cups fresh or frozen whole cranberries. Replace the granulated sugar with an equal amount of dark brown sugar, packed. Increase the almond extract to ½ teaspoon.

FRESH PEACH PIE

The bright yellow-orange color and rich sweet flavor of ripe peaches make them prize filling for fresh fruit pies. Use either freestone or clingstone types, since they are easily prepared. To peel them effortlessly, drop 3 or 4 at a time into a pot of boiling water. Boil about 2 minutes, then remove with a slotted spoon to a bowl of cold water. Drain when cool. The skins should slip off easily. Slice the peaches about ¼ inch to ⅜ inch thick and sprinkle immediately with lemon juice to avoid discoloration.

Advance preparation: The fruit may be prepared, seasoned as described below, and frozen in individual, pie-sized packets in advance (page 56); the pastry can be prepared ahead and frozen (page 53). Complete pies can also be frozen, unbaked or baked (page 56).

Special Equipment: 9-inch pie plate; pastry brush; aluminum foil strips or frame (page 25).

Baking time: 425°F for 10 minutes; 350°F for 35 to 40 minutes.

Quantity: One 9-inch pie.

> *Unbaked pastry for a 2-crust, 9-inch pie,*
> *made with unsweetened Basic All-*
> *Purpose Flaky Pastry, Nut Pastry*
> *Variation (almond, page 35), or other*
> *pastry of your choice*
> Egg glaze: *1 whole egg beaten with 1*
> *tablespoon water*
> *2¼ pounds medium-sized ripe peaches,*
> *peeled and sliced (see introduction*
> *above); about 8 medium-sized*
> *peaches or 5½ cups slices*
> *Juice of 1 lemon*
> *½ to ¾ cup granulated sugar, depending*
> *on sweetness of fruit*
> *⅛ teaspoon each nutmeg, cinnamon,*
> *mace*

3 tablespoons quick-cooking tapioca or
  cornstarch
2 tablespoons unsalted butter, cut up

1. Prepare the pastry, roll it out, and line pie plate (page 38). Trim ½-inch pastry overhang. To moisture-proof the lower crust, brush it with egg glaze. Preheat oven to 425°F.

2. Toss the peaches in a large bowl with lemon juice, sugar, spices, and tapioca or cornstarch. Add fruit to pastry-lined pan, mounding it in the center. Dot with butter. Brush egg glaze over the edge of the lower crust. Roll out top crust (page 40) and fit over fruit. Trim ¾-inch overhang. Fold top edge under bottom crust overhang and pinch together to seal, making a raised rim all around. Flute as desired (page 44). Cut vent holes (page 49). To glaze the pie, if you wish, brush with egg glaze and sprinkle with a little granulated sugar or brush with milk only.

3. Set the pie in the lower third of the preheated oven and bake 10 minutes. Reduce the heat to 350°F, raise the pie to the center of the oven, and bake an additional 35 to 40 minutes, or until the pastry is golden brown. Check the pie after it is half-baked and add foil strips to protect the crust if it is browning too fast. Cool on a wire rack. Serve warm or cold.

VARIATIONS:

Blueberry-Peach Pie. This is the all-time favorite in my house, served by special request on my husband's birthday instead of cake. Prepare Fresh Peach Pie but use only 2 cups peach slices. Add 2 cups fresh blueberries, washed, stemmed, and dried. Use ⅔ cup granulated sugar, the juice of 1½ lemons, and a dash of cinnamon and nutmeg. Omit mace. Thicken with 3 tablespoons quick-cooking tapioca and top fruit with 3 tablespoons butter, cut up. To moisture-proof lower crust, brush with egg glaze and/or sprinkle with 4 tablespoons cornflake crumbs before adding fruit. (*Note:* Since this pie is so colorful, it shows off well with an egg-glazed lattice crust, page 47.)

Nectarine Pie. Prepare Fresh Peach Pie, substituting nectarines (unpeeled) for peaches.

Peach-Plum Pie. Prepare Fresh Peach Pie, substituting 2 cups pitted and sliced (unpeeled) Italian prune plums for 2 cups peach slices.

Deep-Dish Peach Pie. Prepare Fresh Peach Pie or any of the above variations but use 6 cups fruit altogether and add a little more sugar if you wish. Do not adjust thickener as deep-dish pie does not have to slice neatly. Prepare only half the pastry recipe. Omit bottom crust. Place the fruit in a 7- to 8-cup (1½- to 2-quart) oven-proof baking dish, at least 2 inches deep. Cover the fruit with pastry rolled out, fitted to the edge of pan, and cut steam vents as for a regular crust. Glaze and bake as for a regular 2-crust pie, but for a *total* time of 35 to 40 minutes, or until the pastry is golden brown.

Peaches-and-Cream Pie. This divine pastry has a creamy custard filling blended with the peaches. Prepare Fresh Peach Pie using ½ cup sugar. Replace mace with ground ginger, omit lemon juice, and use 2 tablespoons all-purpose flour as thickener instead of tapioca or cornstarch. Pour over fruit in pie just before baking: custard made by whisking together 1 egg plus ¾ cup heavy cream.

FRESH PLUM PIE

Little Jack Horner
Sat in the corner,
Eating a Christmas pie;
He put in his thumb,
And pulled out a plum,
And said, What a good boy am I!

This familiar nursery rhyme has quite a complex history. To begin, one must explain that the plum in question may not be the fruit as we know it, but rather a large currant or raisin, in which case the pie may actually have been Christmas mince, rather than "plum." No matter; whether or not it is true, it still makes a good story, involving King Henry VIII. Henry became furious, it is said, when he learned that the abbot of Glastonbury, Richard Whiting, had used church funds to enhance himself and build an elaborate new kitchen. On hearing of the King's wrath, Whiting commissioned an emissary, one Jack Horner, to take a gift of pie to the King. During the journey, Jack opened the pie and discovered it was not filled with edible plums at all, but with another variety: deeds to various estates or manors. He "stuck in his thumb" and pulled out the deed to the manor of Mells, which he kept for himself, and gave the rest to the king. Mells remains in the Horner family today, and the phrase "political plum," meaning a specially favored office, has become a part of our language.

Advance preparation: Plums may be sliced, seasoned as described on page 140, and frozen in individual pie-sized packets (page 56); pastry can be prepared ahead and frozen (page 53). Complete pies can also be frozen, baked or unbaked (page 56).

Special equipment: 9-inch pie plate; pastry brush; aluminum foil strips or frame (page 25).
Baking time: 425°F for 12 minutes; 350°F for 40 to 45 minutes.
Quantity: One 9-inch pie.

> *Unbaked pastry for a 2-crust 9-inch pie*
> *made with Basic All-Purpose Flaky*
> *Pastry (page 34) sweetened with 2*
> *tablespoons sugar, or other pastry*
> *of your choice*
> *Egg glaze: 1 whole egg beaten with 1*
> *tablespoon water*
> *About 1¾ pounds plums, unpeeled,*
> *sliced, pitted (4 to 5 cups); I prefer*
> *Italian prune plums for tart flavor*
> *and bright color; damsons or*
> *greengages may also be used with*
> *success.*
> *1 tablespoon freshly squeezed lemon*
> *juice*
> *½ to ¾ cup granulated sugar, depending*
> *on tartness of fruit*
> *3 tablespoons quick-cooking tapioca*
> *A pinch of salt*
> *¼ teaspoon each cinnamon and nutmeg*

1. Prepare the pastry, roll it out, and line the pie plate (page 38). Trim ½-inch pastry overhang. To moisture-proof lower crust, brush with egg glaze. Preheat oven to 425°F.

2. In a large bowl, toss the sliced plums with the lemon juice, sugar, tapioca, salt, and spices. Add the fruit to the pastry-lined pan.

3. Roll out the top crust (page 40) and fit over fruit. Trim ¾-inch over-hang. Fold edge under bottom crust and pinch together to seal, making a raised rim all around. Flute the edge as desired (page 44). Cut vent holes (page 49). If you want to glaze the pie top, brush with egg glaze and sprinkle with a little granulated sugar. Or simply brush with milk.

4. Set the pie in the lower third of the preheated oven and bake 12 minutes. Reduce heat to 350°F, raise the pie to the center of the oven, and bake an additional 45 minutes, or until pastry is golden brown. Check the pie halfway through baking time and add foil strips or frame if necessary to prevent the crust from overbrowning. Cool on a wire rack. Serve warm with Custard Sauce (*Crème Anglaise,* page 113).

VARIATIONS:

Plum Good Pie. This is an open-faced pie with a rich yogurt-custard filling added to the fruit. Note that honey replaces sugar; to measure honey easily, oil the measuring cup before using. Use Italian prune plums for best results and use extra brown sugar noted below only if you prefer a very sweet pie.

Prepare Fresh Plum Pie with only half the pastry recipe; use only 2 cups (¾ pound) sliced plums. Omit all other ingredients and replace as follows: Add ⅓ cup chopped walnuts to sliced plums and spread in pastry-lined pan. Pour over fruit before baking: custard made by beating together 3 eggs, 1 cup (8 ounce) plain yogurt, 1 teaspoon vanilla extract, a pinch each nutmeg and cinnamon, and ¾ cup honey (optional extra sweetener: 2 tablespoons brown sugar, packed). Set in center of preheated oven and immediately turn heat down to 375°F. Bake 45 minutes, or until a stainless steel knife inserted into the custard 1 inch from the edge comes out clean. The pastry edging should appear golden brown. Cool on a wire rack. Serve warm and top with a very light sifting of confectioners' sugar just before serving. (*Note:* This pie may also be made with a partially prebaked pie shell [page 43] moisture-proofed with egg glaze [page 121].)

Plum Crumb Pie. Prepare Fresh Plum Pie but omit the top crust. Before baking, top the fruit with Nut Streusel or Oat-Wheat Germ Streusel Topping (page 000).

Grape Custard Pie. Prepare Plum Good Pie, above, as pie or tart, but substitute for the plums 1 pound sweet purple grapes, seeded (about 2 cups prepared grapes).

FRESH PEAR PIE

There are over five thousand varieties of pears and nearly as many theories on how to select and ripen them. Since today's methods of picking and transporting fruit deprive us of ever finding perfectly ripe fruit in the market, the best we can do is to choose overfirm fruit and let it stand in the fruit bowl at home until it smells aromatic and the flesh gives slightly when pressed at the stem end. For pies, you want ripe, flavorful pears that have not yet begun their sadly rapid decline to mush. The best moment can be about a day before you feel the fruit ready to eat fresh, because a slight firmness of flesh gives a better texture to the baked pie. Watch carefully and refrigerate ripe pears; they go bad almost before you notice it.

Advance preparation: Bartlett pears, which have such good flavor, can be tricky when frozen. I have not had great success freezing pear pies and discourage the idea. The pastry can be prepared ahead and frozen (page 55).

Special equipment: 9-inch pie plate; pastry brush; aluminum foil strips or frame
  (see page 25).

Baking time: 425°F for 12 minutes; 350°F for 30 to 35 minutes, until golden
  brown.

Quantity: One 9-inch pie.

> *Unbaked pastry for a 2-crust pie made*
> *with lemon or orange-flavored Basic*
> *All-Purpose Flaky Pastry (page 34) or*
> *Cheddar Cheese Pastry (page 35),*
> *or other pastry of your choice*
> Egg glaze: *1 egg beaten with 1 tablespoon*
> *water, optional*
> *4 tablespoons apricot preserves or orange*
> *or ginger marmalade*
> *6 or 7 medium-sized Bartlett or Anjou*
> *pears, peeled, cored, and sliced,*
> *about 5 cups slices; as soon as pears*
> *are sliced, sprinkle them with juice*
> *of 1 lemon to avoid discoloration*
> *¼ cup granulated sugar*
> *¼ cup brown sugar, packed*
> *¼ teaspoon each ground cardamom,*
> *nutmeg, cinnamon*
> *2½ tablespoons quick-cooking tapioca*
> *or cornstarch*
> *2 tablespoons unsalted butter*

1. Prepare the pastry, roll it out, and line the pie plate (page 38). Trim
½-inch pastry overhang. To moisture-proof the lower crust and to give unique
flavor, spread pastry with preserves or marmalade. Preheat the oven to 425°F.

2. In a large bowl, toss the lemon juice-covered pear slices with sugar, spices,
and tapioca. Spread in the pastry-lined pan and dot with butter. Brush egg glaze
over the edge of the lower crust.

3. Roll out the top crust (page 40) and fit over the fruit. Trim ¾-inch
overhang. Fold the edge under the bottom crust overhang and pinch together to
seal, making a raised rim all around. Flute as desired (page 44). Cut vent holes
(page 49). If you want to glaze the pie top, brush with egg glaze and sprinkle
with a little granulated sugar, or brush with milk only.

4. Set the pie in the lower third of the preheated oven and bake 12 minutes.
Reduce the heat to 350°F, raise the pie to the center of the oven, and bake an

additional 30 to 35 minutes, or until the pastry is golden brown. Check the pie halfway through baking time and add foil edging if necessary to protect the crust from overbrowning. Cool on a wire rack. Serve warm or cold, plain or with a slice of sharp chedder cheese or a dollop of Custard Sauce (*Crème Anglaise*), see page 113.

VARIATIONS:

Pear-Raisin Pie. Prepare Fresh Pear Pie, but add ¾ cup seedless raisins to the pear slices.

Pear-Apricot Pie. Prepare Fresh Pear Pie but add 1 cup cut-up dried apricots to the pear slices.

Ginger-Pear Pie. Prepare Fresh Pear Pie but add 2 to 3 tablespoons (to taste) finely minced crystallized ginger to the pear slices.

Pear Crumb Pie. Prepare Fresh Pear Pie but omit the top crust. Before baking, top fruit with Nut-Crumb Streusel Topping (page 112) made with chopped pecans or walnuts.

RHUBARB PIE

According to Claire Haughton in her book *Green Immigrants* (New York: Harcourt Brace Jovanovich, 1978), it is believed that the first rhubarb plants in America were imported to the territory now known as Alaska by Russian fur traders during the late 1700's. The plant was appreciated for its ability to ward off scurvy, and it endured the cold climate in its new home just as well as it had in the tundra of Siberia.

A native of Asia, rhubarb was originally used by the Chinese as a medicine. For centuries, dried and powdered medicinal forms of rhubarb roots were imported along with spices from Asia to the Mediterranean region. Marco Polo tried to introduce the plant to Europe, but the earliest attempts failed. Other explorers and botanists continued transplanting rhubarb, and eventually, rhubarb was successfully cultivated in many parts of Northern Europe.

Because they so enjoyed eating baked rhubarb in pies and puddings at home, European settlers and travelers to the first American colonies brought rhubarb seeds with them. The plant flourished in New England as it had in Alaska, and was known as "pie plant" for obvious reasons. But beware: only the rhubarb stalks are edible; the leaves contain oxalic acid and are poisonous.

Advance preparation: Fresh rhubarb may be sliced, seasoned as described on page 144, frozen in individual pie-sized packets (page 56); the pastry can be prepared ahead and frozen (page 53). Complete pies can also be frozen unbaked or baked (page 56).

Special equipment: 9-inch pie plate; pastry brush; aluminum foil strips or frame (page 25).

Baking time: 425°F for 10 minutes; 350°F for 40 to 45 minutes.

Quantity: One 9-inch pie.

> *Unbaked pastry for a 2-crust pie made*
>   *with Whole Wheat (page 59) or*
>   *Wheat Germ Pastry (page 36) or*
>   *other pastry of your choice*
> Egg glaze: *1 egg beaten with 1 tablespoon*
>   *water*
> *1½ pounds fresh rhubarb stalks cut into*
>   *1-inch pieces (4 cups pieces)*
> *1 cup granulated or packed light brown*
>   *sugar plus ¼ cup honey, or 1¼ cups*
>   *granulated sugar*
> *4 tablespoons all-purpose flour*
> *½ teaspoon nutmeg*
> *A pinch of salt*
> Optional: *¼ cup strawberry preserves or*
>   *orange or pineapple marmalade*
> *2 tablespoons unsalted butter*

1. Prepare the pastry, roll it out, and line the pie plate (page 38). Trim ½-inch pastry overhang. To moisture-proof the lower crust, brush on egg glaze. Preheat the oven to 425°F.

2. In a large bowl, toss the sliced rhubarb with the sugar and honey, if you are using it, plus flour, nutmeg, and salt. Stir in the optional preserves of marmalade if you wish. Add the fruit to the pastry-lined pan and dot with butter. Brush the edge of the lower crust with egg glaze.

3. Roll out the top crust (page 40) and fit it over the fruit. Trim ¾-inch overhang. Fold the edge under the bottom crust overhang and pinch together to seal, making a raised rim all around. Flute the edge as desired (page 44). Cut vent holes (page 49).

4. If you want to glaze the pie top, brush with egg glaze and sprinkle with a little granulated sugar; or brush with milk only.

5. Set the pie in the lower third of the preheated oven and bake 10 minutes. Reduce the heat to 350°F, raise the pie to the center of the oven, and bake an additional 40 to 45 minutes, or until the pastry is golden brown. Check the pie

after about half the baking time and add a foil edging if necessary to prevent the crust from overbrowning. Cool on a wire rack. Serve warm, topped by custard sauce (*Crème Anglaise,* page 113) or vanilla ice cream or flavored whipped cream (page 107).

VARIATIONS:

Strawberry-Rhubarb Pie. Prepare Rhubarb Pie but substitute 2 cups fresh hulled strawberries, whole or halved, for 2 cups of rhubarb. Omit the preserves or marmalade. Top the pie with pastry strips woven into a lattice (page 47).

Quick and Creamy Rhubarb Pie. This is an open-face pie or tart that combines a sweet creamy filling with the tangy rhubarb. The taste is exceptional, the process quick and easy, the quantity generous; use a 10-inch pie plate or an 11-inch tart pan. Prepare Rhubarb Pie but make only ½ the pastry recipe. Roll out the dough and prepare as for an unbaked single-crust pie or tart shell (page 41). Shape a high fluted edging on the pie shell to hold in the custard. Moisture-proof the shell with egg glaze, then chill while preparing the fruit and custard. For the filling, use the 4 cups cut-up rhubarb but omit all other ingredients in the original recipe. Toss the rhubarb with 2 tablespoons sugar in a bowl and set aside for a few minutes. *Immediately before baking* add the fruit to the prepared pastry shell and pour over it a thick custard batter made by beating together: ½ cup plus 2 tablespoons granulated sugar; ¼ cup dark brown sugar, packed; ⅓ cup all-purpose flour; ¼ teaspoon nutmeg, a pinch of salt, ½ cup heavy cream, 1 egg, and ¼ teaspoon almond extract. (*Note:* The custard can be made ahead and refrigerated several hours.)

Bake in the center of the preheated oven for 30 minutes; then reduce the heat to 350°F and bake 30 minutes longer, or until the top is golden brown and crackled. Check the pie after about half the baking time and add a foil edging if necessary to protect the rim of the crust from overbrowning. Cool on a wire rack. Before serving, you can sift on a light sprinkling of confectioners' sugar if you wish. The flavor is best if served warm. (*Note:* This pie can also be made in partially prebaked pastry shell, page 43.)

NO-BAKE FRESH FRUIT PIE

The recipe for this excellent summer pie was given to me by fellow Montessori mother and food-writing colleague Dede Ely-Singer. It requires no baking, is quick to prepare, and can be varied to suit whatever combination of berries or fruits is in season. The technique is simple: Some of the fruit is first mashed and cooked into a thickened sauce. Then the remaining fresh fruit is stirred in and the entire mixture turned out into a prebaked pastry shell. The filling is so delicious, it can be served as a pudding without any pastry if you are really in a hurry. For the Fourth of July, use equal quantities of strawberries and blueberries and top the pie with whipped cream to make a rousing Red-White-and-Blue pie!

Advance preparation: The pastry can be prepared ahead, prebaked, and frozen (page 53). Thaw before using. The filling can be made early in the day and the pie filled and set to chill until ready to serve.

Special equipment: 9-inch pie plate; food processor or bowl and fork; 2½-quart enamel or stainless steel saucepan.

Cooking time: 7 to 10 minutes to prepare fruit sauce.

Quantity: One 9-inch pie.

> *Pastry for a single-crust 9-inch pie shell*
> *made with Basic All-Purpose Flaky*
> *Pastry (page 34), Egg Yolk Pastry (page*
> *65), or Rich Tart Pastry (page 64),*
> *or other pastry of your choice*
> *4 cups any combination of fresh berries,*
> *picked over, hulled, washed, and*
> *drained dry; and/or cut-up, peeled*
> *fresh fruit (*Note: *Try blueberries*
> *and peaches, or raspberries and*
> *nectarines, or blueberries and*
> *strawberries, or plums and peaches.*
> *Do not peel plums, nectarines, or*
> *pears.)*
> *⅔ to 1 cup sugar, to taste*
> *3 tablespoons cornstarch*
> *1 cup water*
> *1 tablespoon lemon juice*
> *2 tablespoons butter*

1. Prepare the pastry, roll it out, and line the pie plate (page 38). Trim ¾-inch overhang, fold over pastry edge, and flute as desired (page 44). Prick pastry bottom with a fork, chill until firm, then completely blind-bake the shell (page 42).

2. In a food processor or using a fork, mash 1½ cups of cut-up mixed fruit. Measure the sugar, cornstarch and water into a pan and whisk until smooth. Stir

in the mashed fruit and cook over medium-low heat for 7 to 10 minutes, or until the mixture is thick and clear. Stir in the lemon juice.

3. Taste the sauce and correct the balance of sugar and lemon if necessary. Stir in the butter and all remaining cut-up fresh fruit or berries. Firm fruits like apples or plums are best slightly mashed into the cooked sauce, with softer fresh fruits and berries simply stirred in. Chill until partially thickened. Pour into the cooked pastry shell and chill to set. Serve with ice cream or sweetened whipped cream (page 107).

MINCE PIE

Drink now the strong Beere,
Cut the white loafe here,
The while the meat is a shredding;
For the rare Mince-Pie
And the Plums stand by,
To fill the Paste that's a kneading.

Robert Herrick, "Christmas
Mince and Plum Pie"

The future . . . seems to me no unified dream but a mince pie, long in the baking, never quite done.

E. B. White, *One Man's Meat*

"Minc'd" or "shrid" pie has a long and popular history that can be traced to the Crusaders, who brought back a wide variety of spices from the East. Traditionally served at Christmas, mincemeat is made in two forms: with or without shredded ("shrid") meat. All versions contain fruits, spices, sugar, brandy, and beef suet, though the quantity of the last three ingredients varies depending upon whether or not they must serve as a preservative for the long maturing period. Today, you can freeze your mincemeat if you like and thus reduce these ingredients somewhat. Our recipe omits the beef and uses less suet than the eighteenth-century versions, but is generous in all other proportions. It makes enough for three pies and thus should be packed in three separate containers if frozen. Or, instead, pack in covered jars and refrigerate or store in a cool pantry for at least a week or two before using, to allow the flavors to mature. (*Note:* The food processor speeds the task of chopping. Flour for thickening is added to mincemeat just before the pie is baked.)

Advance preparation: The mincemeat filling can be frozen, or it must be aged a minimum of 1 to 2 weeks before baking (see page 147). The pastry can be prepared ahead and frozen (page 53).

Special equipment: Food processor or chopping knife and board; large mixing bowl; wooden spoon; three 1-quart freezer containers or a large crock for storing mincement; 9-inch pie plate(s); pastry brush; aluminum foil strips or frame (page 25).

Baking time: 425°F for 40 to 45 minutes.

Quantity: 3 quarts filling, enough for three 9-inch pies.

Mincemeat Filling

> ¼ *pound blanched almonds, chopped*
> *fine (1 cup)*
> 1 *pound beef suet, ground (3½ cups,*
> *packed)*
> 3 *tablespoons toasted bread or cracker*
> *crumbs*
> ½ *pound mixed candied citrus peel*
> *(orange, lemon, citron), shredded (1*
> *cup, packed)*
> ½ *pound seedless raisins, chopped (1*
> *cup, packed)*
> ½ *pound currants, chopped (1 cup,*
> *packed)*
> 1 *pound (5 large) cooking apples*
> *(Granny Smith, Greening, etc.)*
> *peeled, cored, and chopped (4 cups)*
> *Grated zest and juice of 2 whole lemons*
> *and 1 orange*
> ½ *pound dark brown sugar (1 cup,*
> *packed)*
> 2 *tablespoons cinnamon*
> 2 *teaspoons each cloves, ginger, mace,*
> *ground allspice, nutmeg*
> 1 *teaspoon salt*
> 2 *cups apple cider*
> ½ *cup sherry*
> ½ *cup brandy*

1. If you are chopping the ingredients in a processor, work from dry to moist ingredients for best results. Whatever chopping method you use, chop each ingredient in turn, then add it to the mixing bowl.

First chop the nuts. Have the butcher chop or grind the suet (or grind it yourself by mixing suet with 2 tablespoons of the bread or cracker crumbs to prevent sticking). After grinding, pick out any pieces of suet membrane. Chop the candied peel, then the raisins and currants, in small batches, mixed with a little of the remaining crumbs to prevent sticking. Chop the apples.

2. Add the grated lemon and orange peel, then the juice, to the bowl. Or after grating, slice off white pith, remove seeds, then cut up the entire fruit, chop it in the processor, and add to the filling.

3. Add sugar, spices, salt, and liquids and stir well. Pack in clean, dry containers and refrigerate or freeze until needed.

To Bake a Mince Pie

> *Unbaked pastry for a 2-crust 9-inch pie*
> *made from Basic All-Purpose Flaky*
> *Pastry (page 34) or Lard Pastry*
> *page 62) or other pastry of your choice*
> Egg glaze: *1 egg beaten with 1*
> *tablespoon water*
> *4 cups mincemeat filling measured into a*
> *bowl and stirred with 1 tablespoon*
> *all-purpose flour, for thickener*
> *Hard Sauce (page 114), to serve with pie*

1. Prepare the pastry, roll it out, and line the pie plate (page 38). Trim ½-inch pastry overhang. To moisture-proof the lower crust, brush with egg glaze. Preheat the oven to 425°F.

2. Add mincemeat to the pastry-lined pan. Brush egg glaze over the edge of the lower crust.

3. Roll out top crust (page 40) and fit over pie. Trim ¾-inch overhang, fold edge under bottom crust overhang and pinch together to seal, making a raised rim all around. Flute the edge as desired (page 44). Cut vent holes (page 49). Brush the top with egg glaze.

Set in the lower third of the preheated oven and bake 15 minutes. Raise the pie to the center of the oven and continue baking at this heat for another 25 to 30 minutes. Check the pie after about half the baking time and add a foil edging if necessary to protect the crust from overbrowning. Cool on a wire rack. Serve warm, with Hard Sauce (page 114).

VARIATION:

Quick Mincemeat Pie. To 1 jar prepared mincemeat (1 pound 12 ounces) add: 1 chopped, peeled apple, the juice and grated zest of 1 lemon and 1 orange, ½ cup chopped walnuts. Use as filling without aging. Bake pie as directed above.

CONCORD GRAPE PIE

You'll taste the full flavor of the vine in this pie, its grapey tang pointed up by a citrus accent. This is an unusual and very special fall dessert, but surely part of my pleasure in it comes from the fact that I buy my grapes from Maple Bank Farm in Roxbury, Connecticut, a spot that is the essence of fall in New England. Smoke from the woodstove clouds the frosty air, and orange and scarlet maples crowd fruit-laden orchards surrounding a little red roadside barn, which stands sentinel over the hillside farm. A cow nibbles chrysanthemums beyond the fence while the yard is a cornucopia of pumpkins, gourds, apples, plums, grapes, leeks, carrots, and cider. In the barn, fresh eggs and hand-spun yarn are stacked beside the antique scale upon which copper-haired Cathleen weighs produce when not tending vegetables, babies, or weaving. A daughter of the Hurlbut family, which has owned and worked this farm since the late 1700's when Thomas Hurlbut became the first farmer and settler in the town, Cathy and her husband, Howard Bronson, and their two young children have recently taken over its operation, the tenth generation of Hurlbuts to do so. Howie is the family pie baker, and he talks piecrusts as easily as he picks apples, claiming that the secret of his success is to fill his pies with original combinations of whatever fruits or berries the farm has in season. Concord grapes are no exception, and this is a recipe we have shared and enjoyed together.

Advance preparation: The pastry can be prepared ahead and frozen. Bake the pie
  the day of serving since the crust softens on standing.
Special equipment: Coarse sieve; pastry brush; 2-quart stainless steel or enamel
  saucepan with lid; grater.
Baking time: 425°F for 15 minutes; 375°F for 35 to 40 minutes.
Quantity: One 9-inch pie.

> *Unbaked pastry for a 2-crust 9-inch pie*
> *made with Basic All-Purpose Flaky*
> *Pastry (page 34) or pastry of your*
> *choice*
> Egg glaze: *1 egg beaten with 1*
> *tablespoon water*
> *2 pounds blue grapes (Concord or*
> *other slipskin variety, with seeds),*
> *rinsed well (4 cups, stemmed grapes)*
> *1 tablespoon grated orange zest*
> *1 tablespoon orange juice*

1 teaspoon lemon juice
¾ cup granulated sugar (or 1 cup for a
  sweeter pie)
2½ tablespoons quick-cooking tapioca

1. Prepare the pastry as directed, roll out half the dough and return the rest to the refrigerator. Line the pie plate (page 38) and trim a ¾-inch overhang. Brush moisture-proofing egg glaze over the bottom of the piecrust. Set the pastry-lined pan in refrigerator while you prepare the filling. Preheat the oven to 425°F.

2. Stem, rinse, and drain the grapes. Pinch the grapes between your thumb and forefinger to slip the skin from the pulp. Place the skins in a bowl and the pulp and seeds in a saucepan. Cover and cook the pulp over medium heat for 4 to 5 minutes, until soft. Strain through a coarse sieve to remove the seeds. Combine the pulp with the skins in the bowl.

3. Stir in the grated orange zest, orange and lemon juice, sugar, and tapioca. Allow to stand 5 minutes.

4. Roll out the remaining dough for the top crust, or prepare a lattice crust (page 47). Moisten the rim of the lower crust with egg glaze. Fill the pie with the grape mixture. Set the top crust in place, fold the overhanging crust edges together and pinch them into a raised, fluted rim. Brush the top crust or lattice with egg glaze and sprinkle with a little granulated sugar. Set the pie in the lower third of the preheated oven for 15 minutes. Lower the heat to 375°F, raise the pie to the center shelf, and bake 35 to 40 minutes longer, or until the crust is golden brown. Check the pie after half the baking time and add a foil edging if necessary to protect the crust from overbrowning. Cool on a wire rack.

SEEDLESS GRAPE PIE

Made with fully ripe, sweet seedless grapes, this pie is as easy to prepare as it is to eat—a delectable finale to a late-summer or early fall dinner. One of the best varieties of grape for this pie is Flame Red, which looks inviting beneath a glazed lattice crust; however, you can also use seedless Ribier or Thompson Green grapes, and prepare a full top crust instead of a lattice.

Advance preparation: The pastry can be prepared in advance and frozen. Bake the pie the day of serving since the crust softens on standing.
Special equipment: 9-inch pie plate; 2-quart stainless steel or enamel saucepan with lid; strainer set over 2-cup measure or bowl; grater; pastry brush.
Baking time: 425°F for 12 minutes; 350°F for 25 minutes.
Quantity. One 9-inch pie.

Unbaked pastry for a 2-crust 9-inch pie
 made with Basic All-Purpose Flaky
  Pastry (page 34) plain or nut variation,
  or Whole Wheat Pastry (page 59)
Egg glaze: 1 egg beaten with 1 tablespoon
  water
2 pounds red, blue, or green seedless
  grapes, rinsed well (5 cups, stemmed
  grapes)
¼ cup apple cider or orange juice
2½ tablespoons cornstarch
1 tablespoon lemon juice
3 tablespoons water
2 teaspoons grated orange zest
¼ teaspoon nutmeg
½ cup granulated sugar

1. Prepare the pastry as directed, roll out half the dough and return the rest to the refrigerator. Line the pie plate (page 38) and trim a ¾-inch overhang. Brush a moisture-proof egg glaze coating over bottom of piecrust. Set the pastry-lined pan in the refrigerator while you prepare the filling. Preheat the oven to 425°F.

2. Stem, rinse, and drain the grapes. Place them in a 2-quart stainless steel or enamel saucepan along with the cider or juice. Bring to a boil, cover, and cook over medium heat about 5 minutes. Press the grapes with the back of a wooden spoon to burst about half of them, releasing some juice.

3. Pour the grapes into a strainer set over a 2-cup measure. Measure the juice; you will usually have about 1¼ cups. Return the strained pulp and skins to the saucepan along with 1 cup of juice.

4. In small bowl, dissolve the cornstarch in the lemon juice and water. Add it to the grapes in the pan. Add the grated zest, nutmeg, and sugar. Stir, bring to a boil over medium heat, and cook uncovered until thickened and clear— about 3 minutes total cooking time. Set aside to cool slightly.

5. Roll out the remaining dough to ⅛-inch thickness to make top crust, or prepare a lattice top (page 47). Moisten the rim of the lower crust with egg glaze. Fill the pie with the grape mixture. Set the top crust or lattice in place, fold the overhanging crust edges together, and pinch into a raised, fluted rim. Brush the crust with egg glaze and sprinkle with a little granulated sugar. Set the pie in the lower third of the preheated oven to bake 12 minutes. Lower the heat to 350°F and continue baking for 25 minutes, or until the crust is golden brown. Cool pie on wire rack.

GREEN TOMATO PIE

Although we think of the tomato as a vegetable, it is, botanically speaking, a berry. Filled with pulp and seeds, it is the fruit of a vine. Thus, it qualifies for inclusion with other fruit pies. As a pie filling, it ranks among the least appreciated and most delicious.

With this recipe in hand, you no longer have to wrap all your green garden tomatoes in newspaper before the first frost and hope that they ripen before they rot. Just save them for pie; the green tomato produces a flavor, surprisingly enough, halfway between spicy apple and peach pie. Friends Dick Parks and Jim Garland shared this recipe with us one summer Sunday at the end of a gorgeous corn chowder luncheon in their converted-barn home in eastern New York State. They presented it as Dick's Special Pie, and only after we tasted and acclaimed it, did they reveal the mystery ingredient. You can repeat this precaution if you wish, but be assured that the taste of this pie, if not the idea, will win unanimous praise.

Advance preparation: The pastry can be prepared ahead and frozen. Complete unbaked pies can also be frozen (page 56), though the texture is best when freshly baked.

Special equipment: 9-inch pie plate; pastry brush; large saucepan; colander; aluminum foil strips or frame (page 25).

Baking time: 425°F for 20 minutes; 375°F for 35 to 40 minutes.

Quantity: One 9-inch pie.

> *Unbaked pastry for 2-crust, 9-inch pie*
> *made with Basic All-Purpose Flaky*
> *Pastry (page 34) or Cheddar Cheese*
> *Pastry Variation (page 35) or Whole*
> *Wheat Pastry (page 59)*
> Egg glaze: *1 egg beaten with 1 tablespoon*
> *water*
> *3 tablespoons crushed cornflakes or*
> *Rice Krispies cereal*
> *4 cups peeled, sliced green tomatoes,*
> *prepared as described on page 154*
> *(5 to 6 medium-large tomatoes)*
> *1 cup light brown sugar, packed*
> *Juice and grated zest of 1 lemon*
> *½ teaspoon each cinnamon and nutmeg*
> *5 tablespoons flour plus 1 tablespoon*
> *quick-cooking tapioca*

1. Prepare the pastry as directed. Roll out half of it, and line the pie plate (page 38). Refrigerate the remaining dough. Trim a ½-inch overhang on pie plate. Brush the lower crust with moisture-proofing egg glaze and sprinkle with cereal crumbs. Chill the pastry-lined pan in the refrigerator while preparing the filling.

2. To peel the tomatoes, bring a large pot of water to a boil. Cut a cross-shaped slit in the skin at the bottom of each tomato. Immerse the tomatoes in the boiling water 2 to 3 minutes. Drain in a colander, then cut around the stem ends and peel the skin. Quarter the tomatoes, then cut them in ⅜-inch thick slices and drain them thoroughly in a colander. Put the slices in a bowl. Preheat the oven to 425°F.

3. Add to the tomatoes the sugar, grated zest and juice of lemon, the spices, flour and tapioca. Stir gently. Note that while tomatoes vary greatly, they all contain a lot of water. For this reason, sufficient thickener must be used or the pie will be too runny.

4. Fill the pastry with the prepared tomato mixture. Brush egg glaze around the rim of the lower crust. Roll out the top crust (page 40) and fit it over the fruit. Trim a ¾-inch overhang. Fold the top edge under the bottom crust overhang and pinch together to seal, making a raised rim all around. Flute the edge as desired (page 44). Cut vent holes in the top (page 49). Brush egg glaze over the pie top and sprinkle lightly with a little granulated sugar.

5. Set the pie in the lower third of the preheated oven and bake 20 minutes. Reduce the heat to 375°F, raise the pie to the center of the oven, and bake an additional 35 to 40 minutes or until the pastry is golden brown. Check the pie after half the baking time and add a foil edging if necessary to protect the crust from overbrowning. Cool on a wire rack. Serve warm or at room temperature.

Fresh Berry Pies

Berry pies mean Vermont summer to me: prickly patches of ruby, black, or blue berries, sweet scented, plump and dusty under the hot sun on a dirt road. Scratched ankles to be sure, but full berry baskets proudly delivered to the kitchen of our lakeside log cabin to be transformed into a pie or tart, the only thing better than eating berries directly from the bush.

Fresh berries should always be firm, plump, and clean. Discard bruised or dried-up fruit. Pick over berries to remove hulls, leaves, and unidentified flying objects. *Just before using,* place berries in a colander and spray with cold water to remove dust. Spread berries on several thicknesses of paper toweling to dry. If you do this quickly and do not soak or squash the berries, their flavor will be left intact. Berries can be baked between 2 solid pastry crusts or under a lattice topping, which I prefer as it shows off the colorful filling. (*Note:* You may wish to adjust the amount of sugar and thickening in the basic recipe to allow for variations in the quality of your own berries.)

As a general rule of thumb, the procedure for making baked berry pies is to line a 9-inch pie plate with flaky pastry and fill it with about 4 cups of fresh berries mixed with sugar and thickened with about 2½ to 3½ tablespoons quick-cooking tapioca or cornstarch or 4 tablespoons flour. Cover with plain or lattice top crust, glaze if you wish, and bake in a hot oven at (425°F) at first, to set the pastry quickly. If the pastry browns too much, cover with foil edging. To complete baking, lower heat to moderate (350°F) and continue baking, for a *total* of 50 to 55 minutes. To protect your oven from dripping juices, set a sheet of foil with the edges turned up under the pie on the oven floor itself (not on the oven shelf where it will deflect heat away from the pie).

BLUEBERRY PIE

Use this as a master recipe for whatever type of berries you have. Be sure to select firm, plump, ripe berries, picked over and hulled. Immediately before using, so as neither to soak the berries nor to lessen their flavor, gently rinse them with cold water and drain them on paper towels until dry. Cover the pie with lattice topping for the most attractive presentation.

Advance preparation: Blueberries (or other berry varieties) may be combined with seasonings, sugar, and thickener as described below and frozen in individual pie-sized packets (see page 56); the pastry can be prepared ahead and frozen. Complete *unbaked* pies can also be frozen (see page 56).
Special equipment: 9-inch pie plate; pastry brush; aluminum foil strips or frame (page 25); colander; paper towels.
Baking time: 425°F for 10 minutes; 350°F for 40 to 45 minutes.
Quantity: One 9-inch pie.

> *Unbaked pastry for a 2-crust, 9-inch pie*
> *made with Cream Cheese Pastry*
> *(page 65) or Basic All-Purpose*
> *Flaky Pastry, Orange or Lemon*
> *Variation (page 35), or other pastry*
> *of your choice*
> Egg glaze: *1 egg beaten with 1*
> *tablespoon water*
> *4 cups fresh, picked over berries, rinsed*
> *and dried just before using*
> *½ to 1 cup granulated sugar, amount*
> *depending on the sweetness of the*
> *berries*
> *A pinch of salt*
> *3 tablespoons quick-cooking*
> *tapioca or 3 tablespoons cornstarch*
> *2 tablespoons lemon juice*
> *A dash of cinnamon and ground nutmeg*
> *2 tablespoons butter*

1. Prepare the pastry, roll it out, and line the pie plate (page 38). Trim ½-inch pastry overhang. To moisture-proof the lower crust, brush with egg glaze. Preheat oven to 425°F.

2. In a large bowl, gently toss the berries to coat thoroughly with sugar, tapioca or cornstarch, and flavoring. Add the fruit to the pastry-lined pan and dot with butter. Brush egg glaze over the edge of the lower crust.

3. Roll out the top crust (see page 40), and fit it over the fruit. Trim a ¾-inch overhang. Fold the edge under bottom crust overhang and pinch together to seal, making a raised rim all around. Cut vent holes. Or cut rolled pastry into ½-inch strips and arrange in lattice topping (page 47). Flute edges as desired (page 44). To glaze top of pie, brush egg glaze over solid or lattice pastry.

4. Set the pie in the lower third of the preheated oven and bake 10 minutes. Reduce heat to 350°F, raise the pie to the center of the oven, and bake an additional 40 to 45 minutes, or until the pastry is golden brown. Check the pie after half the baking time and add a foil edging if necessary to prevent the crust from overbrowning. Cool on a wire rack. Serve warm or cold, topped by slightly sweetened whipped cream (page 107) or Custard Sauce (*Crème Anglaise,* page 113).

VARIATIONS:

Deep-Dish Blueberry Pie. Prepare Blueberry Pie above, but use 6 to 8 cups berries. Increase sugar slightly but do not alter other ingredients. Prepare only half the pastry recipe; omit the bottom crust. Place prepared berries in a 1½ to 2 quart ovenproof casserole or a dish at least 2 inches deep and cover with rolled out pastry fitted to the edge of the pan. Cut steam vents; glaze the top if you wish. Bake as for a regular 2-crust pie.

Blueberry-Strawberry or Raspberry Pie. Prepare Blueberry Pie above, but use 2 cups blueberries and 2 cups other berries.

Raspberry Pie. Prepare Blueberry Pie above, substituting 4 cups fresh ripe raspberries. If the berries are very plump and juicy, use 3½ tablespoons quick-cooking tapioca. (*Note:* Be sure the berries are picked over, rinsed, and dried on paper towels *immediately before using*; if this is done in advance they may *get soggy*.)

Blackberry Pie. Prepare Blueberry Pie above, substituting 4 cups fresh ripe blackberries for the blueberries. If the berries are very plump and juicy, use 3½ tablespoons quick-cooking tapioca. (*Note:* Be sure the berries are picked over, rinsed, and dried on paper towels *immediately before using*.)

RUTH LAWRENCE'S BLACKBERRY PIE

The Albany, Vermont, farm of Ruth and Daniel Lawrence stretches for four hundred acres along one of the most beautiful ridges in the northeast corner of the state. From the white clapboard farmhouse nestled in masses of Ruth's carefully tended flowers, the open meadows and rambling red and gray barns stretch down through thickets of blackberries and raspberries, past currant and blueberry bushes, across vast vegetable gardens to a pine forest in the valley below. The view from the kitchen window sweeps across it all, past the sheep in the lower meadow to the distant mountains on the opposite ridge. The sight is almost as spectacular as the kitchen table, covered with quart boxes of freshly picked plump blackberries, or the chest freezer filled to the very top with carefully marked packs of garden vegetables, beef from the farm, berries of all sorts, and pies and piecrusts.

Ruth's pies are famous. The first one I ever tasted was a blackberry pie she was serving at her own fifty-fifth wedding anniversary party, and although all the friends and neighbors brought foods and baked goods, the guest of honor's pie stole the show, and the competition was stiff.

I recalled the blackberry pie vividly some seven years later when I visited Ruth at berry-picking time. Not only did she share her recipe, but she gave me the berries to bake with, as well. It was a morning to remember, as you will her pie, if you try it.

Her technique is to cook the berries in sugar and thickener for a short time before baking them in the crust. This allows some of the juice to be released and thickened in advance, preventing spillovers when the pie is baked. It also allows Ruth to work a little magic with the blackberry seeds, which can be tough. "I add about ½ teaspoon of cider vinegar to the cooking of berries," she said. "It's a good tip, because it softens the seeds." After this mixture is cooled completely, she puts it between unbaked crusts to bake or freeze. "When I first came to this farm as a young bride, I made between eight and eleven pies a week; but sadly people don't eat pies like they used to. Now I make seven or eight at a time and put them right in the freezer. I take them out one at a time and bake them frozen, and they are as fresh-tasting as if I'd just picked the berries."

Advance preparation: Pastry can be prepared ahead and frozen. Complete unbaked pies can also be frozen (page 56).

Special equipment: 9-inch pie plate; pastry brush; potato ricer or large spoon for mashing fruit; 3-quart heavy-bottom enamel or stainless steel saucepan; aluminum foil strips or frame (page 25).

Baking time: 425°F for 10 minutes; 350°F for 40 to 45 minutes.
Berry-cooking time: 5 to 7 minutes.
Quantity: One 9-inch pie.

> *Unbaked pastry for a 2-crust, 9-inch pie*
>   *made with Butter-Lard Pastry (page*
>   *63). (Ruth uses about 2 tablespoons*
>   *milk as part of the liquid when she*
>   *bakes with lard.)*
> Egg glaze: *1 egg beaten with 1 tablespoon*
>   *water*
> *4 cups fresh blackberries, picked over*
>   *and quickly rinsed*
> *1½ to 1⅔ cups granulated sugar*
>   *(depending on sweetness of berries)*
> *½ teaspoon cider vinegar*
> *3 tablespoons cornstarch*
> *1 tablespoon quick-cooking tapioca*

1. Prepare the pastry, roll it out, and line the pie plate (page 38). Trim a ½-inch pastry overhang. To moisture-proof the lower crust, brush with egg glaze. Chill the crust in the refrigerator while you prepare the filling. Preheat oven to 425°F.

2. In a heavy-bottom saucepan, combine berries, sugar, vinegar, and cornstarch, and add 2 tablespoons water (to prevent scorching). Mash the fruit very slightly with a potato ricer or spoon in order to start the juices flowing. Set the pan over medium-low heat and cook, stirring occasionally, just until the mixture nears the boiling point. Remove from heat and cool completely. Stir in tapioca.

3. Add the cooled fruit to pastry-lined pan. Brush egg glaze over the edge of the lower crust. Roll out the top crust (page 40) and fit it over the fruit. Trim a ¾-inch overhang. Fold the top edge under the bottom crust overhang and pinch them together to seal, making a raised rim all around. Flute the edge (page 44). At this point, the pie can be wrapped and frozen, or baked. Before baking, cut vent holes in top crust (page 49).

4. Set the pie in the lower third of the preheated oven and bake 10 minutes. Reduce the heat to 350°F, raise the pie to the center of the oven, and bake an additional 40 to 45 minutes, or until the pastry is golden brown. Check the pie after about half the total baking time and add a foil edging if necessary to protect the crust from overbrowning. Cool on a wire rack. Serve warm or cold.

(*Note:* If the pie was frozen, bake it without thawing. Set the frozen pie in a preheated 375°F oven for the first 35 minutes. Cover the pastry edge with foil to prevent overbrowning if necessary. Raise the heat to 400°F for the last 15 minutes or so if needed to brown the crust; total baking time should be roughly 45 to 55 minutes.)

CURRANT CREAM PIE

Like Blackberry Pie (page 158), Currant Cream is a specialty of Ruth Lawrence, whose Albany, Vermont, farm literally overflows with growing things: beds of prizewinning flowers as well as strawberries, currant and blueberry bushes, raspberry and blackberry patches, and vegetable gardens too vast to contemplate picking. "It's hard farming, but delicious eating," says Ruth with a touch of pride, and I can well believe it. While we leaned on a farm wagon and talked of berries and pie recipes, Ruth's daughter-in-law and able assistant, Delia Lawrence, graciously picked an overflowing basket of jewel-like red currants for me to use in testing this recipe. The pie is actually a custard, and the currants rise to the top during baking to give a delightful tart contrast to the sweet soft filling below.

I have made a few minor modifications in the recipe to suit my own baking methods. The first, as usual, is to reduce the sugar slightly from the original 1 cup. The second is to forgo the unbaked pastry shell Ruth uses for one partially baked, in order to keep the lower crust crisp while baking the custard at a low heat.

Advance preparation: The partially prebaked pastry shell can be prepared in advance and frozen (page 53). Fill and bake the shell shortly before serving, or no more than 3 hours in advance; the lower crust softens on standing.

Special equipment: Mixing bowl and whisk; 9-inch pie plate; pastry brush; stainless steel knife.

Baking time: Partially prebaked pastry shell: 425°F for 10 minutes with pie weights and foil liner, then 5 minutes empty; filled pie: 325°F for 35 to 40 minutes.

Quantity: One 9-inch pie.

> *2 eggs*
> *1 cup heavy cream*
> *Partially prebaked 9-inch pie shell made*
>   *with Basic All-Purpose Flaky Pastry*
>   *(page 34) or other pastry of your*
>   *choice*

⅔ cup granulated sugar
½ teaspoon all-purpose flour
A dash of cinnamon
1 cup fresh currants, stemmed

1. In a mixing bowl, whisk together the eggs and cream and set aside. Prepare the pastry. Preheat the oven to 425°F. Roll out the pastry and fit it into the pie pan (page 38). Trim a ¾-inch overhang, fold over the edge, and flute as desired (page 44). Prick the pastry with a fork, chill until firm, then partially blind-bake (page 42) in the preheated oven for 10 minutes. Remove the liner and weights from the pastry and brush with the egg-cream mixture. Return the pastry shell to the oven to bake an additional 5 minutes, or until the dough is no longer translucent. Cool on a wire rack. Reduce heat to 325°F.

2. Add sugar, flour, and cinnamon to egg and cream mixture. Whisk well, then stir in the currants. Pour the mixture into the prepared pastry shell and bake in the center of the 325°F oven for 35 to 40 minutes, or until the top is golden brown and a knife inserted into the center of the custard comes out clean. Cool on a wire rack. Serve warm or at room temperature.

CONTINENTAL FRUIT TARTS AND GALETTES

The friendly cow all red and white,
I love with all my heart:
She gives me cream with all her might,
To eat with apple-tart.

Robert Louis Stevenson, "The Cow"

It is true that nothing enhances a fruit tart more than cream, whether served alongside, on top, or in a custard filling. But even unadorned, the fruit tart is a splendor unto itself. When the Knave of Hearts stole those tarts made by the Queen ("all on a summer's day") in the nursery rhyme, it was surely a crime of passion, for no one can resist the glamour of a beautifully prepared tart. Tarts, and their smaller relatives, tartlets (page 51), are open-faced, single-crust pastries served free-standing, removed from their baking pans.

While tarts are just as easy to make as pies and use only half the pastry, they make especially elegant and dramatic presentations that can look as if you had done twice the work. Tarts come in all varieties, from classic combinations of neatly arranged fruit slices baked and glazed with preserves, to quickly assembled fruit glacée tarts, in which a prebaked pastry shell is filled with a precooked vanilla or almond custard, topped with fresh fruit or berries, and glazed with fruit jelly. Tart pastry is generally richer and less flaky than pie pastry; it is made with an egg or yolk, plus sugar (*pâte brisée* or *pâte brisée sucrée*, page 33). For special flavor that complements almost every tart filling, add lemon or orange juice and grated zest to your tart pastry (page 64). Puff pastry can also be used for tart shells formed in pans, or shaped into free-standing prebaked shells; for an example of the latter, see Puff Pastry Shells (page 183) and Fruit Flower Tart (page 187). These puff shells have a drama all their own though they are not hard to create, and in a pinch you can even use store-bought frozen puff pastry.

Tarts are either baked in pans with removable bottoms or shaped in flan rings set on a flat baking sheet (page 52). In either case, the tart bottom is perfectly flat, and must therefore be unmolded onto a flat serving platter or tray. If you lack a flat platter of sufficient diameter, simply cover a piece of stiff cardboard with foil, or serve the tart on the metal disk of the pan bottom. The latter alternative is the most reliable, in any case, if the tart is at all delicate, for it prevents its being disturbed or jarred before serving. For a measuring guide to fruit quantities, see page 14.

A galette is literally any flat cake, or pancake. Our first galette is a traditional specialty of Brittany: a crisp buttery shortcake baked in a tart pan and cut into wedges for serving. Our second galette is completely different: a rustic French country fruit tart free-formed on a flat baking sheet and served in wedges like a fruit pizza.

The galette pastry should not contain too much sugar, or it will be have a tendency to overbrown; use Basic All-Purpose Flaky Pastry (page 34) made with no more than 1 tablespoon sugar. Dough made with 2 cups flour will produce a rectangle approximately 10 × 14 inches or a round 14 inches in diameter.

Generously butter a large pizza pan or a 12 × 16 inch cookie sheet. After the dough is prepared and chilled it is ready to roll out. Pat the dough into a flattened ball shape, then set it in the center of a lightly floured surface and roll with a floured rolling pin to a thickness of between $\frac{1}{8}$ and $\frac{1}{4}$ inch and shaped free-form (into a heart or an oval, for example, or a star), or as a rectangle or circle, to fit the size and shape of the pan. If you are shaping the dough in a star or other fairly complex shape, it is best to do the rolling out and cutting on a piece of floured foil or wax paper. Then simply turn the paper upside down over the buttered pan, position the dough for baking, and peel off the paper. For a plain round or rectangular shape, roll the dough up onto the rolling pin, then ease it down onto the buttered pan.

To complete, fill and bake according to the specific recipe. Traditionally, the raw dough is topped with fruit slices, a dough edging is folded onto the fruit, and the galette is baked at 400°F for 50 to 60 minutes, or until pastry is golden brown. The cooled galette is brushed with fruit glaze (page 120) before serving.

FRENCH APPLE TART (*TARTE AUX POMMES*)

In this version of the classic French Apple Tart, the decorative arrangement of glazed apple slices covers a thick applesauce flavored with preserves and brandy.

Advance preparation: The partially baked pastry shell may be prepared ahead and frozen (page 53). The tart is best when freshly made, but it may also be baked, left unglazed, and frozen (page 56). Thaw and warm in the oven, then glaze just before serving.

Special equipment: 11-inch tart shell with removable bottom; pastry brush; food processor fitted with steel blade or knife and cutting board; 2½-quart heavy-bottom enamel or stainless steel saucepan; 12-inch flat serving platter.

Sauce cooking time: About 25 minutes.

Baking time: Partially prebaked shell: 425°F for 12 minutes with pie weights, then 3 minutes empty; completed tart: 375°F for 35 to 45 minutes.

Quantity: One 11-inch tart.

> *Partially prebaked 11-inch tart shell*
> *made with Basic All-Purpose Flaky*
> *Pastry (page 34) prepared with egg*
> *yolk and 2 tablespoons sugar or*
> *Rich Tart Pastry (page 64)*
> *4 pounds apples (firm tart variety such*
> *as Granny Smith or Greening)*
> *2 tablespoons lemon juice*
> *2 tablespoons granulated sugar*
> *3 tablespoons butter*
> *3 tablespoons water*
> *⅓ cup orange marmalade or apricot*
> *preserves*
> Optional: *¼ cup calvados, brandy, or*
> *rum*
> *Plain Fruit Glaze (page 120)*
> *made with apricot preserves and*
> *kirsch, or Firm Fruit Glaze (page 120)*

1. Prepare the pastry, roll it out, and line the buttered pan (page 38). Trim a ¾-inch pastry overhang, and shape the sides of the tart shell (page 41). Prick the bottom with a fork, chill until firm, then partially blind-bake the shell (page 42). Cool on a wire rack.

2. Prepare apples and sauce. First peel and evenly thin-slice about 3 cups of apples. Place them in a bowl and coat them with lemon juice and sugar to prevent discoloration. Peel, core, and chop the remaining apples (using the food processor or knife and cutting board) and place them in a saucepan with the butter and water. Cook over low heat, covered, about 20 minutes, to make the applesauce. Stir in the marmalade or preserves, and the brandy or other flavoring. Raise the heat slightly and cook, uncovered, until so thick the sauce clings to the spoon and resists dripping off. Do not burn. Remove from the heat and stir to cool. Preheat oven to 375°F.

3. Spread the applesauce in the bottom of the partially baked pastry shell. Cover the sauce with neatly overlapping rows of apple slices arranged in concentric circles. Bake in the center of the preheated oven for 35 to 45 minutes, or until the apples are fork-tender (different types require different baking times). While the tart is baking, prepare the glaze. Cool the tart about 5 minutes, then unmold from the pan (page 43), and slide onto a flat serving platter or wire rack to cool completely. Brush the lukewarm glaze over the completely cooled apples. Chill to set the glaze; serve tart at room temperature.

VARIATION:

Apple and Cranberry Sauce Tart (*Tarte aux Pommes et aux Airelles*). Prepare French Apple Tart but omit preserves and brandy. Note that the applesauce is replaced by cranberry sauce. Therefore, use only 1½ pounds cooking apples. To make the sauce, chop coarsely together 1 cup peeled, cut-up apples and 2 cups fresh or frozen cranberries. Put the fruit in a heavy-bottom enamel or stainless steel saucepan with 3 tablespoons water, 3 tablespoons butter, ½ teaspoon each cinnamon and nutmeg, ½ cup sugar, and 2 tablespoons quick-cooking tapioca. Cook gently, uncovered, 10 to 15 minutes or until very thick, stirring occasionally to prevent sticking. While the sauce cooks, thinly slice the remaining apples (about 3 cups) and toss with 2 tablespoons lemon juice and 2 tablespoons sugar. Cool the sauce slightly, spread it on the pastry shell, and cover with overlapping concentric rings of apple slices. Allow the red sauce to show between the rows of apples. Bake and glaze as above.

NORMANDY APPLE TART (*TARTE NORMANDE AUX POMMES*)

Because Normandy produces such a bounty of excellent dairy products, the title of this classic French recipe indicates that the tart contains a rich custard.

Advance preparation: The unbaked pastry shell may be prepared ahead and frozen (page 53), but the tart must be freshly assembled before baking or the custard will soften the lower crust.

Special equipment: 11-inch tart pan with removable bottom; pastry brush; mixing bowl and whisk or food processor; flat, edged baking sheet; aluminum foil strips or frame (page 25); 12-inch flat serving platter.

Baking time: 425°F for 20 minutes; 375°F for 30 minutes.

Quantity: One 11-inch tart.

> *Pastry for an 11-inch unbaked tart shell*
> *made with Basic All-Purpose Flaky*
> *Pastry, Orange or Lemon Variation*
> *(page 35), prepared with egg yolk and*
> *2 tablespoons confectioners' sugar,*
> *or Rich Tart Pastry (page 64)*
> *1 pound apples (firm variety such as*
> *Granny Smith or medium firm such*
> *as Golden Delicious), peeled, cored,*
> *and sliced ⅛ inch thick (3 cups*
> *slices)*
> *⅓ cup plus 1 tablespoon granulated*
> *sugar*
> *⅛ teaspoon cinnamon*
> *¼ teaspoon freshly grated nutmeg*
> *Egg glaze: 1 egg white beaten with 1*
> *tablespoon water*
> *3 tablespoons ground almonds*
>
> **Custard**
> *1 egg plus 1 yolk*
> *3 tablespoons granulated sugar*
> *¼ cup all-purpose flour*
> *½ cup heavy cream*
> *2 teaspoons vanilla extract or 3*
> *tablespoons calvados, applejack, or*
> *dark rum*

1. Prepare the pastry, roll it out, and line the buttered pan (page 38). Trim a ¾-inch pastry overhang and shape the sides of the tart shell (page 41). Do not prick the pastry. Chill the unbaked shell until firm. Preheat oven to 425°F.

2. While the pastry chills, prepare the apples and toss them in bowl with ⅓ cup of the sugar, the cinnamon and nutmeg. When pastry is firm, brush with moisture-proofing egg white glaze and sprinkle with 1 generous tablespoon sugar. Arrange overlapping apple slices in concentric circles over the prepared pastry.

3. Set the tart in the lower third of the preheated oven and bake 20 minutes. This first baking cooks the apples to partial tenderness and prebakes the crust at the same time. While the apples bake, prepare the custard. Beat together in bowl or processor the egg plus yolk, 3 tablespoons sugar, the flour, cream, and vanilla or other flavoring.

4. After 20 minutes, remove the tart from the oven. Reduce heat to 375°F. Set the tart on a flat, edged baking sheet for ease in handling. Pour the custard over apples and sprinkle on a few gratings of nutmeg and the ground almonds. Place foil edging over the pastry rim to prevent overbrowning, if necessary. Place the tart in the center of the oven and bake 30 to 35 minutes, or until the top is puffed and golden and a knife inserted into the custard 1 inch from the edge comes out clean. Cool about 4 minutes, then unmold the tart from its pan (page 43) and slide it onto a flat serving platter. Serve warm or at room temperature.

VARIATION:

Normandy Apple-Pear Tart (Tarte Normande aux Pommes et aux Poires). Prepare Normandy Apple Tart but instead of all apples, use 2 large tart apples plus 2 large ripe pears. Peel, core, and slice apples ⅛ inch. Core and slice, but do not peel, pears, for a total of about 3 cups prepared fruit. Omit ground almonds in custard.

FRANGIPANE PEAR TART

This elegant tart has an almond cream filling that goes especially well with the flavor of pears. A recipe from the classic French pastry repertoire, this version is favored by students and chefs at l'École de Cuisine La Varenne in Paris. It is easy to prepare ahead, and versatile, since peaches or other fruits can be substituted for the pears. Firm pears or peaches should be poached as directed; as a substitute, canned fruit may be used. Note that there are two versions of this recipe: In one, the frangipane filling is baked at the same time as the fruit so that it puffs up around the fruit, making a pretty presentation. The variation at the end of the recipe, in contrast, has a layer of frangipane baked in the pastry shell, then topped by fresh, glazed fruits. The second method is good for tarts that must be prepared far ahead, as the baked frangipane layer prevents fruit moisture from softening the crust.

Advance preparation: The pastry shell can be prepared and chilled in advance, or partially prebaked (page 43) and frozen until needed. Frangipane cream can be made well ahead and refrigerated up to 3 days or frozen. Firm pears can be poached a day ahead and refrigerated in their poaching liquid. Either version of the tart can be made the morning of the day it is to be served, but use Firm Fruit Glaze (page 120) if glazing more than 2 hours before serving.

Special equipment: 11-inch tart pan with removable bottom; 2½-quart heavy-bottom stainless steel or enamel saucepan for fruit poaching; slotted spoon; paper towels.

Baking time: Partially prebaked shell: 425°F for 12 minutes with pie weights, then 3 minutes empty; complete tart: 400°F for 25 to 30 minutes.

Quantity: One 11-inch tart.

> *Partially baked 11-inch tart shell made*
> *with Basic All-Purpose Flaky Pastry*
> *(page 34), sweetened with*
> *3 tablespoons sugar, or Rich Tart*
> *Pastry (page 64), or Cream Cheese*
> *Pastry (page 65)*
> *1 cup Almond Pastry Cream*
> *(Frangipane), (page 103)*
> *Plain Fruit Glaze (page 120) or Firm*
> *Fruit Glaze (page 120); see* Advance
> preparation *above*
>
> *5 to 6 medium-sized firm pears (Anjou or*
> *Bosc) or 1 large can of halved pears*
> *in heavy syrup*
> *Poaching syrup (for use with firm*
> *fresh pears): 2 cups water, ½ cup*
> *granulated sugar, 1 vanilla bean,*
> *one whole lemon, sliced*
> *1 tablespoon granulated sugar*

1. Prepare and partially prebake the pastry shell (page 43). Cool on a wire rack. Prepare the Frangipane cream and Fruit Glaze. If the glaze hardens, it can be rewarmed before using.

2. If you are using fresh pears, they must be poached as follows: Combine the syrup ingredients in 2½-quart stainless steel or enamel saucepan, and bring to a boil. Peel, halve, and core the pears. Immerse them in the boiling syrup, reduce the heat slightly, and poach, uncovered, for 5 to 7 minutes, or until the pears can be pierced with a sharp knife. (*Note:* To poach peaches, leave them whole; peel and pit *after* poaching.) Store the fruit in its poaching liquid and chill until ready to use. If you are using canned pears, drain them well and blot dry with paper towels.

3. To assemble tart: Preheat oven to 400°F. Warm the fruit glaze if it is stiff. Brush a moisture-proofing layer of glaze over the partially prebaked pastry shell. Stir the frangipane cream; if it is too stiff after chilling, soften it with a couple of tablespoons of cream. Spread it over the pastry shell. Lift the poached fruit from its liquid and dry it between several layers of paper towels. When it is dry, set each pear half flat side down and cut it in slices crosswise, but retain the half-pear shape. Slip a knife blade under the pear slices and lift them in one piece. Set them down on the cream filling and arrange like the petals of a flower, wider ends facing out. Put one slice—or an entire half if there is room—in the center of the "flower." Sprinkle the pears *lightly* with about a tablespoon of granulated sugar so they will brown.

4. Bake the tart in the preheated oven for 25 to 30 minutes, or until the frangipane puffs slightly around the pears and looks golden brown. Watch that the pastry does not brown too quickly; cover the edges with foil to prevent them from overbrowning if necessary. Cool on a wire rack.

5. Cool about five minutes, then unmold from the pan (page 43). Slide the tart onto a flat serving plate. Brush warm glaze over the top of the tart. Chill in the refrigerator to set the glaze.

VARIATION:

Frangipane Fresh Fruit Tart. Instead of baking the fruit and frangipane together as above, the frangipane layer can be baked alone. To do this, line the tart pan with pastry, prick the bottom all over with a fork, and chill until firm. Spread the pastry with frangipane cream. Bake at 400°F for 15 to 25 minutes, or until the pastry and cream are a rich golden brown. Cool on a wire rack. Brush fruit glaze over the frangipane, then top with any single or combination of prepared fresh fruit (whole strawberries, washed, hulled, and dried well; sliced ripe peaches, peeled and pitted; blueberries, washed and dried well; fresh raspberries; etc.). Brush fruit glaze over the top of the fruit arrangement. Chill to set the glaze. This tart can be made well in advance.

ALMOND PEAR TART

I first tasted this tart as an art student in Paris years ago. Since then, the memory has been refined by numerous visits and at least as many different versions, the most recent sampled on a trip through Normandy during the pear harvest. Though similar in concept to Frangipane Pear Tart, this recipe is prepared quite differently.

Advance preparation: The pastry shell may be prepared ahead and frozen (see page 53). The tart can be baked ahead but the texture is best if made the day of serving.

Special equipment: 11-inch tart shell with removable bottom; pastry brush; food processor fitted with steel blade or blender; 12-inch flat serving platter.

Baking time: 425°F for 15 minutes, 350°F for 40 to 45 minutes.

Quantity: One 11-inch tart.

Unbaked pastry for 11-inch tart shell
    made with Rich Tart Pastry,
    flavored with orange or lemon (page
    64) or Cream Cheese Pastry (page 65),
    or Basic All-Purpose Flaky Pastry
    (page 34) prepared with egg yolk
    and 2 tablespoons sugar

Almond Filling
2 ounces (½ cup) unblanched almonds,
    whole or slivered
⅓ cup granulated sugar
4 tablespoons unsalted butter, cut up, at
    room temperature
1 large egg
¼ teaspoon freshly grated nutmeg
½ teaspoon each: vanilla extract and
    almond extract

Cream Filling
½ cup heavy or whipping cream
1 whole large egg plus 1 yolk
1 tablespoon granulated sugar

1 teaspoon vanilla extract
Optional: *2 tablespoons Eau de Vie de*
    Poire

4 large ripe pears (Bosc or Bartlett),
    peeled, cored, and quartered

1. Prepare the pastry, roll it out, and line the buttered pan (page 38). Trim a ¾-inch overhang, and form the sides of the tart shell (page 41). Prick the bottom with a fork, and chill until firm while preparing the filling. (*Note:* This recipe can also be made with a partially baked and completely cooled pastry shell, page 43.)

2. Preheat the oven to 425°F. Prepare the almond layer: In a food processor, combine the almonds and sugar and process until nuts are ground fine. Or grind the nuts in a blender after drying in oven (page 32), then combine them with the sugar. Add butter, pulse 2 or 3 times, then add the egg, nutmeg, and both extracts. Pulse 2 or 3 times to blend. Set aside until pastry is chilled.

3. Prepare the Cream Filling: In a food processor or blender combine the cream, egg plus yolk, sugar, vanilla, and brandy if you are using it. Process a few seconds to blend.

4. Finally, prepare the pears just before using them (to avoid discoloration). Spread the almond filling on the chilled pastry. Top with a flower-petal arrangement of pear quarters (thin necks pointing inward). Pour the cream filling over the pears and sprinkle with a few gratings of fresh nutmeg. Bake in the lower third of the preheated oven for 15 minutes. Lower the heat to 350°F, raise the tart to the center of the oven, and continue baking another 40 to 45 minutes, or until the filling is set and looks golden brown. Cool on a wire rack. Unmold the tart (page 43) and slide it onto a flat serving platter. Serve warm or at room temperature.

VARIATION:

Apricot-Almond Tart. Prepare Almond-Pear Tart but omit the almond extract and replace the pears with canned apricot halves, drained and positioned cut side down *after* both the almond filling *and* cream fillings are put into the shell. If you like, brush the cooled apricots with apricot Plain Fruit Glaze (page 120) shortly before serving.

BLUEBERRY CUSTARD TART

This is an irresistible summer party dessert in which fresh berries (any variety or any combination) are baked into a custard. It is a Vermont–French Canadian variation on the classic French Normandy Apple Tart.

Advance preparation: The partially baked pastry shell may be prepared ahead and frozen (page 56). The tart is best when freshly made; custard does not freeze well.

Special equipment: 11-inch tart shell with removable bottom; pastry brush; bowl and whisk or food processor fitted with a steel blade; flat, edged baking sheet; stainless steel knife; 12-inch flat serving platter.

Baking time: Partially prebaked shell: 425°F for 10 minutes with pie weights, then 3 minutes empty; completed tart: 375°F for 40 to 45 minutes.

Quantity: One 11-inch tart.

> *Partially prebaked 11-inch tart shell*
> *made with Basic All-Purpose Flaky*
> *Pastry, Orange Variation (page 35),*
> *or Cream Cheese Pastry (page 64)*
> *or Rich Tart Pastry (page 65)*
> *Egg glaze: 1 egg white beaten with 1*
> *tablespoon water*
> *½ cup granulated sugar*
> *¼ cup all-purpose flour*
> *½ teaspoon cinnamon*
> *¼ teaspoon nutmeg*
> *A pinch of salt*
> *½ cup heavy cream*
> *¼ cup milk*
> *1 egg*
> *4 cups fresh blueberries, stemmed,*
> *rinsed, and dried, or partially*
> *thawed frozen berries (or use half*
> *blueberries, half raspberries or*
> *peeled, sliced peaches)*

1. Prepare the pastry, roll it out, and line the buttered pan (page 38). Trim a ¾-inch pastry overhang, and form the sides of the tart shell (page 41). Prick the pastry with a fork, chill until firm, then partially blind-bake the shell

(page 42). Brush the pastry with egg white glaze after the first 10 minutes and continue baking 3 minutes, or until dough is no longer translucent. Cool on a wire rack. Reduce the oven heat to 375°F.

2. In a bowl or processor, beat together the sugar, flour, cinnamon, nutmeg, salt, cream, milk, and egg. Set the pastry-lined pan on a flat, edged baking sheet for ease in handling. Spread the berries over the shell and top with the custard mix.

3. Set the tart on its baking sheet in the center of the preheated oven and bake 40 to 45 minutes, or until stainless steel knife inserted into the custard 1 inch from the edge comes out clean. Check the tart after about half the baking time and add a foil edging if necessary to protect the crust from overbrowning. Cool about 5 minutes, then unmold the pan (page 43) and slide the tart onto a flat serving platter or wire rack to cool completely. Serve at room temperature.

RASPBERRY YOGURT TART

The picturesque glazed berry topping conceals a flavorful layer of fruit yogurt blended with cream cheese. I devised this filling as an accompaniment for whatever fresh fruits I have available, and I like to select a yogurt flavor that complements the color and flavor of the fruit. *(Note:* A small amount of un-flavored gelatin is added to set the filling so that the tart can be sliced neatly; without gelatin, you have a thick pudding good by itself or for filling individual tartlets.)

Advance preparation: The completely baked pastry shell can be made ahead and frozen (page 53) or the shell can be filled with the yogurt mixture one day ahead and refrigerated. Several hours before serving, top with fresh fruit, glaze, and refrigerate.
Special equipment: 11-inch tart shell; pastry brush; electric mixer or food processor fitted with a steel blade; small saucepan and spoon; paper towels.
Baking time: Completely prebaked shell: 425°F for 10 minutes, then 350°F for 15 to 20 minutes.
Quantity: One 11-inch tart.

> *Completely prebaked 11-inch tart shell*
> *made with Basic All-Purpose Flaky*
> *Pastry, Orange Variation (page 35),*
> *or other pastry of your choice;*
> *or any Crumb Crust (page 72)*
> *baked in a pie plate*

> 2 (8 ounce) packages cream cheese (not
>   whipped), at room temperature,
>   cut up
> 2 tablespoons frozen orange juice
>   concentrate, undiluted
> 1 tablespoon grated orange zest
> 4 tablespoons granulated or
>   confectioners' sugar, sifted
> 1 cup fruit-flavored yogurt, such as
>   raspberry, strawberry, cherry, or
>   orange
> 1 envelope (2 teaspoons) unflavored
>   gelatin
> 4 tablespoons cold water
> 3 to 4 cups fresh raspberries, stemmed,
>   rinsed, and dried well on paper
>   towels (or other berries or sliced
>   fresh fruit; or canned fruit, drained
>   well and dried)
> Plain Fruit Glaze made with red currant
>   jelly and kirsch (page 120), or Firm
>   Fruit Glaze (page 120) if the tart is
>   to be held longer than 2 hours
>   before serving

1. Prepare the pastry, roll it out, and line the buttered tart pan (page 38). Trim a ¾-inch overhang and form the sides of the tart (page 41). Prick the bottom pastry with a fork and chill until firm, then completely blind-bake the shell (page 42). Cool on a wire rack.

2. In a mixer or food processor combine the cream cheese, orange juice concentrate and grated zest, the sugar, and the yogurt. Cream until thick and smooth. Set aside.

3. In a small saucepan, sprinkle the gelatin over the cold water, set it aside about 3 minutes, then stir in 3 or 4 tablespoons of the yogurt mixture. Set the pan over medium heat and slowly bring to a boil, stirring, until the gelatin is completely dissolved. Boil, stirring, about 3 seconds. Remove from the heat and cool. Pour the gelatin mixture into the mixer or processor and beat together with the remaining yogurt mixture.

4. Pour the yogurt mixture into the baked pastry shell. Chill at least 4 hours, or until the filling is set. Then top with an attractive arrangement of

dry, prepared berries and/or fruit slices (instead of raspberries try blueberries and/or strawberries, bananas, pitted grapes or cherries, sliced nectarines or peaches, kiwis, etc.). Brush with glaze and refrigerate until ready to serve. Refrigerate leftovers.

TWO-BERRY ORANGE CREAM TART

This quick-to-prepare summer dessert has a prebaked shell filled with orange-flavored cream cheese topped with colorful rings of fresh glazed berries. For contrasting colors, use alternating circles of blueberries and strawberries, or blackberries and raspberries, for example.

Advance preparation: The completely baked tart shell may be prepared ahead and frozen (page 53); the Orange Cream Cheese Filling may be prepared and refrigerated a day or 2 in advance. Assemble the tart the morning it is to be served, but glaze it as close as possible to serving time (see below). This tart can also be prepared in a pie plate.

Special equipment: 11-inch tart pan; pastry brush; aluminum foil strips or frame (page 25).

Baking time: Completely baked tart shell: 425°F for 12 minutes; 350°F for 10 to 15 minutes.

Quantity: One 11-inch tart.

> *Completely prebaked 11-inch tart shell*
> *made with Basic All-Purpose Flaky*
> *Pastry (page 34), or Cream Cheese*
> *Pastry (page 65), or other pastry*
> *of your choice*
> *Plain Fruit Glaze made with red currant*
> *jelly and kirsch (page 120), or Firm*
> *Fruit Glaze (page 120) if the tart is*
> *to be held longer than 2 hours*
> *before serving*
> *Orange Cream Cheese Tart Filling*
> *(page 104)*
> *4 cups fresh berries (2 cups red berries*
> *plus 2 cups blue or black if*
> *available), hulled, rinsed, and*
> *dried well on paper towels*

1. Prepare the pastry, roll it out, and line the buttered tart pan (page 38). Trim a ¾-inch pastry overhang, and form the sides of the tart shell (page 41). Prick the bottom with a fork, chill until firm, then completely blind-bake (page 42). Cool on a wire rack. Brush moisture-proofing Fruit Glaze over the bottom of the pastry shell.

2. Prepare the Orange Cream Cheese Tart Filling and spread it over the pastry shell. Top with concentric circles of berries, alternating colors: a red ring, a blue ring, etc. Brush the berries with Firm Fruit Glaze (page 120) and chill several hours before serving. Or chill first, then brush with Plain Fruit Glaze just before serving. Refrigerate leftovers.

STRAWBERRY SHORTCAKE TART

This spring dinner party dessert is quick and easy to prepare ahead, fresh and appealing in presentation. For entertaining, the cream cheese-whipped cream filling is a welcome variation on the more traditional shortcake prepared only with whipped cream; the latter tends to get soggy if made too far in advance.

Advance preparation: The completely baked tart shell may be prepared ahead and frozen (page 56); the filling can be made a day ahead. Filling may be added to the shell the morning the tart is to be served, but glazed fruit should be added closer to serving time. This tart can also be prepared in a pie plate.

Special equipment: 11-inch tart pan with removable bottom; pastry brush; electric mixer, blender, or food processor fitted with a steel blade; chilled electric mixer beater and bowl for whipped cream; plastic wrap.

Baking time: Completely baked tart shell: 425°F for 12 minutes; 350°F for 10 to 15 minutes.

Quantity: One 11-inch tart.

> *Completely prebaked 11-inch tart shell*
> *made with Basic All-Purpose Flaky*
> *Pastry, Orange Variation (page 35),*
> *or Cream Cheese Pastry (page 65),*
> *or any Crumb Crust (page 72)*
> *prepared in a pie plate*
> *Lemon Double Cream Tart Filling*
> *with whipped cream (page 104)*

4 cups fresh strawberries, hulled, rinsed,
and dried well (use perfectly formed
large berries for best presentation)
Firm Fruit Glaze made with red currant
jelly and kirsch (page 120)
Optional garnish: *mint sprigs*

1. Prepare the completely prebaked shell, and cool thoroughly (page 43). Prepare Lemon Double Cream Tart Filling with folded-in whipped cream (page 104). Spread the cream mixture into the pastry shell, cover with plastic wrap, and chill.

2. About 4 hours before serving, top the filling with an attractive allover arrangement of perfectly dry berries placed stem end down. Brush on the glaze. Garnish tart with mint sprigs. Chill until ready to serve.

VARIATION:

Peach Shortcake Tart. Prepare Strawberry Shortcake Tart, above, but substitute about 2 pounds fresh ripe peaches for the berries. Peel (page 137) and chop about 1 cup peaches and stir them into the Lemon Double Cream Tart Filling before spreading it over the pastry shell. Top with the remaining peaches, peeled, sliced, and patted dry. Glaze as above. (*Note:* Canned peaches, drained well, can be substituted.)

CRANBERRY-RAISIN TART

A proud native American, the cranberry is highly nutritious and contains calcium and iodine as well as significant amounts of vitamin C, a fact appreciated by the sailors on ninetenth-century clipper and whaling ships, who ate the berries to prevent scurvy. The versatility of the berry was also well known to the Indians, who ground it with venison for pemmican, a dried trail food, as well as using it for dye and as a poultice for poisoned arrow wounds.

Select only unblemished cranberries for pies. Commercial packers pass the berries through a "bouncer" which, as the name implies, separates berries firm enough to leap down a series of 4-inch high hurdles from those too soft or bruised. You should be equally stringent in your standards, so bounce your berries before baking! During fall harvest season, cranberries are widely available, though they can be hard to find at other times. When you find them, put bags of fresh berries directly into your freezer for year-round use.

With its red berries peeking from beneath the lattice crust, this tart makes a festive holiday presentation. The orange-scented filling is tangy, rather than sweet, and is especially good served warm, with vanilla ice cream or Orange Flavored Whipped Cream, (page 108). The recipe can also be used for tartlets, or baked as a pie.

Advance preparation: Cranberries may be frozen (whole and fresh) until needed, then prepared as described below and baked while still frozen. The unbaked pastry shell can be prepared ahead and frozen (page 53). The complete tart can be frozen baked or unbaked, though it is best made fresh (page 56).

Special equipment: 10- or 11-inch tart shell or 8 tartlet pans 4½-inch diameter; pastry brush; pastry wheel for cutting lattice; aluminum foil strips or frame (page 25); 12-inch flat serving platter.

Baking time: 425°F for 15 minutes; 350°F for 30 to 35 minutes for tart or 20 to 25 minutes for tartlets.

Quantity: One 10- or 11-inch tart or 8 tartlets 4½-inch diameter.

> *Unbaked pastry for a 2-crust 10- or*
> *11-inch pie (use 3 cups flour) made*
> *with Whole Wheat Pastry (page 59)*
> *or Basic All-Purpose Flaky Pastry,*
> *Nut Variation (page 35),*
> *sweetened with 2 tablespoons sugar,*
> *or other pastry of your choice*
> *3 cups (12-ounces) fresh or frozen whole*
> *cranberries, picked over, rinsed and*
> *patted dry with paper towels*
> *1 cup seedless raisins*
> *½ cup shelled walnuts, chopped coarse*
> *1 large orange: grated rind plus ½ cup*
> *orange juice*
> *½ cup dark brown sugar, packed*
> *1 cup granulated sugar (if you prefer a*
> *very sweet pie, add ½ cup more*
> *sugar)*
> *2 tablespoons quick-cooking tapioca*
> *½ teaspoon each cinnamon and nutmeg*
> *Egg glaze: 1 egg beaten with 1 tablespoon*
> *water*

1. Prepare the pastry, roll out half the quantity, and line the buttered pan (page 38) or tartlet shells (page 51). Trim a ¾-inch overhang, and form the sides of the tart shell (page 51). Chill until firm while preparing the filling.

2. Preheat the oven to 425°F. In a bowl, combine and stir together the cranberries, raisins, walnuts, juice and rind of orange, sugar, tapioca, and spices. Brush moisture-proofing egg glaze over bottom of the pastry. Fill with the fruit mixture, spread flat.

3. Roll out the remaining dough, cut it into ½-inch strips, and arrange in a lattice top (page 47). Pinch the lattice strip ends into the dough around the edges of the tart. Fold dough up into a raised rim and flute as desired (page 44). Brush the lattice strips with egg glaze and sprinkle lightly with granulated sugar. (*Note:* Tartlets may be left topless or given lattice crust, as you prefer.)

4. Set the tart in the lower third of the preheated oven and bake 15 minutes. Reduce the heat to 350°F, raise the tart to the center of the oven, and bake an additional 30 to 35 minutes (tartlets 20 to 25 minutes), or until the pastry is golden brown. Check the tart or tartlets after about half the baking time and add a foil edging if necessary to prevent the crust from overbrowning. Cool about 5 minutes, then unmold (page 43) and slide the tart onto a flat serving platter or wire rack to cool completely. Serve warm or at room temperature.

LINZERTORTE

This traditional Austrian torte is really a tart, whose rich, sweet-and-spicy, cinnamon-raspberry flavor provides the perfect finish to a fireside dinner on a snowy winter evening. To be authentic, arrange the lattice-strip pastry topping on the diagonal.

The dough for this tart is delicious by itself, baked into cookies. For this reason, the pastry recipe is large enough to make one 11-inch tart plus about 30 round cookies, which, when studded with cloves and rolled in powdered sugar, make an aromatic addition to a holiday cookie platter.

Advance preparation: The partially baked pastry shell may be prepared ahead and frozen, or the plain dough can be frozen (page 55), as can the completely baked tart (page 55). Cookies made with Linzer Pastry can also be frozen.

Special equipment: 11-inch tart pan with removable bottom; wax paper; aluminum foil strip or frame (page 25); pastry brush; 12-inch flat serving platter; flat baking sheet for cookies.

Baking time: Partially prebaked shell: 425°F for 12 minutes; complete tart: 350°F for 40 minutes. Cookies: 350°F for 15 minutes.

Quantity: One 11-inch tart plus thirty 1-inch cookies, or two 9-inch tarts; or one 11-inch plus one 8-inch tart.

> *Unbaked Linzer Pastry (page 67), for*
> *partially prebaked shell made as*
> *described below*
> *1⅓ cups seedless raspberry jam (best*
> *quality); this will fill one 11-inch*
> *tart. If you are making the*
> *additional 8-inch tart, use 1*
> *additional cup jam. For two 9-inch*
> *tarts, use 1 cup jam each.*
> *¼ cup ground almonds or walnuts*
> *Egg glaze: 1 egg beaten with 1 tablespoon*
> *water*
> *Optional: 1 tablespoon confectioners'*
> *sugar*

For Cookies
⅓ cup whole cloves
¾ cup confectioners' sugar, sifted

1. Preheat the oven to 425°F. Prepare the pastry, butter the tart pan, and divide your dough into 2 pieces, one slightly larger than the other. Wrap and refrigerate the smaller piece to use later for lattice top and cookies. Roll out the larger piece of dough between 2 pieces of floured wax paper (page 38) to a generous ⅛-inch thickness. Fit the dough into the tart pan (page 39), and trim ¾-inch pastry hangover. Form the sides of the tart shell (page 41). Or you can simply pat the dough into the buttered pan with lightly floured fingertips instead of rolling it out. Chill dough-lined pan 30 minutes, or until dough is firm.

2. Partially prebake the pastry shell in the lower third of the preheated oven for 12 minutes (*without lining with weights*), or only until the dough begins to change color. Don't let the dough brown; check it after 5 to 6 minutes, and if you see any puffed-up bubbles, prick and deflate them with a fork. Cool the shell on a wire rack. Reduce oven heat to 350°F.

3. When the pastry shell is cool, spread on the preserves, then sprinkle on about 2 tablespoons ground almonds.

4. Remove the remaining dough from the refrigerator and break off golf ball-size lumps, one at a time. Roll each lump on a floured surface into a

pencil-thick rope (roughly ⅜-inch diameter) long enough to reach across the top of the tart. Brush egg glaze around the edge of the tart shell. Position 6 or 7 dough ropes on a diagonal at equal intervals across the top of the tart. Gently press the rope ends onto the glazed pastry rim. Cut off excess dough. Position 6 or 7 more dough ropes going in the opposite direction across the first, setting these also on a diagonal to make diamond-shaped spaces. (*Note:* Cold dough is easier to handle; chill if necessary. Dough ropes rolled too thin will break when lifted.)

To neaten the tart edge after applying the lattice, roll out additional dough ropes. Brush the tart edge again with egg glaze and press a row of connected ropes onto the tart edge to cover the lattice ends and make a neat border. Be sure this border is inside, not overlapping, the pan edge. Brush the border, as well as the entire lattice topping, with egg glaze.

5. Place the tart in the center of the preheated oven and bake 40 minutes, or until the pastry is golden brown and the preserves are bubbling. Check the tart after about half the baking time and add a foil edging if necessary to prevent the crust from overbrowning. Cool on a wire rack before unmolding (page 43) onto a flat serving platter. If you like, just before serving, sift on a delicate coating of 1 tablespoon confectioners' sugar.

6. To make cookies. divide the remaining dough into 1-inch balls and set them on a buttered baking sheet. Stick one whole clove into the top of each ball. Bake the cookies in the center of a preheated 350°F oven for about 15 minutes, or just until golden brown. Cool cookies on a wire rack. While they are still warm, roll the cookies in sifted confectioners' sugar. When cold, sift on more sugar. Store airtight or freeze.

CHEESECAKE FRUIT TART

This recipe combines the best of two worlds: the richness of a baked cheese-cake plus the fresh tangy flavor of a fruit tart. The filling is baked ahead, then topped with glazed fresh fruit in any combination that appeals to you; I prefer sliced peaches or nectarines combined with kiwis and blueberries. This recipe can be baked in and served from a pie plate, or baked in a tart pan and served free-standing.

Advance preparation: The partially prebaked pastry shell can be prepared ahead and frozen (page 53). The complete tart can be prepared several hours before serving, or the cheesecake layer can be baked and refrigerated a day ahead, with the fruits added several hours before serving.

Special equipment: 10-inch pie plate or tart shell with removable bottom (or 10-inch cake pan with removable bottom); pastry brush; small saucepan; electric mixer or food processor fitted with a steel blade; aluminum foil strips or frame (page 25).

Baking time: Partially prebaked shell: 425°F for 10 minutes with pie weights, then 3 minutes empty; cheesecake layer: 350°F for 30 minutes.

Chilling time: At least 1 hour before serving.

Quantity: One 10-inch pie or tart.

> Partially prebaked 10-inch pie or tart
> shell made with All-Purpose Flaky
> Pastry (page 33), prepared with egg
> yolk and 2 tablespoons sugar, or
> Cream Cheese Pastry (page 65), or
> other pastry of your choice
> 12 ounces cream cheese (not whipped) at
> room temperature
> ½ cup granulated sugar
> 2 eggs
> ¼ teaspoon nutmeg
> 4 cups prepared fruit (4 or 5 peaches or
> nectarines, peeled and sliced ¼ inch
> thick, plus 1 cup fresh blueberries,
> stemmed, and 1 kiwi, peeled, sliced,
> and quartered)
> Plain Fruit Glaze (page 120), using
> apricot or red currant glaze
> depending on the color of the fruit,
> or Firm Fruit Glaze (page 120) if
> tart is to be held longer than 2
> hours before serving

1. Prepare the pastry, roll it out, and line buttered pie or tart pan (page 38). Trim a ¾-inch overhang, fold pastry edge inward, and flute it if you are using a pie plate, or press to the sides of the tart pan if you are using that. Trim excess dough. Prick the bottom with a fork and chill at least 30 minutes, until the dough is firm. Preheat the oven to 425°F. Partially blind-bake the shell (page 42). Cool on a wire rack. Reduce oven heat to 350°F. While the pastry shell bakes, prepare the cheesecake batter.

2. In an electric mixer or processor beat together until creamy and smooth: cream cheese, sugar, eggs, and nutmeg. Pour the batter into the cooled pastry

shell and bake in the center of the preheated oven for 30 minutes. After about half the baking time, check the tart and add a foil edging if necessary to prevent the crust from overbrowning. Cool on a wire rack. Chill.

3. Be sure the prepared fruit is perfectly dry. When the cheesecake is cold, top with an attractive arrangement of fruit—a flower petal pattern or concentric circles of overlapping slices. for example. Brush the cold fruit with lukewarm glaze. Chill at least one hour to set the glaze. Unmold the tart (page 43) or serve directly from the pie pan. Serve at room temperature; refrigerate leftovers.

VARIATIONS:

Strawberry Cheesecake Tart. Prepare the Cheesecake Fruit Tart above through step 2. Over the baked and chilled cheesecake, spread 2 cups dairy sour cream. Chill again. Instead of topping with fresh whole fruit, measure 4 cups strawberries (or raspberries or other berries) into an enamel or stainless steel saucepan. Add ½ cup sugar (or to taste), 2 tablespoons cornstarch, and 2 tablespoons fruit-flavored liqueur; a good choice is double cream of cassis (black currant) syrup. Cook over medium heat, stirring, about 5 minues, or until thick and clear. Cool completely, then spread over the tart. Chill about 2 hours before serving.

Strawberries-and-Cream Cheesecake Tart. This is also known as Outrageous! Prepare the Strawberry Cheesecake Tart variation above but cook the berries with only ⅓ cup sugar and 1½ tablespoons cornstarch. Cool the cooked berry mixture. Whip 1 cup heavy cream until nearly stiff, then fold in the fruit-flavored liqueur (optional) and the cooled berry mixture and spread it over the tart. Chill several hours before serving.

(*Note:* You can also omit the cheesecake and sour cream layers and spread this fruit-cream mixture directly into a completely prebaked pastry shell, or tartlet shells.)

FRUIT TART IN PUFF PASTRY SHELL

This is a classic French tart in which a free-standing prebaked puff pastry shell is filled with pastry cream and topped with glazed fresh fruits. I have given here two different shaped shells: the band and the square case; both are easy to form in any size following the step-by-step directions. For a third style, see Fruit Flower Tart, page 187. All cases can be made successfully either with Quick or Classic Puff Pastry (pages 82–89) though the latter will, of course, rise somewhat higher during baking.

Advance preparation: Quick or Classic Puff Pastry can be prepared ahead and
frozen (page 85) or the completely prebaked pastry shell (any style) can be
frozen. Fill the shell with cream and fruit no more than several hours before
serving to prevent a soggy lower crust.

Special equipment: Sharp knife or pizza cutting wheel; ruler; table fork; baking
sheets sprinkled with cold water; pastry brush; heavy-duty aluminum foil.

Baking time: 425°F for 20 minutes, approximately.

Quantity: ½ recipe of Classic Puff Pastry or whole recipe Quick Puff Pastry
rolls to a sheet of dough approximately 13 × 15 inches × a generous ⅛ inch.
From this you can make two bands, each about 4½ × 14 inches to serve
twelve; or you can make nine 3-inch square cases or one 10- or 11-inch
square case. Double quantities of other ingredients if you are using full
recipe of Classic Puff Pastry.

> *½ recipe Classic Puff Pastry (page 85)*
> *or whole recipe Quick Puff Pastry*
> *(page 82)*
> *Egg glaze: 1 egg beaten with 1 tablespoon*
> *water*
> *Plain Fruit Glaze (page 120) or Firm*
> *Fruit Glaze (page 120)*
> *Vanilla Pastry Cream (page 100) or*
> *Almond Pastry Cream Variation*
> *(page 103)*
> *Fresh fruit or berries, about 4 cups;*
> *whole fruit should be peeled, pitted,*
> *sliced neatly and patted dry; berries*
> *should be hulled, picked over,*
> *rinsed quickly and gently, and*
> *patted dry. The amount of fruit*
> *depends on the size and number of*
> *pastry shells. Poached or drained,*
> *canned fruit can also be used.*

Puff Pastry Band

1. On a lightly floured surface—the best is a piece of heavy-duty foil—roll
the dough into a rectangle about 13 × 15 inches by ⅛- to 3/16-inch thick. Without stretching the dough, lift it (on the piece of foil) onto a dry baking sheet, and
refrigerate at least 30 minutes, or until the dough feels firm. If dough has not

softened, you can skip this chilling. (*Note:* If the dough resists rolling, refrigerate it until it relaxes.)

2. Remove the sheet containing the foil and dough from the refrigerator, lift the foil from the sheet, and set it flat on the table. With a sharp knife held against a ruler, or using a pizza cutting wheel, cut the dough in half lengthwise. Cut cleanly without pulling the dough. Cut off about ½ inch on the narrow ends of each piece and freeze these scraps for another use (a).

To make the raised borders of the band, cut a ¾- to 1-inch border strip from both long sides of each band. Carefully lift these border strips off the foil and set them aside (b).

3. Sprinkle the baking sheet with cold water. One at a time, transfer the bands from the foil to the baking sheet as follows: Lift the foil and place it dough side down over the baking sheet, then peel the foil off the back of the dough band. The dough will thus be set *face down* on the sheet.

4. Moisten a ¾- to 1-inch wide border on both sides of the top surface of each of the bands with a pastry brush dipped in water. Place the narrow dough strips on these dampened borders and press them to seal. With the back edge of a knife blade, scallop or indent slightly at ½ inch intervals all around the outer edge of each border. These marks join the 2 layers and help them to rise together evenly.

5. Score the dough lightly along the inside edge of each border strip (heavy line, c). Prick the entire central area with a fork to allow steam to escape and prevent the area from rising too much. Brush egg glaze carefully on the tops of the border strips. Don't let the glaze drip over the sides or they will be glued together and will not rise. Chill the bands until firm. Preheat the oven to 425°F.

6. To bake, set the bands in the preheated oven for 20 minutes, or until well browned. Press down the central (pricked) area if it rises too much. Cool on a wire rack.

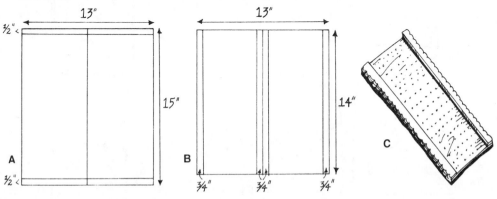

Puff Pastry Square Case

1. On a lightly floured surface—the best is a piece of a heavy-duty foil—roll the dough into a rectrangle about 13 × 15 inches × ⅛- to 3/16-inch thick. Without stretching the dough, lift it (on the piece of foil) onto a dry baking sheet. Refrigerate about 30 minutes, or until the dough feels firm. If dough has not softened, you can skip this chilling.

2. Cut the dough to desired size; note that the dough square is cut 1 inch larger all around than the dimensions of the baked shell. For 3-inch square cases, therefore, cut 4-inch dough squares; for a 10-inch square baked case, cut an 11-inch square of dough. Form as follows, whatever the size.

3. To make the square even, fold the dough in half diagonally (a) forming a right angle triangle. With even, clean slices (don't pull the dough), cut away a border about ¼ inch wide (dotted line) on both open edges. Freeze these scraps for another use.

4. Now, paralleling open edges of the triangle, cut border strips ¾-inch wide as follows: Begin to cut at the fold and cut *only* to within ¾ inch of the corner (b). The edging strips *must* remain attached at the corners as shown.

5. Unfold the square of dough, handling it carefully so as not to stretch it. Brush a line of water along the edge of the inner square of dough (inside the borders, dotted lines, b).

6. Lift half the cut border strip and place it face down over the moistened edge on the opposite side (c). Press the border gently to seal. Lift the remaining border strip and press it onto the opposite side (d). Press to seal. Note that one set

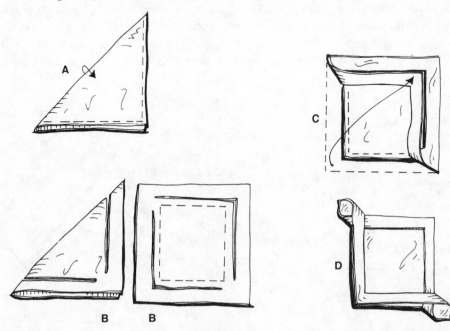

of corners is flat and even and the other has been given a decorative twist as the borders were formed. You can leave the case this way (as I prefer to do) or make all the corners flat and even by trimming off the twisted corners where the strips overlap (e). Score along the inner edge of the dough borders by cutting halfway through the dough with a knife tip (f, heavy line).

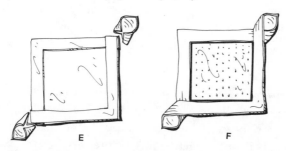

7. Sprinkle the baking sheet with cold water. Carefully transfer the squares to the dampened sheet and re-form the shapes if they have been damaged in moving. Prick the central area of each square all over with a fork. Brush the tops of the borders with egg glaze; do not let the glaze drip onto the sides or the dough won't rise. Refrigerate the dough until firm. Preheat the oven to 425°F.

8. To bake, set the squares in the preheated oven for 20 minutes, or until golden brown. Cool on a wire rack. If the central area is not flat enough, use a knife tip or fork to pry out the inner pricked area; it may have risen too much. Also remove any unbaked layers of dough in this central area.

Assembly Procedure

Brush moisture-proofing fruit glaze over the bottom of the baked and cooled pastry shell, then spread with cold pastry cream filling. Top with an attractive arrangement of prepared fruit and/or berries. Brush with fruit glaze and refrigerate, to set glaze, until ready to serve.

FRUIT FLOWER TART

The Château of Azay Le Rideau is one of the smallest in France's Loire Valley and yet, because of its exquisite delicacy and elegance, it rates two stars in the Michelin Green Guide. Unfortunately, they don't rate pastry, but I do, and in my book there is another treasure that merits the same rating only a block away on a village square: the Boulangerie-Pâtisserie of Monsieur Apolda. Amid the dour gray stone shops and houses, this bakery shop sparkles like a gem, its glass shelves adorned with napoleons, meringues, religieuses, éclairs, gilded bon-

bons, gâteaux, and tartes—all the classic French pastries and candies you ever dreamed of. But the crowning beauty set on the tart shelf is the Tarte Multi-Fruits—a spectacular eight-petaled flower edged with high-rise puff pastry and filled with alternating colored wedges of glazed fruits set on almond pastry cream. Like many other French bakers, M. Apolda jealously guards his "formulas" and would not share the recipes for his own specialties. However, his wife allowed as how this was just a variation on a classic *tarte aux fruits* that she was sure I could duplicate if I thought about it. Well, I did, and I have. And so can you.

Advance preparation: The puff pastry can be made ahead and refrigerated or frozen (page 85), or the tart shell can be baked ahead and stored a day or two in an airtight container, or wrapped and frozen. Do not fill and decorate the shell until a few hours before serving; the pastry may soften on standing.

Special equipment: Heavy-duty foil or 11- to 12-inch wide baking parchment; 10-inch pie plate or ring (for template); sharp paring knife; pastry brush; baking sheet at least 13 inches wide; 12-inch round flat serving platter.

Quantity: One 10-inch tart.

> *½ recipe Classic Puff Pastry (page 85)*
> *Egg glaze: 1 egg beaten with 1 teaspoon*
>   *water*
> *Plain Fruit Glaze (page 120)*
> *1 recipe Vanilla Pastry Cream (Crème*
>   *Pâtissière, page 100) or vanilla*
>   *pudding*
> *4 cups fresh fruit—use a variety of*
>   *colored fruits so each petal will be a*
>   *different or alternating color*
>   *(green seedless grapes, apricot slices,*
>   *strawberries or raspberries, fresh*
>   *blueberries, sliced bananas, etc.)*

1. Preheat the oven to 450°F. After the puff pastry has had six turns and at least a 30-minute chill in the refrigerator, roll it out on a lightly floured surface—the best for ease in handling is heavy-duty foil or wide parchment paper stuck to the countertop with a few drops of water. Roll the dough into a rectangle 13 × 15 inches about ⅛ inch thick. To create the flower shape, the dough is lightly marked into a circle, then divided into sections before being cut out. To do this, turn a 10-inch pie plate upside down in the *center* of the rolled out dough—*not* near the edges. With the back edge of a paring knife or with a

toothpick, lightly trace around the edge of the plate. Don't cut the dough. Then lightly mark lines dividing the circle into quarters, then eighths (a). Following the sketch, draw full half-moons (for the tips of the flower petals) at the *outside* of each wedge (b). At the widest part, the half moons should be about ¾- to 1-inch wide.

2. Now cut out around the *outside outline* (heavy line, c) of the tart. Don't cut the inner lines. When cutting, make clean, straight cuts; don't pull or stretch the dough. Stack up the dough scraps and freeze for another use.

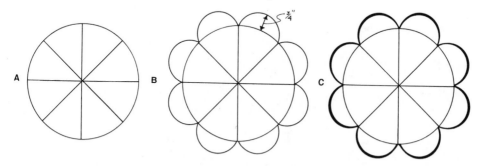

3. Slide the foil or parchment onto a baking sheet, taking care not to stretch the dough. Mark the inner curved edge of each half moon (heavy line, d) with a knife tip. Then cut halfway through the dough's thickness along these lines, taking care to leave enough dough at each petal's edge so the half-moons are not simply cut off. This cut allows the entire half-moon to rise freely, while the inner petal area will stay flatter and be hollowed out after baking to contain the cream and fruit. Prick the entire inner petal area (dots) with a fork to inhibit its rising. Do *not* prick the half-moons.

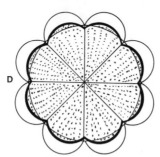

4. With a pastry brush or your fingertip (which gives best control) brush egg glaze over the tops of the half-moons; take care that no glaze runs down the edges, which would prevent rising. Chill the tart on its baking sheet in refrigerator for at least 30 minutes, until firm. During this time, preheat the oven to 425°F.

5. Just before baking, apply a second coat of egg glaze to the half-moon tops. Then bake in the preheated oven for about 35 to 45 minutes, or until the

pastry is a deep golden brown and the edges are well risen. The central pricked area may rise as well—you can either leave it alone or push it down with a pot holder during baking; however, it will be cut out when cool.

6. Slide the baked tart onto a wire rack to cool, removing the foil or paper it was baked on. With a fork or the tip of a paring knife, cut around the outside edge of the inner petal area to release it completely from the half-moons (see sketch, e). Carefully pry and lift this center out. Use a fork to lift out all un-cooked layers of dough beneath the removed central area, leaving intact the crisp shell below. Now the tart shell is ready to be filled and set on a flat serving platter, or it can be set on stiff cardboard and wrapped for freezing.

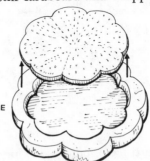

7. To complete, brush a thin layer of plain Fruit Glaze over the central area of the tart. Top with a generous ¼-inch layer of Vanilla Pastry Cream. Trace wedge lines in the cream with a toothpick. Decorate the top by filling each wedge with fruit, alternating various colors. Work from the outer tip to the center of each wedge or petal. Brush on the remaining fruit glaze and chill until serving time. Cut along the wedge (petal) lines to serve.

COMPLETE FLOWER FRUIT TART

FRESH FIG TART

The fig is a native of southwestern Asia and has been cultivated since pre-historic times. The ancient Greeks considered the fruit a delicacy, as did the Romans who spread it throughout their empire. The fig is responsible for two special culinary moments in my life—one, my first experience picking figs, from a tree in the garden outside the kitchen of Sandra Calder Davidson in the Loire

Valley, in France. It was a misty gray October morning, but it seemed suddenly sunny as I delighted in the purple-black pear-shaped fruit and savored their exotic sweetness and rose-hued interior—a moment for the eye of the painter and the palate of the gourmet.

Shortly thereafter, enamored of fresh figs, I discovered the following gem of a fig tart in a small pâtisserie on the Quiberon peninsula of Brittany. It is a classic preparation in this province, wherein the figs are poached in a red wine syrup. I have adapted this method, and now use it at home in New England with pale green figs from California. The red wine-fig flavor combination is sophisticated and satisfying; the presentation is elegant. (*Note:* If your figs have firm or tough skins, peel them before poaching; if the skins are tender, leave the figs unpeeled.)

Advance preparation: The completely baked tart shell may be prepared ahead and frozen (page 56); the figs can be poached a day ahead and left refrigerated in their syrup. Assemble the tart on the day of serving.

Special equipment: 11-inch tart shell with removable bottom; pastry brush; 2-quart stainless steel or enamel saucepan; slotted spoon; wooden spoon; optional: candy or jelly thermometer.

Baking time: Completely prebaked pastry shell: 425°F for 10 minutes with pie weights, then 13 to 15 minutes empty.

Setting time for glazed tart: 2 hours.

Quantity: One 11-inch tart.

> *Completely prebaked 11-inch tart shell*
> *made with Basic All-Purpose Flaky*
> *Pastry, Nut Pastry (almond) or*
> *Orange Pastry Variation (page 35),*
> *or Rich Tart Pastry (page 64) or*
> *other pastry of your choice*
> *18 medium-sized (1½ pounds) purple or*
> *green figs, sliced in half through the*
> *stem ends* (Note: *Peel only if skins*
> *are tough.*)
> *1½ cups granulated sugar*
> *1 cup dry red wine*
> *1 cup water*
> *Zest of one whole lemon, cut in wide*
> *strips*
> *2 tablespoons freshly squeezed lemon*
> *juice*
> *½ cup red currant jelly*

1. One day ahead, or at least several hours before making the tart, poach the figs in wine syrup. To do this, combine in a 2-quart saucepan the sugar, wine, water, lemon juice and strips of lemon zest. Heat slowly until the sugar dissolves, then bring to a boil. Add the halved figs, and allow the syrup to reach nearly to the boiling point. Reduce the heat slightly and slowly cook the figs about 15 minutes, until tender when gently pierced with the tip of a knife, but still holding their shape Remove the pan from the heat and let the figs cool in the syrup. Lift the figs with a slotted spoon and drain them on a plate, cut sides down.

2. You will have about 1¾ cups syrup at this point. Return the syrup to the heat and boil it down until about 1 cup remains. It will become thick and syrupy and should read 210°F on a candy or jelly thermometer. Remove from the heat, add the red currant jelly, and stir until completely melted. Discard the strips of lemon zest and set the glaze aside.

3. Prepare the pastry, roll it out, and line the buttered pan (page 38). Trim a ¾-inch overhang, and form the sides of the tart (page 000). Prick the bottom pastry with a fork and chill until firm, then completely blind-bake (page 000), until pastry is golden. Leave pastry in pan and cool on a wire rack.

4. To assemble the tart, brush a generous layer of wine glaze over the completely baked pastry shell. (*Note:* If the glaze has thickened too much upon standing, you can soften it by warming gently over low heat, stirring constantly until smooth.) Arrange the cooled, halved figs cut side down in concentric circles around the tart. Arrange several halves in the tart center, to fill the space. The fat, rounded ends of the figs should point to the outside, and each fig should touch the next. Brush wine glaze over the figs, then drip the remaining glaze between the figs, filling up the spaces. To set the glaze, allow the tart to stand about 2 hours before removing it from the pan (page 43), and serve at room temperature.

TART LEMON TART (*TARTE AU CITRON*)

This dessert is what tart means in every sense of the word. The piquance of the velvety-smooth lemon custard comes as a surprise to your tongue—sharp and refreshing. I first tasted it at the finale of an extraordinary dinner at the Café du Bec Fin in Old Greenwich, Connecticut. Chef Harvey Edwards shared his recipe with me, and it has become one of my favorites. Aside from slight modifications and my own garnish of glazed lemon slices, what follows is the genuine article. It makes a superb finish for a dinner party, especially if the menu is rich and filling.

Advance preparation: The pastry shell can be prepared ahead, partially baked, and frozen. Defrost before using. Fill and bake several hours before serving time. Glaze the lemon slices for garnish several hours ahead or the day before baking.

Special equipment: 11-inch tart pan with removable bottom; 1½-quart enamel or stainless steel saucepan; slotted spoon; dinner plate; flat baking sheet; toothpick; sifter.

Baking time: Partially prebaked pastry shell: 425°F for 10 minutes with pie weights, then 12 to 13 minutes empty; filled pie: 375°F for 22 to 25 minutes.

Glazing lemon slices: 45 minutes.

Quantity: One 11-inch tart.

> *Partially prebaked pastry shell made*
>   *with Rich Tart Pastry (page 64) or*
>   *Basic All-Purpose Flaky Pastry*
>   *(page 34) prepared with egg yolk*
>   *and 3 tablespoons sugar*
> 2¼ *cups water*
> 1¼ *cups granulated sugar*
> Glazed lemon slices: *10 to 12 thinly*
>   *sliced (3/16 inch) rounds cut from a*
>   *whole lemon, pits removed*
>
> **Custard Filling**
> *4 eggs*
> *1 cup granulated sugar*
> ¾ *cup freshly squeezed lemon juice*
> ¼ *cup freshly squeezed orange juice*
> *Grated zest of* ½ *large orange*
> ¼ *cup heavy cream*
> Garnish: *1 to 2 tablespoons*
>   *confectioners' sugar, sifted*

1. To glaze the lemon slices, combine the water and sugar in saucepan and heat until the sugar is melted. Bring to a boil and add the lemon slices. Reduce the heat slightly and simmer, uncovered, for about 40 to 45 minutes, removing the slices *before* the pulp disintegrates. Lift the slices from the syrup with a slotted spoon and place them around the edges of a dinner plate to drain.

2. Prepare the pastry as directed. Roll it out and line the buttered tart pan (page 38). Trim a ¾-inch overhang, fold the pastry edge inward, and press to

the side of the pan. Run a rolling pin over the top of the pan to trim excess dough. Press the edge straight up so it extends slightly above the pan edge but does not bend over it. Prick the pastry bottom with a fork and chill at least 30 minutes, until the dough is firm. Preheat the oven to 425°F. Partially blind-bake shell (page 42). Cool on a wire rack.

3. In a large bowl (or in a food processor or electric mixer) combine the eggs, sugar, lemon and orange juice, the orange zest, and the cream. Whisk or beat until well blended and pale in color, about 1 minute when whisking by hand.

4. Preheat the oven to 375°F. For ease in handling, set the prepared pastry shell (in its pan) on a flat baking sheet. Pour in the lemon custard, then select the 8 best-looking glazed lemon slices and arrange them in an evenly spaced ring about 1-inch inside the edge of the tart. Put one more slice in the center of the pie. (*Note:* Do not use any slices whose pulp layer is missing; these will sink beneath the filling). Set the tart in the center of the preheated oven and bake for 25 to 35 minutes, or until the filling no longer jiggles when the pan is gently tapped. The custard topping will not be browned, but a toothpick inserted in the center should come out clean. Cool on a wire rack.

5. A few minutes before serving, lightly sift a tablespoon or 2 of confectioners' sugar over the tart. Serve at room temperature. (*Note:* Just before cutting the tart, remove the lemon slice from its center so your knife can cut cleanly through center point of the filling.) Divide the pie so each piece contains a lemon slice.

BRITTANY GALETTE

A specialty of Brittany, this *Galette Bretagne, or Gâteau Breton* as it is also called, is basically a rich tender shortbread baked in a tart pan. Serve it with a glass of port in the late afternoon.

The recipe was shared with me, surprisingly enough, by a French pâtissier, Monsieur Gaudin, in the town of Fougères, located on the border between Brittany and Normandy. I happened into his appealing shop on the Rue de Laval ("Pâtisserie, Confiserie, Glaces, Salon de Thé") seeking edible solace on a bleak and rainy fall day after driving down from Mont St. Michel. The shelves of sunny golden galettes arranged on lace doilies were a welcome and cheerful sight indeed.

Advance preparation: The galette can be baked and frozen; reheat to crisp before serving at room temperature.

Special equipment: Electric mixer; 10-inch tart pan with removable bottom; pastry brush; flat 12-inch serving platter; toothpick or cake tester.

Baking time: 375°F for 35 to 40 minutes, depending upon size of tart.

Quantity: One 10-inch tart.

> *4 egg yolks*
> *1 cup plus 3 tablespoons granulated*
> *sugar*
> *1⅓ cups unsalted butter, softened but*
> *not melted*
> *4 cups all-purpose flour, sifted*
> *Egg glaze: 1 egg beaten with 1 teaspoon*
> *water and 1 teaspoon sugar*

1. Preheat the oven to 375°F. Butter the tart pan and set it aside. In the bowl of an electric mixer, beat the egg yolks and sugar together 3 or 4 minutes, until they are very creamy and light colored and the mixture "ribbons" when the beater is lifted. If correctly beaten, you will see batter fall over on itself like a flat ribbon as it drips from the beater.

2. Add butter and flour alternately, a little at a time, and beat slowly. The batter will be thick, almost like a cookie dough. Press the batter into the buttered pan, flattening the top with the palm of your hand. The batter should be about ¾- to 1-inch thick. Brush egg glaze over the top.

3. The final, decorative touch is given by scoring the surface of the galette with a sharp knife. To do this, cut lightly into the top, making a design of straight parallel or cross-hatched lines.

4. Bake in the center of the preheated oven for 35 to 40 minutes, or until the top is golden brown and the toothpick or cake tester poked into the center comes out clean. If making cookies or smaller tarts, bake 20 to 30 minutes, until golden.

Cool the tart about 5 minutes, then unmold (page 44) onto a wire rack or flat serving platter. Cool completely. Slice with serrated knife. Store in an airtight container to keep crisp.

APPLE GALETTE

This rustic French fruit tart is shaped by hand on a flat baking sheet instead of being molded in a tart pan. It is, in fact, a sweet fruit "pizza" made with tart pastry, ideal for picnics, tailgate parties, or casual dinners. Beginning pie makers and teenagers especially enjoy making galettes since they are less intimidating and more casual than formal tarts.

Because the dough is hand-shaped, the only confining factors are the dimensions of the flat baking sheet. Create any shape you like: ovals, rectangles, or hearts, for example. Any type of fruit may be used, whether fresh, poached, or canned and drained.

Advance preparation: The pastry dough can be prepared ahead and frozen in a
   flat disk (page 56); thaw before shaping. Or shape the galette and freeze it
   before baking. To bake frozen, increase the baking time 10 to 15 minutes.
Special equipment: Flat baking sheet about 14 × 16 inches or a large round pizza
   pan; pastry brush.
Baking time: 400°F for 55 to 60 minutes.
Quantity: One 13-inch round galette.

> *Basic All-Purpose Flaky Pastry (page 34)*
>   *made with 1½ cups flour and*
>   *prepared with egg yolk and 1 or 2*
>   *tablespoons sugar*
> *Egg glaze: 1 egg beaten with 1 tablespoon*
>   *water*
> *5 large cooking apples (Granny Smith,*
>   *Greening, or other tart, firm variety)*
> *6 tablespoons cranberry sauce*
>   *(prepared type chopped and*
>   *warmed in a saucepan until*
>   *spreadable) or orange marmalade*
> *½ cup fine-chopped walnuts*
> *¼ cup granulated sugar*
> *2 to 3 tablespoons lemon juice*
> *¼ teaspoon each cinnamon and nutmeg*
> *4 tablespoons butter*
> *Plain Fruit Glaze (page 120) made with*
>   *apricot preserves, or Firm Fruit*
>   *Glaze (page 120) if tart is to be held*
>   *longer than 2 hours before serving*

1. Prepare the pastry and roll it out (page 38) on a floured surface. Plan the size and shape of galette so it will fit your baking sheet. Butter the baking sheet and set it aside. Roll the dough about ⅛-inch thick and about 2-inches larger around than the finished galette, because the edge will be folded over into a border.

Fold the dough into quarters, lift it, and position it on the buttered baking sheet. Unfold and trim any ragged edges so dough now measures about 1½ inches larger than the finished piece. If the dough looks too thick or uneven, it can be rolled again right on the baking sheet. Preheat the oven to 400°F.

2. Brush egg glaze over the dough, to within 1½ inches of the edges. Peel, core, and slice the apples about ¼-inch thick. Take all uneven apple pieces and chop them together, to be spread beneath the good slices. Over the egg glaze, spoon on a thin layer of the cranberry sauce or marmalade, coming to within 1½ inches of the dough edge. Keep this dough border clean.

Top with chopped nuts. Over this, spread the chopped apples and top them with some granulated sugar and about 1 tablespoon of the lemon juice.

3. Above all, arrange the good apple slices. Starting just inside the clean dough border, set the slices in an overlapping spiral design, or arrange like flower petals closely overlapping. In the center, if you like, you can add a tablespoon of the cranberry sauce or marmalade for color. Over the slices, sprinkle on the remaining lemon juice, sugar, cinnamon and nutmeg.

4. Fold the dough border up and overlap it onto the fruit. Pleat and crimp the dough slightly as you go to fit into your shape. Brush egg glaze over the top of dough border.

5. Bake in the center of the preheated oven 55 to 60 minutes, or until the pastry is golden and the fruit bubbling. Cool on a large wire rack or a wooden board. When the galette is cool, brush on fruit glaze. Serve lukewarm or at room temperature, cut into wedges.

VARIATION:

Peach or Plum Galette. Prepare Apple Galette but use 4 or 5 cups peeled and sliced peaches or plums instead of the apples. Use a marmalade or preserves with compatible flavor.

CUSTARD AND CREAM PIES
AND TARTS

Custard pies and tarts generally have delicately flavored fillings made with eggs, milk, and sugar. They are open-face, and baked in a pastry or crumb shell. The filling is thickened as the egg proteins coagulate and cook gently and slowly at a very low heat; the ideal result is a well-set, creamy custard that cuts neatly and neither "weeps" nor separates into liquid and solid. Overcooking or cooking at too high a temperature causes the custard to separate and become watery.

It is easy enough to bake a custard slowly when it is prepared as a pudding in custard cups. But when baked in a pastry shell, the problem becomes complex: custard requires low heat, but pastry needs high heat to set it quickly and keep it flaky. The various solutions are discussed in the recipe for Custard Pie (page 199). They range from partially prebaking the pastry shell to baking the shell and custard separately (the ideal solution), then slip-sliding the custard into place in the shell.

Cream pies are made with an egg-sugar-milk custard base, but are thickened with flour or cornstarch. They can have an infinite number of flavorings.

The wide variety of pies in this section, from Southern Chess Pies to Lemon Meringue Pie, are all variations on these two basic types—custard and cream.

Because these pies have a high egg content, they should be stored in the refrigerator to avoid bacterial contamination, especially in hot weather. However, you may have already noticed that some pies, custard in particular, tend to get watery when refrigerated. It occasionally happens, and the only way to avoid it seems to be to eat the whole pie so that there are no leftovers to refrigerate—not such a bad fate, really.

CUSTARD PIE

In the Southern United States, this is known as Egg Custard Pie, but whatever you call it, it is delicious and deserves far more attention than it usually gets, reserved as it often is for "family" suppers or for comforting desserts when the children are home sick.

Anyone can bake a fine custard *pudding,* but it takes a little doing to bake that same custard successfully inside a pastry shell—unless you know a few tricks. The problem is that creamy egg custard bakes at a low temperature, while flaky pastry requires high heat. To get around this, you have three choices: (1) Pour the custard into an unbaked pastry shell, bake both simultaneously, and risk a soggy bottom crust, or (2) partially prebake the pastry shell, moisture-proof it with egg glaze, then add the custard and bake again, or (3) use the slip-slide method, the only one that absolutely guarantees a crisp bottom crust and a tender, well-set custard. Our instructions will give both the last two methods; however, I urge you to try the slip-slide even if it sounds silly. It works and is very easy to accomplish.

Advance preparation: The partially or completely prebaked pastry shell may be made ahead and frozen. Do not fill and bake the pie until shortly before serving; standing softens the bottom crust.

Special equipment: 9-inch pie plate; pastry brush; mixing bowl or electric mixer; for slip-slide method: one extra 9-inch Pyrex pie plate.

Baking time: Partially baked shell: 425°F for 10 minutes, with pie weights, then 8 minutes empty; completely prebaked shell: 425°F for 10 minutes with pie weights, then 15 to 20 minutes empty; filled pie: 325°F for 30 to 35 minutes.

Quantity: One 9-inch pie.

> *Partially prebaked (or completely*
> *prebaked, see page 200) 9-inch pie*
> *shell made with Basic All-Purpose*
> *Flaky Pastry (page 34), prepared with*
> *1 whole egg as part of the measured*
> *liquid, or other pastry of your choice*
> Egg glaze: *1 egg white beaten with 1*
> *tablespoon water*

Filling
3 eggs plus 1 yolk (reserve the extra
white for the egg glaze)

½ *cup granulated sugar*
¼ *teaspoon salt*
2 *cups milk, or half milk, half heavy*
    cream
1 *teaspoon vanilla extract*
¼ *teaspoon freshly grated nutmeg*
A dash of cinnamon
Butter for greasing the extra pie plate
    for slip-slide method

1. The first method described will be the one in which a partially prebaked pastry shell is baked along with the custard. The slip-slide method follows.

Prepare the partially prebaked shell. Preheat the oven to 425°F. Make the pastry, roll it out, and line the pan (page 38). Trim a ¾-inch pastry overhang, fold over the edge, and flute as described (page 44). Prick the bottom with a fork, chill until firm, then partially blind-bake (page 42) just until the pastry begins to look golden but is not yet browned. Cool on a wire rack. Reduce oven heat to 325°F.

In the bowl of an electric mixer, combine all filling ingredients and beat well. For ease in handling, and to prevent spills on the oven floor, set the pan containing the pastry shell in the center of a flat baking sheet. Pour the custard mixture into the prepared pastry shell and sprinkle it with a little nutmeg. Set the baking sheet in the preheated oven for 30 to 35 minutes, until a knife inserted into a custard 1-inch from the edge comes out clean. Do not overbake. Cool on a wire rack. Serve the pie at room temperature. Refrigerate leftovers.

2. For the slip-slide method, the pastry shell is completely prebaked. To do this, prepare the pastry, roll it out, and line the pan. Trim a ¾-inch overhang, fold over the edge, and flute as desired. Prick the pastry bottom with a fork, chill until firm, then completely blind-bake until golden brown. Cool on a wire rack.

To prepare the custard, beat all filling ingredients together in an electric mixer. Generously butter a 9-inch pie plate. (*Note:* Be sure this pie plate is the same size as that containing the pastry shell.) Pour the custard into buttered plate and bake in the center of a preheated 325°F oven for 30 to 35 minutes, until a stainless steel knife inserted into the custard 1-inch from the edge comes out clean. Do not overbake. Remove the custard from the oven and cool on wire rack until it is *just lukewarm*. Before it cools further, slide it into the pastry as described below.

The final step, slip-sliding the custard into the baked crust, sounds much trickier than it is, though I confess it took me a year to work up to trying it, I was so skeptical. I am pleased to say I was completely won over on the first try—it's absolutely simple. The trick is that the butter you spread in the baking pan under the custard remains in a separate layer, so, if you work while the custard is still lukewarm before the butter hardens, it acts as a lubricant for the custard to slide on. To do this, first run a knife blade around the edge of the custard to release it from the baking pan. Then lift the custard pan and hold it just a little bit above and directly over the baked pastry shell. Tilt the custard so it faces the far edge of the pastry shell and gently slip-slide the custard out as you pull back on the pie plate. The custard will ease itself into the pastry shell in one piece and look as if it had always been there. (It will, I promise. But if, for some reason, this method fails to work, the pie will still taste good.)

Cool the assembled pie on wire rack. Serve at room temperature. Refrigerate leftovers.

VARIATIONS:

Sugarless Custard Pie. If for dietary reasons you prefer to bake this pie without any sugar at all, it will still have a good, eggy flavor and will slip-slide with ease.

Coconut Custard Pie. Prepare Coconut Crumb Crust (page 73), or use the Coconut Pastry Variation for Basic All-Purpose Flaky Pastry (page 34). Prepare Custard Pie, but just before adding the custard mixture to its baking pan, blend in 1 cup flaked or shredded sweetened coconut. Top the finished pie with a sprinkling of Toasted Coconut Topping (page 113) if you wish.

Lemon Custard Pie. Prepare Custard Pie, but add to the filling: 2 tablespoons lemon juice and the grated zest of 1 lemon.

OLD-FASHIONED PUMPKIN PIE

What moistens the lip, and what brightens the eye,
What calls back the past, like the rich pumpkin pie?
John Greenleaf Whittier, "The Pumpkin."

Here is the answer to Whittier: Every man's Thanksgiving memory, a rich mellow pumpkin custard pie complemented by a topping of Yogurt-Rum Sauce (page 115) or Ginger Whipped Cream (page 108).

To avoid the soggy lower crust familiar to custard pies, carefully prebake and moisture-proof the pastry shell before filling and baking with the custard.

Advance preparation: The partially prebaked pastry shell can be prepared ahead and frozen (page 53). Fill the shell with custard immediately before baking and no more than 3 to 4 hours before serving. (*Note:* The lower crust softens on standing.)

Special equipment: 10-inch pie plate, preferably Pyrex; pastry brush; electric
    mixer or mixing bowl and spoon; flat baking sheet; stainless steel knife.
Baking time: Partially prebaked pastry shell: 425°F for 10 minutes with pie
    weights, then 8 minutes empty; filled pie: 400°F for 45 to 55 minutes.
Quantity: One 10-inch pie.

> *Partially prebaked 10-inch pastry shell*
> *made with Basic All-Purpose Flaky*
> *Pastry (page 34) prepared with*
> *1 whole egg as part of the measured*
> *liquid, or Whole Wheat Pastry*
> *(page 59)*
> Egg glaze: *1 egg white beaten with 1*
> *tablespoon water*

Filling

> *2 eggs plus 1 yolk (reserve extra egg*
> *white for glaze)*
> *2 cups canned pumpkin, or fresh*
> *pumpkin, cooked and mashed*
> *½ to ¾ cup granulated sugar, to your*
> *taste*
> *1½ cups milk or cream (the heavier the*
> *cream the richer the pie)*
> *2 tablespoons butter, melted*
> *½ teaspoon salt*
> *¾ teaspoon cinnamon*
> *½ teaspoon each ground ginger and*
> *nutmeg*
> *⅛ teaspoon cloves*

Topping
Yogurt-Rum Sauce or Ginger-Flavored
Whipped Cream

1. Preheat the oven to 425°F. Prepare the pastry, roll it out, and line the pan
(page 38). Trim a ¾-inch pastry overhang, fold over edge, and flute as desired
(page 44). Be sure the fluted edge is high so it will contain the custard filling.
Prick the bottom with a fork, chill until firm, then partially blind-bake for 10
minutes (page 42). Bake for 8 minutes after removing the foil and pie weights,
until dough is no longer translucent and is beginning to look golden. Cool on a
wire rack. Reduce the oven heat to 400°F.

2. In an electric mixer or bowl, beat the eggs, then add the pumpkin and beat well. Beat in the sugar, milk or cream, the melted butter, salt, and all spices. Set the pan containing the pastry shell on a flat baking sheet for ease in handling. Pour the filling mixture into the prepared pastry shell. Set the baking sheet in the center of the preheated oven for 40 to 50 minutes, or until the top is golden brown and a knife inserted into the custard 1 inch from the edge comes out clean. Do not overbake. When the knife comes clean at the custard's edge, the pie is done even though the center may not yet be set; the internal heat of the pie will complete the baking out of the oven. Cool on a wire rack. Serve at room temperature, topped with Yogurt-Rum Sauce or Ginger-Flavored Whipped Cream.

VARIATIONS:

Vermont Maple Sugar Pumpkin Pie. Prepare Old-Fashioned Pumpkin Pie but replace ¾ cup granulated sugar with ⅔ cup *granulated maple sugar.*

Orange Pumpkin Pie. Prepare Old-Fashioned Pumpkin Pie but add ⅓ cup orange marmalade and 1 tablespoon grated orange zest to the filling.

Southern Sweet Potato Pie. This pie is a specialty of Virginia, but is made throughout the South, where sweet potatoes are popularly used in a variety of baked goods. The preferred pie potatoes are a deep red-gold color, very rich in vitamins A and C and very sweet. You can buy sweet potatoes wherever you live when they are in season, then boil, peel, mash, and freeze them for later use in this recipe. (*Note:* 1 pound raw potatoes = 2 cups, cooked and mashed.)

Prepare Old-Fashioned Pumpkin Pie, above, but instead of pumpkin use 2 cups cooked, mashed sweet potatoes (or a 1 pound can vacuum-packed sweet potatoes). Add ⅓ cup apricot or peach preserves and ¼ cup chopped walnuts to the filling. If you enjoy the flavor of ginger, you can add up to 1 or 2 tablespoons fine-chopped crystallized ginger as well.

New England Squash Pie. New Englanders make this recipe to use up the over-bountiful fall squash harvest. Winter squash such as acorn, butternut, and blue Hubbard can be used; the flavor will be slightly milder than either the pumpkin or the sweet potato versions. (*Note:* All the above mentioned squash can be boiled, peeled, mashed, and frozen when in season for later pie baking. One pound raw squash = 2 cups cooked and mashed.)

Prepare Old-Fashioned Pumpkin Pie, above, but use 2 cups cooked, mashed, and strained squash instead of the pumpkin. Use 1 cup light brown sugar instead of granulated white sugar. Optional flavoring: grated zest of 1 orange and/or ½ cup chopped walnuts. If you are using nuts, sprinkle them over the top of the pie just before baking, to make a crunchy topping.

VANILLA CREAM PIE

If you enjoy a rich vanilla flavor, use the vanilla bean to prepare this pie. It is outstanding unadorned or enhanced by a topping of sweetened maple-flavored whipped cream. However, the recipe is very adaptable and lends itself to any number of flavor variations. (*Note:* For another version of vanilla cream filling, see Vanilla Pastry Cream, page 100.) This Vanilla Cream Pie filling is slightly less stiff than the Vanilla Pastry Cream and is a slightly larger recipe, but they may be used interchangeably, for filling éclairs, cream puffs, or other pastries.

Advance preparation: The completely prebaked pastry shell or crumb crust may be prepared ahead and frozen. Add the cream filling no more than 3 or 4 hours ahead and chill to set. Or top the hot filling with meringue and bake. Then chill until serving time. Alternatively, as close to serving time as is convenient, add whipped cream topping. Refrigerate until serving time.

Special equipment: 9-inch pie plate; 2½-quart heavy-bottom enamel or stainless steel saucepan; electric mixer; rubber scraper; whisk; plastic wrap; spoon or pastry bag fitted with ½-inch star tip for meringue or whipped cream.

Baking time: Completely baked pastry shell: 425°F for 10 minutes with pie weights, 350°F for 10 to 15 minutes empty; *meringue topping:* 350°F for 12 to 15 minutes; *cooking custard:* 12 to 15 minutes.

Quantity: One 9-inch pie.

> *Completely prebaked 9-inch pastry shell*
> *made with Basic All-Purpose Flaky*
> *Pastry (page 34), or Nut Pastry*
> *Variation (page 35); or a 9-inch*
> *crumb crust of your choice (page 72),*
> *preferably baked to give it more*
> *solidity*

> **Filling**
> ⅔ *cup granulated sugar*
> 4 *tablespoons cornstarch*
> Optional: ¼ *teaspoon salt*
> 2½ *cups milk*
> ¼ *cup heavy cream*
> 2 *egg yolks*
> 1 *whole vanilla bean, split lengthwise,*
>   *or 2 teaspoons pure vanilla extract*
> 2 *tablespoons unsalted butter, at room*
>   *temperature*

Meringue Topping

4 egg whites
A pinch of salt
¼ teaspoon cream of tartar
6 tablespoons superfine or granulated
*   sugar*

Alternate Topping

1 cup heavy cream
2 tablespoons confectioners' sugar
½ teaspoon vanilla extract

1. Preheat the oven to 425°F. Prepare the pastry (page 34), roll it out, and line the pan (page 38). Trim a ¾-inch overhang, fold over the edge, and flute as desired (page 44). Prick the pastry bottom with a fork, chill until firm, then completely blind-bake (page 42) by lining pastry with foil and pie weights. Cool on a wire rack. Or, prepare the crumb crust of your choice as directed.

2. To make the filling, combine the sugar, cornstarch, and salt in a heavy-bottom saucepan. In a bowl, whisk the milk and cream into the egg yolks.

3. Whisk egg-milk mixture into the cornstarch-sugar in the pan. Whisk well to be sure all the cornstarch is picked up off the bottom of the pan and dissolved. Add the vanilla bean if you are using it; if you prefer vanilla extract, do not add it until the end of the recipe or cooking will dissipate its flavor.

Set the pan over medium heat and cook the mixture about 12 minutes, until thickened and brought to a boil. To do this, stir on and off for the first 5 minutes, then stir constantly about 7 minutes longer, until the mixture really thickens and reaches a boil, when you will see fat heavy bubbles work up to the surface and burst between stirs. Use the whisk instead of the spoon occasionally to remove lumps. Boil for 1 full minute while stirring constantly. Remove from the heat. Remove the vanilla bean; wash and dry it for reuse. Stir in the butter and/or vanilla extract, if you are using it.

4. Spoon the hot cream into prepared pastry shell. If you are adding meringue topping, do it now, while the cream filling is still hot. To prepare the meringue topping (page 109) beat the egg whites in an electric mixer with the salt and cream of tartar until fluffy. Add the sugar, 2 tablespoons at a time, beating between additions. Beat until the whites are satiny and form stiff peaks. Pinch the meringue between your fingers to be sure no grains of sugar remain undissolved. Preheat the oven to 350°F.

Spoon the meringue over the hot custard in the pastry shell and smooth it onto the edges of the crust all around, to seal it and prevent shrinking. Shape the meringue into peaks with the back of a spoon. Or cover the filling with a flat base layer of meringue, then pipe a decorative design on top with meringue forced through a pastry bag fitted with ½-inch star tip. Bake in the preheated oven for 12 to 15 minutes, until the meringue topping is golden brown. Watch carefully so it does not burn. Cool on a wire rack, then refrigerate.

If you are adding a whipped cream topping to the pie, first cover the top of the hot cream filling with plastic wrap to prevent a skin from forming. Set it aside to cool, then chill until shortly before serving. In a chilled bowl with chilled beaters, whip the cream to soft peaks, add the sugar and vanilla (or other flavoring, page 109), and whip to stiff peaks. Decorate the top of the pie with rosettes of cream piped through a pastry bag fitted with star tip, or spoon mounds of cream around the pie and stripe them with a fork. Chill. Refrigerate leftovers.

VARIATIONS:

Banana Cream Pie. Prepare Vanilla Cream Pie. Thinly slice 1 or 2 bananas and stir them into the finished cream just before turning it into the prepared pastry shell. Top with meringue or whipped cream.

Fruit Cream Pie. Prepare Vanilla Cream Pie. Prepare 1 to 1½ cups fresh fruit slices (well drained and blotted dry) and arrange them on the pie shell before spooning on the cream filling. Successful fruits include sliced strawberries or peaches or berries. Top with meringue or whipped cream.

Chocolate Cream Pie. Prepare Vanilla Cream Pie, but use 1 cup sugar. In a double boiler, melt 4 ounces semisweet chocolate. Stir the chocolate into the finished cream filling along with the butter. For more intense chocolate flavor, add 3 tablespoons Dutch-process cocoa to the cornstarch at the beginning of the recipe in addition to the chocolate added at the end.

Butterscotch Cream Pie. Prepare Vanilla Cream Pie, but substitute ¾ cup dark brown sugar, packed, for the granulated sugar.

Quick Coconut Cream Pie. Prepare Vanilla Cream Pie, but add 1½ cups flaked sweetened coconut to the finished cream along with the butter. Spoon the filling into the pastry shell and top with Toasted Coconut Topping (page 113) or Coconut Meringue (page 111). For this pie, you can also use All-Purpose Flaky Pastry, Coconut Pastry Variation (page 35), for the pastry shell.

Fresh Coconut Cream Pie. This is a variation on Vanilla Cream Pie using grated fresh coconut and canned coconut cream in place of part of the milk. To begin, prepare the coconut as follows: Remove husk (green or brown outer shell) from coconut. Pierce "eyes" of coconut with a screwdriver, then pour out and discard milky liquid. Or, strain and drink it. Set the whole coconut on a baking sheet and bake at 350°F for 30 minutes to crack the shell and facilitate separating the meat. After baking, you may need to hit the shell with a couple of hammer blows to remove it completely. Pry the shell away from the meat, using a screwdriver where necessary. Then remove the brown skin with a vegetable peeler. Grate the coconut meat; you should have about 3½ cups.

Prepare Vanilla Cream Pie, but reduce the sugar to ⅓ cup and in place of the milk and heavy cream use 1¾ cups milk plus 1 cup canned sweetened cream of coconut. After combining the milk-coconut cream with cornstarch-sugar and whisking well, stir in about 1 cup freshly grated coconut and cook as directed. After the cooking is complete, stir in another ½ to 1 cup grated coconut if you wish, at the same time you add the butter, the vanilla extract if you are using it, and to strengthen the flavor, ½ teaspoon coconut extract.

Spoon into the prepared pastry shell and sprinkle on Toasted Coconut Topping (page 113) or top with Coconut Meringue (page 111).

APRICOT-RAISIN-SOUR CREAM PIE

At pie-tasting parties in preparation for this book, this recipe was consistently selected as one of the favorites. The rich custard-cream filling is easy to prepare and has a cheesecakelike texture. The raisins and apricots lend a sparkle of color as well as delicious flavor.

Advance preparation: The unbaked pastry shell can be prepared in advance and frozen; thaw before filling. Fill and bake the pie one day in advance or on the day it is to be served. Refrigerate until 1 to 2 hours before serving; then bring to room temperature.
Special equipment: 10-inch pie plate; strainer or colander; electric mixer; stainless steel knife.
Baking time: 400°F for 40 to 45 minutes.
Quantity: One 10-inch pie.

> *Unbaked pastry for a 10-inch pie shell*
> *made with Basic All-Purpose Flaky*
> *Pastry (page 34) or other pastry*
> *of your choice*

Filling
⅓ cup seedless raisins
⅔ cup (5 ounces) dried apricot halves,
*   packed*
2 cups sour cream
2 eggs

1 cup granulated sugar
¼ cup all-purpose flour
¼ teaspoon salt
Grated zest of one orange
1 teaspoon vanilla extract
Confectioners' sugar

1. Prepare the pastry, roll it out, and line the pie plate (page 38). Trim a ¾-inch overhang, fold over the edge, and flute as desired (page 44). Chill in the refrigerator while the filling is prepared.

2. Preheat the oven to 400°F. Measure the raisins into a small bowl and cover them with boiling water. Let them stand to plump about 20 minutes. Cut the apricots into small pieces (approximately in quarters), then put them into a saucepan and cover with water. Cover pan, bring to a boil, then lower the heat slightly and simmer apricots 10 minutes. Drain the apricots through a strainer or colander.

3. With an electric mixer, beat together the sour cream, eggs, sugar, flour, salt, orange zest, and vanilla. Strain the raisins, discarding the liquid, and add them to the sour cream mixture along with the prepared apricots. Stir well to distribute the fruit evenly. Pour into the prepared pastry shell.

4. Bake in the lower third of the preheated oven for 40 to 45 minutes, or until light golden on top and a stainless steel knife inserted into the custard 1 inch from the edge comes out clean. Cool on a wire rack. The pie filling puffs somewhat as it bakes, then sinks as it cools. Serve at room temperature. Just before serving, sift a light sprinking of confectioners' sugar over the top of the pie. Refrigerate leftovers.

VARIATION:

Rum-Raisin-Sour Cream Pie. Prepare Apricot-Raisin-Sour Cream Pie but omit the apricots and double the quantity of raisins. Plump the raisins in rum instead of boiling water.

VERMONT MAPLE-WALNUT PIE

This recipe comes from Vermont's Northeast Kingdom, a region known both for its extraordinarily picturesque alpine scenery and its delicious maple syrup. As the February thaw begins, there is scarcely a wooded area that doesn't have a sugar shack tucked within, its jauntily angled chimney billowing steam into the frosty air as the sap (thirty gallons for one of syrup) is boiled down over a wood fire. Although horse-drawn wagons hauling sap buckets are increasingly replaced by miles of plastic hose, the final product is still redolent of wood smoke and mountain air.

Vermonters use maple syrup and maple sugar as part of their daily cooking. The recipe for this maple custard pie was shared with me by a neighbor even though, after twenty years of summering, I am still considered a "downstater."

Note: For this recipe, be sure to use *pure* maple syrup, labeled as such, rather than flavored corn syrup blends sold in imitation of the real thing.

Advance preparation: The partially prebaked pastry shell can be prepared ahead and frozen (page 55). The filling should be added and the pie baked no more than 4 hours in advance of serving; the bottom crust softens on standing.
Special equipment: 9-inch pie plate; pastry brush; electric mixer; flat baking sheet.
Baking time: Partially prebaked pastry shell: 425°F for 10 minutes with pie weights, 3 minutes empty; filled pie: 375°F for 35 to 45 minutes.
Quantity: One 9-inch pie.

> *Partially prebaked 9-inch pie shell made*
> *with Lard Pastry (page 62), or*
> *Whole Wheat–Wheat Germ Pastry*
> *Variation (page 60)*

Filling
3 eggs
¼ teaspoon salt
⅓ cup granulated sugar
¼ cup butter or margarine, melted
1 cup pure maple syrup
1 cup walnut halves

1. Preheat oven to 425°F. With a whisk or an electric mixer, beat together the eggs and salt. Set the bowl aside. Prepare the pastry, roll it out, and line the pie plate (page 38). Trim a ¾-inch overhang, fold over the edge, and flute as desired (page 44). Prick the bottom with a fork; chill until firm, then partially blind-bake (page 42). Moisture-proof the crust bottom by brushing with the beaten eggs before baking the empty shell for the final 3 minutes. Cool on a wire rack. Reduce the oven heat to 375°F.

2. To the eggs and salt add the sugar, melted butter, and maple syrup. Beat well, but do not make the mixture too frothy. For ease in handling, set the pan containing the pastry shell on a flat baking sheet.

3. Pour the filling into the prepared pie shell and top with nuts. Bake in the center of the preheated oven for 30 to 40 minutes, or until a stainless steel knife inserted into the filling 1 inch from the edge comes out clean. Cool on a wire rack. Serve at room temperature, topped by plain or Maple Flavored Whipped Cream (page 109).

VARIATION:

Maple-Pecan Pie. Prepare Maple-Walnut Pie, but replace the walnuts with halved pecans.

About Chess Pies

Chess pies are a uniquely Southern specialty, developed during the eighteenth century to utilize the eggs and butter plentiful on plantations and the molasses available at Southern ports catering to the West Indies rum-molasses-slave trade. As refined sugar became available in the beginning of the nineteenth century, brown sugar, and later highly refined white sugar, began to replace the molasses; the greater the sugar content, the longer the keeping quality of the pie. The large amount of sugar also gives these pie fillings their characteristically clear, satiny appearance, hence the name "transparent pies." Among these is the familiar Southern culinary export, pecan pie. Equally delicious but less known are Buttermilk Chess, Kentucky Bourbon Chess, and Date-Nut Chess pies, and all are excellent prepared as individual tartlets.

Where did the word "chess" originate? There seem to be as many answers as there are Southern cooks. One explanation suggests the word is "chest," pronounced with a drawl and used to describe these pies baked with so much sugar they could be stored in a pie chest rather than refrigerated. Another story, probably apocryphal, is about the plantation cook who was asked what she was baking that smelled so good. "Jes' pie," was her answer. The English lemon curd pie filling is very close to lemon chess, and some authorities believe our "chess" is an Americanization of the English word "cheese," refering to curd pie.

BUTTERMILK CHESS PIE

This traditional Southern pie is scented only with vanilla and a hint of cinnamon in order to allow the buttermilk flavor to come through. Some recipes also add lemon juice and peel but this tends to overwhelm the delicate taste of the pie.

Advance preparation: The partially prebaked pastry shell can be prepared in advance and frozen (page 53). Thaw before filling. Fill and bake the pie no more than 3 hours before serving if possible, since the bottom crust softens on standing.

Special equipment: Electric mixer; 9-inch pie plate; pastry brush; flat baking sheet; stainless steel knife.

Baking time: Partially baked shell: 425°F for 10 minutes with pie weights, then 3 minutes empty. Filled pie: 350°F for 30 to 40 minutes.

Quantity: One 9-inch pie.

*Partially prebaked 9-inch pie shell made
with Butter-Lard Pastry (page 63)
or other pastry of your choice*

Filling
3 eggs
1 cup granulated sugar
2 tablespoons all-purpose flour
1½ cups buttermilk
*⅓ cup lightly salted butter or
    margarine, melted*
1 teaspoon vanilla extract
⅛ teaspoon cinnamon

1. In a large bowl with an electric mixer, beat the eggs; set them aside. Preheat the oven to 425°F. Prepare the pastry, roll it out, and line the pie plate (page 38). Trim ¾-inch pastry overhang, fold over the edge, and flute as desired (page 44). Prick the pastry bottom with a fork, chill until hard, then partially blind-bake (page 42). Brush the bottom with moisture-proofing beaten egg before baking empty shell for the final 3 minutes. Cool on a wire rack. Reduce the oven heat to 350°F.

2. Add the sugar to the beaten eggs and beat together until the mixture is thick and very light-colored. Beat in the flour, buttermilk, melted butter, vanilla, and cinnamon. Set the pan containing the pastry shell on a flat baking sheet for ease in handling. Pour the egg-flour mixture into the prepared pastry shell and top with a dash of cinnamon.

3. Bake in the center of the preheated oven for 30 to 40 minutes, or until the top is golden brown and a stainless steel knife inserted into the custard 1 inch from the edge comes out clean. (*Note:* Monitor your oven temperature. If baked at too high a heat, the custard may separate.) Cool on a wire rack. Serve at room temperature.

VARIATION:

Buttermilk-Nut Pie. Prepare Buttermilk Chess Pie, but just before baking, stir into the filling 1 cup coarse-chopped pecans or peanuts or walnuts.

PINEAPPLE CHESS TART

The tangy flavor of pineapple is a refreshing addition to this sweet chess pie. It makes an appealing dinner party dessert when served topped by rosettes of whipped cream garnished with mint sprigs. The same recipe will also make eight 4½-inch-diameter tartlets.

Advance preparation: The partially prebaked tart shell can be prepared ahead and frozen (page 53). Fill and bake the pie no more than 3 to 4 hours before serving, since the bottom crust softens on standing.

Special equipment: 11-inch tart pan with removable bottom (or 10-inch pie plate); pastry brush; strainer; electric mixer or mixing bowl and whisk; flat baking sheet; stainless steel knife; optional: pastry bag fitted with star tip, or spoon for applying whipped cream garnish.

Baking time: Partially prebaked tart shell: 425°F for 10 minutes lined with pie weights, 3 minutes empty; filled tart: 325°F for 50 to 60 minutes.

Quantity: One 11-inch tart (or 10-inch pie).

> *Partially prebaked 11-inch tart shell*
> *made with Basic All-Purpose Flaky*
> *Pastry (page 34) prepared with egg*
> *yolk and 2 tablespoons sugar, or*
> *Butter-Lard Pastry (page 63).*
> *(Note: Butter-Lard Pastry is the more*
> *traditional Southern choice.)*
> Egg glaze: *1 egg beaten with 1 tablespoon*
> *water*

Filling
> *1 (20-ounce) can pineapple chunks,*
> *drained (for 12 ounces prepared*
> *fruit)*
> *1½ tablespoons all-purpose flour*
> *½ cup unsalted butter, at room*
> *temperature, or half butter/half*
> *margarine*

⅓ cup granulated sugar
⅓ cup dark brown sugar, packed
1 teaspoon vanilla extract
¼ teaspoon salt
3 eggs
½ cup sour cream, or plain yogurt
Freshly grated nutmeg

Topping
1 cup heavy cream
2 tablespoons confectioners' sugar
Optional garnish: *mint sprigs*

1. Preheat the oven to 425°F. Prepare the pastry, roll it out, and line buttered pan (page 38). Trim a ¾-inch pastry overhang, fold the edge inward, and shape the sides of the tart shell (page 41). Prick the bottom with a fork, chill until firm, then partially blind-bake (page 42). Brush moisture-proofing egg glaze on pastry shell as soon as it is removed from the oven. Cool on a wire rack. Reduce oven heat to 325°F.

2. Drain the pineapple in a strainer set over bowl. Cut the chunks in thirds, then put the fruit into a bowl and toss with the flour.

3. In an electric mixer, cream together the butter, both sugars, the vanilla, and salt, beating until smooth and light textured. Add the eggs, one at a time, beating after each addition. Beat in the sour cream or yogurt. Stir in the pineapple. Don't worry if the mixture looks curdled; baking will make the filling smooth and creamy.

4. For ease in handling, set the pastry shell in the center of a flat baking sheet. Spoon the filling into the prepared pastry shell and top with a light sprinkling of freshly grated nutmeg. Bake in the center of the preheated oven for 50 to 60 minutes, or until the top looks golden brown. (*Note:* Monitor your oven temperature. If baked at too high a heat, custard may separate.) Cool on a wire rack. A short time before serving, whip the cream until it forms soft peaks, add the sugar, then whip stiff and spoon on the pie in an edging ring or pipe through a pastry bag fitted with star tip, making rosettes over the pie top. Garnish with mint sprigs if you wish.

KENTUCKY BOURBON CHESS PIE

Kentucky-born writer Joan Moore shared this old family recipe with me. She is an excellent cook, and the pie is an authentic Southern specialty right down to the white cornmeal in the filling. The bourbon flavor is pronounced and further enhanced by the touch of bourbon in the whipped cream topping. We affectionately call this "killer pie"—it's rich, marvelous, and a unique dinner party finale. For the faint-hearted, you can cut down the bourbon, or eliminate it entirely and replace it with milk or cream.

Advance preparation: The partially prebaked pastry shell can be prepared ahead and frozen (page 53). Fill and bake the pie no more than 4 hours before serving, since the bottom crust softens somewhat on standing.

Special equipment: 9-inch pie plate; pastry brush; electric mixer; stainless steel knife; aluminum foil strips or frame (page 25); chilled bowl and beater for whipping cream; optional: pastry bag fitted with star tip.

Baking time: Partially prebaked pastry shell: 425°F for 10 minutes with pie weights, then 3 minutes empty; filled pie: 350°F for 30 minutes.

Quantity: One 9-inch pie.

*Partially prebaked 9-inch pie shell made
with Butter-Lard Pastry (page 63)
or other pastry of your choice
Egg glaze: 1 egg white beaten with 1
tablespoon water*

Filling
*4 egg yolks
1 cup granulated sugar
1½ tablespoons white cornmeal
1½ tablespoons all-purpose flour
½ cup lightly salted butter, melted and
    cooled
4 tablespoons Kentucky straight
    bourbon whiskey
4 tablespoons heavy cream or milk
1 teaspoon vanilla extract*

Optional Topping
*½ cup heavy cream
1 tablespoon confectioners' sugar, sifted
1 tablespoon Kentucky straight
    bourbon whiskey*

1. Preheat the oven to 425°F. Prepare the pastry, roll it out, and line the pie plate (page 38). Trim a ¾-inch pastry overhang, fold over the edge, and flute as desired (page 44). Prick the pastry bottom with a fork, chill until firm, then partially blind-bake (page 42). Brush moisture-proofing egg glaze on pastry shell as soon as it is removed from the oven. Cool on a wire rack. Reduce oven heat to 350°F.

2. With an electric mixer, beat the yolks and sugar together until thick and light colored. Beat in the cornmeal and flour. With the machine running slowly, pour in the melted butter, bourbon, cream or milk, and vanilla. Mix well.

3. Pour the mixture into the prepared pastry shell and bake in the center of the preheated 350°F oven for 30 minutes, or until puffed and golden brown, and a stainless steel knife inserted in the center comes out clean. Check the pie after about half the baking time and, if necessary, add a foil edging to prevent the pastry from overbrowning. Cool on a wire rack. The filling will sink as the pie cools.

4. Shortly before serving, whip the cream in a chilled bowl with chilled beaters. When soft peaks form, add the sugar and bourbon, then beat to stiff peaks. Spoon over the top of the pie, or pipe a decorative pattern using a pastry bag fitted with a star tip. Serve at room temperature. Refrigerate leftovers.

DATE-NUT CHESS PIE

This variation on a Southern pie called Jefferson Davis Pie or Plain Chess Pie tastes somewhat like Pecan Pie, but is much less sweet. Chopped pitted prunes or seedless raisins can be substituted for the dates, or you can use all nuts. Cream gives a richer flavor than milk, but either is good. Bake it as a pie, as a tart, or as individual tartlets.

Advance preparation: The partially prebaked pastry shell can be prepared in advance and frozen (page 53). The baked pie or tartlets can also be frozen, though the filling will not have as good a texture as when freshly baked.

Special equipment: 9-inch pie plate or six tartlet pans 4½ inches in diameter (or 8 tartlets 3½ inches); electric mixer; pastry brush; food processor fitted with steel blade or blender to chop fruit; flat baking sheet (if making tartlets).

Baking time: Partially prebaked pastry shell: 425°F for 10 minutes with pie weights, 3 minutes empty; filled pie or tartlets: 375°F for 25 minutes.

Quantity: One 9-inch pie or 6 tartlets.

*Partially prebaked 9-inch pie shell made
with Basic All-Purpose Flaky Pastry,
Nut Pastry Variation (page 35),
prepared with egg yolk and 2
tablespoons sugar, or partially
prebaked tartlet shells made with
the same pastry*

Filling
*2 tablespoons heavy cream or milk
2 eggs
½ cup walnuts, coarsely chopped
½ cup pitted dates
2 tablespoons all-purpose flour
½ cup dark brown sugar, packed
¼ cup granulated sugar
1 teaspoon vanilla extract
4 tablespoons lightly salted butter or
margarine, melted*

1. Preheat the oven to 425°F. In a mixing bowl, beat together the cream or milk and the eggs. Set aside. Prepare the pastry, roll it out, and line the pie plate (page 38). Trim a ¾-inch pastry overhang, fold over edge, and flute as desired (page 44). Or fit the dough into tartlet pans as described on page 41. Prick the bottom with a fork, chill until firm, then partially blind-bake (page 42). Brush the bottom with beaten egg and cream to moisture-proof before baking the empty shell for the final 3 minutes. Cool on a wire rack. Reduce the oven heat to 375°F.

2. In a processor or blender, chop the nuts, then place them in a bowl and chop the dates mixed with 1 tablespoon flour to keep them from sticking. Add to the nuts and set aside.

3. Add both sugars to the egg-cream mixture and beat until light and smooth. Add the vanilla, the remaining 1 tablespoon flour, and the melted butter or margarine and beat well. Stir in the chopped dates and nuts.

4. If making tartlets, set the pans on a flat baking sheet for ease in handling. Spoon the filling into the pie or tartlet shells. Bake in the center of preheated 375°F oven for 25 to 30 minutes, or until the filling puffs up and is golden brown on top. Cool on a wire rack. Serve at room temperature, topped by vanilla ice cream or slightly sweetened whipped cream (page 107).

PECAN PIE

Pecan pie is the prototype of the Southern classic "transparent pie:" a variation on the Chess Pie which is rich in eggs, butter, sugar, and another local specialty—pecans. This recipe contains brown sugar and molasses, traditional Southern sweeteners, as well as corn syrup, a late comer to Chess pie filling. The touch of lemon cuts the sugar and eliminates the cloying taste often associated with pecan pie.

If the sweetness of this pie has always put you off, try the Pecan-Cranberry variation that follows; the tartness of the berries gives a delightful sweet-sour balance to the pie. Or try using a variety of nuts; each will flavor the pie differently—peanuts, black walnuts, or macadamia nuts, for example. Northern Vermont cooks replace the corn syrup with maple syrup, for their own flavor variation. This pie makes an attractive presentation when baked in a tart pan and served free-standing.

Advance preparation: The partially prebaked pastry shell can be prepared ahead and frozen (page 53). Because of the high sugar content, pecan pie will keep well at room temperature. It can be prepared ahead of serving, but be aware that the crust will soften on standing longer than a day.

Special equipment: 9-inch pie plate (or 9- or 10-inch tart pan with removable bottom); mixing bowl and whisk or electric mixer; stainless steel knife.

Baking time: Partially prebaked pastry shell: 425°F for 10 minutes with pie weights. Filled pie: 400°F for 20 to 25 minutes.

Quantity: One 9-inch pie.

> *Partially prebaked 9-inch pie shell made*
> *with Whole Wheat Pastry (page 59)*
> *or pastry of your choice*

Filling
¾ cup dark brown sugar, packed
3 eggs
6 tablespoons unsalted butter, melted
⅔ cup dark corn syrup
1 tablespoon unsulfured molasses
1 teaspoon lemon juice
1 teaspoon vanilla extract
¼ teaspoon salt
1 cup pecans, halved

1. Preheat the oven to 425°F. Prepare the pastry. Roll out the pastry, and line the pan (page 38). Trim a ¾-inch overhang, fold over the edge, and flute as desired (page 44). Prick the bottom with a fork, chill until firm, then partially blind-bake for only 10 minutes (page 42). Cool on a wire rack. Lower the oven heat to 400°.

2. To prepare the filling, measure the brown sugar into the bowl of an electric mixer and beat with the eggs until well blended and free of lumps. Add the melted butter, corn syrup, molasses, lemon juice, vanilla, and salt. Beat well.

3. Pour the filling into the prepared pastry shell and arrange the halved nuts over the top—either carefully positioned in concentric circles or simply scattered at random. Bake the pie in the center of the preheated oven for 20 to 30 minutes, or until a stainless steel knife stuck into the center comes out clean. Cool on a wire rack. Serve at room temperature, topped by vanilla ice cream or slightly sweetened whipped cream (page 107).

VARIATIONS:

Cranberry-Pecan Pie. Prepare Pecan Pie but add ¾ cup coarsely chopped fresh or frozen cranberries and use only ¾ cup pecan halves.

Black Walnut Pie. Prepare Pecan Pie but replace the pecans with 1 cup chopped black walnuts, and use light corn syrup instead of dark.

Hawaiian Macadamia Nut Pie. Prepare Pecan Pie but replace the pecans with 1 cup unsalted macadamia nuts, coarsely chopped.

Peanut Pie. Add ½ cup fine-chopped or ground peanuts to the pastry (page 35, Basic All-Purpose Flaky Pastry, Nut Pastry Variation), and replace the pecans with peanuts as follows: Coarsely chop ½ cup dry roasted, lightly salted peanuts and add to the filling mixture. Sprinkle an additional 1 cup of dry roasted, lightly salted peanuts, whole, over the top of the filled pie before baking. (*Note:* Peanut pie can be made with either dark or light corn syrup.)

PENNSYLVANIA DUTCH SHOOFLY PIE

Shoofly Pie is a well-known Pennsylvania-Dutch specialty with a spicy molasses and gingerbread flavor. It is thought that the name comes from the fact that flies love molasses and have to be shooed away when you make this pie. The pie filling can be assembled and baked in different ways: when the pastry lining is topped by alternating layers of crumbs and molasses custard, with the crumbs ending up on top, the texture is cakelike and the title is "Gravel Pie," for obvious reasons. When the molasses custard remains in a layer by itself beneath the crumb topping, the result as described in the following directions, is "Wet

Bottom Shoofly Pie," also for obvious reasons. Either way, serve it plain for breakfast as a coffee cake, or for afternoon tea topped with Vanilla Yogurt-Rum Sauce (page 115), or sweetened whipped cream (page 107).

Advance preparation: The unbaked pie shell can be prepared ahead and frozen (page 53). The pie can be filled and baked ahead, though the texture is best when warm from the oven.

Special equipment: 9-inch pie plate; electric mixer; 2 mixing bowls; toothpick or cake tester.

Baking time: 375°F for 35 to 40 minutes.

Quantity: One 9-inch pie.

> *Unbaked pastry for a 9-inch pie shell*
> *made with Basic All-Purpose Flaky*
> *Pastry (page 34) or Butter-Lard*
> *Pastry (page 63)*

Crumb Topping
1 cup all-purpose flour
½ cup dark brown sugar, packed
¼ teaspoon each salt, ground nutmeg,
*   cloves, mace, cinnamon, ground*
*   ginger*
5 tablespoons margarine or butter

Molasses Custard
½ cup unsulfured molasses
2 eggs
½ cup boiling water
½ teaspoon baking soda

1. Prepare the pastry, roll it out, and line the pie plate (page 38). Set the pastry-lined pan in the refrigerator to chill while preparing the filling. Preheat the oven to 375°F.

2. In one large bowl, combine the flour, brown sugar, and spices for the topping. Cut in the shortening until the mixture looks like coarse meal. Spoon about ⅓ cup of this mixture into an even layer in the pastry-lined pan.

In a second bowl or an electric mixer, beat together the molasses and eggs. (*Note:* Oil the measuring cup first for ease in pouring out the molasses.) In a small bowl, measure ½ cup boiling water and stir in the baking soda until it is dissolved. The mixture will bubble up. Immediately, stir the soda-water into the molasses-eggs, beat well, then pour over crumbs in the pastry-lined pie plate. Sprinkle on all the remaining crumb topping, making an even coating with a nearly bare spot in the pie's center to allow the filling to rise and expand. Don't delay in getting this into the oven or the rising power of the baking soda will be dissipated.

3. Bake the pie in the center of the preheated oven for 35 to 40 minutes, or until well browned and a cake tester inserted into the center comes out clean. Serve warm, or at room temperature, plain, with Vanilla Yogurt-Rum Sauce (page 115), or with sweetened whipped cream (page 107).

VARIATION:

Gravel Pie. Prepare Shoofly Pie, but add ½ cup seedless raisins, sprinkled over the pastry-lined pan before adding the filling. Add filling in alternate layers, beginning with custard (over the raisins) and ending with crumbs on top.

LEMON MERINGUE PIE

This is everybody's favorite, and it is equally good, if not better, flavored with orange for Orange Meringue Pie, with a little orange liqueur adding sparkle to the meringue.

Advance preparation: The completely prebaked pastry shell can be prepared ahead and frozen (page 53). The baked shell can be filled with custard and chilled a few hours before serving (but be careful; the crust will soften if the custard stands in it too long). Add the meringue shortly before serving, or in any case no more than 4 hours ahead, for best results.

Special equipment: 9-inch pie plate; double boiler with cover; whisk; electric mixer; mixing bowl and small bowl.

Baking time: Completely prebaked pastry shell: 425°F for 10 minutes with pie weights, 350°F for 15 to 20 minutes longer; meringue: 350°F for about 15 minutes.

Custard Cooking time: About 25 minutes.

Quantity: One 9-inch pie.

> *Completely prebaked 9-inch pie shell*
> *made with Basic All-Purpose Flaky*
> *Pastry, Orange or Lemon Pastry*
> *Variation (page 35), prepared with*
> *1 egg yolk and 1 tablespoon sugar*

Filling

3 egg yolks
1 cup granulated sugar
6 tablespoons cornstarch
¼ teaspoon salt
2 cups water
3 tablespoons butter
⅓ cup lemon juice
2 teaspoons grated lemon zest

Meringue

3 egg whites
¼ teaspoon cream of tartar
A pinch of salt
6 tablespoons granulated sugar
Optional: *2 tablespoons Grand Marnier*
        or Triple Sec

1. Preheat the oven to 425°F. Prepare the pastry, roll it out, and line the pan (page 38). Trim a ¾-inch overhang, fold over the edge, and flute as desired (page 44). Prick the bottom with a fork, chill until firm, then completely blind-bake (page 42). Cool on a wire rack.

2. To prepare the filling, put the egg yolks in one small bowl, the whites in large mixing bowl, and set them aside for the meringue. Beat the yolks, then set them aside.

Measure the sugar, cornstarch, and salt into the top of a double boiler and set over boiling water on high heat. Slowly stir in the 2 cups water, whisking to make the mixture smooth. Continue to whisk, or stir with a wooden spoon, as the mixture heats and thickens—it takes about 7 to 10 minutes to get really thick and look clear. At this point, cover the double boiler and cook mixture on medium heat for 7 to 10 minutes longer, stirring every once in a while. When done, it should look clear and thick. Turn off the heat.

3. When cornstarch mixture is cooked, spoon about ½ cup of it into the beaten egg yolks and *immediately* beat vigorously (or you will get hard-boiled eggs!). Then pour all the warmed yolk mixture into the cornstarch mixture in the double boiler and whisk hard until it is well blended.

4. Set double boiler over medium heat and cook the custard mixture about 5 minutes, stirring constantly. Remove from the heat. Stir in the butter, lemon juice, and grated zest. Whisk well and stir until it cools slightly. Set aside on a wire rack to cool. Preheat the oven to 350°F.

5. To prepare the meringue topping, beat the egg whites in an electric mixer with the cream of tartar and pinch of salt until fluffy. Add the sugar 2 tablespoons at a time (and the liqueur if you are using it), beating between additions. Beat the whites until they are very satiny and form stiff peaks. Pinch the meringue between your fingers to be sure no grains of sugar remain undissolved.

6. Spoon the lemon custard into the baked pastry shell. Spoon the meringue over the custard (it is all right if the custard is still warm). Smooth the meringue onto the edges of the crust to seal it and prevent shrinking. Shape the meringue into medium-high peaks with the back of a spoon. Or pipe the meringue onto the pie with a pastry tube, after first covering it with a flat base layer of meringue. Bake the pie in the preheated oven for 12 to 15 minutes, until the meringue topping is golden brown. Watch carefully so it does not burn. Cool on a wire rack, and serve at room temperature. Store leftover pie in the refrigerator.

VARIATIONS:

Orange Meringue Pie. Prepare Lemon Meringue Pie, above, but replace the lemon juice with orange juice and use 2 tablespoons grated orange zest instead of the lemon zest. Use orange-flavored liqueur in the meringue.

Lime Meringue Pie. Prepare Lemon Meringue Pie, above, but replace the lemon juice with lime juice and replace lemon zest with lime zest. Omit the liqueur in the meringue.

ALMOND MERINGUE PIE

For this unusual dessert, prepare a flaky pastry crust and fill it with any one of several delicately flavored baked meringues. The texture is delightfully light and chewy with a crisp topping. Serve with a dollop of sweetened whipped cream.

Advance preparation: The partially baked pastry shell may be prepared ahead and frozen. The completely baked pie may be made one day in advance or several hours before serving. Store the pie in an airtight container.

Special equipment: 9-inch pie plate; aluminum foil strips or frame (page 25); electric mixer.

Baking time: Partially prebaked shell: 425°F for 10 minutes with pie weights, then 3 minutes empty; complete tart: 350°F for 25 to 30 minutes.

Quantity: One 9-inch pie.

Partially prebaked single-crust 9-inch pie
     or tart shell made with Basic
     All-Purpose Flaky Pastry (page 34)
     prepared with egg yolk and
     1 tablespoon sugar, or other pastry
     of your choice
2 egg whites
A pinch of salt
½ teaspoon each vanilla and almond
     extract
⅔ cup confectioners' sugar
⅔ cup blanched almonds, toasted and
     ground (Note: *To toast almonds,*
     set them on a pie pan in a 300°F
     oven for about 4 to 5 minutes, or
     just until they turn light golden.
     Watch carefully; they can burn fast!
     Then grind.)

1. Preheat the oven to 425°F. Prepare the pastry, roll it out, and line the buttered pan (page 38). Trim a ¾-inch pastry overhang, fold over and flute the edge (page 44). Prick the bottom with a fork, chill until firm, then partially blind-bake the shell (page 42). Cool shell on a wire rack.

2. Reduce the oven heat to 350°F. In the bowl of an electric mixer, combine the egg whites with a pinch of salt and beat until fluffy. Add the extracts and sift on the sugar a little at a time, beating between additions until the whites are satiny and very stiff. Fold in the ground nuts.

3. Turn egg white mixture into the prebaked and cooled shell and bake in the center of the preheated oven 25 to 30 minutes, or until the top of the tart is lightly browned and a cake tester inserted in the center comes out clean. Check after about half the baking time and add a foil edging if necessary to protect the crust from overbrowning. Cool on a wire rack. Serve at room temperature.

VARIATIONS:

Chocolate Meringue Pie. Prepare Almond Meringue Pie, above, but add to the
     filling 1 ounce grated semisweet chocolate, folded in along with the nuts.
Butterscotch Meringue Pie. Prepare Almond Meringue Pie, above, but replace
     the almonds with ½ cup fine-chopped pecans and use 1 teaspoon vanilla
     extract; omit the almond extract. Replace the confectioners' sugar with ⅔

cup dark brown sugar, packed; after measuring the sugar, crumble it and sprinkle it over the fluffy, partially beaten whites, then continue beating until stiff. Fold in the nuts. Serve with Butterscotch Flavored Whipped Cream (page 109).

KEY LIME PIE

This recipe is considered a quick pie because the filling is not a cooked custard but rather is made with condensed milk. Gail Borden first produced this product in 1858, and after the Civil War, it supplied many food deficiencies for the war-ravaged South. In Key West, Florida, it was used as the basis for this "new" pie. The flavor and texture of this recipe is excellent, and it only takes a moment to prepare. I make it every winter, during my annual Southern migration, with Key limes freshly picked from the trees of Bea and Jordan Joslin, my uncle and aunt, in Hollywood, Florida. The pie is so outstanding, and the limes are so flavorful, they always send me home with a bag of limes to share "up north." If you prefer the cooked custard variety, see Lime Meringue Pie, page 222.

Advance preparation: The crumb crust can be prepared ahead and frozen. The custard can be added to the pie and chilled several hours in advance. Add the meringue shortly before serving, or in any case no more than 3 hours ahead, for best results.

Special equipment: 9-inch pie plate; electric mixer fitted with a steel blade; rubber spatula; optional: pastry bag fitted with star tip.

Baking time: Crumb crust: 350°F for 8 minutes; meringue topping: 350°F for 12 to 15 minutes.

Chilling time: Completed pie: 2 to 3 hours.

Quantity: One 9-inch pie.

Graham Cracker Crumb Crust for a
9-inch pie, baked 8 minutes
(page 73)

Filling
4 egg yolks
1 (14-ounce) can sweetened condensed
*   milk*
½ cup freshly squeezed Key lime juice
(or juice of regular limes)

2 teaspoons grated lime zest (Note: *Key*
limes are yellow-green rather than
dark green in color. If you feel your
pie is not really "lime" unless it
looks green, you can add a drop of
green food coloring to the cream
filling, although it goes against my
better judgment

Meringue Topping
4 egg whites
A pinch of salt
¼ teaspoon cream of tartar
6 tablespoons superfine or granulated
sugar

1. Preheat the oven to 350°F. Prepare the Graham Cracker Crumb Crust and bake it as directed. Set on a wire rack to cool.

2. In an electric mixer or processor, combine egg yolks, condensed milk, lime juice, and grated zest. Blend until thick and smooth. Scrape the filling into the prepared crust and refrigerate several hours, until set. Serve with sweetened whipped cream (page 107) or top with meringue as follows:

3. To make meringue, combine egg whites, salt, and cream of tartar in an electric mixer. Beat until fluffy. Add sugar, 2 tablespoons at a time, beating between each addition. Beat the whites until very satiny and stiff peaks form.

4. Spoon the meringue over the filled pie and smooth onto the edges of the crust to seal it and prevent shrinking. Make peaks with the back of a spoon or pipe meringue onto the pie from a pastry bag fitted with star tip, after first covering the pie with a flat base layer of meringue. Bake in the preheated oven for 12 to 15 minutes, until the meringue topping is golden brown. Watch carefully so it does not burn. Cool on a wire rack and serve at room temperature. Store in the refrigerator.

VARIATION:

Key Lime Cheese Pie. Prepare Key Lime Pie, above, but omit the egg yolks. Use only ⅓ cup lime juice, but add 8 ounces dairy cream cheese, at room temperature, beaten into the mixture along with the condensed milk and grated lime zest. Top with meringue made with 3 or 4 egg whites (as above), or with sweetened whipped cream (page 107).

ITALIAN RICOTTA CHEESE PIE (*TORTA DI RICOTTA*)

Torta di Ricotta is an Italian cheesecake pie made with ricotta cheese and flavored with either chopped candied fruits or small chunks of bittersweet chocolate (my favorite). In many regions, it is served as a Christmas specialty.

Advance preparation: The partially prebaked pie shell may be prepared ahead and frozen (page 53). Bake the pie shortly before serving, as it is best warm, though it may also be chilled and served cold.

Special equipment: 9-inch pie plate or quiche pan; strainer set over bowl; mixing bowl or electric mixer; pastry brush; food processor fitted with a steel blade, or a wooden board and chopping knife.

Baking time: Partially prebaked shell: 425°F for 10 minutes with pie weights, then 3 minutes empty; completed tart: 350°F for 40 to 45 minutes.

Quantity: One 9-inch pie.

> *Partially prebaked 9-inch pie shell made*
> *with Basic All-Purpose Flaky Pastry,*
> *either Sherry Pastry Variation or*
> *Nut Pastry Variation (page 35), or*
> *Cream Cheese Pastry (page 65)*

Filling
1 pound ricotta cheese (2 cups)
3 eggs
1 cup granulated sugar
1 (3-ounce) package cream cheese (not
*   whipped), at room temperature*
1 teaspoon almond extract
1 cup candied mixed fruits, chopped, or
*   1/2 cup chopped semisweet pure*
*   chocolate, or a combination of half*
*   fruit, half chocolate*

1. Prepare the pastry, roll it out, and line the pie plate (page 38). Trim a 3/4-inch pastry overhang, fold over the edge, and flute as desired (page 44). Be sure the fluted rim is high, as it must contain a generous amount of filling. Preheat oven to 425°F. Prick the pastry bottom with a fork, chill until firm, then partially blind-bake (page 42). Cool on a wire rack. Reduce oven heat to 350°F.

2. Measure the ricotta into a strainer set over a bowl and press out the excess fluid. (*Note:* Freshly made dairy ricotta often has much more liquid in

it than commercially processed ricotta; either one works well in this pie, as long as the liquid is completely drained.)

3. In an electric mixer or mixing bowl, beat the eggs well. Then brush some of the beaten eggs over the bottom of the pie shell to moisture-proof it. Add the sugar to the remaining eggs and beat 2 or 3 minutes, until thick and a light yellow color. Add the drained ricotta, cream cheese, and almond extract and beat until smooth.

4. Sprinkle about half the fruit and/or chocolate mixture over the glazed pie shell. Stir the remaining fruit and/or chocolate into the egg-cheese mixture, then spoon this into the pie shell. Bake in the center of the preheated oven for 40 to 45 minutes, until the top is puffy and golden brown. Cool on a wire rack. Serve warm or chilled.

CHEESECAKE PIE

The filling for this rich creamy cheesecake is prepared in minutes with a blender or food processor. It is a great party pie, which can be baked ahead and chilled until ready to serve. Top it with whipped cream, fresh whole berries, or cooked berry glaze.

Advance preparation: The crumb crust may be prepared ahead and frozen; the complete pie can be prepared ahead and chilled for several hours or until serving. Add the topping no more than 2 hours before serving, or it may soften the filling.

Special equipment: 9-inch pie plate; blender or food processor fitted with a steel blade; rubber scraper; optional: saucepan and wooden spoon for cooked sauce.

Baking time: Filled pie: 325° For 40 minutes.

Chilling time: Crumb crust: 30 minutes; baked pie: 2 to 3 hours before serving.

Quantity: One 9-inch pie.

Graham-Nut Crumb Crust (page 73),
made with almonds, chilled

Filling
2 eggs
½ cup granulated sugar
2 teaspoons vanilla extract
1½ cups sour cream
2 tablespoons butter or margarine,
     melted

2 (8-ounce) packages cream cheese (not
   whipped), at room temperature

Optional Fruit Glaze
3 to 4 cups fresh strawberries or
   raspberries (or others)
½ cup granulated sugar
2 tablespoons cornstarch
½ cup orange (or other fruit) juice

Optional Topping
½ cup heavy cream, whipped and
   sweetened with 2 tablespoons sugar
   and/or 3 cups fresh whole berries

1. Prepare and chill the crumb crust until firm. Preheat the oven to 325°F. In a blender or food processor, combine the eggs, sugar, vanilla, and sour cream. Blend until smooth. Add melted butter or margarine and about ⅓ of the cream cheese. Blend again until smooth. Add the remaining cream cheese and blend until free of lumps, thick, and creamy.

2. Use a rubber scraper to turn the mixture into the prepared crumb crust. Bake in the preheated oven for 40 minutes. Cool on a wire rack, then chill in the refrigerator at least 3 hours before serving.

3. For topping, whip ½ cup heavy cream, sweetened with 1 or 2 tablespoons sugar, and pipe it decoratively from a pastry bag fitted with a star tip, or spoon over the pie and stripe with a fork. Or top with whole berries, hulled, washed, and dried carefully, then set stem end down on the pie. Or prepare a glaze of cooked berries as follows:

To make fruit glaze, hull and rinse the berries, then mash them in a stainless steel or enamel saucepan along with the sugar. In a cup, stir the cornstarch into the fruit juice, then stir into the fruit in the pan and cook over medium heat, stirring, about 5 minutes, until the mixture is thick and clear. Cool completely, then spread over the baked and chilled cheesecake. Chill 1 or 2 hours longer, to set the glaze somewhat (it does not get stiff).

DOUBLE CHOCOLATE CHEESECAKE PIE

This is a chocolate-lover's pleasure: rich velvety chocolate cheesecake punctuated by chocolate bits. The filling puffs up during baking, then sinks down and crackles on the top as it cools to a dense texture perfect for cutting in narrow wedges and topping with vanilla ice cream.

Advance preparation: This pie can be made well ahead and chilled. Serve at
room temperature.

Special equipment: 10-inch pie plate; double boiler; electric mixer; rubber scraper.

Baking time: Partially prebaked pastry shell: 425°F for 10 minutes with pie
weights, then 10 minutes empty (until nearly golden); filled pie: 325°F for
40 minutes, then left to cool in oven for 30 minutes with heat off.

Quantity: One 10-inch pie.

> *Partially prebaked pastry shell for a*
> *10-inch pie prepared with Basic*
> *All-Purpose Flaky Pastry, Nut Pastry*
> *Variation (almond, page 35) baked*
> *as directed below; or, 10-inch*
> *Chocolate-Almond Crumb Crust*
> *(page 74), chilled 30 minutes or*
> *until firm*

Filling
8 ounces semisweet chocolate
1⅞ large packages (15 ounces) cream
    cheese at room temperature, cut up
3 eggs
1 teaspoon vanilla extract
¾ cup granulated sugar
3 tablespoons Baker's unsweetened cocoa
⅛ teaspoon salt
⅛ teaspoon cinnamon
4 tablespoons milk or cream
¾ cup semisweet mini chocolate bits or
    coarsely chopped pieces of block
    chocolate

1. To prepare the pastry shell, preheat the oven to 425°F. Prepare the pastry,
roll it out, and line the pan (page 38). Trim a ¾-inch overhang, fold it over,
and flute it as desired (page 44). Prick the bottom with a fork, chill until firm,
then partially blind-bake (page 42). Cool on a wire rack. Or prepare Chocolate-
Almond Crumb Crust (page 74), and chill.

2. Measure 8 ounces of chocolate in the top of a double boiler and set to
melt over hot (not boiling) water. Remove from the heat before completely
melted and stir to complete the melting process. Preheat the oven to 325°F.

3. In an electric mixer, beat the cream cheese until soft and fluffy. Add the
eggs, vanilla, and sugar and beat smooth.

4. Add the melted chocolate, the cocoa, salt, cinnamon, and milk or cream. Beat until smooth but do not overwork. The mixture will be thick. Stir in the semisweet minibits, or coarsely chopped chocolate.

5. Spread the mixture in the prepared pastry shell. (*Note:* If you have left-over filling, bake it into a tartlet or two; no need for the pastry liner.) Bake the pie in the center of the preheated oven for 40 minutes. Then turn off the heat but do not open the door. Leave the pie in the oven an additional carefully timed 30 minutes. Remove from the oven and cool on a wire rack. Chill. Serve at room temperature; the texture will be too stiff if served cold. Top each serving with a scoop of vanilla ice cream if you wish.

VARIATIONS:

Double Chocolate Amaretto Cheesecake Pie. Prepare Double Chocolate Cheese-cake Pie, page 228, but in step 3, add ½ teaspoon almond extract and 2 tablespoons amaretto liqueur to the cream cheese mixture.

Chocolate-Mocha Cheesecake Pie. Prepare Double Chocolate Cheesecake Pie but in step 4, dissolve 3 teaspoons instant powdered espresso coffee in the milk or cream before beating it into the chocolate mixture.

MISSISSIPPI MUD PIE

This pie is fun to make both because it is easy to prepare and because its name always stimulates dinner table conversation. The flavor is a chocoholic's dream, although it looks rather like what you might expect: a mudpie that has dried in the sun, crusty and cracked on top, soft inside. The touch of coffee in the filling is not overwhelming, just enough to take the edge off the sweetness. Serve at room temperature with a dollop of vanilla yogurt or vanilla ice cream, or sweetened whipped cream (page 107).

For such a pedestrian-sounding pie, this has a rather complex pedigree, but one that merits recognition for the fine results. Mississippi Mud Pie was shared with me by Connecticut friend, good cook, and artist-in-clay Elizabeth McDonald, who had refined it over the years from a New York Sunday *Times* classic by Dorothy Ann Webb. I have further modified it, by adding the coffee flavoring. For Frozen Mud Pie made with ice cream, see page 262.

Advance preparation: The unbaked pastry shell can be prepared ahead and frozen (page 53); thaw before filling. The filled, baked pie can also be frozen, although it never tastes as good as when freshly baked.

Special equipment: 10-inch pie plate; double boiler; electric mixer or mixing bowl
or food processor fitted with a steel blade; rubber scraper.
Baking time: Filled pie: 350°F for 35 to 45 minutes.
Quantity: One 10-inch pie.

> *Unbaked 10-inch pie shell made with*
> *Basic All-Purpose Flaky Pastry, Nut*
> *Pastry Variation (walnut or almond,*
> *page 35), or pastry of your choice*

Filling
½ *cup unsalted butter (or half butter/*
   half margarine)
2 *ounces unsweetened chocolate*
1 *ounce semisweet chocolate*
3 *eggs*
1 *tablespoon instant coffee dissolved in*
   2 *tablespoons sour cream*
1⅓ *cups granulated sugar*
3 *tablespoons light Karo syrup*
1 *teaspoon vanilla extract*

1. Prepare the pastry, roll it out, and line the pie plate (page 38). Trim a
¾-inch overhang, fold over the edge, and flute as desired (page 44). Chill the
pastry-lined pan until the filling is prepared. Preheat the oven to 350°F.

2. Measure the butter and chocolate into the top of a double boiler and melt
over hot (not boiling) water. Remove from the heat and cool.

3. With an electric mixer or processor, beat together all remaining ingredients
until well blended. Stir in the melted chocolate-butter mixture. Pour into prepared pie shell.

4. Bake in the lower third of the preheated oven for 35 to 45 minutes, or
until the filling puffs up and forms a crisp, deeply crackled crust and the pastry
edges look golden brown. Cool on a wire rack. The filling will sink down as it
cools, and the inner layer will set but remain softly chewy. (*Note:* The shorter
baking time of 35 minutes leaves the inner layer more creamy than chewy, an
effect some people prefer.) Serve at room temperature, topped by vanilla yogurt
or vanilla ice cream or whipped cream (page 107).

CHIFFON PIES

A chiffon pie is a light fluffy confection in which flavoring, usually in an egg-yolk base, is supported by stiffly beaten egg whites and/or whipped heavy cream. Often gelatin is added as well, as a stabilizer. Without gelatin, the chiffon is essentially a *mousse,* a French term meaning literally "froth" or "foam." Dessert mousses and mousse pies are served chilled from the refrigerator, or frozen, in which case they are called frozen soufflés and have a texture similar to creamy ice cream. When gelatin is added to the mixture along with whipped cream, but without egg whites, it becomes, strictly speaking, a Bavarian cream. Bavarian creams may be frozen, but should be thawed overnight in the refrigerator before serving cold.

Because these pies can be made ahead and refrigerated or frozen, they are ideal for entertaining. With this in mind, many of the recipes in this section are large, 10 inches, for party serving.

Crumb crusts are the traditional choice for chiffon pies for two reasons. First, they absorb less moisture than pastry crusts and can be filled and held longer without getting soggy. Second, crumb crusts are less brittle and taste better when served frozen than do pastry crusts.

The basic procedure for making chiffon pies with gelatin is the same in most cases. If you understand what is happening, you will see that there is a reason for the order of things here. To begin, a flavor base containing yolks and sugar is beaten together and combined with gelatin that has (usually but not always) been softened in water in advance. This mixture is cooked (usually in a double boiler) until the gelatin completely dissolves, an essential step if the filling is to set properly.

At this point, the mixture is removed from the hot pan or double boiler and set to cool in a clean bowl. Before proceeding, this mixture must be cooled and partially set. To accomplish this, you have two choices. You can set the mixture into the refrigerator, stirring occasionally to prevent its setting hard on the bottom, and chill until it mounds on a spoon. This takes about 30 minutes. Or you can use the speedy ice water method recommended in the recipes of this section. In this case, the gelatin mixture is set into a large bowl containing ice water and whisked about 15 minutes, until chilled and thickened to the consistency of raw egg whites, at which point it will mound on the spoon rather than drip off as a liquid. Remove the bowl from the ice water at once to avoid overchilling and hard-setting the gelatin. If, however, this happens by accident and the mixture stiffens, do not worry. Simply set it over a bowl of very hot water and stir until it melts and softens again. Then rechill, stirring, over ice water. Watch carefully; though, it will set faster the second time.

Whip the egg whites stiff, but beat the cream only until medium-stiff peaks form, just slightly beyond Chantilly stage (page 106). If the cream is overbeaten, the finished filling will taste heavy or buttery, and the fat may separate from the liquid.

Once the gelatin mixture is cooled and partially jelled, it should be folded into the whipped cream and egg whites as soon as possible, before it solidifies further. If you wish, you can even whip the cream and whites in advance to stand ready while you prepare the gelatin over ice water. In any case, fold the mixture first into the whipped cream and second into the whites, which are more fragile. Finally, spoon the filling into the prepared shell and refrigerate until set, which takes about three hours.

RUM-PUMPKIN CHIFFON PIE

This light but richly flavored pie is a family favorite, made by my mother, Frances Joslin Gold. It has been part of our Thanksgiving since I can remember. Equally good without the rum, it is an elegant variation on the traditional pumpkin custard pie.

Advance preparation: The crumb crust may be prepared in advance and frozen, or the complete pie can be made a day ahead and refrigerated. The complete pie may also be frozen, then thawed overnight in the refrigerator. Add the whipped cream garnish shortly before serving.

Special equipment: 9-inch pie plate; double boiler; small saucepan; large mixing bowl containing ice cubes and cold water; bowl and beater set in freezer or

refrigerator to chill for whipping cream; rubber scraper; plastic wrap; optional:
pastry bag fitted with ½-inch star tip.

Chilling time: Crumb crust: 30 minutes minimum; filled pie: 3 hours or overnight in refrigerator, or freeze for convenience.

Quantity: One 9-inch pie.

*9-inch Gingersnap Crumb Crust (page
73) prepared without additional
sugar; chilled until firm*

Filling
*1 envelope (2 teaspoons) unflavored
gelatin*
¼ cup very hot water
3 eggs
⅔ cup granulated sugar
½ teaspoon salt
*Generous ½ teaspoon each cinnamon,
nutmeg, ground ginger; or to taste*
*Optional: 3 to 4 tablespoons dark rum
(or Triple Sec), to taste*
1¼ cups canned pumpkin
½ cup heavy cream

Garnish
Rum-flavored Whipped Cream (page 107)
Almond slices or slivers of candied ginger
Freshly grated nutmeg

1. Prepare the Gingersnap Crumb Crust, and set it in the refrigerator to chill
while you prepare the filling. Sprinkle the gelatin over cool water in a small saucepan, let sit 2 minutes to soften, then stir over low heat until thoroughly dissolved.
Set gelatin aside to cool. Separate the eggs (page 31), placing the yolks in the top of
a double boiler and the whites in the large bowl of an electric mixer.

2. Add ⅓ cup granulated sugar to the yolks and whisk until the mixture is
thick and light lemon-colored. Add salt, spices, rum, and dissolved gelatin. Whisk
together, then set double boiler over (not touching) boiling water and stir constantly over medium heat until the mixture becomes very thick and generously
coats a spoon.

3. Remove from the heat and stir in the pumpkin; whisk to combine thoroughly with the custard. Turn the mixture into a clean, cool mixing bowl. Then set it into a large bowl containing ice water. Whisk about 15 minutes to cool the mixture until it feels thick, mounds on the spoon, and looks as if it is beginning to set—about the consistency of raw egg whites. Do not chill until it sets hard; remove it from the ice water. (*Note:* The ice water speeds this process, but if you are not in a hurry, you can simply leave the mixture in the refrigerator until it cools and thickens; however, do not let it set completely.)

4. Beat the egg whites until fluffy, then add the remaining 1/3 cup sugar a little at a time, beating after each addition until stiff peaks form and the whites are very satiny. With chilled bowl and beaters, whip the heavy cream until medium stiff peaks form.

5. Fold the cooled, thickened (but not hard-set) pumpkin mixture into the whipped cream, then into the stiffly beaten whites. Spoon the mixture into the prepared shell. Cover with plastic wrap to protect the flavor. Then chill at least 3 hours to set. Or chill overnight, or top with plastic wrap and fast freeze; then, when firm, wrap airtight with foil and store in the freezer. Defrost overnight in the refrigerator before serving.

6. Garnish the pie shortly before serving with Rum-flavored Whipped Cream (page 107) spooned into a ring around the edge of the pie or piped into rosettes through a pastry bag fitted with star tip. Decorate with almond slices or slivers of candied ginger and sprinkles of freshly grated nutmeg.

PINA COLADA PIE

Like the cocktail for which it is named, this light refreshing chiffon pie is redolent of tropical island flavors: rum, coconut, lime, and pineapple.

Advance preparation: The crumb crust can be prepared ahead and frozen. The complete pie can be prepared a day ahead and refrigerated; or it can be frozen, then thawed overnight in the refrigerator.

Special equipment: 10-inch pie plate; 2½-quart heavy-bottom enamel or stainless steel saucepan; large bowl containing ice cubes and cold water; electric mixer; chilled bowl and beater for whipping cream; plastic wrap; paper towels; strainer; pastry bag fitted with ½-inch star tip, or spoon and fork, for applying whipped cream.

Baking time: Coconut crust: 325°F for 20 minutes.

Chilling time: Filled pie: 3 hours minimum, or freeze until set.

Quantity: One 10-inch pie.

*One 10-inch Coconut Crumb Crust (page
    75) prepared with 2½ cups flaked
    or shredded coconut and ⅓ cup
    melted butter*
1 can (20 ounces) crushed pineapple
*½ cup canned sweetened coconut cream
    (Coco Lopez, for example)*
3 eggs
⅓ cup granulated sugar
1 tablespoon cornstarch
*1½ envelopes (1 tablespoon) unflavored
    gelatin*
4 tablespoons dark rum
2 tablespoons freshly squeezed lime juice
Optional: *½ teaspoon coconut extract*
⅓ cup confectioners' sugar, sifted
1 cup heavy cream

Topping

½ cup heavy cream
1 tablespoon confectioners' sugar
*1 tablespoon dark rum or ½ teaspoon
    coconut extract*

Garnish

Fresh mint sprigs
Toasted Coconut Topping (page 113)
Thin-sliced cartwheels of fresh lime

1. Prepare the Coconut Crust and set aside to cool on a wire rack while you make the filling. Put the pineapple into a strainer set over a bowl. You should have about 1⅔ cups fruit and ¾ cup pineapple juice. Set the fruit aside. Stir the canned coconut cream into the juice.

2. Separate the eggs (page 31) putting the whites in the bowl of an electric mixer and the yolks into the pineapple juice mixture. Whisk the yolks and juice.

3. In a saucepan, combine the granulated sugar, cornstarch, and gelatin. Stir, then whisk in the pineapple juice-yolk mixture. Set over medium heat and stir constantly with a wooden spoon for about 5 minutes, until the mixture comes to a boil and thickens. Stir constantly while boiling one full minute. Remove from the heat. Stir in 3 tablespoons rum, all the lime juice and the coconut extract if used. Measure and add 1½ cups pineapple pieces. Reserve the remaining pineapple for a garnish.

4. Turn the pineapple mixture into a clean mixing bowl, then set it into a large bowl containing ice water. Whisk about 15 minutes until the mixture feels thick and looks as if it is beginning to set—about the consistency of raw egg whites. Then remove from the ice water. Do not allow it to set hard. The ice water speeds this process, but if you are not in a hurry, you can simply leave the mixture in the refrigerator until it cools and thickens; however, do not let it set completely.

5. Beat the egg whites until they are foamy, then add the confectioners' sugar and beat until stiff peaks form. In a chilled bowl with chilled beaters, whip the heavy cream until it forms soft peaks, then stir in the remaining 1 tablespoon rum and whip medium-stiff. Fold the cream into the pineapple mixture, then fold in the beaten whites.

6. Turn the filling into the prepared shell. Cover with plastic wrap and refrigerate at least 3 hours, until set.

Shortly before serving, garnish with *either* reserved pineapple pieces (blotted well on paper towels) arranged around the edge of the pie and alternating with sprigs of mint *or* whip the ½ cup cream, stir in the sugar and rum or coconut extract, and decorate the pie with rosettes of cream piped through a pastry bag fitted with a star tip, or spoon mounds of cream around the pie and stripe them with a fork. Garnish with Toasted Coconut Topping, mint sprigs, and thin lime slices alternating with bits of pineapple, for color. Serve directly from the refrigerator.

LEMON MOUSSE PIE

This light, tart, refreshing dessert is especially appreciated after a heavy meal, though it is also an appropriate finale for a spring luncheon, when the slices of pie can be served alongside whole, fresh strawberries. For easy entertaining, prepare the pie a day ahead and refrigerate it until serving time. For variety, replace the lemon with orange, lime, or tangerine zest and juice. Strictly speaking, this is a Bavarian cream, rather than a mousse, since it is stabilized with gelatin, whipped cream, and egg whites.

Advance preparation: The crumb crust can be prepared ahead and frozen; the complete pie may be prepared in advance and refrigerated overnight or at least 3 hours before serving. Or, the complete pie can be frozen in advance, then thawed overnight in the refrigerator before being served cold.

Special equipment: 9-inch pie plate; grater; strainer; cup; double boiler; electric mixer; whisk; optional: large mixing bowl containing ice cubes and cold water; rubber scraper; medium-sized bowl; plastic wrap; chilled bowl and beater for whipping cream.

Chilling time: Crumb crust: 20 minutes minimum; filled pie: 3 hours minimum.

Quantity: One 9-inch pie.

9-inch Graham Cracker or Graham-Nut
    Crust (page 72)

Filling

3½ lemons, for 3 tablespoons grated zest
    and ½ cup freshly squeezed juice;
    plus grated zest of ½ lemon (1½
    teaspoons) reserved for garnish
1 envelope (2 teaspoons) unflavored
    gelatin
¼ cup cold water
2 eggs, separated, plus 1 yolk
1 cup superfine sugar
1 teaspoon cornstarch
3 tablespoons orange-flavored liqueur
    (Grand Marnier, Cointreau)
A pinch of salt
½ cup heavy cream
2 tablespoons confectioners' sugar, sifted

1. Prepare the Graham Cracker or Graham-Nut Crumb Crust and set it in the refrigerator to chill while you prepare the filling. Grate the lemons, reserving about 1½ teaspoons zest to garnish the completed pie and putting the rest in a cup or small bowl. Squeeze the lemons, strain the juice, and add to the zest in the cup. Set aside.

2. In the top of a double boiler, sprinkle the gelatin over the cold water, stir, and let the gelatin sit, to soften, about 2 minutes. Then set over hot water on medium heat and stir until the gelatin dissolves.

3. Put the 3 egg yolks in the bowl of an electric mixer and the two whites in another bowl. Add the sugar to the yolks and beat about 5 minutes, until thick and light colored, and the mixture forms a flat ribbon, falling back upon itself when the beater is lifted. (*Note:* If the mixture seems too dry and granular to become creamy after beating 3 minutes, add 2 or 3 teaspoons water and continue beating.)

4. Add the cornstarch to lemon juice and zest. Stir until the cornstarch is dissolved, then remove the top of the double boiler from the heat and pour the

lemon-cornstarch into the melted gelatin. Whisk well. Little by little, whisk in the egg-sugar mixture, then set the pan back over medium heat and cook *over* (not in) hot water, whisking constantly, about 9 to 12 minutes, or until the mixture thickens enough to coat a spoon. Stir in the liqueur and cook about 1 minute longer. Do not boil. Remove from the heat and spoon into a clean, cool medium-sized bowl.

5. To chill the lemon mixture, set it into a larger bowl containing ice water. Whisk about 10 to 15 minutes until it feels thick, will mound on a spoon, and looks like it is beginning to set—about the consistency of raw egg whites. Immediately remove it from the ice water. Do not chill the mixture until it sets hard. (*Note:* The ice water speeds the chilling process, but if you are not in a hurry, you can simply refrigerate the mixture about 30 minutes, stirring occasionally until it cools and thickens; do not let it set completely.)

6. When the lemon mixture reaches the correct consistency, set it aside while you whip the egg whites with a pinch of salt until stiff peaks form. Use a chilled bowl and chilled beater to whip the cream to soft peaks, then add the confectioners' sugar and whip the cream medium-stiff. Fold the lemon mixture, a little at a time, into the cream, then into the whites. Spoon the filling into prepared shell. Garnish with the reserved lemon zest. Refrigerate to set at least 3 hours. When the top of the pie is set, cover it with plastic wrap to protect the flavor, especially if the pie will be refrigerated longer. Serve directly from the refrigerator.

GRASSHOPPER PIE

This elegant company pie has an attractive green color, a richly mellow mint-chocolate flavor, and a creamy texture enhanced by the addition of grated solid chocolate. It is traditionally served with a chocolate crumb crust, but a nut or graham cracker crust goes equally well. To ensure the best flavor, use the best quality liqueur possible.

(*Note:* This recipe is prepared as a true Bavarian cream set with gelatin, unlike some Grasshopper Pie recipes, which are set with melted marshmallows.)

Advance preparation: The crumb crust may be prepared ahead and frozen. The complete pie may be prepared in advance and refrigerated overnight, or the pie may be frozen, then thawed overnight in the refrigerator. Garnish shortly before serving.

Special equipment: 9-inch pie plate; small saucepan; large mixing bowl containing ice cubes and cold water; chilled mixing bowl and beaters for whipping cream; rubber scraper; wax paper; plastic wrap; pastry bag fitted with ½-inch star tip, or spoon and fork, for applying whipped cream.

Chilling time: Crumb crust: 30 minutes minimum; filled pie: 3 hours minimum, or overnight for convenience.

Quantity: One 9-inch pie.

9-inch Chocolate Wafer or Chocolate Almond Crumb Crust (page 74) or other crumb crust of your choice

Filling
¾ envelope (1½ teaspoons) unflavored gelatin
1⅓ cups heavy cream
¼ cup granulated sugar
4 egg yolks
¼ cup crème de cacao
¼ cup green crème de menthe
2 tablespoons grated unsweetened chocolate

Topping
½ cup heavy cream
1 tablespoon confectioners' sugar, sifted
1 teaspoon green crème de menthe

Garnish
Chocolate Leaves (page 116) or Curls (page 118), or additional grated chocolate

1. Prepare the Chocolate Wafer or Chocolate-Almond Crumb Crust and set in the refrigerator to chill while you prepare the filling. Sprinkle the gelatin over ⅓ cup heavy cream in small saucepan and let it sit about 2 minutes to soften. Then set over low heat and stir constantly until the gelatin is completely dissolved. Set aside.

2. In a mixing bowl, combine the sugar and egg yolks and beat until thick and light colored. Stir in both liqueurs and the dissolved gelatin. Set this bowl into a bowl of ice water and whisk 10 to 15 minutes until the mixture feels thick, mounds on the spoon, and looks as if it is beginning to set—about the

consistency of raw egg whites. Remove it from the ice water. Do not allow it to set hard. The ice water speeds this process, but if you are not in a hurry, you can simply leave the mixture in the refrigerator until it cools and thickens; however, do not let it set completely.

3. Grate the chocolate onto a piece of wax paper and set it aside. With chilled bowl and chilled beaters, whip the remaining 1 cup heavy cream until stiff. Fold the cooled and thickened gelatin mixture into the whipped cream. Fold in the grated chocolate. Spoon the mixture into the prepared shell. Cover with plastic wrap to protect the flavor and chill at least 3 hours to set. Or chill overnight, or top with plastic wrap and fast-freeze; then when firm, wrap airtight with foil and store in the freezer. Defrost overnight in refrigerator before serving.

4. Shortly before serving, whip the 1/2 cup heavy cream until soft peaks form. Add the sugar and crème de menthe (green will tint your cream; if you prefer white cream, use white crème de menthe or peppermint extract). Whip until the cream forms stiff peaks. Spoon it onto the pie, or pipe rosettes through a pastry bag fitted with a star tip. Garnish with Chocolate Leaves or Chocolate Curls or simply grate some solid chocolate over the cream. Serve cold, directly from the refrigerator.

RASPBERRY BAVARIAN CREAM PIE

This delightful summertime pie is rich and creamy, light but with a full fruit flavor. Serve it garnished with rosettes of raspberry liqueur-flavored whipped cream and topped with whole fresh berries.

You can be creative with this recipe and substitute different berries or whole fruit purée. Or prepare the recipe in the form of eight 4½-inch tartlets.

Advance preparation: The crumb crust can be prepared ahead and frozen, or the complete pie can be prepared in advance and refrigerated overnight. Garnish with whipped cream shortly before serving.

Special equipment: 9-inch pie plate (or 8 tartlets, 4½ inches wide); enamel or stainless steel heavy-bottom saucepan; strainer; large mixing bowl filled with ice cubes and cold water; chilled mixing bowl and beater for whipping cream; rubber scraper; plastic wrap; pastry bag fitted with ½-inch star tip, or spoon for applying whipped cream.

Chilling time: For crumb crust: minimum 30 minutes; for filled pie: 3 hours minimum, or overnight for convenience.

Quantity: One 9-inch pie or eight 4½-inch tartlets.

9-inch Hazelnut or Almond Crumb
Crust (page 74) or other crumb
crust of your choice (or tartlet pans
lined with crumb crust)

Filling

1½ envelopes (1 tablespoon) unflavored
gelatin
¼ cup cold water
½ cup boiling water
1½ tablespoons lemon juice
⅛ to ¼ cup granulated sugar, depending
upon sweetness of fruit
¼ teaspoon salt
1 cup fresh raspberry purée, sieved; or 1
(10 ounce) package frozen raspberries,
thawed, drained, and sieved (use
fruit and juice to make 1 cup)
3 tablespoons fruit-flavored liqueur (for
raspberry pie use Chambord
raspberry liqueur or double crème
de cassis)
¾ cup heavy cream

Topping

½ cup heavy cream
1 tablespoon confectioners' sugar, sifted
2 tablespoons fruit-flavored liqueur
(same as in pie)
½ cup fresh whole berries, washed and
dried, for garnish

1. Prepare Hazelnut or Almond Crumb Crust and set in refrigerator to chill while you prepare the filling. Sprinkle the gelatin over the cold water in a small enamel or stainless steel heavy-bottom saucepan. Let it sit 3 or 4 minutes to soften, then stir in ½ cup boiling water and stir until dissolved. Stir in the lemon juice, sugar, salt, and berry purée. Taste and add more sugar if necessary. Set the pan over low heat and stir well until the sugar is dissolved.

2. Transfer the fruit mixture to a medium-sized bowl and stir in the fruit-flavored liqueur. Set the bowl over ice water and stir or whisk for 10 to 15 minutes, until the mixture feels thick, mounds on the spoon, and looks as if it is beginning

to set—about the consistency of raw egg whites. Remove it from the ice water. Do not allow it to set hard. The ice water speeds this process, but if you are not in a hurry, you can simply leave the mixture in the refrigerator until it cools and thickens; however, do not let it set completely.

3. With a chilled bowl and chilled beaters, whip the ¾ cup heavy cream until *nearly* stiff. Fold the whipped cream into the cooled and thickened raspberry mixture. Spoon the filling into the prepared shell. Cover with plastic wrap to protect the flavor and chill at least 3 hours, or overnight.

Shortly before serving, whip the ½ cup heavy cream until soft peaks form. Add the confectioners' sugar and 2 tablespoons of the same liqueur used in the pie. Beat to stiff peaks, and spoon into a decorative ring around the edge of the pie. Or pipe rosettes of cream through a pastry bag fitted with a star tip. Garnish with whole berries set into the whipped cream.

NESSELRODE PIE

Often served at Christmas time, this very rich pie contains chopped candied fruit as well as whipped cream and rum. It is a 10-inch pie that really serves ten, because the richness dictates small servings. For the holidays, serve it topped with whipped cream rosettes trimmed with red and green candied cherries.

Advance preparation: The Graham-Nut crust can be prepared ahead and frozen; the complete pie may be prepared in advance and refrigerated overnight. Or the pie may be frozen in advance, then thawed overnight in refrigerator. Garnish shortly before serving.

Special equipment: 10-inch pie plate; 2-quart heavy-bottom enamel or stainless steel saucepan; large mixing bowl containing tray of ice cubes and cold water; rubber scraper; chilled mixing bowl and beaters for whipping cream; plastic wrap; pastry bag fitted with ½-inch star tip or spoon and fork, for applying whipped cream.

Chilling time: Crumb crust: 30 minutes minimum (or bake 8 minutes, then chill); filled pie: 3 hours minimum, or overnight for convenience, or freeze 4 hours or longer.

Quantity: One 10-inch pie.

> *10-inch Graham-Nut Crust (page 73)*
> *prepared with 1¼ cup crumbs and*
> *¾ cup ground walnuts plus ⅓ cup*
> *sugar and 7 tablespoons melted*
> *butter. Bake as directed, or chill*
> *until firm*

Filling

2/3 cup mixed candied fruit, chopped
    (or 1/3 cup mixed fruit plus 1/3 cup
    candied cherries)
Optional: 1 or 2 tablespoons crystallized
    ginger, chopped fine
3 tablespoons dark rum
1/2 cup plus 2 tablespoons granulated
    sugar
1/4 teaspoon salt
2 tablespoons cornstarch
2 envelopes (4 teaspoons) unflavored
    gelatin
3 eggs
1 1/3 cups milk
1 teaspoon vanilla extract
1 cup heavy cream

Topping

1/2 cup heavy cream
2 tablespoons confectioners' sugar, sifted
1 tablespoon dark rum
Chocolate Leaves (page 116) or Curls
    (page 118) or candied red and
    green cherries, for garnish

1. Prepare Graham-Nut Crust as directed above. In a small bowl, combine the candied fruit and ginger with the rum and set it aside to macerate.

2. In a saucepan, combine 1/2 cup of the granulated sugar, the salt, cornstarch, and gelatin. Stir to break up lumps. Separate the eggs (page 31), putting the yolks into a mixing bowl and the whites into the bowl of an electric mixer. Measure the milk into the yolks and whisk until blended. Then whisk the milk-yolks into the sugar-cornstarch mixture.

3. Set the saucepan over medium heat and whisk constantly for about 5 or 6 minutes, until the mixture thickens, smooths, and comes to a bubbling boil. Stir constantly with a wooden spoon while boiling for 1 full minute. Lift the pan from the heat from time to time to avoid scorching. When sufficiently cooked, the mixture should generously coat the spoon. Remove from the heat. Stir in the vanilla extract and fruit-rum mixture. Turn into a clean bowl and set into a larger bowl of ice water. Whisk the mixture until it feels thick, mounds on the spoon, and looks as if it is beginning to set—about the consistency of raw

egg whites. Remove it from the ice water. Do not allow it to set hard. The ice water speeds this process, but if you are not in a hurry, you can simply leave the mixture in the refrigerator until it cools and thickens; however, do not let it set completely.

4. Beat the egg whites until fluffy, then add the remaining 2 tablespoons granulated sugar. Beat until stiff peaks form. In chilled bowl with chilled beaters, whip the 1 cup cream until medium-stiff peaks form. Fold the cooled and thickened fruit mixture into the cream, then into the whites. Spoon into the prepared shell, cover with plastic wrap to protect the flavor, and refrigerate at least 3 hours, to set. Or fast freeze, then when firm, wrap airtight with foil and store in the freezer. Defrost overnight in the refrigerator before serving.

5. Shortly before serving, whip the ½ cup cream to soft peaks. Add sugar and rum and whip stiff. Decorate the pie with rosettes of cream piped through a pastry bag fitted with a star tip, or spoon mounds of cream around the pie and stripe them with a fork. Garnish with Chocolate Leaves or Curls or quartered pieces of red and green candied cherries arranged in flower-petal groupings. Serve cold, from the refrigerator.

QUICK MOCHA CREAM PIE

This is one of the easiest, quickest, and best-tasting chocolate pies ever, made basically of melted chocolate folded into coffee-flavored whipped cream. The only way it could be simpler to prepare is to have a crumb crust or prebaked pastry shell in your freezer. For entertaining, make the pie days or weeks ahead and freeze it, but thaw it overnight in the refrigerator before serving. Or if you prefer a texture closer to ice cream, remove it from the freezer about 10 minutes before serving. Add the whipped cream topping shortly before serving. The recipe is a favorite of Michele Peasley, good friend, professional baker, and tester of many of the recipes in this book.

Advance preparation: The prepared crumb shell can be made ahead and frozen (page 53); the completely filled pie can be prepared and frozen until needed, or thawed overnight in refrigerator before serving, or frozen until 10 minutes before serving.

Special equipment: 9-inch pie plate; double boiler; electric mixer; chilled bowl and beater for whipping cream; rubber scraper; optional: pastry bag fitted with ½-inch star tip for decorating.

Chilling time: Crumb crust: 30 minutes; filled pie: about 3 to 4 hours in refrigerator, or 2 hours in freezer, or longer for convenience.

Quantity: One 9-inch pie.

9-inch Chocolate Wafer Crumb Crust
    (page 74), chilled, or other crumb
    crust of your choice, or one
    completely prebaked 9-inch pie
    shell made with pastry of your
    choice

Filling

8 ounces semisweet chocolate, or one 8-
    ounce semisweet or milk chocolate
    candy bar
1 cup heavy cream
3 teaspoons instant espresso coffee
    dissolved in 2 tablespoons hot water

Topping

½ cup heavy cream
2 teaspoons instant espresso coffee
    dissolved in 2 tablespoons heavy
    cream
2 tablespoons confectioners' sugar, sifted

1. Prepare the crumb shell as directed and chill until the filling is prepared.

2. To make the filling, measure the chocolate into the top of a double boiler and melt over hot (not boiling) water. Remove from the heat just before completely melted, and stir to complete the melting process. Set aside, off the heat, to cool slightly while you prepare the cream.

3. In a chilled bowl with chilled beaters, whip the heavy cream until it fluffs softly. Add the dissolved coffee and beat until the peaks hold their shape well; stop beating before the cream feels really stiff. Test the temperature of the chocolate: It should be comfortable to the touch when you stick your finger into it (80° to 90°F) and appear soft, satiny, and easy to stir. If it has chilled and stiffened, set it over a pan of warm water for a few seconds while you stir it soft again. (*Note:* If the chocolate is too hot, it will melt the whipped cream; if too cold, it will cause the cream to become grainy when folded in.)

Little by little, gently fold and stir the chocolate into the coffee cream until it is evenly colored. Don't worry if a few flecks of solid chocolate are visible, this only adds texture to the cream.

4. Spoon the mixture into the prepared shell, and refrigerate several hours before serving, or place the pie in the freezer, uncovered, to set. When hard, wrap airtight in foil and store in the freezer. Thaw overnight in the refrigerator

or, for an ice cream texture, leave it frozen until 10 minutes before serving. The pie should be served cold.

5. To make the topping, whip the cream until it holds soft peaks. Add the dissolved coffee and sifted sugar and beat until the cream holds firm peaks. Spread in a ring around the edge of the pie, or pipe a decorative design through a pastry bag fitted with a star tip. Garnish with grated unsweetened chocolate or Chocolate Leaves (page 116) or Curls (page 118). (*Note:* The flavor of the cream is best if added shortly before serving; however, you can add whipped cream to the pie before freezing.)

VARIATION:

Quick Chocolate Cream Pie. Prepare Quick Mocha Cream Pie but omit the coffee in the filling and in the whipped cream.

CHOCOLATE HONEY CHIFFON PIE

There are two surprises in this light, creamy pie: the honey, which adds richness to the chocolate flavor, and the lack of sugar and cream, which means fewer calories than in other chiffon pies (not exactly dietetic, but the thought is there).

Advance preparation: The crumb crust can be prepared ahead and frozen (as can the completely prebaked pastry shell, if you prefer). The complete pie may be prepared in advance and refrigerated overnight.
Special equipment: 9-inch pie plate; rubber scraper; electric mixer with largest balloon beater; double boiler; plastic wrap.
Chilling time: Crumb crust: 30 minutes, minimum; filled pie: 3 hours minimum or overnight for convenience.
Quantity: One 9-inch pie.

> *9-inch Chocolate-Almond Crumb Crust*
> *(page 74), or completely prebaked*
> *9-inch pastry shell made with Basic*
> *All-Purpose Flaky Pastry, Nut*
> *Pastry Variation (almond, page 35)*

Filling
2 eggs
½ cup sour cream
6 ounces semisweet chocolate

¼ teaspoon salt
⅓ cup honey

Topping
*Chocolate Curls (page 118) or grated
    chocolate*

1. Prepare the Chocolate-Almond Crumb Crust and set in the refrigerator to chill while you prepare the filling. Separate the eggs (page 31), and place the yolks in a small bowl and the whites in the bowl of an electric mixer fitted with the largest balloon beater available. Spoon the sour cream into a measuring cup and place near the stove along with egg yolks; you'll need them handy when working with the double boiler.

2. Melt the chocolate in the top of a double boiler over hot (not boiling) water. While the chocolate is melting, begin preparation of the egg whites. Add salt to the whites; measure the honey, and set it nearby.

Beat the whites until stiff but not dry, then very gradually add honey while continuing to beat until stiff peaks form. Do not despair if the whites look soft after you add the honey. Beat 4 or 5 minutes, and they will stiffen beautifully. The bigger the beater and the more powerful the mixer the easier and quicker this job becomes; but no matter what type beater you use, it will work if you just keep at it.

3. As soon as the chocolate is melted, remove it from heat, add the yolks, and whisk vigorously. Then replace over heat and whisk for about 30 seconds or slightly more, until the mixture forms a ball and pulls away from the sides of the pan. Immediately remove the top of the double boiler from the heat. Stir in the sour cream and beat until smooth.

4. When the egg whites are stiff, gently fold them into the chocolate mixture, adding a little chocolate at a time to the whites. Spoon the mixture into the prepared shell and cover with plastic wrap to protect the flavor. Chill in the refrigerator at least 3 hours or overnight, to set. Garnish with Chocolate Curls or grated chocolate and serve cold, directly from the refrigerator.

AMARETTO CHOCOLATE PIE

I first tasted this creamy chocolate chiffon pie at a parents' potluck supper at the Washington, Connecticut, Montessori School. It confirmed my opinion that Montessori families appreciate excellence in cuisine as well as in education. This pie will satisfy even the most jaded chocoholic. For best flavor, use the finest quality amaretto liqueur, or if you prefer, substitute Kahlua, or another coffee liqueur.

Advance preparation: The crumb crust can be prepared ahead and frozen; the complete pie may be prepared in advance and refrigerated overnight. Or the pie may be frozen in advance, then thawed overnight in the refrigerator. Garnish shortly before serving.

Special equipment: 10-inch pie plate; double boiler; electric mixer; large mixing bowl containing tray of ice cubes and cold water; rubber scraper; chilled bowl and beaters for whipping cream; plastic wrap; pastry bag fitted with a ½-inch star tip, or spoon and fork, for applying whipped cream.

Chilling time: Crumb crust: 30 minutes minimum (or bake at 350°F for 8 minutes); filled pie: 3 hours minimum, or overnight for convenience.

Quantity: One 10-inch pie, 12 servings; it is very rich.

10-inch Chocolate-Almond Crust (page 74) made with 1 cup crumbs and ¾ cup ground almonds, plus 2 tablespoons sugar and 7 tablespoons melted butter

Filling
1 envelope (2 teaspoons) unflavored gelatin
1 cup sugar
⅛ teaspoon salt
2 eggs
1 cup milk
12 ounces semisweet chocolate chips or block chocolate, chopped fine
¼ cup amaretto liqueur
½ to 1 teaspoon almond extract, depending upon the flavor strength of the amaretto
1 teaspoon vanilla extract
1 cup heavy cream

Optional Topping
Chocolate Leaves (page 116) or Curls (page 118), or grated chocolate, for garnish
½ cup heavy cream
1 tablespoon confectioners' sugar, sifted
1 tablespoon amaretto liqueur

1. Prepare the Chocolate-Almond Crust as directed, and set in the refrigerator to chill while you prepare the filling. In the top of a double boiler, combine the gelatin, ¼ cup of the sugar, and salt. Separate the eggs (page 31), placing the yolks in the top of the double boiler and the whites in the bowl of an electric mixer. Add the milk to the yolks, then whisk to combine well and remove lumps.

2. Place top of double boiler over (not in) hot water and cook, stirring with a wooden spoon 7 to 10 minutes or until thickened enough to coat the spoon. Remove from the heat and add the chocolate, stirring until melted. Then stir in the amaretto liqueur and the almond and vanilla extract.

3. Turn the mixture into a clean bowl and set into a bowl of ice water. Stir 10 to 15 minutes, until the mixture feels thick and mounds on the spoon. It will look as if it is beginning to set—about the consistency of raw egg whites. Immediately remove it from the ice water and set aside. Do not allow mixture to set hard. The ice water speeds this process, but if you are not in a hurry, you can simply leave the mixture in the refrigerator about 30 minutes until it cools and thickens; however, do not let it set completely.

4. Beat the egg whites until fluffy, then add ½ cup of sugar and beat 5 to 10 minutes until stiff. Set aside. With chilled bowl and beaters, whip the cream until soft peaks form; add the remaining ¼ cup sugar, then beat stiff.

Fold the cooled, thickened (but not set) chocolate mixture into the cream, then into the whites. Spoon into the prepared shell. Cover with plastic wrap to protect the flavor, then chill at least 3 hours, to set. Or fast freeze; when firm, wrap airtight with foil and store in the freezer. Defrost overnight in the refrigerator before serving.

5. Shortly before serving, grate chocolate over the pie top. Or whip ½ cup heavy cream with sugar and amaretto until stiff, and decorate the pie with rosettes of cream piped through a pastry bag fitted with a star tip, or spoon mounds of cream around the pie and stripe them with a fork. Garnish with grated chocolate, or Chocolate Leaves or Curls. Serve cold, from the refrigerator.

CHOCOLATE MOUSSE-CREME DE MENTHE PIE

A grand finale dinner party dessert! The rich velvety texture, heavenly flavor, and elegant presentation of this pie belie the fact that it's a breeze to prepare ahead and store in the freezer. Predictably, chocolate lovers will swoon, but the rest of the world will enjoy it too, because the mint flavor cuts the sweetness of the traditional chocolate mousse. Serve topped with whipped cream rosettes and chocolate leaves.

Advance preparation: The chocolate crumb crust may be prepared ahead and frozen. The complete pie can be prepared ahead and refrigerated overnight. Or it can be frozen and thawed overnight in the refrigerator. Garnish with whipped cream shortly before serving.

Special equipment: 10-inch pie plate; double boiler; mixing bowl and beater chilled in refrigerator or freezer for whipped cream; rubber scraper; pastry bag fitted with ½-inch star tip for decorating; plastic wrap.

Chilling time: Crumb crust: 30 minutes minimum; filled pie: 6 hours in refrigerator or 2 hours in freezer, minimum.

Quantity: One 10-inch pie.

> *10-inch Chocolate Wafer or Chocolate-*
> *Almond Crumb Crust (page 74)*
> *prepared with 1¾ cups crumbs and*
> *½ cup melted butter*

Filling
12 ounces semisweet chocolate
½ cup unsalted butter
4 eggs
7 tablespoons green crème de menthe
2 tablespoons confectioners' sugar, sifted
½ cup heavy cream
¼ teaspoon peppermint extract

Garnish
½ cup heavy cream
2 tablespoons confectioners' sugar, sifted
2 teaspoons crème de menthe
Chocolate Leaves (page 116) or Curls
* (page 118)*

1. Prepare the Chocolate Wafer or Chocolate-Almond Crumb Crust and set in the refrigerator to chill while you prepare the filling. Measure the chocolate and butter into the top of a double boiler and set to melt over hot (not boiling) water. Stir to blend, then remove from the heat.

2. Separate the eggs (page 31). Place the whites in a mixing bowl and vigorously whisk each yolk into the melted chocolate mixture. Stir 6 tablespoons of the crème de menthe into the yolk-chocolate mixture and set aside to cool.

3. Beat the egg whites until foamy, then add 1 tablespoon of the confectioners' sugar and beat until stiff peaks form. In a chilled bowl with chilled beaters, whip the cream until soft peaks form. Add the remaining 1 tablespoon confectioners' sugar, and stir in the remaining 1 tablespoon crème de menthe along with the peppermint extract. Whip until nearly—but not completely—stiff.

4. To lighten the chocolate mixture, stir in about 3 tablespoons each of the whipped cream and whipped whites. Then fold in all the remaining whipped whites and whipped cream. Spoon the chocolate mixture into the prepared shell, cover with plastic wrap to protect the flavor, and refrigerate at least 6 hours, or overnight. Or freeze the pie ahead and thaw it overnight in the refrigerator before serving cold.

5. Shortly before serving, garnish the pie. Beat the cream with the sugar and crème de menthe until stiff. Place the green-tinted cream in a pastry bag and pipe rosettes around the pie; or, spoon the cream in a circle covering about 2/3 of the center of the pie, leaving a ring of plain filling exposed at the edge. Stripe the spooned-on cream with fork tines. Decorate with Chocolate Leaves or Curls, or grate chocolate over the cream.

(*Note:* Since this is a mousse and not stiffened with gelatin, in very hot weather it is best to serve it directly from the refrigerator. At room temperature, it may become too soft to slice neatly. Return leftovers to the refrigerator or freezer.)

ORANGE CHOCOLATE SILK PIE

The orange lightens and refreshes, the chocolate thickens and enriches, and the silk describes the luxurious texture. What more could you ask? This recipe can be prepared as a chiffon pie, or as six individual tartlets.

(*Note:* People have been known to substitute frozen nondairy whipped topping, thawed, for the whipped cream in this recipe. You are on your own.)

Advance preparation: The crumb crust can be prepared ahead and frozen. The complete pie can be prepared a day ahead and refrigerated.

Special equipment: 9-inch pie plate; double boiler; electric mixer; rubber scraper; chilled bowl and beater for whipping cream; plastic wrap; pastry bag fitted with 1/2-inch star tip, or spoon and fork, for applying whipped cream; paring knife.

Chilling time: Crumb crust: 30 minutes minimum; filled pie: 3 hours, or overnight.

Quantity: One 9-inch pie.

9-inch Chocolate Wafer, or Chocolate-
  Almond Crumb Crust (page 74) or
  six 4½-inch tartlets prepared with
  crumb crust

Filling

2 ounces semisweet chocolate, melted
  and cooled
½ cup unsalted butter, at room
  temperature
¾ cup confectioners' sugar, sifted
2 eggs
4 tablespoons orange-flavored liqueur
  (Cointreau, Grand Marnier, etc.)
1 cup heavy cream

Topping

½ cup heavy cream
1 tablespoon confectioners' sugar, sifted
1 tablespoon orange-flavored liqueur
  (same as above)

Garnish

Chocolate Leaves (page 116) or Curls
  (page 118)
Thin-sliced cartwheels of fresh orange

1. Prepare the Chocolate Wafer, or Chocolate Nut-Crumb Crust (page 74) and set in the refrigerator to chill while you prepare the filling. Measure the chocolate into a double boiler and melt over hot (not boiling) water. Stir and set aside to cool.

2. With an electric mixer, cream together the butter and ¾ cup confectioners' sugar until fluffy. Blend in the melted and cooled chocolate. Add the eggs one at a time, beating a full 5 minutes after each addition. Don't cheat; the texture developed in the beating is important. Beat in the orange liqueur.

3. In a chilled bowl with chilled beaters, whip the cream until medium-stiff peaks form. Fold the whipped cream into the chocolate mixture. Spoon into the prepared crumb crust. Cover with plastic wrap to protect the flavor and chill in the refrigerator at least 3 hours, to set.

4. Shortly before serving, whip the ½ cup of cream until soft peaks form. Add the sugar and liqueur and beat stiff. Decorate the pie with rosettes of cream piped through a pastry bag fitted with a star tip, or spoon mounds of cream around the edge of the pie and stripe them with a fork. Garnish with chocolate curls or leaves combined with very thin slices of orange cut through to the center at one point, then twisted in opposite directions to form an S curve. Refrigerate leftovers.

BLACK BOTTOM PIE

This traditional pie has something for everybody: a creamy chocolate layer on the bottom and a vanilla-rum-scented Bavarian cream on top. Neither layer is excessively rich, and the total effect is very agreeable.

The technique is simple once you understand the plan: First you prepare a vanilla pastry cream, then you divide this, adding chocolate to one part and gelatin, rum, and stiffly beaten egg whites to the other. Serve garnished with whipped cream rosettes and Chocolate Leaves or Curls.

Advance preparation: The completely prebaked pastry shell can be prepared ahead and frozen; the complete pie can be prepared in advance and refrigerated overnight. Garnish shortly before serving.

Special equipment: 9-inch pie plate; 2-quart heavy-bottom enamel or stainless steel saucepan; electric mixer; large bowl containing ice cubes and cold water; rubber scraper; plastic wrap; pastry bag fitted with a ½-inch star tip, or spoon.

Baking time: Completely prebaked pastry shell: 425°F for 10 minutes with pie weights; 350°F for 15 to 20 minutes empty.

Chilling time: Filled pie: 3 hours minimum or overnight for convenience.

Quantity: One 9-inch pie.

*Completely prebaked 9-inch pie shell
made with Basic All-Purpose Flaky
Pastry, Sherry Pastry Variation (page
35), or other pastry of your choice*

Filling
*¾ cup granulated sugar
1 tablespoon cornstarch
3 eggs*

2 cups milk

6 ounces semisweet chocolate, fine-
   chopped, or 1 cup semisweet
   morsels

1 envelope (2 teaspoons) unflavored
   gelatin

¼ cup cold water

2½ tablespoons dark rum

1 teaspoon vanilla extract

Topping

½ cup heavy cream

1 tablespoon confectioners' sugar, sifted

1 tablespoon dark rum

Garnish

Chocolate Curls (page 118) or Leaves
   (page 116), or grated chocolate

1. Preheat the oven to 425°F. Prepare the pastry, roll it out, and line the pie plate (page 38). Trim a ¾-inch pastry overhang, fold the edge inward, and flute as desired (page 44). Make sure the rim is high enough to contain the generous filling. Prick the bottom with a fork, chill until firm, then completely blind-bake (page 42). Cool on a wire rack; chill before filling.

2. In a saucepan, combine and stir ½ cup of the sugar with the cornstarch. Separate the eggs (page 31), putting the yolks in the pan with the sugar and cornstarch and the whites in the bowl of an electric mixer. Add the milk to the yolks and whisk well to avoid lumps.

3. Set the pan over medium heat and stir or whisk constantly about 5 minutes, until the mixture thickens and comes to a full rolling boil. Lift the pan from the heat from time to time to avoid scorching. Stir and boil one full minute. Remove from the heat.

4. Measure the chocolate into a small bowl and stir in 1 generous cup of the hot custard. Stir vigorously until the chocolate melts and cools somewhat. Then pour this mixture into the prepared pastry shell and set it in the refrigerator to chill. This is the famous "black bottom."

5. Sprinkle the gelatin over the cold water in bowl and let it soften about 2 minutes. Add the softened gelatin to the remaining vanilla custard in the saucepan. Set the pan over medium heat and stir constantly until the gelatin dissolves; test the custard by pinching it between your fingers to be sure it is not

grainy. Remove from the heat and stir in the rum and vanilla extract. Turn the custard into a mixing bowl and set into a large bowl of ice water. Whisk 10 to 15 minutes, until the mixture feels thick, mounds on the spoon, and looks as if it is beginning to set—about the consistency of raw egg whites. Remove it from the ice water. However, do not allow it to set completely.

6. Beat the egg whites in the electric mixer until soft peaks form. Add the remaining ¼ cup sugar, a little at a time, beating after each addition until stiff peaks form, then fold in the cooled and thickened custard. Spoon over the chocolate layer in the prepared pastry shell. Cover with plastic wrap to protect the flavor and refrigerate at least 3 hours, or overnight.

7. Shortly before serving, whip the ½ cup of cream, in a chilled bowl with chilled beaters, until soft peaks form. Add the sugar and rum and whip stiff. Decorate the pie with rosettes of cream piped through a pastry bag fitted with a star tip, or spoon mounds of cream around the pie and stripe with a fork. Garnish with Chocolate Curls or Leaves, or grate chocolate over the cream. Serve cold, directly from the refrigerator. Refrigerate leftovers.

QUINCE PUDDING PIE

This unusual dessert is my autumn creation, inspired by some quince purée left after making quince paste, that glorious specialty of the south of France. The pie has the texture of a creamy pudding, though it is really a chiffon pie without gelatin—or, to be strictly correct, a fluff pie, which is the name farm women a century ago gave to pies lightened and risen only with stiffly beaten egg whites. The tartness of the quince is mellowed by baking with spices and honey in a cream custard; the flavor is rich and somewhat reminiscent of home-made apple sauce with heavy cream on top.

This pie is especially good served warm on a cold winter night, so if you are making quince paste or quince jam in the fall, freeze several 1 cup portions of unsweetened purée for later use in this recipe.

Advance preparation: The unbaked pastry shell can be prepared ahead and frozen. For best texture and flavor bake the pie on morning of the day it is to be served.

Special equipment: 9-inch pie plate; 2-quart heavy-bottom enamel or stainless steel saucepan; food mill; electric mixer (with 2 bowls if possible); rubber scraper; stainless steel knife.

Baking time: 400°F for 15 minutes; 350°F for 30 to 35 minutes.

Quantity: One 9-inch pie.

Unbaked 9-inch pastry shell made with
Basic All-Purpose Flaky Pastry
(page 34) or Butter-Lard Pastry (page
63), or other pastry of your choice

Filling

2 large ripe quinces (or 1 cup
  unsweetened quince purée)
3 eggs
3 tablespoons honey
½ cup granulated sugar
2½ tablespoons all-purpose flour
⅛ teaspoon salt
2 tablespoons butter or margarine, at
  room temperature
⅛ teaspoon each cinnamon and nutmeg
1 cup heavy or light cream
  (depending upon how rich you
  wish the pie to be)

1. Prepare the pastry, roll it out, and line the pie plate (page 38). Trim a ¾-inch overhang, fold over the edge, and flute as desired (page 44). Be sure to make the rim high enough to contain the generous filling. Set the pastry-lined pan in the refrigerator to chill while you prepare the filling. Preheat the oven to 400°F.

2. To make the quince purée, wash and quarter the quinces. Place them in a saucepan with about ⅓ cup water. Cover and cook on medium heat until the quinces are tender. Drain. Put the fruit through a food mill. You should have about 1 cup pulp. (*Note:* Homemade unsweetened apple sauce can be substituted for the quince purée or used to augment your purée supply.)

3. Separate the eggs (page 31), putting the whites into a small bowl and the yolks into the large bowl of an electric mixer. To the yolks, add the honey, sugar, flour, salt, and butter or margarine. Beat until creamy. Add the quince purée, cinnamon and nutmeg, and beat well. Slowly stir in the cream, then beat until combined; the mixture will be thick and creamy.

If you do not have 2 bowls for your mixer, turn quince mixture into a clean bowl and wash the mixer bowl in order to use it for the egg whites.

4. Place egg whites in a clean bowl. Add a pinch of salt, stir, then dip a pastry brush into whites and brush it over the bottom of the chilled pastry to form a moisture-proof coating. With clean beaters, whip the whites until stiff peaks form. Fold the quince mixture little by little into the whites. Spoon into

the prepared pastry shell and bake in the lower third of the preheated oven for 15 minutes. Reduce the heat to 350°F, raise the pie to the center of the oven, and continue baking 30 to 35 minutes longer, until the filling is puffed up and browned on top and a knife inserted in the center comes out clean. Cool on a wire rack. The filling will be high right after baking, but will sink down as the pie cools. Serve warm or cold.

VELVET RUM CREAM PIE

This recipe was shared with me by my sister, Nancy Gold Lieberman. A delectable blend of egg yolks, cream, and rum, it is sinfully rich, and so easy to prepare, you will wish you had made two. It has become a tradition in my family to serve this pie on New Year's Eve as a good luck charm for a sweet New Year.

Advance preparation: The nut-crumb crust can be prepared ahead and frozen; the complete pie can be prepared one day ahead and refrigerated or frozen in advance and thawed overnight in the refrigerator.

Special equipment: 10-inch pie plate; whisk; chilled bowl and beater for whipping cream; large mixing bowl containing ice cubes and cold water; rubber scraper; plastic wrap; pastry bag fitted with ½-inch star tip, or spoon and fork, for applying whipped cream.

Chilling time: Crumb crust: 30 minutes minimum (or bake this crust 8 minutes); filled pie: 4 hours minimum, or overnight.

Quantity: One 10-inch pie.

> *10-inch Graham-Nut Crumb Crust (page 73) prepared with 1 cup graham cracker crumbs and ¾ cup ground almonds plus 5 tablespoons sugar and ½ cup melted butter. Or, one 10-inch completely prebaked pastry shell of your choice*

Filling
1 envelope (2 teaspoons) unflavored gelatin
½ cup cold water
6 egg yolks

1 cup granulated sugar
⅓ cup dark rum
1½ cups heavy cream

Topping
½ cup heavy cream
1 tablespoon confectioners' sugar, sifted
1 tablespoon dark rum
Chocolate Leaves (page 116) or Curls
    (page 118), or grated chocolate

1. Prepare the Graham-Nut Crumb Crust and set it in the refrigerator to chill while you prepare the filling. Sprinkle the gelatin over the cold water in small saucepan. Place over low heat and stir constantly while bringing to just below the boiling point to dissolve the gelatin. Remove from the heat.

2. In a mixing bowl, beat the yolks with the granulated sugar until thick and light-colored and the mixture forms a flat ribbon falling back upon itself when the beater is lifted. Stir in the hot gelatin, which will melt the sugar. Then gradually add the rum while beating slowly.

3. In a chilled bowl with chilled beaters, whip the cream until stiff peaks form. Fold the cream into the gelatin-yolk mixture. Set this bowl into a larger bowl of ice water and whisk for 10 to 15 minutes, until the mixture feels thick, mounds on the spoon, and looks as if it is beginning to set—about the consistency of raw egg whites. Immediately remove this bowl from the ice water; do not allow mixture to set hard. Spoon mixture into the prepared pastry shell. Cover it with plastic wrap to protect the flavor, and chill it at least 4 hours, to set. Or wrap and freeze it, but thaw overnight in the refrigerator before serving cold.

4. Shortly before serving time, whip the ½ cup heavy cream. When soft peaks form, add the sugar and rum (or omit rum if you prefer), then beat the cream medium-stiff. Spoon it into a ring around the edge of the pie or pipe it into rosettes through a pastry bag fitted with a star tip. Decorate with Chocolate Leaves or Curls, or some grated chocolate sprinkled over the cream.

VARIATION:

Eggnog Chiffon Pie. Prepare Velvet Rum Cream Pie but beat 3 egg whites until stiff and fold them into the mixture in step 3 along with 1½ teaspoons vanilla extract and ½ teaspoon freshly grated nutmeg. Sprinkle a little grated nutmeg over the top of the finished pie. The mixture will make one 10-inch pie plus an 8-inch pie or several small tarts.

CHESTNUT MOUSSE PIE

Some years ago Craig Claiborne published a recipe in the *New York Times* for a molded chestnut mousse developed by Marcel Gosselin, former owner of Manhattan's L'Armorique restaurant. As chestnuts are a holiday specialty in my family, I have prepared this recipe many times, ultimately adapting and transforming it into this velvety, rum-scented elegance far too chic to be called simply a pie. Perhaps Mousse en Croûte would be more fitting.

Advance preparation: The completely prebaked pastry or crumb shell can be prepared ahead and frozen. The complete pie can be prepared one day ahead and refrigerated.

Special equipment: 10-inch pie plate; pastry brush; 2-quart heavy-bottom enamel or stainless steel saucepan; strainer set over a bowl; chilled bowl and beaters for whipping cream; rubber scraper; pastry bag fitted with ½-inch star tip, or spoon, for applying whipped cream; plastic wrap.

Baking time: For pastry shell: 425°F for 10 minutes lined with pie weights; 350°F for 15 to 20 minutes empty.

Chilling time: Filled pie: 3 hours minimum, or overnight.

Quantity: One 10-inch pie.

Completely prebaked 10-inch pastry shell made with Basic All-Purpose Flaky Pastry, Nut Pastry Variation (almond, page 35), or Nut Crumb Crust (page 74)

Egg glaze: 1 egg white beaten with 1 tablespoon water

Filling

1 (15½ ounce) can unsweetened chestnut purée

2 cups milk

½ cup plus 2 tablespoons granulated sugar

2 envelopes (4 teaspoons) unflavored gelatin

1 teaspoon vanilla extract

6 egg yolks (reserve 1 egg white for the glaze)

3 tablespoons dark rum
1 cup heavy cream

Topping
½ cup heavy cream
1 tablespoon confectioners' sugar, sifted
1 jar of candied chestnuts in syrup
 (marrons glacés) or Chocolate
 Leaves (page 116) or Curls
 (page 118)

1. Preheat the oven to 425°F. Prepare the pastry, roll it out, and line the pie plate (page 38). Trim a ¾-inch overhang, fold over the edge, and flute as desired (page 44), making a high rim to contain the generous filling. Prick the bottom with a fork, chill pastry until firm, then completely blind-bake (page 42). After removing liner and pie weights, brush moistureproofing egg white glaze over bottom of pastry shell before reducing oven heat to 350°F and baking shell for final 15 to 20 minutes, or until golden brown. Cool on a wire rack. (If you are making the crumb crust instead, prepare as directed in recipe.)

2. In a large saucepan, mash the chestnut purée with a fork. Add the milk and sugar and whisk until fairly smooth. Sprinkle on the gelatin, then set the pan over medium heat and bring to a boil while stirring with a wooden spoon. Don't worry if there are some lumps; the mixture will be strained later. As soon as the mixture reaches a boil, remove it from the heat and stir in the vanilla extract.

3. Beat the yolks together in a mixing bowl. When frothy, stir in about ½ cup of the hot chestnut mixture while whisking constantly (to avoid hard boiling the eggs). Add the warmed yolks back into the hot chestnut mixture, again stirring constantly so the eggs do not poach. Cook, stirring, over medium heat until the mixture thickens slightly. Do not boil. When thick, remove from the heat and stir in the rum. Strain through a sieve set over a bowl. Let mixture cool in refrigerator until thickened but not quite jelled. If by accident jelling occurs, simply set the chestnut mixture over hot water and stir until it softens.

4. Whip the cream until medium-stiff peaks form. Fold the cream into the cooled and thickened (but not jelled) chestnut mixture. Turn into the prepared pastry shell, cover with plastic wrap to protect the flavor, and refrigerate at least 3 hours, until set.

5. Shortly before serving, whip the ½ cup heavy cream in a chilled bowl with chilled beaters. When soft peaks form, add the sugar, then beat stiff. Decorate the pie with rosettes of cream piped through a pastry bag fitted with a star tip, or spoon mounds of cream around the pie and stripe with a fork. Cut the candied chestnuts in halves or quarters and set pieces into the whipped cream. Or garnish with Chocolate Leaves or Curls.

FROZEN PIES

The following four pies are all designed for easy entertaining; they can be prepared well in advance and frozen until a few minutes before serving.

FROZEN MUD PIE

This easy-to-prepare ice cream dessert comes entirely from the freezer, is a perfect last-minute concoction, and tastes infinitely better than its name would suggest.

Advance preparation: Keep an extra crumb or nut-crumb crust on hand in the freezer for making this pie. The crumb shell may be filled with ice cream wrapped, and stored frozen until needed. To serve, simply add Rich Chocolate Sauce (page 118) and whipped cream, if you wish.

Special equipment: 9- or 10-inch pie plate; plastic wrap; foil.

Chilling time: Crust: 30 minutes minimum; filled pie: 2 or 3 hours in freezer, or longer for convenience.

Quantity: One 9- or 10-inch pie.

> *9- or 10-inch Chocolate Wafer or*
> *Chocolate-Pecan Crumb Crust (page*
> *74)*
> *1 quart coffee ice cream (or 1 pint dark*
> *chocolate and 1 pint coffee), left at*

room temperature for about 5
minutes to soften
1 cup pecan halves, broken

Topping
Rich Chocolate Sauce (page 118), warmed
Grated Chocolate (page 118)
Optional: *Sweetened plain or Maple or*
Butterscotch Whipped Cream (page
109)

1. Prepare the crumb shell of your choice and chill it well, or freeze. Soften the ice cream to spreading consistency. Line the shell with ice cream or line with half the ice cream, spread a layer of pecans, then top with the remaining ice cream. If you are using 2 different flavors, put nuts between them. Cover the top of the pie with plastic wrap and fast-freeze until hard.

2. Wrap the pie in freezer foil and store frozen until needed. To serve, bring to room temperature 5 to 10 minutes before slicing. Top with grated semisweet chocolate and serve with warm chocolate sauce and a dollop of flavored whipped cream.

BAKED ALASKA PIE

The mystique of Baked Alaska lingers from the days of ice chest coolers. With today's excellent home freezers the making of this dessert is a breeze, although the magical effect of combining fire and ice is as stunning as ever.

This dazzling finale is really a busy cook's secret weapon: It comes almost entirely from the freezer and is ready to serve in only a few minutes. For best results, the meringue really should be made and baked on the pie immediately before serving, and as the entire process takes no more than 15 minutes, it's good enough to ask your guests to wait for. However, if the last-minute idea makes you feel too pressed, you can complete the entire procedure and return the pie to the freezer before sitting down to dinner. Serve as soon as possible.

Advance preparation: Nearly everything can be made ahead: egg whites separated and frozen, defrosted at room temperature before whipping; pie shell made ahead and frozen; pie shell filled with ice cream, covered airtight, and frozen for a minimum of 4 hours or as long as convenient. Prepare meringue just before serving, for best flavor, or return the pie to the freezer after browning the meringue. Remove from the freezer 10 minutes before serving.

Special equipment: 9- or 10-inch metal pie plate; plastic wrap; electric mixer for meringue; spatula; broiler; pastry bag and ½-inch star tip, only for meringue scrolls or latticework. Optional: wooden board slightly larger than the pie plate to set it on in the oven so heat will not be conducted to pie; aluminum foil.

Quantity: One 9- or 10-inch pie.

> *9- or 10-inch pie shell made of either side-by-side slices of store-bought ladyfingers or sponge cake sprinkled with sweet sherry or brandy or rum, or a completely prebaked pie shell made with the pastry or baked crumb crust of your choice*
>
> *1 quart ice cream, any flavor, or 2 pints different flavors, plus chopped nuts or chopped fruits if desired to spread between the ice cream layers. Let the ice cream stand at room temperature about 5 minutes, to soften enough to spread*
>
> *Meringue Topping: (page 110), made with 4 large egg whites, ¼ teaspoon cream of tartar, a pinch of salt, and ½ cup superfine or granulated sugar*

Optional Garnish
Chopped pistachio nuts or sliced almonds

1. Prepare the cake, crumb, or pastry shell ahead and be sure it is chilled, or frozen, until just before it is lined with ice cream. Bring the ice cream to spreading consistency, then smooth it into the shell. To make different layers, you may need to return the pie to the freezer to harden between each layer. Smooth the top, cover with plastic or foil, and freeze hard—for at least 4 hours, or as long as convenient.

2. Just before serving, preheat the broiler. Prepare Meringue Topping. Use a spatula to spread a smooth ¾-inch thick coating of meringue over the top of the pie and seal it to the edges of the crust and pie plate all around. Then add

the remaining meringue and decorate the pie top by making peaks with the back of a spoon or by piping scrolls or latticework over the top using a pastry bag fitted with a ½-inch star tip. Sprinkle with chopped pistachio nuts or almonds if you wish, and set the pie on wooden board. (*Note:* Wood is not essential, but since it does not conduct heat, it prevents the hot oven shelf from melting the ice cream.) Brown the meringue under the preheated broiler about 3 minutes, but watch! Cover any quick-browning spots of meringue with flat pieces of aluminum foil to prevent burning. Turn the pie under the broiler if necessary for even browning. Remove pie as soon as it turns golden, and serve at once. Or if you must, return the pie to the freezer. Remove from the freezer 10 minutes before serving.

FROZEN PRALINE MOCHA PIE

Excellent for entertaining, this light but richly flavored pie combines toasted almonds, coffee, and chocolate with a blend of meringue and whipped cream. Hard to resist! It is easy to prepare, however, and can be frozen well ahead. For additional elegance, you can make a Nut-Meringue Shell (page 78) instead of the crumb crust. Or, if you are short of time, forget the pastry shell altogether and freeze the filling alone, in individual foil muffin cup liners, or premade Chocolate Shells (page 76). Serve garnished with grated chocolate or Chocolate Leaves (page 116) or Curls (page 118).

Advance preparation: Prepare the Nut-Crumb Crust ahead and freeze, or prepare crust and fill pie, then freeze, well wrapped, until 15 minutes before serving.

Special equipment: 9-inch pie plate; electric mixer with 2 bowls (and 2 beaters if possible); one mixer bowl and beaters chilled, for whipped cream; rubber scraper; blender or food processor to chop nuts; small frying pan (to toast nuts).

Chilling time: 2 or 3 hours in freezer (until filling is set), or longer, for convenience.

Quantity: One 9-inch pie or six 3-inch tartlets.

> *9-inch Nut Crumb Crust (almonds, page*
> *74), baked 8 minutes (or simply*
> *chilled, if you prefer); or crumb*
> *crust for about six 3-inch tartlets*

Filling

1 egg white
⅛ teaspoon salt
1 tablespoon instant espresso coffee
¼ cup plus 2 tablespoons confectioners'
*   sugar, sifted*
1 cup heavy cream
1 teaspoon vanilla extract
¼ teaspoon almond extract
¼ cup almonds, toasted and fine
*   chopped; to toast nuts, see page 32*
3 tablespoons almond praline powder (broken
*   nut brittle ground in processor)*
3 tablespoons unsweetened Baker's
*   cocoa, sifted*
Grated Chocolate (page 118)

1. Prepare the pastry shell. In the bowl of an electric mixer, combine the egg whites, salt, and instant coffee. Beat until fluffy, then add 2 tablespoons sifted confectioners' sugar. Beat until stiff peaks form and the mixture looks satiny and light beige in color. Set aside.

2. In a clean, prechilled mixer bowl with chilled beaters, whip the cream until soft peaks form. Add the remaining ¼ cup confectioners' sugar, the vanilla and almond extracts, and whip until stiff peaks form.

3. Fold the toasted, chopped nuts into the whipped cream, then fold in the coffee meringue. Remove about 1¾ cups of this mixture to one of the mixing bowls, sift into it the Baker's cocoa, and stir gently.

4. Spread the cocoa-cream mixture in the bottom of the prepared pastry shell, then top with the remaining cream. Garnish with Grated Chocolate, top with plastic wrap, and fast-freeze. When firm, wrap airtight with foil to store in the freezer. Fifteen minutes before serving, remove from the freezer. Garnish with whipped cream or Chocolate Leaves (page 116), if you wish.

FROZEN STRAWBERRY FLUFF PIE

Taste the essence of springtime here: fresh strawberries whipped into a creamy froth and served frozen in a crisp meringue shell! And it tastes even better than it sounds—a perfect dinner party finale made in advance.

The "fluff" in the title is the real surprise in this recipe. I admit when I first heard the procedure for making it from a friend in Vermont, I did not think it would work. I had to try it to believe that egg whites containing so much fruit at the start would whip this high, but they do and then some. The lemon juice helps stabilize the egg white foam, whose volume is stupendous but reduces somewhat when the whipped cream is folded in. The mixture is frozen in a premade meringue shell. Shortly before serving, the pie is garnished with whipped cream and whole fresh berries with perhaps a mint sprig or two for color contrast.

Advance preparation: The meringue pie shell can be made ahead and stored, covered airtight, for several days, or frozen in a protective box. The pie filling must be made ahead and frozen overnight, or longer. Just before serving, garnish with whipped cream and fresh berries.

Special equipment: 10-inch pie plate; mixing bowl; paring knife; electric mixer with large bowl (and balloon beater if available); chilled bowl and beater for whipping cream; plastic wrap and heavy-duty aluminum foil; spoon, or pastry bag fitted with 1/2-inch star tip for applying whipped cream.

Baking time: Meringue shell: 275°F for 60 to 65 minutes.

Chilling time: Pie filling: overnight, in freezer.

Quantity: One 10-inch pie.

10-inch baked Meringue Shell (page 77), made with 4 egg whites

Filling

1 pint fresh strawberries, or 1 (10-ounce) package frozen strawberries, thawed and drained

1/4 cup granulated sugar

2 egg whites

1 tablespoon lemon juice

1 cup heavy cream

Topping

1/2 cup heavy cream

2 tablespoons confectioners' sugar, sifted

Garnish

1 pint fresh strawberries

Mint sprigs

1. Prepare the 10-inch Meringue Shell and freeze or store it in a cool dry place, wrapped airtight until needed. To prepare the filling, wash, hull, and mash up the strawberries, to make about 1½ cups, mashed fruit. Don't worry about the size of the pieces, the beater will whip them smaller. Add the sugar and stir well.

2. In the large bowl of an electric mixer, combine the egg whites, lemon juice, and mashed and sweetened berries. Whip on medium (not high) speed until stiff peaks form. This may take 10 minutes or more with small beaters, or 5 minutes at speed #6 on a Kitchenaid fitted with a balloon beater. (*Note:* Speed is not the important thing here; just whip slowly and steadily until the volume mounts.) It will surprise you how high the volume will rise. Stop when the peaks are really stiff, but not dry.

3. In a chilled bowl with a chilled beater, whip the cream until nearly stiff. Fold this, little by little, into the strawberry fluff. The volume will decrease somewhat at this point. Turn the mixture into the prepared meringue shell, top with plastic wrap, then wrap it airtight in foil and freeze until about 15 minutes before serving.

4. Shortly before serving time, whip the ½ cup heavy cream with chilled bowl and chilled beater. When soft peaks form, add the sugar, then whip stiff. Decorate the frozen pie with spooned on mounds of cream or rosettes piped through a pastry bag fitted with a star tip. Garnish with halved or whole strawberries (washed, dried, and hulled) placed in the cream alongside a few sprigs of mint. Serve immediately, before the strawberry fluff melts. Return leftovers to the freezer.

INDIVIDUAL SWEET PASTRIES, TARTLETS, AND TURNOVERS

A wide variety of single-serving pastries fit this category. Cream Puffs, Profiteroles, and Éclairs, all made with the same Puff Shell Dough (page 80); small individual Meringue Shells, or nests (page 78) filled with ice cream or pastry cream and fresh fruit; Chocolate Shells (page 76) filled with fruit sherbet or flavored frozen creams; and miniature pastry tarts baked in fancy shapes and filled with anything you might put in a regular size tart. You should consider, when making tartlets, that any full size tart or pie can also be baked in individual tartlet shells. Good candidates for this treatment are fruit pies and tarts, chess pies, custard pies, and cream pies. For example, try Blueberry-Peach Tartlets (page 138), or Mincemeat Tartlets (page 147), Vermont Maple-Walnut Tartlets (page 208), Pecan Pie Tartlets (page 217), or Cranberry-Raisin Tartlets (page 177)—all made with pie or tart fillings. To convert a pie or tart recipe into tartlets, remember that a pastry recipe made with 2 cups flour = one 2-crust 9-inch pie = one 11- or 12-inch tart shell = approximately nine 4-inch tartlets, or eight 4½-inch tartlets. Filling for a 9-inch pie = about 4 cups; enough to fill 8 tartlets 4½-inch diameter with ½ cup filling each. To form individual sweet pastry cases of Puff Pastry, see page 183.

QUICK MERINGUE ICE CREAM TARTLETS

Prepare 3-inch Meringue Tartlet Shells (page 78). When the shells are cold, fill with ice cream (flavor of your choice) and serve topped with Rich Chocolate Sauce (page 118) or complementary fresh or frozen berries, puréed in blender or food processor with a tablespoon or two of rum or kirsch. If you are feeling excessive, pipe a rosette of flavored whipped cream (page 107) on the top and garnish with a Chocolate Leaf (page 116) or a sprig of fresh mint leaves.

ANGEL TARTLETS

Prepare Orange Angel Pie (page 284) forming the shells into 3-inch meringue nests, as described on page 79. Fill with Angel Pie filling—Orange, Tangerine, or Lemon—and top with whipped cream and a mint leaf. Or garnish with a slice or 2 of mandarin orange (canned, drained well) brushed with Plain Fruit Glaze (page 120) and a sprig of fresh mint leaves.

PASTRY TARTLETS

Pastry tartlet shells can be filled with anything you would put into a large tart shell—you are limited only by your imagination. If the shells are unbaked, or partially baked, add any regular fruit, cream, or custard filling and bake as for a full-size pie or tart, but reduce baking time according to tart size. If shells are completely baked, add any chiffon or cold, precooked custard filling. (*Note:* As a rule of thumb for filling tartlets: ½ cup filling = one 4½-inch tartlet; 4 cups filling = one 9-inch pie = 8 tartlets 4 to 4½ inches.)

Follow instructions on page 51 to shape and completely prebake tartlet shells made with Rich Tart Pastry (page 64), or Cream Cheese Pastry (page 65), or Basic All-Purpose Flaky Pastry, Lemon or Orange Pastry Variation (page 35), prepared with 1 egg yolk and 1 tablespoon sugar. Fill and garnish these tartlets as follows. Be sure to refrigerate cream-filled tartlets.

VARIATIONS:

Berry Custard Tartlets. Prepare completely prebaked tartlet shells. Fill with Vanilla or other Pastry Cream (page 100) and top with fresh berries. Brush the berries with Plain Fruit Glaze (page 120) shortly before serving. Or top with any combination of berries and fresh, peeled, sliced fruit. (*Note:* Canned fruits, well drained, may be substituted.)

Kiwi Cream Tartlets. Prepare completely prebaked tartlet shells. Fill with Almond Pastry Cream (page 102). Top with overlapping slices of peeled kiwi fruit. Brush with Plain Fruit Glaze (page 120) shortly before serving.

Almond-Pear Tartlets. Prepare completely prebaked tartlet shells. Fill with Frangipane (page 103) or Almond Pastry Cream (page 102). Top with ½ of a well drained poached pear (page 167) or half a canned pear, drained. Brush with Plain Fruit Glaze (page 120) shortly before serving and garnish with a sprig of mint or a sprinkling of freshly grated nutmeg.

Whipped Cream Tartlets with Chocolate Curls or Leaves. Prepare completely prebaked tartlet shells. Fill with flavored whipped cream of your choice (page 107) and top with Chocolate Curls (page 118) or Chocolate Leaves (page 116). These may be frozen in advance, and served partially thawed, for an ice creamlike texture.

Frozen Praline Mocha Tartlets. Prepare either completely prebaked pastry shells or Chocolate Shells (page 76) or simply use paper muffin cup liners. Fill with Frozen Praline Mocha filling (page 265). Freeze. Makes approximately 6 tarts, 4-inch diameter. Garnish with grated chocolate or Chocolate Curls (page 118).

Orange Cream Tartlets. Prepare completely prebaked tartlet shells. Fill with Orange Cream Cheese Tart Filling (page 104) and top with freshly peeled orange segments or canned mandarine orange sections, well drained. Brush with Plain Fruit Glaze (page 120) shortly before serving.

Strawberry Shortcake Tartlets. Prepare completely prebaked tartlet shells. Fill with sweetened whipped cream (page 107) or Lemon Double Cream Tart Filling (page 104). Top with hulled fresh strawberries and brush with Plain Fruit Glaze (page 120) shortly before serving.

Jam Tartlets. Prepare completely prebaked tartlet shells. Fill with a thin layer of Orange Cream Cheese Tart Filling (page 104) and top with a generous layer of your favorite fruit preserves. Sift on a light sprinkling of confectioners' sugar just before serving.

Apricot Tartlets. Prepare completely prebaked tartlet shells. Prepare Orange Cream Cheese Tart Filling (page 104) or Lemon Double Cream Tart Filling (page 104) but add 1 cup canned apricot halves, drained and chopped, to the filling. Spread the filling in the shells and top with canned apricot halves, well drained. Brush with Plain Fruit Glaze (page 120) shortly before serving.

PENNSYLVANIA DUTCH MILK TARTLETS
(*SCHLOPP* OR *MILLICH BOI*)

One of the nicest things about writing this book was the delightful response from my friends. Pies—the word brings to mind Grandmother's house, nurseries on rainy days, nostalgia. So many people contributed stories and treasured recipes. One lovely incident involved Dick Gackenback, the well-known children's book illustrator. We were having lunch one winter day when he asked what I was working on. When I told him pies, his face beamed. "Milk pie is my favorite, do you know it?" I didn't, but I do now—a delicious milk custard that absolutely sings of home and comfort.

"My Pennsylvania Dutch grandmother made milk pie for the kids," explained Dick, "to keep them out of the grown-ups' apricot pies. But my grandfather preferred the milk pies and was forever snitching them from the kids. Grandmother made her pies in alarming number, with dough as big as a basketball and homemade butter. She just made the little milk pies to use up leftover scraps of dough."

Our afternoon pie talk led to correspondence with Dick's aunt in Pennsylvania, who sent a cryptic file card with few hints. It took seven or eight attempts, with Dick tasting, before he proclaimed, "Fine, this is the way I remember it!" Authentic schlopp pie should have custard lightly set, with just a slight bit of milk visible around the edges and the barely golden top sprinkled with cinnamon.

Advance preparation: The partially baked tartlet shells may be prepared ahead and frozen (page 53). Bake the custard shortly before serving.

Special equipment: Four 4½-inch diameter tartlet pans; flat baking sheet.

Baking time: Partially prebaked tartlet shells: 400°F for 5 to 6 minutes, with pie weights, then 8 to 12 minutes empty, or until a light golden color; complete custard tart: 400°F for 30 to 35 minutes.

Quantity: Four 4½-inch diameter tartlets.

> *Four partially prebaked 4½-inch*
> *diameter tartlet shells made with*
> *Basic All-Purpose Flaky Pastry*
> *(page 39) or Cream Cheese Pastry*
> *(page 65)*
> *6 tablespoons granulated sugar*
> *7 tablespoons all-purpose flour*
> *2 tablespoons lightly salted butter, cut*
> *up and softened at room*
> *temperature (not melted)*
> *2 cups milk*
> *1 teaspoon vanilla extract*
> *A pinch of cinnamon*

1. Prepare and partially prebake the tartlet shells (page 52). Cool the shells while you prepare the custard. Preheat the oven to 400°F.

2. In a mixing bowl, cream together the sugar, flour, and butter, then whisk in the milk and the vanilla. Set the tartlet shells on a flat baking sheet for

ease in handling. Divide the mixture among the pastry shells, sprinkle with a bit of cinnamon, and bake in the center of the preheated oven for 30 to 35 minutes, until the tops are slightly golden and the filling almost set, with a little milk visible at the edges. Serve warm or at room temperature.

PORTUGUESE BEAN-CUSTARD TARTLETS (*PASTEIS DE FEIJAO*)

Provincetown, Massachusetts, is a seaside resort full of surprises, from the surging tides of flamboyant summer tourists who pack the narrow streets to the deserted expanses of windswept dunes, punctuated only by driftwood, bayberries, and wild roses. But the biggest surprise of all, to outsiders, is the delightful cuisine of the large year-round Portuguese population.

The focal point of this cuisine is the Provincetown Portuguese Bakery, which supplies bread to virtually every restaurant in the Cape area. The successful bakery is run by Antonio (Tony) Alves Ferreira and his wife, Guilhermina. Originally from Lisbon, they came to the United States and took over the bakery in 1975. With a large Portuguese staff of friends and relatives, they produce an astonishing variety and quantity of authentically Portuguese baked goods. As fast as they come from the ovens in the rear, the delicacies are brought out front to the café-shop where a steady stream of customers wait in a line that often reaches right out the front door. It is no accident that the line is routed past the glass pastry case, for customers thus have plenty of time to make their selections from the carefully labeled items.

One of Tony's specialties, prominently displayed in the case, is *Pasteis de Feijão,* attractive tartlets which, according to the label, contain a "mystery ingredient." "I thought Americans might be put off if I called it Bean Tart, though that is the Portuguese name," explained Tony. And although the pastry filling does in fact contain mashed white kidney beans, which give the sweet custard its unique texture, the effect is delicious and visually appealing, with a jaunty cap of crisp melted sugar on top.

Advance preparation: The Portuguese Lard Pastry may be prepared ahead and frozen, or the completely baked tartlets can be stored airtight in a cool place for several days, or wrapped airtight and frozen.

Special equipment: Two trays of imported Portuguese tartlet tins 2-inch diameter, 1-inch deep, with straight sides (regular 2-inch muffin tins make successful substitutes); 2-quart heavy-bottom enamel or stainless steel saucepan; candy thermometer; sieve; sifter.

Baking time: 400°F for 35 minutes.

Quantity: 21 tartlets, 2 inches in diameter.

Unbaked Portuguese Lard Pastry (page 63)

Filling
2½ *cups minus 1 tablespoon*
    granulated sugar
1 cup water
¼ *cup canned whole white kidney*
    beans, drained well
½ *cup unbleached all-purpose flour,*
    sifted
3 large eggs

Topping
Confectioners' sugar

1. Prepare the Portuguese Lard Pastry, roll it out, and line the buttered muffin tins (page 51). Set the pastry-lined pans in the refrigerator to chill while you prepare the filling.

2. Make a syrup by combining the sugar and water in a heavy-bottom saucepan. Stir, then, without stirring, bring the mixture to a boil. Add a candy thermometer to the side of the pan and boil the syrup gently 15 to 20 minutes, to 227°F, just under the soft ball stage, when 2 drops of syrup will slide off the edge of a spoon simultaneously. Remove the syrup from the heat and set it aside to cool.

3. While the syrup cools, press the kidney beans through a sieve into a small bowl. You should have about 2 tablespoons bean paste. Stir the flour into the paste, making a crumbly-textured mixture.

4. In a separate bowl, whisk the eggs together and set them aside. When the syrup is cool, but before it is cold enough to crystallize, pour it into the flour-bean paste mixture, whisking hard to produce a smooth, thick syrup. Do not use any of the sugar that may have crystallized on the pan sides. Beat in the eggs. Pass the entire mixture through the sieve.

5. Preheat the oven to 400°F. Ladle the filling into the pastry-lined tins, filling each cup to within ⅛-inch of the rim. Wipe spills off the pan. Over each cup, sift on a generous ⅛-inch layer of confectioners' sugar. With your fingertip, wipe excess sugar from the pan.

(*Note:* Do not skimp with the sifted sugar as it plays a double role in creating the pastry topping: when the batter rises, part of the sugar melts into a crisp glaze. This glaze makes the flat raised cap that is topped by the decorative coating of still-unmelted sugar on the baked tartlet.)

6. Bake the tartlets in the lower third of the preheated oven for 35 minutes, or until the pastry filling rises and the sugar forms a raised golden-brown cap on the top; this cap will be coated with a sprinkling of the undissolved confectioners' sugar. Let the tartlets cool 2 or 3 minutes, then tip them out of the baking tins with the point of a small knife. Cool the tartlets on a wire rack. Store them airtight.

CREAM PUFFS, PROFITEROLES, AND ECLAIRS

These three pastries are baked with the same light eggy Puff Shell Dough (*Pâte à Choux*, page 80); the only differences are in the shaping and filling. Cream Puffs are formed into large or small balls, filled with plain or flavored pastry cream or whipped cream, and topped by a sprinkling of confectioners' sugar or glazed with frosting. Profiteroles are shaped into small balls, filled with vanilla ice cream, and served topped with warm Chocolate Sauce. Éclairs are shaped into long narrow rectangles, filled with plain or flavored pastry cream or whipped cream, and frosted with Chocolate Icing.

Advance preparation: The pastry shells can be baked and stored airtight for a day or two before filling. However, they always have the best texture and flavor the day they are baked. Unfilled shells can be baked, wrapped airtight, and frozen. Ice cream-filled Profiteroles can be stored frozen, but should be wrapped carefully to avoid loss of flavor (page 53). Once filled, Cream Puffs and Éclairs should not be stored more than a few hours (refrigerated) before serving, or the pastry shells will soften.

Special equipment: Sifter; pastry brush; baking sheets; 2 tablespoons or teaspoons or a pastry bag fitted with a ½- to ¾-inch plain tip.

Baking time: 400°F for 25 to 35 minutes.

Quantity: 12 to 15 Cream Puffs about 3 inches diameter; 12 Éclairs 4 inches long; 24 Profiteroles about 2 inches in diameter.

> *Puff Shell Dough (page 80)*
> Egg glaze: *1 egg beaten with 1*
>   *tablespoon water*
>
> **Filling**
> *For Cream Puffs and Éclairs use plain*
>   *or flavored pastry cream (page 100)*
>   *or plain or flavored whipped*
>   *cream (page 107)*
> *For Profiteroles, use small balls of*
>   *vanilla ice cream*

Frosting
*Vanilla Icing Glaze (page 115) or Chocolate
Icing (page 119), or sift on a little
confectioners' sugar after the shells
are filled*

Topping
*Rich Chocolate Sauce (page 118),
for Profiteroles*

1. Preheat the oven to 400°F. Prepare Puff Shell Dough (page 80). Generously butter baking sheets and sprinkle them with cold water to add moisture that aids dough in rising.

2. Beat the batter a few extra times before using it, especially if it has been sitting for a while. Put the batter into a pastry bag, then twist the end of bag to close it, and compress the batter into the tip. Or instead of using the bag, shape the pastry with 2 spoons as explained below.

3. To shape Cream Puffs, which will be about 3 inches when baked, pipe balls of dough about 1½-inches diameter on to the prepared baking sheet. Or shape the balls with 2 tablespoons. Be sure to leave a good space between shapes so they can rise well and dry out as the air circulates.

To shape Profiteroles, pipe balls about 1- to 1¼-inches diameter, or shape balls with 2 teaspoons.

To shape Éclairs, pipe dough into stripes about ½-inch wide and 4-inches long.

4. Dip your fingertip into cold water and gently smooth over any pointy dough peaks that might overbrown in the oven before the dough bakes through. Then brush the tops of the dough shapes with egg glaze, but try not to drip glaze onto the bases or the dough will not rise properly.

5. Bake in center of the preheated oven for 25 to 35 minutes, depending upon the size of the shapes. When done, the puffs should be well-rounded, golden brown, and very crisp. They often appear to be done before their interiors are baked through; if not crisp enough on the outside, they may collapse when they cool. It is a good idea to check one piece, after baking at 400°F for 25 minutes. Open it and test. If it's too raw inside, bake a few minutes longer. (*Note:* The inside will always have some soft layers of dough clinging to the crisper edges. They may be left as is or picked out with a fork.)

6. Cool the baked puffs on a wire rack. As soon as the pieces come from the oven, prick them in the center area where they will later be split or filled. The pricking releases steam and helps keep them crisp as they cool.

7. When cool, split the Cream Puffs in half and spoon in pastry cream or

whipped cream. Top with icing or sifted on confectioners' sugar. Refrigerate. Split Profiteroles in half and fill with small balls of ice cream. Reassemble and freeze until hard on tray. Then remove from the tray and store in a plastic bag. Serve with warm Chocolate Sauce poured over the top. Fill and frost Éclairs as you did Cream Puffs, or pipe cream filling into the Éclairs without splitting them.

HAMANTASCHEN

Hamantaschen are prune or poppyseed-filled turnovers traditionally served during the Jewish holiday of Purim. The pastry is given a triangular, or tricorne, shape to recall the hat of Haman, the villain of Purim who plotted to eliminate the Jews living in Persia under King Ahasuerus. The Jewish community was saved when Queen Esther discovered Haman's plan and had him hanged on the gallows he had prepared for his enemies. During the celebration of this holiday, the wearing of costumes and the eating of Hamantaschen recall the principal figures of the story.

This is an old family recipe, which has been refined through the years to its present lemon-flavored, prune-filled version. It owes its development to the late Mrs. Bessie Fierstein of Philadelphia. She was a wonderful lady and a great baker.

Advance preparation: The pastry may be prepared ahead and frozen. Or the completely baked Hamantaschen can be frozen.
Special equipment: Teacup or round cutter about 3½ to 4 inches in diameter; pastry brush; grater; blender or food processor; flat, edged baking sheet.
Baking time: 375°F for 12 minutes.
Quantity: 24 Hamantaschen.

> *Unbaked Hamantaschen pastry (page 66)*
> *1 (12 ounce) can or jar Lekvar prune butter or pastry filling; or the same quantity cooked, pitted dried prunes drained, then put through food mill or puréed in a food processor*
> *1 large lemon for grated zest, pulp, and juice*
> *½ cup walnuts, chopped coarse*
> *½ cup crushed cornflakes*
> *½ cup honey*

1. Prepare the pastry and set it to chill while you prepare the filling. In a mixing bowl, combine the prune butter (or purée stewed and drained prunes) with grated zest of the lemon. Pit the lemon, then slice it and chop the entire lemon (pulp and juice) in a blender or processor. Add this to the prune mixture. Stir in the nuts and cornflakes. Preheat the oven to 375°F. Butter a baking sheet and set it aside.

2. Roll out the dough (page 38) on a lightly floured surface, or work with half the dough while refrigerating the rest until needed. Roll dough about ⅛-inch thick, then cut into rounds about 3½ to 4 inches diameter using a flour-dipped cookie cutter or the rim of a teacup or jar.

3. In the center of each pastry round, place approximately 1 heaping teaspoon of filling. Dip a pastry brush in water, then moisten the rim of the pastry round. Lift up three sides of the pastry and bring them to the center so that their edges touch. Pinch dough edges together to seal, making a tricorne shape. Set the pastries on the buttered baking sheet. Repeat, using up all dough and filling. If you have time, refrigerate the pastries about 30 minutes, or bake immediately. Drip a little honey over the top of the pastries before setting them in the preheated oven. Bake for about 12 minutes, or until the pastry is golden on top. Cool on a wire rack.

RUGELACH

These traditional Middle-European tea pastries, also known as *Kipfel*, are made with a flaky cream cheese dough filled with poppy seeds, jam, or cinnamon nuts, and shaped into crescents or envelopes.

Advance preparation: Cream Cheese Pastry can be made ahead and frozen; defrost before using. Or completely baked rugelach can be frozen.
Special equipment: 2 flat baking sheets; pastry brush; 3 small bowls; ruler; pizza cutter or pastry jagger or paring knife.
Baking time: 375°F for 15 to 20 minutes.
Quantity: Forty-eight 4-inch crescents.

> *Cream Cheese Pastry (page 65) prepared*
> *as directed, plus 1 egg yolk, a pinch*
> *of salt, 2 teaspoons sugar, and 1*
> *teaspoon plain yogurt or sour cream*
> *Add additional flour if dough is*
> *sticky. Chill as directed before rolling*

Egg glaze: *1 egg white beaten with 1*
tablespoon water
Granulated sugar, for sprinkling over
pastries before baking

Filling
Each variety will fill half the dough

POPPYSEED

⅓ cup poppy seeds
2 tablespoons brown sugar
2 tablespoons granulated sugar

NUT

½ cup walnuts or blanched almonds,
chopped fine
¼ cup granulated or brown sugar
½ teaspoon cinnamon
¼ teaspoon ground nutmeg

JAM

½ cup raspberry, plum, apricot, or other
variety fruit preserves or jam
Confectioners' sugar, for sifting over
baked pastries

1. Butter baking sheets and set them aside. Preheat oven to 375°F. Select and prepare ingredients for 2 (or 3 if you wish more variety) of the fillings and set them aside in separate small bowls. Work with half the dough at a time, leaving the remainder in the refrigerator until needed.

2. Roll out dough (page 38) about ⅛-inch thick on a lightly floured surface. (*Note:* If dough feels too soft, work in a little more flour or chill it a little longer.)

To make crescents, cut dough into triangles roughly 4-inch at the base and 4-inch tall; to make envelopes (traditionally filled with jam), cut 2-inch squares. For all shapes, brush cut dough with egg white glaze; then sprinkle about 1 teaspoon poppy seed or nut filling over triangles or spoon ½ teaspoon jam in center of small squares. To form crescents, roll up triangles from the 4-inch base toward the tip; set the rolls tip down on a buttered baking sheet, then bend the ends down, forming the crescent. To form envelopes pinch together 2 opposite corners of each jam-filled square, then place on buttered baking sheet.

3. Brush tops of all shapes with egg white glaze, then sprinkle with a little granulated sugar. Bake in preheated oven for 15 to 20 minutes or until golden brown. Cool on a wire rack. When cool, you can sift a little confectioners' sugar over the tops of jam-filled envelopes; leave crescents plain.

FRUIT TURNOVERS

These are really individual covered fruit pies, as delicious as the larger version but more convenient to serve, especially on picnics, in lunch boxes, or even for dinner, hot from the oven and topped with ice cream. Turnovers are a good way to use up any ripe fruit you have; combine the fruit with puff pastry scraps and you have a delightful creation no one would suspect came from leftovers.

Advance preparation: The Classic or Quick Puff Pastry (or puff pastry scraps) can be frozen (page 85), and thawed as directed. Better yet, use up puff pastry scraps by rolling out and filling them with fruit slices, then freeze until ready to bake. Bake unthawed, but increase the baking time slightly.

Special equipment: Pastry brush; ruler; sharp knife or pizza cutting wheel; flat, edged baking sheet.

Baking time: 425°F for about 17 to 25 minutes.

Quantity: About 6 large turnovers.

> *Quick Puff Pastry (page 82), or ½*
> *recipe Classic Puff Pastry (page 85),*
> *or puff pastry scraps. (Note:*
> *Turnovers can also be made with*
> *Basic All-Purpose Flaky Pastry*
> *[page 34] or Cream Cheese Pastry*
> *[page 65])*

Egg glaze: *1 egg beaten with 1 tablespoon*
    water
Half the fruit filling (about 2 to 2½
    cups) for any 9-inch fresh fruit pie
    (for example, Apple Pie, Apple-
    Cranberry-Walnut Pie, Cherry Pie,
    Peach-Blueberry Pie, Mince Pie, any
    berry pie)
Icing glaze: *½ cup confectioners' sugar,*
    sifted, mixed with 2 teaspoons milk
    and ¼ teaspoon vanilla extract

1. Prepare the pastry according to directions on pages 82 or 85. On a lightly floured surface, roll out the dough to a thickness of about ⅛-inch. Depending upon the quantity of dough you have, cut as many 5- or 6-inch squares as possible. Reroll the scraps and cut more. You should get about 6 squares from a rectangle of dough 12 × 18 inches. Make 5-inch squares, or even smaller, bite-sized ones, as your dough permits.

2. Brush the inner edge of each pastry square with egg glaze; don't drop the glaze on outer edge, or the dough will be glued together and will not rise. In the center of the square place between 1 tablespoon and ⅓ cup fruit filling, depending upon the size of the dough square; the filling should be generous. Fold two opposite corners together making a triangle. Seal the edges by pressing with a fork. Brush the top of the turnover with a little egg glaze, and cut a steam vent with the tip of a knife.

3. If you are using Classic or Quick Puff Pastry, sprinkle cold water on an unbuttered baking sheet. If you are using All-Purpose Flaky Pastry, butter the baking sheet and omit the water. Set the turnovers on the baking sheet and refrigerate about 30 minutes. Preheat the oven to 425°F.

4. Bake the turnovers for about 17 to 25 minutes, or until the pastry is puffed up and a rich golden brown. Cool on a wire rack. Drip on icing glaze. Serve warm, with vanilla ice cream or slightly sweetened whipped cream (page 107).

MERINGUE SHELL PIES

Meringue Shell Pies, as the name implies, actually have a crisp meringue pastry shell. These can be filled with any combination of ingredients your imagination suggests: Pastry cream topped with fresh raspberries, softened ice cream or fruit purée sauce, puréed berries folded into whipped cream (Raspberry Fool, see below), or citrus custards, as in Angel Pies. The latter are indeed heavenly, topped with clouds of whipped cream or even, to gild the angel, delicately browned meringue topping. Meringue Shell Tartlets (page 78) can be prepared exactly like the larger versions, with the same fillings.

HAZELNUT MERINGUE PIE WITH RASPBERRY FOOL FILLING

This elegant confection is simply a hazelnut-flavored meringue pie shell filled with a frothy blend of puréed berries and cream called a fool. You'll be anything but if you serve this to company; the blend of flavors is delectable and the pie can be made well in advance of serving. The recipe is adapted, with an appreciative nod, from an elaborate layer cake version prepared at l'École de Cuisine La Varenne in Paris.

Advance preparation: The meringue shell can be baked ahead and kept crisp overnight in the oven with the heat off. Or the baked shell can be stored a day or two, airtight, or frozen. Fill the shell and refrigerate it at least 3 to 4 hours before serving, or as long as 24 hours in advance. Decorate the top with whipped cream as close to serving time as possible.

Special equipment: Well-buttered 10-inch pie plate; optional: pastry bag fitted
   with ½-inch star tip; food processor or blender; sifter; rubber scraper; chilled
   mixer bowl and beater for whipping cream.
Baking time: Meringue shell: 275°F for 60 minutes, plus 45 minutes left in oven
   with heat off and door ajar.
Chilling time: Filled pie: 3 to 4 hours.
Quantity: One 10-inch pie.

> *One 10-inch Meringue Pie Shell (page*
>   *78), made with 4 egg whites, ¼*
>   *teaspoon cream of tartar, ⅛*
>   *teaspoon salt, ¾ cup superfine*
>   *sugar, ½ teaspoon vanilla extract,*
>   *plus ¾ cup shelled hazelnuts,*
>   *toasted, ground, and folded into*
>   *the stiffly beaten whites. See Nuts*
>   *(page 32)* (Note: *Reserve 6 to 8*
>   *whole toasted nuts for garnishing*
>   *the pie.)*
> *1 pint fresh raspberries or 1 package*
>   *(10 ounces) frozen berries, thawed*
>   *and drained*
> *¾ cup heavy cream plus ¼ cup reserved*
>   *for garnishing the pie*
> *2 tablespoons confectioners' sugar, sifted*
> *1 teaspoon vanilla extract*

1. To toast nuts, set them on a pan in a 300°F oven for about 8 minutes,
until aromatic and golden. To remove hazelnut skins, wrap hot toasted nuts in a
textured towel for several minutes to steam, then rub off skins.

2. Preheat the oven to 275°F. Prepare the meringue as described on page 78,
folding in ground hazelnuts just before turning it into a well-buttered pie plate.
For a fancy shell, pipe on an edging of rosettes using a pastry bag and ½-inch
star tip. Bake in the preheated oven for 60 minutes, then turn off the heat, prop
the oven door ajar with a wooden spoon, and leave the shell in the oven an
additional 45 minutes to dry out. Or leave the shell in the oven overnight (with
heat turned off). Cool on a wire rack before filling. See *Advance preparation,*
above, for storing instructions.

3. In a blender or processor, purée all the drained, frozen berries or all but a
handful of the fresh berries, reserving some for garnishing the top of the pie.
With chilled bowl and beaters, whip ¾ cup of the cream until soft peaks form,

add the sugar and vanilla, and beat a few seconds longer. Then fold in the puréed berries. Spread the fruit cream into the meringue shell and smooth the top. Cover with plastic wrap and refrigerate 3 or 4 hours before serving to allow the cream to soften the meringue slightly.

4. Before serving, whip the remaining ¼ cup of cream in chilled bowl with chilled beaters until stiff peaks form. Spoon a cream edging around the pie and garnish with fresh berries and nuts, or pipe cream rosettes through a pastry bag fitted with a star tip. Set a whole berry atop each rosette. Make a ring of cream rosettes in the center and top with whole hazelnuts.

ORANGE ANGEL PIE

The tangy citrus custard contrasts dramatically with the crisp meringue shell in this refreshing "company" pie. Serve topped by heavenly clouds of sweetened whipped cream, garnished with mint sprigs and orange cartwheels or grated orange rind. This recipe is equally successful made into individual tartlets (page 269).

Advance preparation: The Meringue Shell can be baked ahead and kept crisp overnight in the oven with the heat off. Or the baked shell can be frozen. Fill the shell with custard on the morning it is to be served, and chill. In any case, it must be chilled at least 2 hours before serving. Pie can also be prepared a day ahead and refrigerated, though the meringue shell will soften slightly as it stands.

Special equipment: 9-inch pie plate; double boiler; whisk; electric mixer; rubber scraper; chilled bowl and beaters for whipped cream; knife; optional: pastry bag fitted with ½-inch star tip; grater.

Baking time: Meringue Shell: 275°F for 1 hour.

Chilling time: Completed pie: at least 2 hours.

Quantity: One 9-inch pie.

Meringue Shell (page 78) for 9-inch pie,
made with 3 egg whites

Filling

4 egg yolks
½ cup granulated sugar
¼ cup freshly squeezed orange juice
1 tablespoon grated orange zest
½ cup heavy cream
1 tablespoon confectioners' sugar, sifted

Topping and Garnish

½ cup heavy cream
2 tablespoons confectioners' sugar
Fresh mint sprigs
Grated orange zest

1. Prepare the meringue shell and bake in a buttered pie plate as described on page 79. Cool the shell.

2. In the top of a double boiler set over hot (not boiling) water, whisk the egg yolks until very light and thick—about 3 minutes. Add the sugar and whisk a minute or two, then add the orange juice and zest. Whisk constantly for 7 to 8 minutes, until the mixture is smooth, thick, and creamy. It should leave a thick coating on a spoon. Remove from the heat and set aside to cool while you prepare the whipped cream.

3. In a chilled bowl with chilled beaters, whip the heavy cream to soft peaks. Add the confectioners' sugar and beat to stiff peaks. Fold into the *cooled* orange custard, then spoon into the meringue shell. Chill until ready to garnish.

4. To garnish the pie, beat the cream until soft peaks form. Sift in the confectioners' sugar and whip stiff. Spoon the cream into an edging ring on top of the pie, or pipe rosettes of cream through a pastry bag fitted with a star tip. Top with grated orange zest or very thin cartwheels of fresh orange; cut through the rind to the center, then twist in opposite directions to make an S-curve. Chill until ready to serve. Garnish with mint sprigs.

VARIATIONS:

Tangerine Angel Pie. Prepare Orange Angel Pie but replace the orange juice and
   grated orange zest with tangerine. (*Note:* If you cannot find fresh tangerines,
   use frozen concentrated tangerine juice and use grated orange or lemon zest.)
Lemon Angel Pie. Prepare Orange Angel Pie but replace orange juice and grated
   orange zest with lemon.

DUMPLINGS, COBBLERS, CRISPS, AND KUCHEN

Dumplings, Cobblers. Crisps, and Kuchen are all old-fashioned country kitchen desserts. They are easy to prepare, casual to serve, and have universal appeal.

Dumplings are whole fruits (apples or peaches, for example) baked in pastry jackets and basted with a syrup glaze. Cobblers (also called grunts, slumps, or spoon pies) are deep-dish pies with biscuit dough topping. Crisps are deep-dish fruit pies with streusel-crumb toppings, and kuchen is a coffee cake/tart topped by fresh fruit and a streusel-crumb topping. All are enhanced by being served warm from the oven with heavy cream, plain or whipped, alongside.

APPLE DUMPLINGS IN PASTRY

Nothing warms an icy New England fall evening like the sweet smell of pastry-wrapped apples baking in maple syrup sauce. Wherever you live, in whatever climate, this is an easy-to-make dessert everyone will enjoy, and even the youngest children can help you prepare it.

Advance preparation: The pastry dough can be prepared ahead and frozen. The apples can be stuffed, wrapped in dough, and refrigerated one day in advance. Bake the apples just before serving.

Special equipment: Ruler and sharp knife; pastry brush; vegetable peeler; apple corer; paring knife; small bowl; baking pan about 1½ inches deep and large enough to hold 6 apples (or 2 smaller pans).

Baking time: 375°F for 45 minutes.

Quantity: 6 large pastry-covered apples.

*Unbaked pastry for a 2-crust 9-inch pie
made with Basic All-Purpose Flaky
Pastry (page 34), or Vinegar Pastry
(page 36), or Whole-Wheat Pastry
(page 59)*

*6 large firm baking apples (Ida Red,
Jonathan, Granny Smith, for example)*

6 tablespoons brown sugar

6 tablespoons seedless raisins

¼ cup chopped walnuts

6 tablespoons butter

¼ teaspoon cinnamon

*Egg glaze: 1 egg beaten with 1 tablespoon
water*

6 large whole cloves

Syrup

4 tablespoons pure maple syrup

2 tablespoons brown sugar, packed

⅔ cup water or apple cider

1 tablespoon lemon juice

A pinch of cinnamon

1. Prepare the pastry (page 38). Set the pastry in the refrigerator to chill while you prepare the fruit. To begin, wash, dry, and core the apples, leaving about ½ inch of bottom core intact, to hold in the filling. Then cut away about half the peel beginning at the stem end; leave the bottom half intact. Preheat the oven to 375°F.

2. In a small bowl, combine the brown sugar, raisins, walnuts, butter, and cinnamon. Pack a generous teaspoon full of this mixture into the center of each cored apple. Use more filling if there is room. Set apples aside.

3. Roll out the pastry dough (see page 38) on a lightly floured surface to about ⅛-inch thick. Measure the circumference of an apple so you will know how large to cut the pastry squares. As a guide, an 8-inch circumference, 3½-inch diameter (medium-large) Ida Red apple needs a 7-inch square of dough. Cut the rolled dough into six equal squares.

One at a time, set an apple right side up in the center of a dough square. Moisten the edges of the pastry square with egg glaze, then bring up opposite corners of the pastry and pinch the edges to seal, making 4 pastry seams, poking out around the apple. Brush the top of the pastry with egg glaze. Cut the dough scraps into oval-shaped leaves, mark veins with the back of a knife, and press 3 or 4 leaves onto the top of the apple, curving them in a natural-looking way. Stick one whole clove, stem up, in the center of the apple leaves, to look like a stem. Brush the tops of the pastry again with egg glaze, then set the apples in a well-buttered baking pan.

4. Bake in the preheated oven for 30 minutes while you prepare the syrup. To make syrup, combine in a saucepan the maple syrup, brown sugar, water or cider, lemon juice, and cinnamon. Stir over low heat until the sugar dissolves. Remove from heat.

5. After the apples have baked about 30 minutes, pour the syrup over them, then continue baking about 15 minutes longer while basting frequently with the syrup. Serve warm with Hard Sauce (page 114) or Custard Sauce (page 113) or Maple-Flavored Whipped Cream (page 109).

VARIATION:

Whole Peach Dumplings in Pastry. Prepare Apple Dumplings in Pastry but replace the apples with 6 large whole freestone peaches. Peel the peaches after first dipping them for a minute or two in boiling water, then cooling in cold water. Remove the pit from the stem end only, if you can, in order to keep the peaches whole. Or, reassemble peach after halving it to remove pit. You may use the raisin-nut filling, or omit it, though it helps to keep the peaches in shape. Wrap with pastry and bake, basting with syrup, as for apples. Serve warm, with Ginger-Flavored Whipped Cream (page 108) or Yogurt-Rum Sauce (page 115).

BLACKBERRY GRUNT, BLUEBERRY SLUMP, CRANBERRY COBBLER

Whether you call it grunt, slump, or cobbler, steaming fruit topped with biscuit dough is true country fare—easy and quick to prepare, hearty and heavenly to eat.

This recipe is a New England specialty, although "cobbler," a universal term, is known to berry pickers across the country. The word is also known to my American Heritage Dictionary, which suggests it comes from "mender"— perhaps because of the way the dough is patched over the fruit? I prefer to think my 1890 Century Dictionary comes closer to the mark, defining a cobbler as "something put together coarsely." This same source defines slump as a "soft, boggy place," which certainly describes the dish so-named in Maine and Vermont. "Grunt" is a Massachusetts term, possibly coming from the sound made by the bubbling hot fruit beneath the dough.

Colonial settlers first made this recipe in a covered pot over an open hearth and served it for breakfast. It wasn't until the nineteenth century that it became popular as a dessert. Whatever you call it and wherever you serve it, make sure it is warm, and pass a pitcher of heavy cream.

(*Note:* This is a creative dish; you can use any fruit or berry or combination of the two that appeals to you. Out of season, canned or frozen—thawed and drained—fruits or berries can be substituted for fresh. Fruit canned in sugar syrup should be drained to measure and the reserved drained syrup or juice substituted for water in the recipe. Taste before adding extra sugar.)

The fruit filling is prepared on the stovetop. After the dough topping (page 71) is added, the cooking can be completed either on the stovetop or in the oven. Select a baking dish that suits your purpose; I prefer one that can go from stovetop to oven to table. In this recipe, some of the fruit juice is absorbed by the dough; if you prefer more liquid, double the fruit recipe (don't double the topping).

Advance preparation: Fruit filling can be made ahead; add topping to re-warmed filling and bake shortly before serving for best flavor.

Special equipment: 2- to 3-quart stovetop oven-proof casserole or 9-, 10- or 11-inch deep-dish baking pan or oven-proof skillet. (*Note:* For cooking on stovetop, be sure the skillet has a tightly fitting lid.)

Fruit cooking time: 10 minutes.

Baking time with topping: 425°F for 20 to 25 minutes; or stovetop cooking time with topping: 12 to 15 minutes.

Quantity: About 1½ quarts, to serve 6.

Cobbler Topping (page 71)
made with 2 tablespoons sugar

Fruit Filling
1⅓ cups water
⅓ to 1 cup granulated sugar
*   (depending upon sweetness of fruit)*
1 tablespoon cornstarch
2 tablespoons lemon juice (omit if
*   fruit is very tart)*
3 to 4 cups fresh berries, washed, picked
*   over, and hulled.*

1. In a large skillet or stovetop casserole, combine the water, sugar, cornstarch, and lemon juice. Stir, then add the fruit. Set over heat, cover, and bring to a boil. Reduce the heat and simmer 10 minutes.

2. Meanwhile, prepare the topping dough. As soon as the fruit is cooked, remove it from the heat. If you plan to bake the topping in the oven, transfer the fruit to an oven-proof casserole if necessary. Preheat the oven to 425°F. Spoon the topping over the *hot* fruit. For dumplings, place separate tablespoonfuls of dough slightly apart all over the fruit; or spoon out dough in even dabs, then spread it gently into a single layer.

3. Bake in the preheated oven, uncovered, for 20 to 25 minutes, or until golden. Or cover the pan and bring to boil on the stovetop. Reduce the heat immediately and simmer 12 minutes without lifting the cover. Then peek; the topping should be puffed up and dry inside. Cover and cook a little longer if necessary. To serve, spoon the topping into a dish, cover with hot fruit, and serve with heavy cream poured from a pitcher passed at table.

VARIATIONS:

Raspberry-Peach Grunt. For fruit use 2 to 3 cups peeled and sliced fresh peaches plus 2 cups fresh raspberries, washed and picked over.

Strawberry-Rhubarb-Peach Grunt. For fruit use 2 cups fresh rhubarb stalks, washed and cut into 1-inch pieces, plus 2 cups fresh strawberries, washed, hulled, and halved, plus 1 cup peeled, sliced peaches added. Use ¾ to 1 cup sugar.

Apricot Cobbler. For fruit use 1½ pounds washed fresh apricots, pitted and halved.

Cranberry Cobbler. For fruit, use 1 cup cranberries plus 3 cups apples, peeled and sliced. Add sugar and simmer 15 minutes, until fruit is soft.

Other Combinations. Peach-Plum, Blueberry-Peach, Sour or Sweet Cherry-Pear; Apricot-Apple; Apple-Pear-Plum, Plain Apple, Peach, or Cherry.

APPLE CRISP

Fruit crisps are friendly, deep-dish pies with crisp crumb toppings. They are effortless to prepare and can be made with apples or any other fresh fruit, alone or in combination. Serve them warm from the oven, with a dollop of (unwhipped) slightly sweetened heavy cream poured over the top.

Advance preparation: The crumb topping can be made ahead and refrigerated. The fruit can be covered with topping and baked in advance, but is best when cooked no more than 1 or 2 hours before serving. If baked earlier (which you certainly can do) rewarm it in the oven before serving; this also crisps the topping, which softens on standing.

Special equipment: Mixing bowl; 9- or 10-inch pie plate or 1½-quart oven-proof casserole.

Baking time: 350°F for 45 to 50 minutes.

Quantity: One 9- or 10-inch pie; serves 6. (*Note:* If you double the amount of fruit filling to make this a deep-dish pie, you can serve 8 or more.)

Filling

4 cups tart cooking apples peeled, cored,
* and sliced*
3 tablespoons brown sugar
½ teaspoon cinnamon
2 tablespoons lemon juice
Oat-Wheat Germ Streusel (page 112)

1. Preheat the oven to 350°F. Butter the pie plate or casserole and slice into it the prepared fruit sprinkled with sugar, cinnamon, and lemon juice.

2. In a separate bowl, combine the ingredients for the streusel topping. Spread the topping over the fruit and pat it flat with the palm of your hand.

3. Bake in the preheated oven for 45 to 50 minutes, or until the fruit is fork-tender and the topping is browned and crisp.

VARIATIONS:

Cranberry-Apple Crisp. Prepare Apple Crisp but use only 2 cup apples plus 2 cups whole cranberries (fresh or frozen) for a total of 4 cups prepared fruit.

Peach-Berry Crisp. Prepare Apple Crisp but instead of apples substitute peeled sliced peaches (or nectarines) combined with any type of fresh, stemmed berries, for a total of 4 cups prepared fruit.

APPLE-PLUM PANDOWDY

As a child, I fondly remember singing the song "Shoofly Pie and Apple Pandowdy, make your eyes light up and your stomach say 'Howdy!'" I was always intrigued by these colorful dishes and wondered what they could possibly taste like to produce such a great reaction. Now I know—and guarantee *your* eyes will light up as soon as you try them.

Shoofly Pie (page 218) is of Pennsylvania Dutch origin, but Pandowdy is a down-home New England farm recipe, related to Cobblers, Slumps, and Grunts. Pandowdy consists of a layer of cut-up fruit—traditionally apple, though I like peaches as well, or combinations such as the apple-plum in this recipe—sweetened with brown sugar or maple syrup and topped by either a biscuit or short crust dough. After partial baking, the crust is cut up and pressed down into the fruit juices, a process (according to the *American Heritage Cookbook*) called "dowdy-ing," which flavors and enriches the texure of the crust. When the juice-soaked crust is completely baked, it regains its crispness and should be served warm in a shallow bowl with fruit, juice, and a dollop of heavy cream.

Advance preparation: Pastry may be made in advance and frozen. Thaw before setting over fruit. Pandowdy can be baked ahead and warmed before serving, but texture of crust is best served freshly baked and warm from the oven.

Special equipment: 10-inch pie plate; large mixing bowl; paring knife; vegetable peeler; pastry brush; spatula or pancake turner.

Baking time: 400°F for 25 to 30 minutes; "dowdy," then bake additional 20 to 25 minutes.

Quantity: One 10-inch pie.

*Unbaked pastry for a single 10-inch pie
crust made with Basic All-Purpose
Flaky Pastry (page 34) or
Butter-Lard Pastry (page 63)*
Milk—for glaze
*4 medium-sized Granny Smith apples,
or other tart variety, peeled and
sliced (3 cups)*
*12 Italian prune plums, quartered and
pitted (2 cups)*
½ cup pure maple syrup
*Optional: 1 tablespoon unsulfured
molasses*
2 tablespoons lemon juice
*½ teaspoon each ground nutmeg and
cinnamon*
A pinch of mace
2 tablespoons unsalted butter, cut up

Topping
Heavy cream or vanilla ice cream

1. Prepare pastry and set it in refrigerator to chill. Preheat oven to 400°F.

2. In large mixing bowl, combine and gently toss the fruit with the maple syrup, molasses, lemon juice, spices, and butter.

3. Turn fruit into the pie plate. Roll out pastry (page 38) and fit it over the top of the fruit. With a sharp paring knife, cut pastry off just *inside* the rim of the plate. Do not crimp the pastry edge. Brush top of pastry with milk and sprinkle with granulated sugar to give it a crisp glaze. Cut several steam vents in the top.

4. Bake in the center of the preheated oven for about 25 to 30 minutes, or until the crust is a *light* golden color. Remove the pan from the oven and set it on a heat-proof surface while you "dowdy" pastry by cutting about 4 slices across the pie in opposite directions, dividing the crust into cookie-size squares. Use a spatula or pancake turner to press these squares gently down into the fruit so the pan juices bubble up and moisten the crust. Return the pan to the oven and bake an additional 20 to 25 minutes, or just until the crust is a deep golden brown. Serve warm, scooping up fruit and juices, and topping with heavy cream or vanilla ice cream.

HUNGARIAN PLUM KUCHEN

This Hungarian specialty uses sour cream in the batter, to make one of the most delicious fruited cake-pies we know. Bake it in a 10-inch pie plate, or a round or square cake pan; whether you call it a coffee cake, a cake-pie, or a kuchen, you will enjoy the way it tastes.

Advance preparation: This recipe can be prepared ahead, baked, and frozen; but the flavor and texture are best when freshly baked.
Special equipment: Mixing bowl and spoon or electric mixer; sifter; 10-inch pie plate or 10-inch round or square cake pan; knife; rubber spatula; cake tester or toothpick.
Baking time: 350°F for 40 to 45 minutes.
Quantity: One 10-inch cake-pie.

> *1 large egg yolk*
> *¾ cup butter or margarine, at room*
> *   temperature*
> *1 cup granulated sugar*
> *⅓ cup sour cream (or plain yogurt)*
> *2 to 2¼ cups all-purpose or cake flour*
> *½ teaspoon baking powder*

⅛ *teaspoon salt*
1 pound (about 12) Italian prune plums

Topping
3 tablespoons butter or margarine
3 tablespoons wheat germ or flour
¼ *cup granulated sugar*
¼ *cup chopped hazelnuts or walnuts*
¼ *teaspoon each cinnamon and nutmeg*

1. Preheat the oven to 350°F. Butter the pan and set it aside. In a mixing bowl combine the egg yolk, butter or margarine, the sugar, and sour cream. Beat well. Sift 2 cups of the flour, baking powder, and salt into the bowl directly over the butter mixture. Beat in the flour mixture slowly until well incorporated. The dough should hold together in a soft ball; it will be softer than a cookie dough and less dry, but if it feels sticky, add more flour, a little at a time, up to ¼ cup.

2. Using a rubber spatula, press the dough onto the buttered pan—on the bottom and up against the sides, into an even layer about ¼-inch thick.

3. Wash, dry, halve, and pit the plums. Arrange the plums skin side down in an all-over pattern on the dough. Press on the plums to push them down into the dough slightly.

4. Without washing the dough-mixing bowl, use it to prepare the topping by combining in it the butter, wheat germ or flour, sugar, nuts, and spices. Crumble the mixture and sprinkle it over the fruit. If it seems like too much topping, use only as much as you wish, or omit it altogether if you prefer.

5. Bake the kuchen in the preheated oven for 40 to 45 minutes, or until the cake is golden around the edges and a toothpick or cake tester inserted about 1-inch in from the edge comes out clean. Cool on a wire rack. Cut in wedges or squares and serve directly from the baking pan.

VARIATIONS:

Apple Kuchen. Prepare Hungarian Plum Kuchen but substitute 5 or 6 medium-sized cooking apples, peeled, cored, and thickly sliced, for the plums.

Peach Kuchen. Prepare Hungarian Plum Kuchen, but substitute 1½ pounds ripe peaches, peeled (page 137), pitted, and sliced, for the plums.

CAKE PIE, CAKE FLAN, AND CLAFOUTIS

Strictly speaking, these are neither cakes nor pies, though all are close relatives. Boston Cream Pie is really a frosted sponge cake filled with pastry cream. Cake flans are sponge cakes baked with a lowered center that one fills with pastry cream and glazed fruit. The Clafoutis is a French country tart baked without a lining crust; it is a simple crepe batter baked with a fruit mixture to create a dessert that resembles nothing so much as a sweet, fruited Yorkshire Pudding.

BOSTON CREAM PIE

Although it really is a cake, no pie book would be complete without Boston Cream Pie. My research has so far failed to clarify the exact origin of this recipe though several New England restaurants would like to claim it for their own. We do know it traces its lineage to the early cake-pies, which were cake batters baked in piecrust. Sometimes, as in this case, the piecrust was simply omitted and the batter baked directly in the pie plate. My 1930 Boston Cooking School Cook Book by Fannie Merritt Farmer says to bake the cake in a heavy frying pan, split it into 2 filled layers, then cut it into pie-shaped pieces for serving.

Traditionally, this is a plain somewhat dense vanilla butter cake, but the version I prefer has stiffly beaten egg whites folded in to lighten the texture. The filling can be Vanilla Pastry Cream made from scratch and used plain or with added banana slices, or, if you are in a hurrry and have the cakes in your freezer, you can prepare a package of cooked-type French vanilla pudding and pie filling with an extra teaspoon of vanilla extract. There seem to be two schools of thought about chocolate icing versus confectioners' sugar as the authentic topping. I favor those who consider a rich, satiny high-gloss chocolate icing the genuine article, while I find confectioners' sugar best complements raspberry jam filling in the variation known as Washington Pie.

Advance preparation: The cake layers can be made in advance, wrapped airtight, and frozen. Thaw before assembling the pie. The cream filling can be made a day ahead, or at least several hours before using, so it can cool and thicken properly. The cake can be assembled a day in advance, but its texture is best if assembled on the day of serving. Allow an hour or so for the icing to set before serving the cake. Store leftovers in the refrigerator to protect the cream filling, but bring to room temperature before serving.

Special equipment: Electric mixer; two 8- or 9-inch round cake pans; rubber scraper; extra mixing bowl; wire rack; double boiler; spatula; wax paper; cake tester or toothpick; flat serving platter.

Baking time: 350°F for 30 minutes.

Quantity: One 8-inch 2-layer cake.

Filling

½ recipe Vanilla Pastry Cream (page
*   100) chilled*

Cake

Butter and flour for preparing pans
2 eggs, separated
6 tablespoons unsalted butter
1 cup granulated sugar
1 teaspoon vanilla extract
½ teaspoon almond extract
2 cups cake flour
2½ teaspoons baking powder
½ teaspoon salt
¾ cup milk

Icing

3 ounces semisweet chocolate
2 tablespoons water
2 egg yolks
1 teaspoon vanilla extract
4 tablespoons unsalted butter, softened
*   at room temperature and cut up*

1. Prepare the Vanilla Pastry Cream and set it in the refrigerator to chill. Butter both cake pans and dust them lightly with flour; shake out excess flour and set the pans aside, Preheat the oven to 350°F.

2. Beat the egg whites in an electric mixer until stiff peaks form. Transfer the whites to another bowl, using a rubber scraper. Set the whites aside and return the first bowl to the mixer. In this unwashed bowl, cream together the butter and sugar until smooth. Add the egg yolks, and vanilla and almond extracts, and beat well.

3. Sift the flour, baking powder, and salt together on a piece of wax paper. With the mixer on slow speed, blend the dry ingredients into the egg yolks alternately with the milk. When the mixture is smooth, remove it from the mixer. Stir in about ¼ of the beaten whites, then gently fold in the remaining whites. Divide the batter evenly between the prepared pans and bake in the center of the preheated oven for 30 minutes, or until a cake tester inserted in the center comes out clean. After about 5 minutes, invert the cakes to remove them from the pans and cool on a wire rack.

4. To prepare the Chocolate Icing, combine the chocolate and water in the top of a double boiler and set over hot (not boiling) water until the chocolate is melted. Stir to blend, then turn the mixture into a small electric mixer bowl and beat in the egg yolks, vanilla and cut-up, softened butter. When smooth and creamy, set the icing aside.

5. To assemble, set one cake layer flat on the serving platter; generously spread the top with Vanilla Pastry Cream, making a thick layer. Set the second cake layer lightly atop the cream filling and spread chocolate icing over the top. Use a spatula to smooth the top and allow some icing to drip down over the edges; do not ice the cake sides. Allow the icing to set for about one hour before slicing and serving the cake.

VARIATIONS:

Banana Cream Pie. Prepare Boston Cream Pie as above, but add 1 large sliced
   banana to the cream filling between the layers.
Washington Pie. Prepare Boston Cream Pie as above but omit the Vanilla Pastry Cream and Chocolate Icing. Fill the cake with a thick layer of raspberry
   jam and sift a generous coating of confectioners' sugar on the top.

FRUITED CAKE FLAN

This cousin of the pastry tart is made with a sponge, or Génoise, cake batter baked in a specially designed pan with a raised bottom (page 23). When inverted, the baked cake has a depression in the center of its raised edging that is filled with custard and glazed fruit.

The pastry cream filling is optional; it can be replaced by a layer of crushed cookies, or simply a layer of jam. This cake recipe is large enough to make two; use one and freeze the other. The reserved frozen cake flan can make an elegant last-minute dessert when defrosted and topped with canned fruit, drained, and brushed with apricot glaze.

Note: Because of its raised bottom, a 10-inch cake flan tin holds 2 cups batter, about half the batter of a regular 10-inch cake pan.

Advance preparation: The cake can be baked ahead and frozen until needed. Thaw before topping with fruit. The completed cake can be prepared and chilled several hours before serving.

Special equipment: Two 10-inch cake flan tins with plain or fluted edges (available in specialty cookware shops); electric mixer; pastry brush; warmed mixing bowl; sifter.

Baking time: 350°F for 10 to 15 minutes.

Quantity: Two 10-inch cakes.

3 large eggs (warmed in a bowl of warm
water for 10 minutes)
⅛ *teaspoon salt*
⅔ *cup granulated sugar, sifted*
½ *teaspoon vanilla extract*
⅔ *cup cake flour, sifted*
3 tablespoons unsalted butter, clarified
(by melting and discarding milky
solids)

To fill one cake flan
Firm Fruit Glaze (page 120) made with
apricot preserves, dark rum, or
brandy
½ *recipe Vanilla Pastry Cream (page 100)*
or ½ cup ground cookie crumbs or
nuts

*2 cups prepared fresh fruit (whole
berries, washed, dried, and hulled;
or pitted cherries or grapes; or
sliced bananas; or peeled, pitted,
and sliced peaches, nectarines, etc.)*

Topping
Sweetened whipped cream (page 107)

1. Preheat the oven to 350°F. Generously butter 2 flan tins, spreading the butter into each flute of the edging, then sprinkle them with flour. Tap out the excess flour and set the pans aside.

2. Warm the mixing bowl by rinsing it with hot water. Dry the bowl well. Add warmed eggs, salt, sugar, and vanilla. Beat on high speed about 3 to 4 minutes, or until the mixture is very thick and light colored. It should form a flat ribbon falling back on itself when it drips from the beater.

3. Resift about half the flour directly onto the egg batter. With a very light touch, fold this flour into the batter in 8 to 10 strokes. Sift on and fold in the remaining flour in the same way. Then dribble on the clarified butter and gently fold it in. Do not overmix the batter or it will lose its original volume and characteristic lightness. Do not worry if the batter sinks somewhat after the butter is added, that is normal.

4. Divide the batter between the 2 prepared pans. Bake in the preheated oven for 12 to 15 minutes, or until the cake is golden, springs back when touched lightly, and a cake tester inserted 1-inch from the edge comes out clean.

5. With the tip of a knife, loosen the edges of the cake from the pan. Invert the cake onto a wire rack to cool. The side now up is the top of the cake; it should have a depression in the center and a raised edging. When cold, the cakes may be wrapped and frozen, or stored in an airtight container for a day or two.

6. To complete, spread the depressed central area of each cake with a coating of brushed-on Firm Fruit Glaze, then top this with a layer of Vanilla Pastry Cream if you are using it, or a layer of crushed cookie crumbs or nuts.

7. Arrange the fruit in a decorative pattern on top of the central area of each cake. Slices, for example, can go in overlapping concentric circles; mixed fruits can be arranged in wedges of alternating colors. Be sure the fruit is drained and dry. Brush fruit with the remaining glaze and refrigerate to set. Serve with sweetened whipped cream (page 107).

MIXED FRUIT CLAFOUTIS

The clafoutis is a casual sort of fruit tart with a thick pancakelike batter that bakes to the texture of Yorkshire pudding. Native to the Limousin region of France, where it is traditionally made with unpitted cherries, the clafoutis is one of the quickest, easiest, and most delicious of all tarts to prepare with whatever fruit you have available.

Advance preparation: The clafoutis is best served freshly baked; it may, however, be prepared several hours in advance and rewarmed before serving.
Special equipment: 10-inch Pyrex pie plate; bowl and whisk or electric mixer or food processor or blender; sifter.
Baking time: 350°F for 35 to 40 minutes.
Quantity: One 10-inch tart.

Fruit
3 cups prepared mixed fresh fruit
*   (such as 4 or 5 prune plums pitted*
*   and thinly sliced, plus 1 banana,*
*   peeled and sliced, plus 1 large pear,*
*   cored and sliced; or use peaches and*
*   blueberries, or apples and*
*   cranberries, or pears and raspberries)*
3 tablespoons granulated sugar
¼ cup rum or brandy or fruit-flavored
*   liqueur*

Batter
¾ cup milk
¼ cup cream (light or half-and-half)
3 eggs
2 teaspoons vanilla extract
3 tablespoons granulated sugar
A pinch of salt
⅔ cup all-purpose or cake flour
A pinch of nutmeg

Topping
Confectioners' sugar

1. Preheat the oven to 350°F. Generously butter a pie plate and set it aside. Prepare the fruit and combine it in a mixing bowl with the sugar and the liqueur or brandy or rum. Macerate the fruit for about 30 minutes, or at least while you prepare the batter.

2. In whatever mixing device you choose to use, combine the milk, cream, eggs, vanilla, 3 tablespoons sugar, salt, flour, and nutmeg. Beat until smooth. If the batter looks too lumpy, pass it through a sieve.

3. Pour about ½ cup batter into the buttered pie plate and set it in the oven for about 4 minutes. This bakes a coating on the pan bottom to prevent the sugared fruit from sticking or burning. Remove the pan from the oven, top with prepared fruit and all its sweetened and flavored juices, then pour on the rest of the batter. Return the pan to the center of the oven and bake about 35 to 40 minutes, or until the top is golden and puffed up. Cool on a wire rack. Just before serving, sift on a fine coating of confectioners' sugar. Cut into wedges and serve warm or at room temperature.

VARIATION:

Cherry Clafoutis. Prepare Mixed Fruit Clafoutis, above, but for the fruit use 3 cups fresh sweet cherries, washed and dried, stemmed and pitted. Or substitute canned and drained sweet Bing or tart cherries; macerate the cherries in kirsch plus the usual 3 tablespoons sugar.

PASTRY SPECIALTIES

The following three pastries qualify for the pastry shop specialty shelf. All require a little more time and effort than a rustic fruit pie, but all are well worth it for the dazzling results and the equally dazzling praise you will receive!

GATEAU PARIS-BREST

Baked in a ring, then sliced open and filled with sweetened cream, this delightful pastry is really a decorative cream puff and no more difficult to make. Both use Puff Shell Dough (*Pâte à Choux*), a quick-to-prepare, light eggy batter that puffs into a crisp shell in the heat of the oven.

You can vary the filling of your *gâteau* to suit your mood and occasion: whole or puréed strawberries or raspberries blended with sweetened whipped cream, for example, or Mocha Whipped Cream (page 108), Praline Pastry Cream (page 102), Pastry Cream St. Honoré (page 102), or pastry cream enriched by folding in whipped cream (page 107). Traditionally, the Paris-Brest is baked with almond slices on top, and finished just before serving with a sprinkling of sifted confectioners' sugar.

Note that the pastry recipe makes 2 ring cakes; fill one now as described below and freeze the second for later use.

Advance preparation: The Puff Shell ring may be baked in advance and frozen. To use, thaw, split, and recrisp in a warm oven if necessary. Add the cream filling as close as possible to serving time. Refrigerate.

Special equipment: Two 11 × 17-inch baking sheets or round pizza pans; pastry
   bag and ½-inch plain or star tip or 2 teaspoons; 8-inch round pie plate,
   bowl, or pan lid for template, serrated knife.
Baking time: 400°F for 30 to 35 minutes.
Quantity: Two 8-inch ring cakes.

> *Puff Shell Dough (*Pâte à Choux, *page*
>   *80)*
> Egg glaze: *1 egg beaten with 1 tablespoon*
>   *milk*
> *⅓ cup sliced almonds*
>
> **For filling one cake**
> *Vanilla Pastry Cream (page 100, made*
>   *ahead and chilled) or plain or flavored*
>   *whipped cream (page 107) or Pastry*
>   *Cream St. Honoré (page 102)*
>
> **Topping**
> *Confectioners' sugar*

1. Prepare the Puff Shell Dough. Preheat the oven to 400°F. Butter two
baking sheets, then sprinkle them lightly with water. For each cake, invert an
8-inch plate (the template) in the center of the buttered surface and draw around
it with a fingertip. Remove the template without marring the prepared pan
surface.

   Spoon the batter into a pastry bag fitted with a ½-inch plain or star tip. To
form one cake, first pipe a ring of dough just inside the marked circle on the
pan. Then pipe a second ring of dough touching the first but outside the marked
circle. Finally, pipe a third ring on top of the first two, right between them.
Alternatively, the ring can be formed with teaspoons full of batter set side-by-side
around the marked circle. Repeat to make the second cake. Use up leftover batter
by making an extra ring on the second cake or by forming several individual
cream puffs.

2. Brush the rings of dough with egg glaze, then sprinkle on the sliced
almonds. Bake the rings in the center of the preheated oven for 30 to 35 minutes,
or until the pastry is golden brown and very crisp. As the pastry surface often
appears to be done before the interior is baked through, at this point remove it
from the oven, prick it with a fork in several places in the side to let the steam
escape, and return it to the oven for about 5 minutes, leaving the door ajar,
propped open with the handle of a wooden spoon if necessary. Cool on a wire
rack. While cooling, again prick the sides with a fork to release steam and keep

the shells crisp. When cool, freeze one ring for later use. Split the second ring in half crosswise with a serrated knife. With a fork, lift out any very soft layers of dough that may cling to the inner crust.

3. Prepare the filling of your choice and spoon or pipe it through a star tip onto the bottom half of the ring. Replace the top, setting it lightly over the filling. Sift on a light coating of confectioners' sugar. Serve immediately, or refrigerate for a short while. The pastry softens on standing.

BAKLAVA

Baklava is surely one of the most famous of Greek pastries: sheets of buttered phyllo dough layered with chopped nuts and cinnamon-sugar, cut into diamonds, and soaked in sugar syrup. Like many Middle Eastern pastries, Baklava is intensely sweet, though the touch of lemon juice in this recipe cuts the sweetness a bit. Serve Baklava for dessert, or as a midafternoon snack as they do in Greece, preferably under the shade of a silvery olive tree beside a whitewashed café with a tall glass of ice water and a thimble-sized cup of thick black Greek coffee at your side. This recipe was shared with me by Greek friends in Connecticut, Mary Katsiaficas and her mother, Mrs. Elpis Kertiles, a native of the isle of Lesbos. They bake marvelous Greek specialties for all the holidays and are as generous about sharing the results as they are with the recipes.

Advance preparation: Phyllo pastry leaves can be purchased frozen, then thawed overnight in the refrigerator, as described on page 98. The Baklava can be frozen after it is completely assembled but before it is baked and coated with syrup; simply wrap the pan in freezer foil and freeze. Bring to room temperature before baking as described below, or bake frozen, at 350°F for 1½ hours, then lower the heat to 300°F and bake 20 to 30 minutes longer if necessary, until golden. Cover with foil if it browns too quickly.

Baked and syrup-coated Baklava can also be frozen after soaking 8 hours. Lift the pieces from the syrup, drain, and set in a freezer container. Freeze. Remove pieces as needed and bring them to room temperature before serving. Without freezing, syrup-coated baked Baklava can be stored from several days to a week, covered, at room temperature.

Special equipment: 2-quart heavy-bottom saucepan; rectangular or round baking pan with an area roughly 9 × 13 inches × 1½ inches thick; flat tray about 14 × 20 inches (to hold phyllo); sharp knife; ruler; small saucepan; medium-sized mixing bowl; dampened tea towel to cover phyllo; 1-cup measure; nut chopper or blender or food processor; aluminum foil; pastry brush; wax paper or plastic wrap.

Baking time: 350°F for 1 to 1¼ hours.
Quantity: 30 pieces.

> *1 (1 pound) package frozen phyllo leaves,*
> *thawed as in note below. This recipe*
> *uses about 22 leaves of phyllo 9 ×*
> *13 inches. See page 96 for further*
> *information on buying and using*
> *phyllo. You can also substitute fresh*
> *strudel dough (page 91) cut to fit*
> *your Baklava pan*

Syrup
3 cups granulated sugar
3 cups water
½ cup honey
1 tablespoon lemon juice

Filling
1½ cups unsalted butter, melted
3 cups (12 ounces) walnuts, chopped fine
*   or pistachio nuts or blanched*
*   almonds, chopped*
½ cup granulated sugar
1½ teaspoons cinnamon
Optional: ½ teaspoon ground cloves

A note about phyllo: Thaw as directed on the box, by setting in refrigerator overnight. (*Note:* Prepare syrup, melted butter, and nut mixture before unwrapping thawed phyllo to prevent it from drying out in the air.) Remove phyllo from the inner plastic bag by slitting one end carefully and saving the bag so it can be reused for refreezing leftover phyllo.

1. To achieve the proper texture, the hot, freshly baked Baklava must be topped by syrup that has been previously made and cooled to room temperature. To prepare the syrup, combine the sugar and water in a heavy-bottom saucepan and stir. Bring to a boil, then lower the heat slightly and boil gently and steadily for 30 minutes. The temperature of the syrup will be about 100°F. Remove from the heat and stir in the honey and lemon juice. Set aside to cool, or transfer to a cold bowl and refrigerate. The syrup should be cool and thick enough to coat a spoon.

2. To prepare the Baklava, melt the butter in saucepan and set it aside, along with a pastry brush. The melted butter can be used as is, without clarifying, a method I prefer. Many Greek cooks, however, prefer to clarify the butter after melting by resting it a few minutes, then skimming off the foam on top and pouring the butter into another pan to separate it from the milky residue that sinks to the bottom. You can facilitate this process by using a gravy-fat separator.

3. Chop the nuts in a blender or processor and combine them with the sugar and spices in a bowl. Stir well and set aside. Brush melted butter on the bottom and sides of the baking pan. Preheat the oven to 350°F.

4. Unwrap the phyllo and set the stack of leaves flat on your tray. Measure the leaves if this information is not indicated on the box, as commercial phyllo comes in varying quantities and sizes and you need to cut the leaves to fit your pan. One pound phyllo can contain between 21 and 30 leaves varying from 12 × 17 inches to 14 × 18 inches. If your leaves are the latter size, simply cut through the entire stack, dividing it in two to fit your 9 × 13-inch pan. If your leaves are smaller, turn your baking pan over onto the stack of phyllo and cut around the edge, shaping leaves to fit. Immediately after cutting the phyllo, cover it with plastic wrap or wax paper topped with a dampened, well-rung-out tea towel to protect it from drying. Use as much phyllo as required for this recipe, then rewrap and refreeze the rest for another use.

5. To assemble the Baklava, remove one leaf of phyllo from the stack, re-cover the rest, and set it on the bottom of the buttered baking pan. Brush melted butter over the phyllo, then top with another leaf. Brush on more butter. Tuck in any overhanging edges. Repeat, building up 7 to 8 buttered layers in all, ending with butter.

6. Dip a 1-cup measure into the nut mixture, fill it, and sprinkle this over the buttered phyllo, making an even layer. Top the nuts with 3 buttered phyllo leaves. Sprinkle on another 1 cup of nuts in an even layer and top with 3 more buttered phyllo leaves. Sprinkle on the remaining nuts in an even layer and top with 7 to 8 buttered phyllo leaves. Be sure the top layer is free of tears and looks neat; brush the top layer with butter.

7. With a sharp knife cut through the Baklava right down to the bottom, making 7 diagonal cuts in each direction to divide the pan into 2-inch diamond-shaped pieces. Cut with a sharp jabbing motion rather than pulling or dragging, which will disarrange the pieces. Cutting through the Baklava now facilitates the absorption of the syrup immediately after baking.

8. Bake the Baklava in the center of the preheated oven for about 1¼ hours, or until the top is golden brown and the layers are puffed up. Cover the pan with foil if browning occurs too soon. As soon as Baklava is baked, set it on a heatproof surface and immediately pour on about half the cool syrup. Allow this to penetrate about 5 minutes, then pour on the remaining syrup and allow it to

stand at least 8 hours, or overnight, before serving. As soon as pan is completely cool, you can cover it with foil. Do not refrigerate. To serve, lift pieces from the pan, drain them on a rack if necessary, then set them on a serving platter or serve in individual fluted paper muffin cups.

Strudel Fillings

A discussion of Strudel, the Strudel dough recipe, and the step-by-step stretching procedure are given on page 91. The following filling recipes for Cheese, Cherry, and Apple-Apricot-Nut Strudel utilize that recipe and basic method.

CHEESE STRUDEL

Advance preparation: Make Strudel dough (page 91), and set the dough to rest at least 30 minutes *before* stretching, while you prepare the filling. This filling can also be made ahead and refrigerated several hours, or overnight. Bring it to room temperature before using.

Special equipment: Read About Strudel (page 89); set out one buttered baking sheet at least 12 × 16 inches; pan of melted butter with a pastry brush.

Quantity: To fill one recipe Strudel dough. Serves 15 to 16.

> *1 (1-pound) package cottage cheese,*
> *whole milk type, either small or*
> *large curd (if you are using an*
> *electric mixer, sieve the cheese; if*
> *you are using a food processor, do*
> *not)*
> *8 ounces cream cheese (not whipped)*
> *¼ cup sour cream*
> *2 large eggs*
> *½ cup granulated sugar*
> *Juice and grated zest of 1 large lemon*
> *(2 teaspoons zest, 2 tablespoons*
> *juice)*
> *½ teaspoon vanilla extract*
> *¾ cup unsalted butter, melted*
> *⅓ cup graham cracker crumbs*

Topping
Confectioners' sugar

1. If you are using an electric mixer, put the cottage and cream cheese, the sour cream, eggs, sugar, lemon zest and juice, and vanilla into the mixer bowl and beat until smooth. If you are using a food processor, combine the cheese, sour cream and eggs in the work bowl fitted with a steel blade. Process until smooth and creamy. Add the sugar, lemon juice and zest, and the vanilla, and process only to blend smooth. Refrigerate until needed, but bring to room temperature to spread.

2. Read About Strudel (page 89). Stretch the dough, then trim as indicated, steps 1 to 6. Sprinkle or lightly brush the dough with melted butter. Then sprinkle on an even layer of crumbs.

3. Beginning about 1 inch down from the top edge and leaving a 1- to 2-inch border along the side edges, drop spoonfuls of cheese mixture in an even pattern, covering 2/3 of the dough. With the back of a spoon, spread the cheese into an even layer. Leave the edges and the remaining 1/3 of the stretched dough covered *only* by butter and crumbs.

4. To roll up and bake the Strudel, review steps 7 to 11 (pages 95–96). Fold the clean top and side edges over the filling, then roll up the Strudel by lifting the cloth under one end, allowing the Strudel to fall over onto itself like a jelly roll, as described. Cut the rolled Strudel in half, or leave it whole and curve it into a horseshoe. Brush the top with more melted butter and set it on a buttered baking sheet.

5. Chill the Strudel on its baking sheet 20 to 30 minutes, if you have time. Bake in the lower third of a preheated 425°F oven for 20 minutes, then reduce the heat to 350°F and bake 20 minutes longer, or until the pastry is a rich golden brown. Cool on a wire rack. To keep it crisp, cut the hot Strudel into 2-inch thick slices to allow steam to escape. Sift on a light sprinkling of confectioners' sugar and serve warm. To store or freeze Strudel, see step 12 (page 96).

CHERRY STRUDEL

Advance preparation: Make 1 recipe Strudel dough, (page 91) and set the
dough to rest at least 30 minutes *before* stretching while you prepare the
filling.

Special equipment: Read About Strudel, page 89; set out one buttered baking
sheet at least 12 × 16 inches; pan of melted butter with a pastry brush.

Quantity: To fill one recipe Strudel dough. Serves 15 to 16.

> 2 *(1-pound) cans pitted tart red cherries,*
> *drained*
> 2 *(1-pound) cans pitted sweet Bing*
> *cherries, drained (or use 4 cans tart*
> *red cherries)*
> ½ *cup walnuts, chopped*
> *Grated zest of 1 lemon (about 2*
> *teaspoons)*
> ½ *teaspoon freshly grated nutmeg*
> ½ *cup granulated sugar*
> ¾ *cup unsalted butter, melted*
> 6 *tablespoons unflavored dry bread*
> *crumbs or graham cracker crumbs*

Topping
Confectioners' sugar

1. Combine the drained cherries in a bowl. Discard the juice. Measure the
nuts into a cup and set them aside. Stir the lemon zest and nutmeg into the
sugar and set it aside.

2. Read About Strudel, page 89. Stretch and trim the dough as indicated,
steps 1 to 5 (pages 92–95). Sprinkle or lightly brush melted butter all over the
stretched dough. Then sprinkle on an even layer of crumbs. Now, beginning
about 1 inch down from the top and leaving a 1- to 2-inch border along the side
edges, scatter an even layer of the sugar mixture, then nuts, then cherries, over
⅔ to ¾ of the dough. Leave the edges and the remaining ⅓ to ¼ of the
stretched dough covered *only* by butter and crumbs. See Strudel, step 6.

3. To roll up and bake the Strudel, review Strudel, steps 7 to 11 (pages 95–
96). Fold the clean top and side edges over filling, then roll up the dough by
lifting the cloth under one end, allowing the Strudel to fall over into itself like
a jelly roll, as described. Cut the rolled Strudel in half, or leave it whole and

curved into a horseshoe. Brush the top with more melted butter and set it on a buttered baking sheet.

4. Chill the Strudel on its baking sheet 20 to 30 minutes, if you have time. Bake in the lower third of a preheated 425°F oven for 20 minutes, then reduce the heat to 350°F and bake 20 minutes longer, or until the pastry is rich golden brown. Cool on a wire rack. To keep it crisp, cut the hot Strudel into 2-inch thick slices to allow steam to escape. Sift on a light sprinkling of confectioners' sugar and serve warm. To store or freeze Strudel, see step 12 (page 96).

APPLE-APRICOT-NUT STRUDEL

Advance preparation: Make Strudel dough (page 91) and set the dough to rest at least 30 minutes *before* stretching while you prepare the filling.

Special equipment: Read About Strudel, page 000; set out one buttered baking sheet at least 12 × 16 inches; pan of melted butter with a pastry brush.

Quantity: To fill one recipe Strudel dough. Serves 15 to 16.

Filling

*1⅓ cups apricot preserves or 1 (12-ounce)
   can apricot pastry filling
1 or 2 tablespoons water or fruit juice
¾ cup currants
¾ cup golden raisins
3 tablespoons port or brandy or sweet
   apple cider
⅔ cup granulated sugar
½ cup dark brown sugar, packed
Juice and grated zest of 1 lemon (about
   2 teaspoons zest, 2 tablespoons juice)
5 to 6 large tart cooking apples
   (Greenings or Granny Smith, for
   example), peeled, cored, sliced fine
   or chopped coarse (about 6 cups)
½ cup walnuts or almonds, chopped
1 teaspoon ground cinnamon
¾ cup unsalted butter, melted
¼ cup unflavored dry bread crumbs or
   graham cracker crumbs*

Topping

Confectioners' sugar

1. If the apricot preserves (or pastry filling) feels too stiff to be easily brushed over the dough, warm it in a saucepan over low heat, stirring in 1 or 2 tablespoons water or juice to thin the mixture. Set aside to cool. In a small bowl, plump the currants and raisins in port, brandy, or cider for at least 10 minutes. In another bowl, combine the sugars and stir in the lemon zest to distribute it evenly. Sprinkle the lemon juice over the sliced apples in a large bowl. Measure and set out the nuts and cinnamon.

2. Read About Strudel page 89. Stretch the dough, then trim as indicated, steps 1 to 5 (pages 92–95). Sprinkle or lightly brush the stretched dough with melted butter. Then sprinkle on an even layer of crumbs.

3. Beginning about 1 inch down from the top edge and leaving a 1- to 2-inch border along the side edges, lightly brush or sprinkle dabs of preserves or pastry filling over ⅔ of dough. Leave side edges and the remaining ⅓ of stretched dough covered *only* by butter and crumbs. Over the jam-covered area, spread on an even layer of currants and raisins topped by the sugar mixture, the apples, cinnamon, and nuts.

4. To roll up and bake the Strudel, review Strudel steps 7 to 11 (pages 95–96). Fold the clean top and side edges over the filling, then roll up the dough by lifting the cloth under one end, allowing the Strudel to fall over onto itself like a jelly roll, as described. Cut the rolled Strudel in half, or leave it whole and curved into a horseshoe. Brush the top with more melted butter and set it on a buttered baking sheet.

5. Chill Strudel on its baking sheet 20 to 30 minutes, if you have time. Bake in the lower third of a preheated 425°F oven for 20 minutes, then reduce the heat to 350°F and bake 20 minutes longer, or until the pastry is a rich golden brown. Cool on a wire rack. To keep it crisp, cut the hot Strudel into 2-inch thick slices to allow steam to escape. Sift on a light sprinkling of confectioners' sugar and serve warm. To store or freeze Strudel, see step 12 (page 96).

SAVORY PIES
AND TARTS

QUICHES, VEGETABLE AND CHEESE PIES, AND PIZZA

A quiche is an open-faced pie or tart containing a savory custard filling. Quiches are sometimes baked in tart pans and served free-standing, but more commonly, they are served directly from their baking pans, which may be metal, china, or ceramic.

The quiche is a very versatile dish: You can make it with whole eggs or yolks, and milk or cream, or any combination of the two, depending upon the richness desired. Because a quiche is basically a custard, it requires cooking at a low heat. To insure that the pastry shell remains crisp, it is best prebaked and moisture-proofed in advance.

The classic quiche comes from Lorraine, France, but the number of variations on this theme are nearly infinite; once you see our list, you will want to improvise quiches of your own.

Vegetable and cheese pies are more or less variations on the quiche, though some have distinctly different fillings. Pizzas—those rounds of yeast dough topped by nearly anything you can think of—have a history and a life all their own, every bit as international and varied as that of the quiche.

All the recipes in this section are served warm or hot and are suitable for luncheon or supper entrées. When baked in small tartlet shells, they may also be served as hors d'oeuvre. For additional hors d'oeuvre, see page 391.

QUICHE LORRAINE

This is the classic quiche, which originated in Lorraine, France. It consists only of bacon, eggs, cream, salt, pepper, and nutmeg, although—as the many following variations illustrate—the contents can be as creative as your imagination.

Advance preparation: The partially prebaked pastry shell can be prepared ahead and frozen. Thaw before filling. For best flavor and texture, fill and bake the shell shortly before serving. (*Note:* Baked quiches may be frozen successfully, though occasionally they get watery when thawed. Thoroughly heat the thawed quiche in a 300°F oven before serving.) Be aware that bottom crusts soften on standing.

Special equipment: 10-inch quiche pan or 11-inch tart pan with removable bottom, or 10-inch pie plate; pastry brush; saucepan; heavy-bottom 12-inch frying pan; stainless steel knife; paper towels (for draining bacon). For variations: grater; optional: food processor with slicing and grating blades.

Baking time: For the partially prebaked pastry shell: 425°F for 10 minutes with pie weights, 3 minutes empty; for the filled quiche: 375°F for 25 to 30 minutes.

Quantity: **One 10- or 11-inch quiche; serves 8.**

> *Partially prebaked 10-inch pastry shell*
> *made with Basic All-Purpose Flaky*
> *Pastry (page 34) or Nut Pastry or*
> *Herb Pastry Variation (page 35).*
> *Omit the sugar, but prepare with*
> *either 1 yolk or 1 whole egg*
> *as part of the measured liquid*
> Egg glaze: *1 egg beaten with 1*
> *tablespoon water*

Filling
6 to 8 slices bacon
4 eggs
1½ cups heavy cream (or half milk,
    half cream)
½ teaspoon each salt and white pepper
A pinch of freshly grated nutmeg
1 tablespoon butter, cut up

1. Prepare the pastry, roll it out, and line the buttered quiche pan (page 41). Trim a ¾-inch overhang, fold the pastry edge inward, and press to the sides of the pan. Run a rolling pin over the top of the pan to trim the excess dough. Prick the bottom of the pastry with fork, chill until firm, then partially blind-bake the shell (page 42). Remove liner and weights and brush bottom of warm shell with moisture-proofing egg glaze before baking an additional 3 to 4 minutes. Cool on a wire rack. Reduce oven heat to 375°F.

2. Blanch the bacon by simmering it in water for 5 minutes. Then drain it on paper towels, pat it dry, and sauté in a frying pan over low heat until crisp. Drain on paper towels, then crumble the bacon into the bottom of the prepared pastry shell.

3. In mixing bowl, beat together the eggs, cream, salt, pepper, and nutmeg. Pour this custard over the bacon and dot with cut-up butter. Bake the quiche in the center of the preheated oven for 25 to 35 minutes, until the filling is puffed up and lightly browned, and a knife inserted into the center comes out clean. Cool on a wire rack. The filling will sink down as it cools. Serve warm.

VARIATIONS:

Ham and Cheese Quiche. Sauté 1 cup diced baked ham in a frying pan for about 3 minutes with 2 tablespoons minced shallots and 2 tablespoons butter. Remove from the heat and set aside to cool. Prepare ¼ cup minced fresh parsley, ½ teaspoon Dijon mustard, ½ cup grated Gruyère or cheddar cheese, and 2 tablespoons grated Parmesan cheese.

Prepare a custard as for Quiche Lorraine but omit bacon. Stir the ham, shallots, parsley, mustard and both cheeses into the egg custard. Pour this into the prepared pastry shell and dot with cut-up butter. Or top with thin slices of cheese, set out in a pinwheel or star shape. Bake as directed for Quiche Lorraine.

Spinach Quiche. Prepare Quiche Lorraine but omit the bacon. Add spinach prepared as follows: In frying pan sauté 2 tablespoons minced shallots with 2 tablespoons butter for 2 or 3 minutes. Add 1½ cups fresh spinach leaves. washed, patted dry, and torn up into small pieces (or 1 package frozen spinach leaves, thawed and well-drained). Stir and sauté the mixture over medium heat until excess moisture has evaporated from the spinach. Remove from heat, cool to lukewarm, then combine with the egg custard and pour into the prepared pastry shell. Dot with cut-up butter and bake as directed.

Smoke Salmon Quiche. Prepare Quiche Lorraine but omit the bacon and use only 3 eggs. Add 1 teaspoon each chopped chives and chopped fresh dill and 1 tablespoon chopped fresh parsley or 1 teaspoon, dried, plus 8 thin pieces (about 4 ounces) of Nova Scotia salmon (not lox, which is too salty for this recipe) chopped or sliced into ¼ inch strips. Blend into the custard and bake as directed. (*Note:* Ask for end pieces of salmon; they are less expensive than center slices but equally flavorful.)

Zucchini Quiche. Prepare Quiche Lorraine using the bacon, but only 3 eggs. Add: ⅓ cup grated Gruyère or Swiss cheese and zucchini prepared as follows:

Wash 2 small zucchini and cut into ¼-inch slices (about 2 cups, sliced). In a heavy-bottom frying pan, sauté 2 tablespoons minced shallots or yellow onion in 3 tablespoons butter for 2 minutes, then add the zucchini slices and 1 teaspoon dried basil (or 2 tablespoons chopped fresh basil leaves). Cook, stirring until the zucchini is slightly tender. Spread the zucchini mixture in the prepared shell, cover with crumbled bacon, add egg custard, and top with grated cheese. Bake as directed.

Michele's Scallion Quiche. Prepare Quiche Lorraine but omit the bacon. Add 12 scallions, chopped or diagonally sliced and sautéed for 3 or 4 minutes with 3 tablespoons butter plus 1 tablespoon oil. Stir in 1 tablespoon flour and 1 teaspoon oregano, then remove from heat. Spread the scallion mixture in the prepared shell, pour on the egg custard, and top with ¾ cup grated Gruyère or Swiss cheese. Bake as directed.

Leek and Mushroom Quiche. Prepare Quiche Lorraine, but omit the bacon and use only 3 eggs. Add 1½ pounds leeks and ½ pound fresh mushrooms, 5 to 6 tablespoons butter or margarine, ¼ cup water, and ⅓ cup grated Gruyère or Swiss cheese prepared as follows:

To prepare the leeks, cut away and discard the root ends and green stems. Cut the remaining white stalks into quarters lengthwise and rinse well under cold water. Gather the pieces on a board and cut into thin (¼-inch) crosswise slices; you should have about 2 cups of slices. Melt 3 tablespoons butter or margarine in a large heavy-bottom frying pan over medium heat. Add the leeks, stir, and cook about 2 minutes. Add ¼ cup water, cover, reduce the heat to low, and simmer the leeks about 15 minutes, or until tender. Uncover and bring to a quick boil for a minute to evaporate any excess water. Place the leeks in a bowl to cool slightly. Wipe out the frying pan.

To prepare the mushrooms, rinse them quickly, then slice through the stems lengthwise. Melt 2 tablespoons butter or margarine in the wiped out frying pan set over medium-high heat. Add the mushrooms and sauté, stirring constantly, 1 to 2 minutes, until the mushrooms are barely cooked through, but no longer raw. Using a slotted spoon, lift out the mushrooms and add them to the leeks. Prepare the egg custard.

Set the partially baked pastry shell on a cookie sheet for ease in handling. Spread the grated cheese in the bottom of the shell, top with leek-mushroom mixture, then pour on the custard filling carefully so the shell does not overflow. Dot with butter and bake as directed. Serve warm.

Seafood Quiche. Prepare Quiche Lorraine but omit the bacon. Add 3 tablespoons dry sherry, a pinch of cayenne pepper, and 2 cups cut-up prepared seafood, such as precooked flaked crabmeat and halved lightly cooked shrimp, or briefly sautéed tiny scallops combined with shrimp or flaked cooked fish. Spread the seafood on the shell and top with custard. Bake as directed. Serve warm.

Fresh Vegetable Quiche. This recipe is very popular in the class I teach called Summer Garden Cooking; the variety of vegetables can be adapted to your seasonal produce or you can substitute frozen vegetables.

Prepare Quiche Lorraine with 4 eggs but omit the bacon and nutmeg. Add ½ teaspoon dry mustard and a dash of cayenne pepper to the custard. Grate ½ cup sharp cheddar cheese and set it aside. Prepare vegetables as follows:

Measure and set aside ½ cup each of fresh or frozen thinly sliced carrots, cut-up green beans, corn kernels and fresh thinly sliced mushrooms. You need 2 cups vegetables, in all. In addition, thinly slice half a yellow onion. First, cook the carrots and beans together in a saucepan with a small amount of water for 4 or 5 minutes, until tender. Add corn kernels and cook all together for the last 2 minutes cooking time. Drain and set aside. In a heavy-bottom frying pan, sauté the onion in 2 tablespoons oil until golden. Add the mushrooms and sauté over medium-high heat for about 2 minutes. The medium-high heat seals the juices into the mushrooms, instead of letting them release their liquid. As soon as the mushrooms are barely tender add them to the other vegetables. Sprinkle cheese over the prepared pastry shell, pour on the custard, and top with vegetables and onion-mushroom mixture. Bake as directed. Serve warm.

CARROT QUICHE

This colorful quiche makes a perfect country luncheon dish when accompanied by a tossed green salad and a dry white wine. It is equally successful as a vegetable course for a holiday buffet. The flavor in the basic recipe is delicate and quite bland; if you prefer to jazz it up, you can add the sharp cheese and mustard. Quantities can be doubled to make a large, party-size quiche.

Advance preparation: The partially prebaked pastry may be made ahead and frozen. Thaw before filling. Carrots can be grated and blanched a day ahead, then drained, covered, and refrigerated. For best flavor and texture, bake the quiche shortly before serving. The quiche can, however, be baked and then frozen. Thaw, then warm in the oven at 300°F for 20 minutes before serving.

Special equipment: 9-inch quiche pan or pie plate; rolling pin; pastry brush; colander; grater (or food processor with grating disk); 3-quart heavy-bottom saucepan; mixing bowl and whisk.

Baking time: The partially prebaked pastry shell: 425°F for 10 minutes with pie weights; 3 to 5 minutes empty; filled quiche: 375°F for 30 to 35 minutes.

Quantity: One 9-inch quiche; serves 6.

> *Partially prebaked 9-inch pastry shell*
> *made with Cream Cheese Pastry*
> *(page 65) or Basic All-Purpose Flaky*
> *Pastry, Herb Variation (page 35) or*
> *Vinegar Pastry (page 36), prepared*
> *with 1 egg yolk and no sugar*

> **Filling**
> *2 eggs plus 1 yolk*
> *¾ cup heavy cream*
> *½ teaspoon salt*
> *¼ teaspoon ground ginger*
> *⅛ teaspoon ground allspice*
> *¾ pound (3 or 4 large) carrots*
> *3 tablespoons lightly salted butter,*
> *   melted*
> *2 teaspoons granulated sugar*
> *2 tablespoons fresh parsley, minced, or*
> *   1½ teaspoons dried*
> *Optional extra seasoning: ⅓ cup sharp*
> *   cheddar cheese, grated, plus ½*
> *   teaspoon Dijon-style mustard or ½*
> *   teaspoon dry mustard*

1. In a mixing bowl, beat together eggs, yolk, and cream, then set aside for use as a moisture-proofing glaze. Prepare the pastry according to recipe instructions. Preheat the oven to 425°F. Roll out the dough and line the quiche pan (page 38). Trim a ¾-inch overhang, fold over the edge, and press to the sides of the pan. Run a rolling pin over the top of the pan to trim excess dough. Prick the pastry bottom with fork and chill until the dough is firm, then partially

blind-bake (page 43). Remove from the oven, remove the liner and weights, and brush moisture-proofing glaze of egg-cream over the bottom of the crust. Return to the oven to bake 3 to 5 minutes longer, until the dough is no longer translucent.

2. To complete the custard mixture, add salt and spices to the egg-cream mixture and whisk well. Add optional seasonings if desired. Set aside.

3. Peel and grate the carrots; you will need roughly 1¾ to 2 cups, grated. Fill a saucepan ½ full with water, bring to a boil, and add the carrots. Boil 1 full minute after the water returns to the boil. Then immediately drain the carrots into a colander and set them into a bowl of ice water, or run cold water over them to stop the cooking. When chilled, drain the carrots well, pressing out *all* excess water.

4. Add butter and sugar to the saucepan, set over medium heat, and melt and stir them together. Then remove the pan from the heat, stir in the carrots, and toss them to coat well.

Arrange the glazed carrots in the bottom of the prepared pastry shell. Pour custard mixture over them, then sprinkle on the parsley.

5. Bake in the center of a preheated 375°F oven for 30 to 35 minutes, or until the filling is puffed and golden and a stainless steel knife inserted in the center comes out clean. Cool slightly on a wire rack; serve warm.

FIDDLEHEAD OR ASPARAGUS QUICHE

This recipe was first given to me by our friend, Seth Bredbury, who enjoys studying, finding, and (judiciously) eating wild foods. As it was June and fiddleheads—as the tightly curled buds of ostrich ferns are called—were past their prime and beginning to unfurl, I was lucky enough to discover them for sale in a local Connecticut supermarket. They were imported from Canada where the growing season is about a month behind that of New England.

Sitting there on the vegetable counter, the mound of little green coils looked as awkward as a country bumpkin perched between the fancy rows of waxed cucumbers and cellophane-wrapped carrots. As it turned out, they were as out of place as they looked. Apparently, I was the first taker, for the checkout girl couldn't figure out what to charge for my bag of fern buds ("Is that what they *really* are?" she asked incredulously). And when I returned for more a few days later, that same basket was as full as it had been the first time, though the contents were sadly wilted. My conclusion is that the number of cooks clamoring for fiddleheads is not statistically significant. In fact, there are not too many people who know what to do with one, let alone a bushelful.

Michael La Croix, good friend and chef/owner of the excellent Michael's

Restaurant in Derby Line, Vermont, explained to me that the growing interest in regional American cuisine emphasized in establishments like his own was just beginning to awaken public enthusiasm for regional foods, even wild foods like the fiddlehead fern. To prove his point, Michael introduced me to one of his part-time waiters, Gary Johnson, who to my mind is fast becoming the Fiddle-head King of the East. With Deborah, his wife, Gary runs a new business called Season's Harvest. This past spring, with the help of his family, he picked over 1,500 pounds of fiddleheads in the Vermont woods and delivered them to some of the most prestigious restaurants and vegetable purveyors in New York City and New England. Among Gary's customers are Manhattan's Balducci's Market and Dean and DiLuca as well as the River Café, the Fours Seasons Restaurant, and Le Perigord East.

When Gary talks about fiddleheads, you are inclined to pay attention. "I took my fiddleheads door to door, when I was first getting started," he explained. "I had to introduce them to more than one chef." And how do you, exactly, introduce an adult chef to a baby fern? The not altogether expected answer: "I told them to treat them the same as asparagus—in Cream of Fiddlehead Soup, for example, or marinated in a vinaigrette." The chefs were impressed, and by now a considerable number of diners have also made the acquaintance of the wild ones. The important thing is the cooking technique, according to Gary. "Blanch them in boiling water to remove any trace of bitterness," he suggests, "pick or rub off the silky brown husk that sometimes clings to the button, or tightest part of the curl, then sauté them in butter to bring out their sweetness."

If you know your ferns and are fiddlehead hunting in your own woods of an early spring day, pick tightly curled buttons, but avoid any that are uncurling to the point where they resemble mature ferns; they are too bitter to eat. Ostrich ferns (*Mattueccia struthiopteris*) are widely available in the northeastern United States, but if you are doubtful about a particular species being edible, ask an expert *before* you taste.

My recipe for Fiddlehead Quiche employs Gary's method of blanching and sautéeing the fiddleheads. The resulting flavor is somewhere between a woodsy mushroom and a sweet young asparagus spear. One other note about this recipe: It breaks one of my self-imposed rules because it uses a packaged mix. But it is Bisquick, a relatively benign buttermilk baking mix, and my excuse is that it is great! The batter produces its own "crust," the mixing method is easy and quick, and it is just plain practical when you are in a hurry. Try it.

Advance preparation: None. For best texture and flavor, prepare and bake this quiche shortly before serving. No pastry crust is required, since the batter makes its own. Leftovers are good cold, though the texture changes slightly.
Special equipment: 3-quart saucepan; colander; 12-inch frying pan; paper towels;

food processor fitted with steel blade or blender or mixing bowl with whisk; 10-inch quiche pan or pie plate;; stainless steel table knife.
Baking time: 400°F for 35 to 40 minutes.
Quantity: **One** 10-inch quiche; serves 6.

> *2 cups salted water*
> *1 cup (4 ounces) fiddleheads (tightly*
> *curled small to medium buds of*
> *ostrich fern); or substitute young*
> *asparagus spears*
> *2 ounces (6 slices) bacon*
> *2 tablespoons vegetable oil or butter*
> *¼ cup yellow onion, chopped fine*
> *2 cups milk (or use half heavy cream)*
> *4 eggs*
> *1 cup Bisquick brand buttermilk baking*
> *mix*
> *¼ teaspoon salt*
> *⅛ teaspoon each white pepper and*
> *dried thyme leaves*
> *½ cup each grated Swiss and sharp*
> *cheddar cheese*

1. Bring salted water to a boil in a 3-quart saucepan. Add the fiddleheads (or asparagus) and blanch by boiling for about 3 minutes (timed from the moment the water returns to a boil), until just tender, but not soft. Drain, rinse immediately in cold water to stop cooking, and spread to dry on paper towels. Pick off any brown husks clinging to the fiddleheads.

2. Preheat the oven to 400°F. In a frying pan, cook the bacon on low heat until crisp. Drain on paper towels, crumble, and set aside. Remove the bacon fat from the pan. Wipe out the pan with paper towel, then add oil or butter and sauté the onions until pale golden in color. Add the fiddleheads (or asparagus) and sauté about 2 minutes longer, stirring and tossing with a wooden spoon. Turn the mixture out into a bowl.

3. In a processor, blender, or bowl, beat together the milk, eggs, buttermilk baking mix, salt, pepper, and thyme.

Generously butter a quiche pan. Arrange the fiddleheads (or asparagus) and onions in the bottom of the pan. Top with half the cheese and all the crumbled bacon. Pour on the egg mixture, then top with the remaining cheese. Set in the center of the preheated oven for 35 to 40 minutes, until browned on top and a stainless steel knife inserted in the custard 1 inch from the edge comes out clean. Cool 5 minutes on a wire rack; serve warm.

MUSHROOM PIE

This mushroom pie is one of the house specialties served at Franni, a delightful café-pâtisserie in Montreal, Québec. The owner-chefs are our good friends Frances and Wally Sheper, a warm and enthusiastic couple who have actually done what so many lackadaisical epicures only talk of—changing careers in midstream for the love of . . . pastry! Following a dream, they gave up another business to prepare and serve a menu of brasserie-style fare that includes salads, quiches, sweet and savory pies, and over twenty-two varieties of cheesecake. They are bakers you can believe in, and their mushroom pie has a sharp, well-seasoned flavor that makes it an excellent choice for an hors d'oeuvre, luncheon entrée, or after-dinner savory.

Advance preparation: The partially prebaked pie shell can be prepared ahead and frozen; thaw before filling. Prepare the filling and bake the pie shortly before serving warm. The pie can be reheated before serving, but the crust tends to soften on standing.

Special equipment: 9-inch pie plate; pastry brush; 12-inch heavy-bottom frying pan; whisk; mixing bowl; knife; aluminum strips or frame (page 25).

Baking time: Partially prebaked pastry shell: 425°F for 10 minutes with pie weights, 3 minutes empty; complete pie: 325°F for 30 minutes.

Quantity: One 9-inch pie; serves 6.

> *Partially prebaked 9-inch pie shell made*
> *with Cream Cheese Pastry (page 65),*
> *Basic All-Purpose Flaky Pastry (page*
> *34), or another recipe of your*
> *choice*
> Egg glaze: *1 egg beaten with 1*
> *tablespoon water*

> **Filling**
> *5 tablespoons unsalted butter or*
> *margarine*
> *2 cups yellow onions, sliced thin*
> *½ cup heavy cream*
> *1 egg*
> *1 pound fresh mushrooms, sliced*
> *1 tablespoon all-purpose flour*
> *⅛ teaspoon salt, or to taste*

¼ teaspoon freshly ground pepper
½ teaspoon dried dill or thyme
1 teaspoon lemon juice
2 tablespoons Madeira wine or cognac

1. Prepare the pastry, roll it out, and line the pie plate (page 38). Trim a ¾-inch overhang, fold the pastry edge under, and flute (page 44). Prick the pastry shell with a fork and chill at least 30 minutes. Preheat the oven to 425°F. Partially blind-bake the shell (page 42) 10 minutes, then remove the pie weights and liner and brush with moisture-proofing egg glaze before baking an additional 3 minutes. Cool on a wire rack. Lower the oven heat to 325°F.

2. To prepare the filling, melt the butter in a frying pan over low-medium heat. Add the sliced onions and cook until golden. While the onions cook, whisk together the cream and egg in a bowl, then set this aside. Stir the mushrooms into the onions and raise the heat slightly. Sauté, stirring, about 2 minutes. (*Note:* Do not let the mushrooms simmer until they release their liquid.) Add the flour, salt, spices, and lemon juice to the pan and stir until well blended. Add the reserved cream-egg mixture and cook with the onions and mushrooms, stirring constantly over medium heat for a minute or two. Remove the pan from the heat and stir in the cognac or Maderia. Set the mixture aside to cool slightly.

3. Spoon the cooled mushroom filling into the prepared pastry shell and bake in the center of the preheated oven for 40 to 45 minutes or until browned on top and a knife inserted into the filling 1-inch from the edge come out clean. Check after half the baking time and add a protective foil edging if necessary to prevent the crust from overbrowning. Cool the pie about 5 minutes on a wire rack, then serve warm.

TOMATO-PESTO TART

Ripe plum tomatoes and fresh, aromatic basil leaves are the quintessence of an August garden, and both are brought to life in this unusual tart. It combines a quiche custard filling with halved tomatoes filled with pesto (basil) sauce and topped with grated cheese. Serve this as a luncheon or light supper dish, with a dry white country wine and a green salad.

(*Note:* While the recipe can be prepared in a tart pan and served freestanding, I prefer to bake and serve it in a 10-inch pie or quiche pan, which holds a somewhat deeper layer of filling. The pesto sauce recipe makes enough for 2 tarts; it can also be tossed with cooked pasta for six generous servings. The pesto recipe is large because it is convenient—and just as easy—to make extra and have it on hand.)

Advance preparation: The pastry can be prepared in advance and frozen. The pesto sauce can be prepared in advance and frozen; defrost at room temperature before using. Fill and bake the tart shortly before serving.

Special equipment: 10-inch pie plate (or 11-inch tart pan with removable bottom); pastry brush; paring knife; broiler with rack; stainless steel table knife; blender or food processor fitted with steel blade.

Baking time: For the partially baked pastry shell: 425°F for 10 minutes with pie weights, then 3 minutes empty; for the filled pie: 375°F for 25 to 30 minutes.

Broiling time for the tomatoes: 4 to 5 minutes.

Quantity: One 10-inch tart, serves 6 to 8.

> *Partially prebaked 10-inch pie shell*
> *made with Basic All-Purpose Flaky*
> *Pastry, Nut Pastry Variation*
> *(almond, page 50) prepared with*
> *1 egg yolk and no sugar; or recipe*
> *of your choice*
> Egg glaze: *1 egg or egg white beaten*
> *with 1 tablespoon water*
>
> **Pesto sauce (enough for 2 tarts or**
> **6 servings of pasta)**
> *2 cups fresh basil leaves*
> *½ cup olive or vegetable oil*
> *2 tablespoons shelled pine nuts or*
> *walnuts*
> *2 large cloves garlic, peeled and crushed*
> *½ teaspoon salt*
> *½ cup freshly grated Parmesan*
>
> **Filling**
> *3 small plum tomatoes*
> *Olive or vegetable oil*
> *Salt and pepper, for seasoning tomatoes*
> *3 tablespoons minced chives*
> *2 tablespoons fresh oregano leaves,*
> *minced, or ½ teaspoon dried*
> *3 tablespoons fresh basil leaves, minced,*
> *or 1 teaspoon dried*
> *2 tablespoons butter, cut up*
> *3 eggs (plus 2 extra yolks, optional, for*
> *richer filling)*

1½ cups heavy cream (or use half milk)
½ teaspoon salt
⅛ teaspoon freshly ground pepper
A dash of nutmeg
3 tablespoons freshly grated Parmesan
3 tablespoons grated cheddar cheese
1 tablespoon butter or margarine

1. Preheat the oven to 425°F. Prepare the pastry, roll it out, and line pie or quiche pan (page 41). Trim a ¾-inch overhang, fold over the edge, and flute as desired (page 44). Make a high fluted rim to contain the generous filling. Prick the bottom with a fork, chill until firm, then partially blind-bake (page 42) for 10 minutes. Remove liner and weights, brush shell with moisture-proofing egg glaze, then bake for additional 3 minutes. Cool on a wire rack.

2. Prepare the Pesto Sauce: Remove the stems from the basil leaves. Rinse the leaves and pat them dry. Put in a blender, a few at a time, or in a food processor. Add some oil, pine nuts or walnuts, garlic, and salt. Blend, pushing down from the container sides when necessary with a rubber scraper. Purée the mixture, turn it out into a small bowl and repeat, using up all the leaves, oil, nuts, garlic, and salt. When all ingredients are blended together, stir in the grated cheese. Use half this pesto for one tart; freeze the rest for later use.

(*Note:* To freeze pesto for long-term, blend together only the basil leaves, oil, nuts, and salt. For best flavor, add garlic and cheese to the base sauce just before using. You can also toss a full recipe of pesto into 1½ pounds cooked, drained pasta and serve hot, with extra grated cheese on the side.)

3. To prepare the tomatoes, cut them in half lengthwise and scoop out pulp and seeds; cut away the stem end with a paring knife. Brush the insides with a little oil and sprinkle them lightly with salt and pepper. Set them, cut sides up, on a broiling rack and broil about 4 to 5 minutes. Turn cut sides down on a wire rack and drain while cooling about 10 minutes. Turn the oven to 375°F.

4. Mince the chives, oregano, and basil in processor or blender. Whisk together the eggs, cream, salt, pepper, and nutmeg in a mixing bowl or food processor, combining them with the minced herbs. Pour this custard into the prepared pastry shell. Sprinkle the grated cheeses evenly over the custard. Put about 1 teaspoon prepared Pesto Sauce inside each halved tomato. Then arrange the tomatoes, cut sides up, in a flower-petal arrangement, with the pesto showing and the wide-end of each tomato facing out. Dot the tart with bits of butter.

5. Bake in the center of the preheated oven for 25 to 30 minutes, until puffed up and slightly browned on top, and a stainless steel knife inserted into the center comes out clean. Cool slightly on a wire rack; serve warm.

CHEDDAR CHEESE PIE (*FLAN AU FROMAGE*)

Cross a savory custard pie with a quiche, and you have this delectable Cheddar Cheese Pie, as at home in France as it is in New England.

Rich and sharp in flavor, this makes a lovely summer luncheon dish when served with a green salad and a chilled, dry white country wine. For a flavor variation, try grated Gruyère cheese instead of cheddar, or combine the grated cheese with ½ cup sieved cottage cheese, or add a little Dijon-style mustard.

Advance preparation: The pastry can be prepared ahead and frozen; thaw before using. The custard can be prepared a few hours ahead and refrigerated in a covered bowl; fill the pie just before baking. Refrigerate leftovers. The pie can be reheated at 350°F for 20 minutes before serving. For best flavor and texture, bake shortly before serving. (*Note:* The crust softens on standing.)

Special equipment: 9-inch pie plate; pastry brush; small frying pan; grater or food processor fitted with a grating disk; flat, edged baking sheet; stainless steel knife.

Baking time: Partially prebaked shell: 425°F for 10 minutes with pie weights, 5 to 8 minutes empty; filled pie: 325°F for 40 to 45 minutes.

Quantity: One 9-inch pie, serves 6 to 8.

*Partially prebaked 9-inch pastry shell
made with Basic All-Purpose Flaky
Pastry, Cheddar Cheese Pastry
Variation (page 35), and prepared
with one egg yolk and no sugar*

Filling
1 cup milk
½ cup light or heavy cream
3 eggs
*1 tablespoon shallots or yellow onion,
    minced*
1 clove garlic, pressed
1 tablespoon butter, or margarine or oil
¼ teaspoon salt
*A pinch each of white pepper and
    cayenne pepper*
2 tablespoons grated Parmesan cheese
1 cup grated sharp cheddar cheese

Garnish

1 tablespoon minced parsley or a dash
of paprika

1. In a mixing bowl, beat together the milk, cream, and eggs, then set aside for use as a moisture-proofing glaze. Prepare the pastry as directed. Preheat the oven to 425°F. Roll out the dough and line the pie plate (page 38). Trim a ¾-inch overhang, fold the edge over, and flute as desired (page 44). Make a high-fluted rim to contain the generous filling. Prick the bottom with fork, chill until the dough is firm, then partially blind-bake (page 42) for 10 minutes. Remove liner and pie weights, and brush the reserved egg-milk glaze over bottom of crust. Return pastry-lined pan to oven to bake 5 to 8 minutes longer or until lightly golden. Cool on a wire rack. Reduce the oven heat to 325°F.

2. In a small frying pan, sauté the shallots or onion with the pressed garlic in butter or oil for 2 or 3 minutes, until a light golden color. Remove from the heat and set aside.

3. Add the sautéed shallots or onions to the milk-egg mixture, along with the salt and peppers. Whisk to combine. Sprinkle both cheeses over the bottom of the prepared pastry shell. Set the pie plate on a flat, edged baking sheet for ease in handling, then pour the custard over the cheese. Top with minced parsley or a dash of paprika for color, and bake in the center of the preheated oven for 40 to 45 minutes, or until the custard is set and a stainless steel knife inserted 1-inch from the edge comes out clean. Cool slightly on a wire rack; serve warm.

CARROT UPSIDE-DOWN TART

Like a plain woman who's done herself up in an exotic fashion, this recipe calls for an explanation by a friend. Like the lady, it's a savory tart to be sure— a plain carrot and potato pie in fancy dress, beautiful in presentation and unusual in texture and flavor.

This tart is the hit of my Savory Pie cooking classes, with everyone eagerly awaiting the moment after baking when it is inverted to display the decorative scale-pattern of carrot slices.

The food processor makes preparation a breeze; use the slicing disk to cut the carrots, and the steel blade to purée the filling. You can use your own imagination to dream up new filling combinations. Try broccoli with potatoes, for example, instead of the carrots.

Because of its decorative appearance and bright color, Carrot Upside-Down Tart is appealing as the vegetable course for a party, or as the entrée for a vegetarian dinner. For brunch or lunch, serve it with spicy sausage patties, green salad, and a dry white country wine.

Advance preparation: The pastry can be prepared ahead and frozen. Thaw before using. The vegetable tart *without the pastry* can be prepared a day in advance, covered, and refrigerated. When ready to bake, top with pastry and set it in the oven. (*Note:* Refrigerate leftovers; freezing the complete pie is unsuccessful, since the texture changes.) If the pie is prepared ahead, it can be reheated before serving. Reheat the unmolded tart covered with foil, for 15 minutes at 350°F, then brush freshly melted unsalted butter over the carrots to restore the glaze and freshen their appearance.

Special equipment: Heavy-duty aluminum foil; 9-inch Pyrex pie plate; food processor fitted with 2mm or 3mm slicing disk, plus steel blade (or knife and cutting board and blender for purée); 2½-quart heavy-bottom saucepan; colander; paper towels; cake tester; 10- to 12-inch flat round serving platter.

Baking time: 425°F for 15 minutes then 375°F for 20 to 25 minutes; vegetables: 15 minutes.

Quantity: One 9-inch tart.

> *Unbaked pastry for a single-crust 9-inch*
> *pie made with Basic All-Purpose*
> *Flaky Pastry (page 34) or*
> *Sour Cream Pastry (page 66)*

Filling
1½ pounds (8 large) raw carrots
1 medium-sized potato, peeled and cut
into 1-inch cubes
2 tablespoons butter, at room
temperature
2 eggs
¼ cup sour cream
Grated zest of 1 orange
¼ teaspoon salt
⅛ teaspoon each ground ginger and
white pepper
½ teaspoon ground cumin or ½
teaspoon dry dill if you don't enjoy
cumin flavor
A dash of cayenne pepper
Parsley sprigs for garnish

1. Prepare the pastry dough according to recipe instructions. Roll out the dough into a 9-inch round about ⅛-inch thick on a floured piece of heavy-duty foil. Invert a 9-inch pie plate over the dough and cut around the edge, making a 9-inch dough disk. Peel up excess dough and freeze for another use. Refrigerate the dough disk on its foil backing until needed.

2. Wash and peel all the carrots; cut off the stem and tip ends. Cut them to fit into the feed tube of a processor fitted with a slicing disk, and cut 4 of the largest carrots into thin (⅛-inch) slices; or cut them neatly by hand. In a saucepan containing salted boiling water, cook the sliced carrots for 3 minutes, until crisp-tender, but not soft. Drain, then spread them on paper towels to blot dry and cool.

3. Slice remaining carrots, though evenness is not important as they will be puréed. Combine them with the cubed potato, put the vegetables into a saucepan of water and bring to a boil. Boil 12 to 15 minutes, until both potatoes and carrots are fork-tender. Drain and set aside.

4. Generously butter the sides and bottom of the pie plate with at least 2 tablespoons butter. This butter coating is covered with dried and cooled carrot slices as follows: Place one carrot slice in the center bottom of the pie plate. Around this center, place slightly overlapping concentric circles of slices, working from the center out. Save the largest slices for the edging. Press the carrots into the butter as you go, and cover all the plate. Fill in any small cracks with broken carrot bits, as holes allow the filling to seep through and stick to the plate, hindering unmolding. To make the edge, set a single row of overlapping large slices, standing upright and leaning against the plate edge. Refrigerate while you purée the filling.

5. Preheat the oven to 425°F. Fit the processor with a steel blade, or use a blender. Add the drained boiled potato and carrots to the work bowl. Pulse a few times to mince the vegetables. Scrape down the sides once or twice, as needed. (If you are using a blender, you may prefer to work with a small quantity at a time.) To the minced vegetables add the eggs, sour cream, grated zest, salt, and spices or herbs. Process until you have a *textured purée*—do *not* process absolutely smooth.

6. Spoon the purée into carrot-slice-lined pie plate. Top with the rolled out round of chilled pastry, which you can simply invert over the plate while you peel off the foil backing. Press gently on the pastry to compress the filling.

Bake in the center of the preheated oven for 15 minutes, then reduce the heat to 375°F and continue baking 20 to 25 minutes, or until the pastry is golden brown and a cake tester inserted through the pastry to the center of the filling comes out clean.

7. Let the pie stand 3 to 5 minutes on a heat-proof surface to settle the bubbling filling. Then run the tip of a sharp knife around the pan edge to

release the carrot slices. Cover the tart with a flat serving platter, hold in place with potholders, and invert. Lift off the pie plate; the pastry layer is now on the bottom. (*Note:* If the tart is either too hot or too cold, it will not unmold easily. If too hot, wait a few minutes and try again. If too cold, return to the oven to warm slightly, softening the butter. Correctly done, it will unmold with perfect ease, in one solid piece.) Reposition any carrot slices that stick to the pie plate. Garnish with parsley sprigs and serve warm, cut into wedges.

GREEK SPINACH PIE (*SPANAKOPITTA*)

An internationally appreciated Greek specialty, this savory Spinach Pie is usually served as an appetizer. Served with sliced tomatoes and a dry white wine, it also makes a delightful luncheon entrée. Prepare the *spanakopitta* in the form of a flat pie, as described below, or as individual pastry-wrapped envelopes for bite-size hors d'oeuvre (page 401).

Advance preparation: Frozen phyllo pastry leaves are available commercially (page 96). Thaw as directed on the package (overnight in refrigerator); or you can substitute homemade strudel leaves (page 91). The filling may be prepared a day in advance and refrigerated in a covered bowl. The prepared *spanakopitta* can be wrapped and frozen unbaked. Bake unthawed, for about 15 minutes longer than usual.

Special equipment: Paper towels; large 12-inch frying pan with lid; large mixing bowl; flat tray; wax paper; dampened tea towel; sharp knife; two 8-inch square baking pans or lasagna-style baking pan 13½ × 8½ × 1¾ inches or equivalent size; pastry brush; small saucepan.

Baking Time: 350° F for about 60 minutes.

Quantity: 16 appetizer-size servings or 8 luncheon entrées.

> *½ pound commercial phyllo leaves,*
> *thawed overnight in refrigerator as*
> *directed on the package; or*
> *substitute homemade Strudel*
> *dough, cut to fit the pans in this recipe*

Filling
2 pounds fresh spinach leaves
¾ cup yellow onions, chopped fine
6 tablespoons lightly salted butter

2 tablespoons vegetable oil, optional
5 eggs, lightly beaten
¾ pound feta cheese, drained and
crumbled
⅓ cup fresh dill, minced, or 1¼
tablespoons dried
¼ cup fresh parsley, minced
Salt and pepper, to taste
1¾ cups unsalted butter, melted

1. Wash and stem the spinach and tear it into small pieces. Drain it on paper towels. In a frying pan, sauté the chopped onions in the butter until golden. Add the prepared spinach and sauté 2 or 3 minutes. Cover and cook one minute until leaves are wilted. Add the oil only if necessary to keep the mixture moist.

2. Turn into a large mixing bowl and add the eggs, feta, dill, and parsley. Salt and pepper to taste. Stir well to blend.

3. Read About Phyllo (page 96). Set the thawed phyllo leaves flat on a tray and cover them with wax paper topped with a dampened tea towel. Whenever using phyllo, remember to re-cover the remaining leaves as you work or they will get too brittle to handle. Preheat the oven to 350°F.

4. Butter the two 8-inch square pans or one large pan. Remove 1 leaf of phyllo, re-cover the rest, and cut the leaf to fit the pan. Set leaf on pan bottom and brush it with melted butter. Cover with another leaf of phyllo, repeating until you have built up about 12 buttered layers.

If you are using 2 small pans, spread half the spinach-feta mixture over the top layer in each pan; if you are using one large pan, spread all the mixture over the top phyllo layer. Cover the spinach-feta with 12 more buttered phyllo layers. Butter the top layer.

5. With a sharp knife, score through the first few phyllo layers marking 2-inch squares. At this point, the *spanakopitta* can be foil-wrapped and frozen. Or it can be baked immediately. To bake, set the pan(s) in the center of the preheated oven and bake about 60 minutes, until puffed up and golden brown on top. Cut through the squares, and serve hot. (*Note:* If the Spinach Pie is frozen, bake the unthawed pie about 15 minutes longer than usual, to be sure the inside is hot.)

CREATIVE PIZZA

Pizza is a pie—in fact pie in one of its earliest, most primitive forms: a round of flat dough with topping. In ancient times, this dough was served sprinkled with a few herbs or seeds, and oil. Time and the age of exploration added new ingredients; Italy's Neapolitan population is credited with perfecting the pizza in its modern guise: thin-crusted, tomato-sauced, and exported to America. The pizza, however, appears throughout all of Italy, in many sizes and shapes, with myriad toppings for nearly every feast day and surely every ordinary day. It is the ultimate peasant food, adapted to the needs, provisions, and creative skills of cooks everywhere.

Until recently, pizza (page 9) in the United States always meant to me variations on the theme of red (tomatoes), white (mozzarella cheese), and green (basil or oregano). At least, that's what pizza meant until I visited Wolfgang Puck's Spago Restaurant, in Los Angeles. There, in brick, wood-burning ovens that contained not only several pizzas at a time, but whole smoldering tree-lengths, Puck and his bright young crew produce a creative—even outrageous—array of pizzas that would make the most imaginative Neapolitan envious. Among the more exotic choices are, for example, pizzas topped with fresh lamb sausage, scallops, or rare duck breast. And with a nod to tradition, I declare them superb. Let that be an inspiration to *your* adventure into creative pizza-making.

Advance preparation: The pizza dough can be prepared ahead (it needs 1 hour to rise) and refrigerated overnight in a bowl topped with a weight or frozen. Bring the dough to room temperature before shaping and baking. The tomato sauce can be prepared ahead and frozen. Or you can partially pre-bake the pizza crust, cover it with unbaked topping, and freeze. Bake un-thawed.

Special equipment: 14 × 17-inch cookie sheet or large round pizza pan; large 12-inch heavy-bottom skillet; garlic press; pizza cutter or large knife; cutting board and knife; small bowls for toppings.

Cooking time for sauce: 25 minutes, minimum.

Baking time: Pizza: 425°F for 20 to 25 minutes (slightly longer if frozen).

Quantity: One 13 × 16-inch rectangular or 14- or 15-inch round pizza; about 4 servings; 8 slices of pizza.

Dough

2 packages granular dry yeast (¼ ounces
    each)
1 cup warm water
1 tablespoon granulated sugar
1 teaspoon salt
1 tablespoon vegetable oil
2¾ to 3 cups all-purpose flour

Tomato Sauce

1 to 2 large yellow onions, chopped fine

3 tablespoons vegetable or olive oil

1 or 2 cloves garlic, pressed

4 tablespoons tomato paste

1½ cups tomato purée

1 teaspoon each oregano and basil, dried

¼ teaspoon each salt and freshly ground
*   black pepper*

2 tablespoons Parmesan cheese, grated

Basic Topping

1 package (10 ounces) mozzarella
*   cheese (whole milk or partially*
*   skimmed milk)*

3 to 4 tablespoons Parmesan cheese
*   grated*

1 tablespoon dried oregano and/or
*   basil*

Optional: *½ teaspoon red pepper flakes*

2 tablespoons olive oil

Creative Additions (use singly or in combination as you wish):

Seafood (add during last 5 minutes
*   cooking time): 1 pound cooked*
*   crabmeat, flaked; 1 pound raw*
*   shrimp, peeled, deveined, sliced,*
*   and tossed in olive oil; 1 pound*
*   shelled mussels, tossed in oil and*
*   minced garlic*

1 green bell pepper, sliced thin

½ pound fresh mushrooms, sliced
*   lengthwise*

6 to 8 ounces pepperoni, sliced thin

1 pound hamburger or sweet Italian
*   sausage, precooked until brown and*
*   crumbled*

1 large can pitted black olives, sliced

Zucchini and fresh red bell peppers,
*   sliced and tossed in oil*

1. Prepare dough according to instructions on page 69–70.

To prepare the tomato sauce, add the chopped onion to the oil in a large frying pan and sauté over medium heat until the onion is golden. Add the garlic and sauté about 1 minute. Add the tomato paste and purée, stirring well. Cook about 2 minutes on high heat, then lower the heat and stir in the oregano, basil, salt, and pepper, and 2 tablespoons Parmesan cheese. Simmer over low heat about 20 to 25 minutes. Taste and adjust seasoning.

2. Remove the rising dough from the oven (if that is where it is rising); preheat the oven to 425°F. Oil a baking sheet and slice or shred the mozzarella cheese; set both aside.

When the dough has doubled in bulk, punch it down with your fist to remove excess gas bubbles. Then flatten the dough ball on the oiled baking sheet, pressing it with the palm of your hand until the dough is about ¼-inch thick. The dough will form one 13 × 16-inch rectangle, or 14 or 15-inch round. Pinch up a fat edge, or lip, all around, to contain the sauce.

3. Spread a generous layer of tomato sauce on top of the flattened area of the dough. Top with shredded or sliced mozzarella cheese, then add a generous layer of creative addition(s) of your choice. Or add these on the tomato sauce and top them with cheese. Finally, sprinkle on a light coat of Parmesan cheese, 1 tablespoon oregano and basil, and if you like spicy flavor, red pepper flakes. Drizzle 2 tablespoons oil over top and bake in the preheated oven for 20 to 25 minutes (longer if the pizza is frozen) or until crust edging is golden brown and the top is bubbling, with the cheese melted and golden. Serve hot.

(*Note:* To achieve the crisp crust texture produced in a brick oven, you can line a shelf in your oven with fire bricks or the special pizza tiles or baking stones sold in specialty cookware shops. Preheat the tiles, then place the pizza directly on them, without a baking pan. Form the pizza on a cornmeal-sprinkled counter top and transfer it to the oven with a large floured spatula or flat, edgeless cookie sheet. Pull out the spatula or cookie sheet as the pizza is slid into place. Read the manufacturer's directions before using commercial tiles.)

VARIATIONS:

Greek Pizza. Prepare Creative Pizza, above, but omit the oregano, basil, and Parmesan cheese. Add 1 pound raw shrimp, shelled, halved lengthwise, and deveined, plus 6 ounces feta cheese, drained and crumbled, plus 1 or 2 tablespoons dried rosemary. Toss the shrimp in 2 tablespoons olive oil or rosemary-flavored olive oil. Cover the pizza dough with shredded mozzarella cheese *before* adding the tomato sauce. Then top with the shrimp and sprinkle with feta and rosemary. Lightly drizzle some oil over the top and bake as directed.

Provençale Pizza (Pissaladière). This is pizza as served in the South of France. I prefer it made with tomato sauce as well as onions and anchovies, as I have enjoyed it in Nice; however, some purists prefer to "hold" the tomatoes. Prepare Creative Pizza, above, but omit the mozzarella and Parmesan cheeses. Use only about 1 cup tomato sauce. In addition, prepare 5 to 6 cups very thin-sliced yellow onions, sautéed in 3 or 4 tablespoons olive oil until lightly golden. Add and sauté 3 minutes 4 pressed cloves of garlic and a dash of salt and pepper. Press the pizza dough into the rectangular shape and top with a light coating of tomato sauce. Cover this with an even layer of onion-garlic mixture. Open 3 cans (2 ounces) of anchovy fillets and drain them. Arrange the fillets in criss-crossing diagonal lines 2 to 2½ inches apart on top of the onions. Garnish with slices of pitted Greek olives or plain pitted sweet black olives, set into the diamond-shaped openings between the anchovy lines. Sprinkle the top with a little olive oil and oregano, and bake as directed. Serve at room temperature or warm.

MEAT AND FISH PIES
AND PATES

Since earliest times, cooks have been serving mixtures of meat and thickened gravy set between or on top of pastry crusts. The ancient Romans elevated this technique to dizzying heights, as shown in this excerpt from a recipe attributed to a first century gourmand, Marcus Gavius Apicius:

> For Patina à la Apicius: Make in the following way. Pieces of cooked sow's udder, fillets of fish, chicken meat, fig-peckers, cooked breasts of turtle-dove, and whatever other good things you can think of. Chop all this, apart from the fig-peckers, carefully. Then stir raw eggs into oil. Pound pepper, lovage, moisten with *liquamen* [a fish-based sauce], wine, and *passum* [a sweet wine sauce], put in a saucepan, heat, and thicken with cornflour. But first add all the different meats and let them cook. When cooked, transfer with the sauce using a ladle, into a pan in layers, having added peppercorns and pine-kernels. Place under each layer as a base an oil cake, and put on each oil-cake one ladleful of the meat mixture. Finally pierce the oil cake with a reed stalk and place this on top. Sprinkle with pepper. Before you put all these meats with the sauce into the saucepan you should have bound them with the eggs.*

Apicius' pie is basically a meat-herb concoction in a custard binding between pastry crusts, but with the addition of interior pastry layers, the oil-cakes. Today, these are known as three-crust pies. While the general concept is not unique, the contents are rather creative by today's standards, and the literary style is a fine

---

* Apicius, *The Roman Cookery Book*, translated by Barbara Flower and E. Rosenbaum (London: George G. Harrap, 1958).

example of the worst of recipe-writers, giving as it does, one of the critical instructions last, long after it was needed.

Today's descendants of these ancient pies still have as their principal ingredients meat or fish set in one or two crusts. The pastry in Apicius' time was usually flour blended with oil; our meat pies developed from those of the British, who prefer the easily molded and sturdy Hot Water Pastry. The French make a version of casing dough called a *pâte à croûstade,* whose fat is butter, or butter and lard, and whose liquid is partially made up of eggs or yolks. Pastry cases containing moist savory fillings are nearly always moisture-proofed with an egg glaze, to retain crispness and to prevent leaky juices from softening the crust. Puff Pastry, Quick or Classic, is often used for meat or fish pies, because of both its high-rising attractive appearance and its crisp flaky texture, which is an excellent foil for soft moist fillings. Occasionally, a country or peasant pie will skip right over all pretensions and go directly to a down-home mashed potato topping, as in a Shepherd or Cottage Pie, or Hasty Pie.

Ground meat mixtures enveloped by pastry can be served cold, as for English Veal and Ham Pie, or they can be filled with colorful egg or vegetable layers to make attractive slices, as in the Torta Rustica, which is molded into a loaf resembling its French cousin, the *pâté en croûte.* Pâtés may be served hot or cold, molded or unmolded.

CHICKEN POT PIE

If it's roast chicken for Sunday Dinner, then it's Chicken Pot Pie on Monday! With this old-fashioned recipe, you will feel as if you are still on the weekend holiday!

Advance preparation: The chicken can be poached in advance and kept refrigerated in a covered bowl, in its broth or separately, for a day or two. Or leftover roast chicken, vegetables, and gravy can be used. The pastry can be prepared ahead and frozen; thaw before using. Assemble and bake the pie shortly before serving, since the pastry lid softens on standing.

Special equipment: Dutch oven with lid; paring knife; colander or strainer; frying pan; 2-quart heavy-bottom enamel or stainless steel saucepan; 10-inch diameter dish 2 inches or more deep, or a 2½ to 3-quart oven-proof casserole; pastry brush.

Cooking time: For poaching the chicken: about 2 hours. For baking the complete pie: 425°F for 35 minutes.

Quantity: 2½-quart casserole; serves 6.

Unbaked pastry for a single-crust 10-inch
*   pie made with Basic All-Purpose*
*   Flaky Pastry, Sesame Seed or Herb*
*   or Cheddar Cheese Pastry*
*   Variation (page 35), or Potato Pastry*
*   (page 63), or Butter-Lard Pastry*
*   (page 68), or Quick Puff Pastry*
*   (page 82)*
Egg glaze: *1 egg beaten with 1*
*   tablespoon water*

Filling

3 to 5 pound fowl or stewing chicken
*   (or small roaster)*
5 to 6 cups water
6 large carrots, peeled and cut in 4-inch
*   lengths*
1 large onion, peeled and halved
1 bunch fresh parsley
2 to 3 stalks celery, with their leafy tops,
*   washed and cut into 4-inch lengths*
1 tablespoon butter or margarine plus 1
*   tablespoon vegetable oil*
2 or 3 tablespoons onion, diced
1 cup sliced fresh mushrooms
¼ cup sweet red bell pepper, diced
⅔ cup fresh or frozen green peas
⅔ cup fresh or frozen corn kernels
¼ teaspoon dried dill, or 1 tablespoon
*   fresh, chopped*
¼ teaspoon dried thyme
⅛ teaspoon celery salt
⅛ teaspoon each salt and pepper
6 tablespoons butter
6 tablespoons all-purpose flour
2 cups reserved chicken stock (reduced,
*   from poaching)*
1 cup heavy cream, or milk
Optional: *½ teaspoon lemon juice, or*
*   to taste*

1. To prepare the chicken: Rinse under cold running water, remove any fat clumps from inside the carcass and under skin. Place the chicken in a Dutch oven with 5 or 6 cups of cold water. Add the carrots, onion, parsley, and celery. Set over high heat and bring to a boil. Boil about 6 minutes, skimming off any foam that rises to the top. Reduce heat, cover, and simmer the chicken about 2 hours, or until fork-tender. Remove from the heat and cool in its broth.

2. Prepare the pastry as directed, and chill while you prepare the filling.

3. Remove the chicken from its broth, cut off the skin, and pull the meat from the bones. This is often easiest if done with your fingers. Cut the chicken into bite-sized pieces. For the pie you will need about 4 cups chicken meat; set this aside.

Strain the chicken broth, and reserve the carrots and celery. Discard the parsley and onion, then return the broth to the pot and boil hard until reduced to about 2 cups. Remove from the heat and cool. Set aside.

4. In a frying pan, melt 1 tablespoon butter or margarine and 1 tablespoon vegetable oil. Add 2 or 3 tablespoons diced onion and sauté until transparent. Add the mushrooms and peppers, and sauté on medium heat, tossing, for 2 or 3 minutes. Add the peas, and corn. Sauté one minute and remove from the heat.

Take the carrots and celery left from poaching the chicken and slice both of them into ¼-inch rounds. Add them to the vegetable mixture in the frying pan. Season all the vegetables with dill, thyme, celery salt, salt and pepper. Set the mixture aside.

5. Reheat the reduced chicken stock, and keep it handy. To make the gravy, melt 6 tablespoons of butter in a heavy-bottom saucepan. Stir in 6 tablespoons of flour and cook them together over low-medium heat for about 2 minutes, making a *roux* that is quite thick. Remove from the heat and all at once stir in the 2 cups hot chicken broth. Immediately whisk the mixture vigorously until it is smooth. Then return the pan to medium heat and whisk 4 or 5 minutes longer, bringing the sauce just to a boil as you whisk. When thick and smooth, whisk in the cup of cream or milk. Set over low heat and whisk for another 5 or 6 minutes, until smooth and thick. Season with salt and pepper to taste. Add a sprinkle of lemon juice to brighten the flavor if you wish. Remove from the heat and set aside. You should have about 3 cups of gravy. Preheat oven to 425°F.

6. Add 2 cups of gravy to the vegetable mixture in the frying pan. Stir in as much of the chicken as will fit; reserve the rest.

Butter the deep dish or casserole and add the unsauced cut-up chicken. Top this with the vegetable-gravy-chicken mixture.

7. On lightly floured surface, roll out the pastry ⅛-inch thick and about 1-inch larger in diameter than the casserole or pie plate. Brush egg glaze around the rim of the casserole; fold the pastry in quarters, lift, and position it over the

filling. Pinch or crimp the pastry to the edge of the pan. Cut steam vents in the top. Brush the pastry with egg glaze. If you wish, cut oval leaves or other decorative shapes from rolled pastry scraps. Position them on the glazed crust, then glaze the cut-outs. (*Note:* The crust can also be made in a woven lattice, (page 47).

8. Bake the pie in the center of the preheated oven for 30 to 35 minutes, until the crust is golden. Serve hot, with the remaining gravy thinned slightly with cream or broth and passed at table.

ENGLISH COTTAGE PIE

The mashed potato topping identifies this beef stew as a Cottage Pie; if the meat were lamb, it could be called a Shepherd's Pie. But whatever its title, this simple country dish is great to prepare ahead, as the flavors mellow and mature after a day or two in the refrigerator. The stew (without the potato topping) may also be frozen in advance. This recipe adds a touch of flavor and color to the dish by glazing the mashed potatoes with melted cheese, an easy and worthwhile trick.

Advance preparation: The stew may be made a day or two ahead and refrigerated, or frozen. The mashed potatoes may be made early in the day and refrigerated. Assemble and bake the pie shortly before serving.

Special equipment: 2-quart saucepan; Dutch oven with lid; paring knife; slotted spoon; food processor fitted with slicing disk or knife and cutting board; 3-quart casserole or oven-proof deep dish; potato ricer.

Cooking time: Beef stew: 2½ to 3 hours.

Baking time: Complete pie: 375°F for 10 to 15 minutes, plus 2 to 3 minutes under the broiler, optional.

Quantity: Serves 6.

Stew
6 ounces bacon
3 pounds beef (round or top round) cut
*   in 2-inch squares*
½ cup margarine
Vegetable oil
All-Purpose flour
1 bunch fresh parsley, chopped
3 large carrots, peeled and cut in ½-inch
*   sections*

1 large onion, sliced
1 large clove garlic, crushed
Optional: *2 leeks, whites only, washed*
well and sliced
2 tablespoons tomato paste
3 cups dry red wine, or beer
3 cups beef stock, or water
Bouquet garni: marjoram, thyme, bay
leaf, and parsley stems wrapped in
cheesecloth bag
½ pound fresh mushrooms, sliced

Topping

2 pounds raw potatoes
2 tablespoons butter or margarine
6 tablespoons milk
½ cup grated cheddar cheese
½ cup grated Parmesan cheese
Salt and pepper, to taste

1. To prepare the stew: Cut the bacon into thin strips and boil it in a saucepan of water for about 5 minutes to remove the salt. Drain, then sauté the pieces in a Dutch oven over low heat. While the bacon sautés, dredge the beef cubes in flour in a mixing bowl.

2. Remove the bacon to another bowl with a slotted spoon. Remove all but 2 tablespoons bacon fat from the pot. Add ½ stick (4 tablespoons) margarine and 1 tablespoon oil to the pot, heat, then add the dredged beef cubes, a few pieces at a time. Over medium heat, stirring with wooden spoon, sear and brown the beef. Remove the pieces as they brown and place them in the bowl with the bacon.

3. Preheat the oven to 350°F. Add 2 to 3 tablespoons of the chopped parsley to the prepared carrots, reserving the rest for later use.

Add 1 to 2 tablespoons oil to the pot and stir in the sliced onions and garlic. Sauté over medium heat, stirring, until the onions are pale gold. Add the remaining vegetables and sauté all together for 3 or 4 minutes, stirring to prevent sticking. Stir in the tomato paste and beef-bacon mixture.

4. Add wine and stock, the bouquet garni tied into a cheesecloth bag, and a generous pinch of salt and pepper. Cover the pot and set it in the preheated oven for 2½ to 3 hours, until the meat is fork-tender. Or you can cook the stew on top of the stove over medium-low heat. While the stew cooks, prepare the mashed potato topping: Boil, peel, and mash the potatoes, then put them through

a ricer. Add the butter and milk and stir until smooth. You should have about 4 cups of mashed potatoes. Set them aside.

During last 30 minutes of stewing time, remove the bouquet garni, then stir in the mushrooms and ½ cup of mashed potatoes, for a thickener. When the cooking is complete, taste the sauce and correct the seasoning. The hot stew may now be topped with mashed potatoes and baked at once. Or it may be set aside to cool, then refrigerated, or frozen without topping. (*Note:* If the pie has been refrigerated or frozen, heat it through completely before topping with potatoes and baking.)

5. To bake, preheat the oven to 375°F. Top the heated stew with all but 1 tablespoon reserved parsley. Spread as much mashed potatoes as will comfortably fit in an even layer on top of the stew, then sprinkle on grated cheese. Bake in the preheated oven for about 10 to 15 minutes, until the cheese is melted and golden. Or finish the cooking with a minute or two under the broiler to brown cheese slightly. Sprinkle the remaining tablespoon of parsley on top and serve hot.

HASTY PIE

This old English country pie is similar to Cottage Pie, as it is topped with mashed potatoes instead of a pastry crust. The difference is that Hasty Pie has a lower "crust" of mashed potatoes as well.

It is an old-fashioned peasant pie created to use up leftovers from the Sunday roast. It is quick to prepare, flavorful to eat, and elegantly disguises the most commonplace ingredients.

Advance preparation: The mashed potatoes can be leftovers or prepared early in the day and refrigerated, covered. The meat mixture (precooked leftovers) can be prepared ahead and refrigerated. Assemble and bake the pie shortly before serving.

Special equipment: Potato ricer or electric mixer; 12-inch skillet; 3-quart saucepan; 9-inch pie plate; optional: pastry bag fitted with ¾-inch star tip.

Baking time: 350°F for 45 to 50 minutes.

Quantity: 9-inch pie; 4 to 5 servings.

Topping
*4 cups mashed potatoes, prepared from
2 pounds raw potatoes, boiled and
put through ricer or gently stirred
in electric mixer*

1 egg
¼ teaspoon salt
⅛ teaspoon white pepper
6 tablespoons milk

Filling
1 large yellow onion, chopped
1 tablespoon butter plus 1 tablespoon
  vegetable oil
1 cup fresh mushrooms sliced
2 cups (12 ounces) cooked meat, cut in
  ½-inch cubes (baked ham plus
  lamb, or veal and pork, or poultry,
  for example)
½ cup frozen or fresh green peas, or
  other cut-up vegetable
3 to 6 tablespoons gravy (below), to
  moisten the filling
¼ teaspoon dried thyme
Salt and pepper, to taste

1½ cups gravy, leftover from a roast, or
  made from cream combined with
  glace de viande or beef broth

1. Put the mashed potatoes into a large bowl. Beat in the egg, salt and pepper, and milk. Stir well, then set aside while preparing the filling.

2. In frying pan, sauté the onion in butter and oil until golden. Add the mushrooms and sauté 2 minutes over medium heat, stirring. Add the meat and peas and cook over low heat 4 or 5 minutes until the vegetables are *partially* cooked. Stir in 3 tablespoons gravy, adding more as needed to moisten the filling. Add thyme, and salt and pepper to taste. Remove the pan from the heat,

3. Preheat the oven to 350°F. Butter the pie plate generously, then spread 2 cups of the mashed potatoes in an even layer over the bottom and sides. Top with the meat filling. To make a decorative topping, pipe the remaining potatoes through a pastry bag fitted with a star tip, beginning in the center of the pie and working a close-fitting spiral out to the rim. Or simply spread the potatoes with a spoon and stripe them with a fork.

4. Bake in the center of the preheated oven for 45 to 50 minutes, until the potatoes are a light golden brown, and the filling is steaming hot. Serve immediately, accompanied by the remaining gravy.

FIDGET PIE

Why the title? Perhaps the farmer fidgeted while waiting impatiently for his wife's pie to bake because he knew how delectable it would be. You make it up. The recipe, we do know, comes from the north counties of England, an old farm recipe whose origins are lost to us. Fortunately, the flavor is not, for it is worth preserving. The combination of ingredients may seem unlikely at first, but the blend is felicitous: the apple giving tartness, the potatoes mellowing into the smoky ham and bacon. It is peasant fare, a country dish designed for economy, and it really stretches meat leftovers; you need only 2 cups meat plus a few potatoes, onions, and apples to serve four comfortably, with second helpings. And when topped with a decorated, glazed pastry crust, it is good enough to be a company pie.

Advance preparation: The pastry can be prepared ahead and frozen. Thaw before using. The meat leftovers can be diced, covered, and refrigerated. The pie may be assembled and refrigerated an hour or two before being baked.

Special equipment: 12-inch frying pan; paper towels; 2-quart oven-proof casserole; paring knife; cutting board; apple corer; vegetable peeler; optional: food processor fitted with steel blade plus slicing disk; aluminum foil; pastry brush.

Baking time: 425°F for 30 minutes; 375°F for 60 minutes.

Quantity: One 9-inch deep-dish pie, serves 4 to 6.

> *Basic All-Purpose Flaky Pastry (page 34),*
> *or Sesame Seed or Herb Pastry*
> *Variation (page 35)*

Filling

> *5 to 6 thick slices of smoked bacon*
> *2 tablespoons margarine or oil*
> *2 medium-sized yellow onions, sliced thin*
> *2 cups cooked ham, about ¾ pound,*
> *   diced*
> *2 tablespoons parsley leaves, minced*
> *1 pound (5 medium-sized) potatoes,*
> *   parboiled until barely fork-tender*
> *   but not totally soft; peeled and*
> *   sliced ⅛-inch thick*

1 pound (3 large) firm cooking apples,
*   peeled, cored, and sliced ¼-inch*
*   thick*
Salt and pepper, to taste
1 cup well-seasoned veal or beef broth,
*   or leftover gravy*
Egg glaze: 1 egg beaten with 1
*   tablespoon water*

1. Prepare the pastry as directed and chill while you make the filling. To make the filling, sauté the bacon in a frying pan until partially crisped. Remove and drain on paper towels. Crumble the bacon and set it aside. Remove all but 2 tablespoons of bacon fat from the pan. Add 2 tablespoons margarine or oil and the onion slices. Sauté over medium heat, stirring with a wooden spoon, until a pale golden color.

2. Add the diced ham to the onions and sauté over high heat, stirring, for 2 minutes. Remove from the heat and stir in the parsley.

3. Butter the casserole, then add the ingredients in alternating layers as follows: Begin with some of the potatoes, top with crumbled bacon, then apples, then ham, then onions. Repeat. Sprinkle each layer with a little salt and pepper. End the layering with apples on top. Pour on the broth or gravy.

4. Brush egg glaze around the lip of the pan. Roll out the pastry on a lightly floured surface (page 41), to 9-inch round, ⅛-inch thick. Fold the pastry in quarters, lift, and position it over the pan. Crimp the pastry to the glazed rim. Cut slits in the top for steam vents. With a sharp paring knife, cut decorative oval leaves or other shapes from the pastry scraps. Brush egg glaze over the top of the pastry, then apply decorative cutouts and glaze their tops. Refrigerate an hour or two before baking and serving. Preheat the oven to 425°F.

5. Bake in the center of the preheated oven for 30 minutes. Cover the top of the pastry lightly with foil to protect it from overbrowning. Reduce the oven heat to 375°F and continue baking about 60 minutes longer, until well browned and bubbling hot. Serve at once.

FRENCH CANADIAN PORK PIE (*TOURTIERE*)

In France, the traditional Christmas Eve after-mass supper known as *Le Réveillon* features *tourtière*, a savory, spice-scented pork pie as versatile as it is delicious. Wherever in the world there are French cooks, there are personal interpretations of this recipe. In the predominately French Canadian province of Québec, the *tourtière* is practically the national dish, and though featured at Christmas, it is served year-round, either as an entrée or baked into individual tartlets as an hors d'oeuvre.

The dish takes its name from the earthenware or metal *tourtière,* or pie dish, used in France to make *tourtes.* Purists declare a true *tourtière* must contain only pork, or perhaps pork and veal; but my research, and that of my friend Frances Sheper, a professional cook and a resident of Montreal, proves otherwise. *Tourtière* always contains *some* pork but, orthodox or not, it is often combined with beef, veal, poultry, or even game. This is essentially a peasant pie, and thus you can be fairly creative about the contents, using leftover cooked meat if you have it, or cooking the meat specially if you don't. In addition to the meat, a *tourtière* will always contain onions, cubed or chopped potatoes or bread crumbs to absorb the pork fat and mellow the flavor, and a touch of clove and/or cinnamon and allspice, to give its characteristic flavor. In Québec, the most common pastry is one shortened with lard or lard-butter, though in France a basic *pâte brisée* is usually used. The pastry shell is moisture-proofed with egg glaze before the filling is added, to keep the lower crust crisp. For convenient serving at holiday time, you can prepare the unbaked *tourtière* and freeze it ahead, then when needed bake it unthawed.

Advance preparation: The pastry can be prepared ahead and frozen; the prepared pie can be frozen and baked unthawed.

Special equipment: 10-inch pie plate; pastry brush; 12-inch frying pan with lid; slotted spoon; paring knife and/or food processor fitted with a steel blade; aluminum foil strips or frame (page 25).

Baking time: 425°F for 15 minutes; 375°F for 45 to 55 minutes.

Quantity: One 10-inch pie; serves 4 to 5.

> *Unbaked pastry for a 10-inch 2-crust pie*
> *made with Lard Pastry (page 62) or*
> *Butter-Lard Pastry (page 63) or*
> *Hot Water Pastry (page 61) or*
> *Potato Pastry (page 68)*
> *Egg glaze: 1 egg beaten with 1*
> *tablespoon water*

Filling
1 large yellow onion, chopped
2 or 3 tablespoons oil or margarine
1 clove garlic, minced

*1½ pounds raw pork, trimmed of fat
    and minced or ground, or use 1
    pound pork plus ½ pound veal*
*1 cup pork gravy or stock or rich
    bouillon (chicken or beef)*
*1 pound (3 medium) potatoes, boiled,
    peeled, and chopped coarse*
Optional: *1 tablespoon chopped celery
    leaves*
2 tablespoons parsley, chopped
*¼ teaspoon each thyme, and either
    rosemary or savory*
1 teaspoon salt, or to taste
*⅛ teaspoon each ground allspice and
    pepper*
⅛ teaspoon ground cloves
A dash of cinnamon

1. Prepare the pastry according to recipe directions. Chill as directed, then divide the dough in half. Chill one part, and roll the other out (page 38) on a lightly floured surface to ⅛-inch thickness. Fold in quarters, lift, and position in the pie plate. Trim a ½-inch overhang, brush with egg glaze, then refrigerate the pastry-lined pan while you prepare filling.

2. In a frying pan, sauté the onion in the oil until transparent. Add garlic, sauté 1 minute, then add the minced pork. Sauté about 3 minutes, then add the veal if you are using it and sauté until the meats are browned. Break up any clumps with a wooden spoon. Add about ½ cup stock. cover the pan, and simmer about 15 minutes to cook the meat through. Preheat the oven to 425°F.

3. Uncover the frying pan and check the liquid. Remove all but 2 or 3 tablespoons of meat juice and stock. Add the potatoes, celery leaves, parsley, herbs and spices, and stir to blend. Add salt, taste and adjust the seasoning. Add, if necessary, just enough additional gravy or stock to moisten mixture well without making it watery.

4. Spoon the mixture into the prepared pastry shell. Brush egg glaze on the overhang of the lower crust. Roll out the top crust on a lightly floured surface, fold in quarters, lift and position it over the pie. Trim a ¾-inch overhang, then fold the top edge under the bottom crust overhang and pinch the two together to seal, making a raised rim all around. Flute the edge as desired (page 44). At this point, you can foil-wrap and freeze the pie. Or bake it immediately. To bake, cut vent holes in the top crust. Brush on milk or egg glaze, and if you wish, sprinkle the top with *a little* coarse salt.

5. Bake in the lower third of the preheated oven for 15 minutes. Reduce the heat to 350°F, raise the pie to the center of the oven, and continue baking about 45 to 55 minutes longer, until golden brown. Check halfway through the baking time and add a foil edging to protect crust from overbrowning if necessary. Cool slightly on a wire rack, then serve hot or warm. Leftovers are also good cold.

STEAK AND KIDNEY PIE

This venerable British standby deserves far better treatment than the insipid versions commonly offered in its name. Prepared properly, it is an outstanding deep-dish entrée, elegantly presented with a decorative pastry lid. The trick is to cook the filling in advance, then, just before serving, top with the pastry and bake.

Advance preparation: The pastry can be prepared in advance and frozen; thaw before using. The filling can be prepared in advance and refrigerated, covered, overnight, or frozen. Assemble and bake shortly before serving.

Special equipment: 9- or 10-inch pie plate; 12-inch frying pan; ovenproof casserole with lid; sharp knife and cutting board; mixing bowl; pastry brush.

Baking time: Filling alone: 350°F for 1½ hours; pastry-topped pie: 400°F for 25 to 30 minutes.

Quantity: One 9- or 10-inch pie, serves 4.

> *Unbaked pastry for a single-crust 9-inch*
> *or 10-inch pie made with Basic All-*
> *Purpose Flaky Pastry (page 34) or*
> *Quick Puff Pastry (page 82). (Note:*
> *the larger amount of pastry gives*
> *scraps for decorative cutouts.)*
>
> Egg glaze: *1 whole egg beaten with 1*
> *tablespoon water*

Filling
1 large yellow onion, diced
2 tablespoons butter or margarine
10 fresh mushrooms, sliced
1 pound tender beefsteak such as London
*   broil, cut into 1-inch cubes*
All-purpose flour
Vegetable oil

1 large whole beef kidney (about 1
  pound), membrane removed, cut
  up, and soaked in cold, salted water
  for 2 hours
2 tablespoons minced parsley
4 to 6 tablespoons Madeira or port or
  cognac
1½ tablespoons Worcestershire sauce
½ cup beef stock or rich bouillon or
  brown sauce
1 teaspoon tomato paste
Salt and pepper to taste

1. Prepare the pastry as directed and refrigerate while preparing the filling.

2. In frying pan, sauté the diced onion in butter or margarine until golden. Add the mushrooms and sauté together 2 minutes. Spoon the onion and mushrooms into an oven-proof casserole. Dredge the cubed beef in flour in a mixing bowl. Add a couple of tablespoons of oil to the frying pan and sauté the dredged beef, about a third at a time, over medium-high heat to seal in the juices. Spoon the cooked beef into the casserole. Preheat the oven to 350°F.

3. Drain the soaked kidney on paper towels. Be sure all the membrane is cut away, and that the pieces are cut to about the same size as the beef. Dredge the kidney pieces in flour in a bowl. Add a little more oil or butter to the frying pan and sauté the kidneys about 2 or 3 minutes, stirring to brown on all sides. Add to the casserole along with the pan juices.

4. Add to the ingredients in the casserole the parsley, Madeira, port, or cognac, Worcestershire sauce, stock, tomato paste, and salt and pepper, to taste. Stir well, taste and correct seasoning. Cover the casserole (or top with crimped-on foil) and bake at 350°F for between 1 and 1½ hours, until the meat is fork-tender.

5. When the meat is tender, remove the casserole from the oven and raise the oven temperature to 400°F. Taste the sauce and add a touch of Madeira or cognac if necessary. If the sauce is too thin and watery, combine 2 teaspoons flour with a tablespoon of soft butter, stir well, then stir into sauce for thickener. (If you prefer a thicker gravy, use 1 tablespoon flour.) Brush egg glaze around the rim of the casserole. Roll out the pastry ⅛-inch thick and 1-inch larger around than the diameter of the casserole. Fold the pastry in quarters, lift, and position it on top of the casserole. Pinch or crimp to the glazed edge and seal in position. Cut a ½-inch circle in the center for a steam vent. Brush the pastry with egg glaze. Cut oval leaves or other shapes from the dough scraps and apply them to the glazed dough. Brush the shapes with egg glaze. Bake the pie in the center of the preheated 400°F oven for 25 to 30 minutes, until the pastry is golden brown and

the filling is steaming hot. (*Note:* Be sure the pan is deep enough that the dough lid is raised well above the level of the filling; if it's too close, the sauce can bubble up and soften the dough. If this should happen, don't worry, the flavor will still be delicious.) As an alternative method, the egg-glazed, cut-to-size pastry lid may be baked *by itself* on a buttered baking sheet while the foil-covered filling is reheated in the oven at the same time. To serve, slip the baked pastry lid in place over the filling. This method is especially successful with puff pastry, which rises best when not dampened by the filling below.

CLAM PIE

This is a Cape Cod specialty, meant to be served for lunch on a silvered-wood deck within sight of sand dunes and crashing waves, the salt breeze in your face as you open a bottle of chilled dry white wine and toast the summer sun.

Advance preparation: The pastry may be prepared ahead and frozen; thaw before using. The chopped fresh clams may also be frozen, then thawed before using. Assemble and bake the pie shortly before serving.

Special equipment: 9-inch pie plate; pastry brush; 12-inch frying pan; paper towels; paring knife; aluminum foil edging (page 25).

Baking time: 400°F for 25 to 30 minutes.

Quantity: One 9-inch pie, serves 4 to 6 as a main course.

> *Unbaked pastry for a 2-crust 9-inch pie*
> *made with Butter-Lard Pastry (page*
> *63) or other pastry of your choice*
> Egg glaze: *1 egg beaten with 1*
> *tablespoon water*

Filling
4 slices (4 ounces) bacon
2 tablespoons butter or margarine
1 yellow onion, chopped fine
3 tablespoons all-purpose flour
1½ cups heavy cream
½ cup milk
¼ cup reserved clam liquor or bottled
clam juice
¼ teaspoon Worcestershire sauce

¼ teaspoon salt
⅛ teaspoon white pepper
1⅓ cups (12 ounces) fresh clams, shelled
    and chopped (plus reserved liquor)
3 tablespoons fresh parsley, minced

1. Prepare the pastry according to recipe directions, and divide it in half. Refrigerate one piece and roll out the other on a lightly floured surface (page 40) to a thickness of ⅛-inch. Fold it in quarters, lift, and position it on the pie plate. Trim a ½-inch overhang. To moisture-proof the lower crust, brush it with egg glaze. Refrigerate the pastry-lined pan while you prepare the filling.

2. Preheat the oven to 400°F. In a frying pan, sauté the bacon over low heat until crisp. Drain on paper towels, then crumble the bacon and set it aside. Remove all but 2 tablespoons bacon fat from the pan. Add 2 tablespoons butter or margarine and the chopped onion. Sauté the onion on medium heat, stirring with a wooden spoon, until golden.

3. To the onion in the pan, add the flour, cream and milk, the clam liquor or clam juice, Worcestershire sauce, salt and pepper. Stir, and cook over low-medium heat until the mixture thickens somewhat. Add the clams and cook 1 minute. Remove from the heat, taste, and correct the seasoning. The mixture should be the consistency of *softly* whipped cream, neither runny nor stiff; if too thick, add a tablespoon or two of milk and stir well. Add parsley and reserved bacon.

4. Pour the mixture into the prepared pastry shell. Brush egg glaze on the edge of the lower crust. Roll out the remaining dough on a lightly floured surface and fit it over the pie. Trim a ¾-inch overhang. Fold the edge under the bottom crust overhang and pinch the two together to seal, making a raised rim all around. Flute as desired (page 44). Cut vent holes in the top. Brush the top crust with egg glaze. If you wish, cut decorative leaves or clam shell shapes from the dough scraps; score naturalistic lines on the "shells" with a knife blade. Apply the shapes to top crust and brush them with egg glaze.

5. Bake the pie in the bottom third of the preheated oven for 10 minutes; raise it to the center shelf and bake 15 to 20 minutes longer, or until the pastry is golden brown. Check halfway through the baking time and cover the crust with foil to protect it from overbrowning if necessary. Serve the pie hot.

RUSSIAN FISH PIE (*KOULIBIAC*)

This is a classic Russian *pirog*, or pie, traditionally consisting of flaked cooked fish layered with rice, hard-boiled eggs, and mushrooms. Additional ingredients may include onions, capers, and dill; in some regions of Russia, semolina replaces the rice. *Koulibiac* appears in a variety of forms: small, bite-sized pastries shaped like half-moons and served as hors d'oeuvre, full-size squares, or rectangles. In all instances, the cases, whether made of puff pastry, short paste, or yeast dough are glazed and decorated with pastry cutouts. The regional variations of *koulibiac* are almost as numerous as the ways its name is transliterated into the Roman alphabet: *coulibiac, kulebiaka,* or *kulybyak,* for example.

Actually, it is much easier to make than to spell, and if you are lucky enough to have leftover fish, rice, and mushrooms at the same time, there is virtually no preparation at all. But even freshly prepared, it is not very time-consuming, and the result is a festive piece of work: a decorative glazed pastry envelope whose crisp texture complements the light, savory blend of the filling. It makes an excellent do-ahead party dish, for it can be assembled and refrigerated in advance, then baked shortly before serving, garnished with sour cream and a sprig of fresh dill.

Advance preparation: The pastry may be prepared ahead and frozen; thaw before using. All the filling ingredients can be either leftovers or freshly prepared in advance and refrigerated. The assembled *koulibiac* can be refrigerated several hours before baking.

Special equipment: Two 2½-quart heavy-bottom enamel or stainless steel sauce-pans, one with lid; slotted spoon; medium-sized frying pan; 3 mixing bowls; sharp paring knife; flat, edged baking sheet (jelly roll pan); pastry brush; ruler.

Baking time: 450°F for 30 to 40 minutes.

Quantity: One loaf, serves 4 to 5; recipe can be doubled for one large party-sized loaf or 2 regular-sized loaves.

> *Quick Puff Pastry (page 82), or one*
> *package (1¼ pounds) store-bought*
> *frozen puff pastry, thawed*
> *according to package directions. Or*
> *unbaked pastry for a 2-crust 10-inch*
> *pie made with Basic All-Purpose*
> *Flaky Pastry (page 34), prepared*
> *with one whole egg*
> *Egg glaze: 1 egg beaten with 1 tablespoon*
> *water and a pinch of salt*

Filling

12 ounces cooked *salmon or white fish*
    fillets, boned and flaked; or 12
    ounces fresh salmon or white fish
    fillets such as turbot, sole, scrod, or
    cod, plus court-bouillon (poaching
    liquid): consisting of 1 cup water, 1
    cup dry white wine, ½ cup chopped
    shallots or onion, 10 whole
    peppercorns or ⅛ teaspoon pepper,
    ¼ teaspoon thyme leaves, and 2
    sprigs fresh dill
2 tablespoons butter or margarine
½ cup onion, chopped
1 cup cooked *white (or brown) rice*
    mixed with 3 tablespoons chopped
    parsley; or ⅓ cup raw long-grain
    white rice and ⅔ cup water or
    chicken stock, salt and pepper to
    taste, 3 tablespoons parsley, chopped
½ pound fresh mushrooms, sliced thin
4 tablespoons butter or margarine
Reserved fish poaching liquid (or 1 cup
    bottled clam juice)
2 tablespoons all-purpose flour
1 teaspoon lemon juice
Salt and pepper
Optional: *1 teaspoon capers or 1*
    tablespoon chopped gherkins
2 eggs, hard-boiled, peeled, and chopped
    coarse

Garnish
Sour cream and fresh dill sprigs

1. Prepare the pastry and set it in the refrigerator to chill while preparing the filling. If you are using store-bought frozen puff pastry, be sure it is thawed as directed on the package. If you are using precooked fish and rice, set them out. If you are preparing fresh fish and rice, proceed as follows:

2. To poach the fish, combine the court-bouillon ingredients in a shallow, heavy-bottom pan, bring to a boil, then add the fish fillets and reduce the heat. Cover and poach gently about 5 minutes, depending upon the thickness of the fillets; cook *only* until the fish feels tender and begins to flake when poked with a fork. Check often. Do not overcook. When the fish is done, remove it with a slotted spoon and place in a bowl; strain the poaching liquid and reserve one cup for the sauce. In a bowl, bone and flake the fish; discard any skin. Set the fish aside.

3. Sauté the onions in 2 tablespoons butter or margarine using a heavy-bottom saucepan set over medium heat. Stir and cook onions until they are golden, then add them to precooked rice along with the parsley.

Or, if you are preparing raw rice, cook it along with the onions after they are sautéed. To do this, add the ⅓ cup raw rice to the pan containing the golden-cooked onions. Stir to coat the rice grains with butter. Add water or chicken stock and bring to a boil. Cover pan, lower the heat, and cook about 20 minutes, until the rice is tender to the bite and the liquid is absorbed. If necessary, add a little more liquid and cook slightly longer. Remove from the heat. Add salt and pepper to taste, stir in the parsley, and set aside.

4. To prepare the mushrooms, melt 2 tablespoons of butter or margarine in a medium-sized frying pan. Add the mushrooms and sauté over medium-high heat, stirring with a wooden spoon to sear (do *not* steam and release the liquid) for about 2 minutes. Turn up the heat and quickly boil off any liquid in the pan, stirring constantly. Remove from the heat and set aside.

5. Return the fish-poaching liquid to the stove and boil rapidly until reduced to 1 cup (or heat the clam juice). Keep warm over low heat. To make the sauce, melt the remaining 2 tablespoons butter or margarine in a medium-sized heavy-bottom saucepan over medium heat. Stir in the flour and cook them together, stirring constantly over low-medium heat for about 2 minutes, making a roux. Remove the pan from the heat and, all at once, stir in the hot fish-poaching liquid (or clam juice) and lemon juice. Whisking constantly, cook over medium heat 2 or 3 minutes longer, until thickened and very smooth. Season to taste. If you wish, you can stir in the capers and chopped gherkins for additional flavor. Remove the sauce from the heat, pour over the flaked fish, toss gently to coat, and set aside. Or refrigerate until ready to assemble the *koulibiac*.

6. To assemble, be sure you have all the ingredients prepared and at hand. Lightly sprinkle cold water on an ungreased jelly roll pan and set it nearby. On lightly floured surface, roll out the pastry to a 14-inch square about ⅛-inch thick. (If using store-bought puff pastry in 2 pieces, join them side-by-side and roll to required size.) In a 4-inch wide strip down the center of the dough, spread in an even layer all of the chopped hard-boiled eggs. Leave about 1-inch of dough clean at each end. Top this with all the mushrooms (drain first with

slotted spoon if they have accumulated any juice while sitting), and cover with the fish. Finally, top with the parsleyed rice and onions. Gently pat all layers into an even, neat rectangle. Clean off the pastry on the sides. Brush egg glaze over the exposed ends of dough. Fold one pastry side over the filling. Brush egg glaze over the side flap remaining on the table, then bring this flap up and overlap it onto the first. Press the edge gently to be sure it is well sealed. Pinch the pastry ends together to seal them. You now have a neat, elongated, seamed rectangular case enclosing the filling.

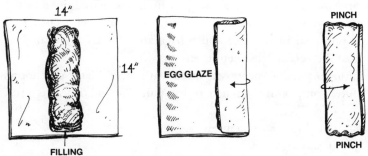

Bring the dampened baking sheet alongside the *koulibiac* and roll the rectangular form over onto the baking sheet, seam side down. Slide the loaf into the center of the pan. Fold under pinched ends. Brush the top of the dough with egg glaze and cut one or two small holes for steam vents.

7. To decorate the top of the *koulibiac*, cut leaves, flowers, vines, or fish shapes from the rolled pastry scraps. Position these on the glazed pastry and brush them with egg glaze.

8. Refrigerate the prepared loaf for at least 30 minutes, until dough is firm, or until 1 hour before serving.

One hour before serving, preheat the oven to 450°F. Bake the *koulibiac* in the center of the preheated oven for 30 to 40 minutes, until the pastry is puffed up and a rich golden brown. Serve hot, cut in slices and garnished with a spoonful of sour cream topped by a dill sprig.

ITALIAN SAUSAGE AND SPINACH TURNOVER (*CALZONE*)

Calzone is a savory mixture served in a pizza-dough pocket. The filling can be meat, vegetables, and cheese, as in this recipe, or any combination of the three. It's a marvelous blend of textures and flavors, with the crisp dough wrapped around the warm, spicy filling making an ideal luncheon or late supper entrée when served with salad and a dry red or white country wine.

Advance preparation: The pizza dough can be prepared in advance and re-frigerated overnight; bring it to room temperature before using. The filling can be prepared in advance and refrigerated, covered, overnight. Assemble and bake the *calzone* just before serving.

Special equipment: Food processor fitted with steel blade or chopping board and knife; sharp knife; 12-inch frying pan; flat baking sheet; ruler; pastry brush.

Baking time: 400°F for 15 to 20 minutes.

Quantity: 4 to 6 servings.

> ½ *recipe for Pizza Dough (page 69)*
>
> **Filling**
> *1 pound sweet Italian sausage, casings*
> *   removed (garlic flavored or hot*
> *   sausage may be substituted)*
> *½ cup fresh mushrooms, chopped coarse*
> *3 scallions, chopped*
> *1 pound fresh spinach leaves, stemmed,*
> *   washed, torn into small pieces, and*
> *   drained on paper towels, or*
> *   substitute 1 (10-ounce) box of frozen*
> *   spinach leaves, thawed and drained*
> *   completely*
> *3 tablespoons grated Parmesan cheese*
> *1 teaspoon dried oregano, plus extra to*
> *   sprinkle over dough*
> *Salt and freshly ground pepper*
> *Olive oil*
> *6 ounces mozzarella cheese*

1. Prepare the dough and set it aside to rise while you prepare the filling. First chop the sausage meat, on a board or in the food processor. In a frying pan over medium heat, sauté the sausage meat until it is brown. Add the chopped mushrooms and scallions and sauté 2 minutes longer. Remove from the heat.

2. Chop or tear the spinach coarsely (do not purée). Add to the mixture in the frying pan and set over heat to cook about 2 minutes. Stir to toss the ingredients until the spinach wilts. Stir in the Parmesan cheese and 1 teaspoon oregano; salt and pepper to taste. Preheat the oven to 400°F.

3. Roll out the dough on a lightly floured surface. Press with your fingers, forming a rectangle roughly 12 × 10 inches. Set the dough on an oiled baking sheet and pat to re-form the shape. Spread the filling over half the dough in a lengthwise strip. Top with the mozzarella cheese. Fold the other half of the dough over the filling and pinch the edges together to seal. Twist or flute (page 44) or press the edges with a fork dipped in flour, to ensure the seal.

Brush olive oil over the top, then sprinkle with some oregano, a pinch of salt, and freshly ground pepper. Cut several diagonal slits in the top to allow steam to escape. Bake in the lower third of the preheated oven for 15 to 20 minutes, or until it turns a rich golden brown. Serve hot.

COUNTRY MEATLOAF IN CRUST (*TORTA RUSTICA*)

While the filling recipe for this "pie" originated years ago with Angela, my aunt Sesyle Hine's Roman cook, I have molded it into a loaf and enveloped it in an herb-scented crust to give it the appearance of its more refined cousin, the French *pâté en croûte*. Unlike the classic pâté, the meat here is cooked before being layered into the pastry for the final baking.

Served cold, it is perfect for a picnic—sliced, garnished with *cornichons* (a variety of pickle), and accompanied by a green salad and a hearty red jug wine. Either hot or cold, it is also ideal for entertaining because the entire pie can be made completely in advance. The presentation is elegant, with each slice revealing a round of hard-boiled egg embedded in spinach.

Advance preparation: The pastry can be prepared ahead and frozen; thaw before using. The complete, baked loaf can be refrigerated for two days, then served cold, or reheated.

Special equipment: 12-inch frying pan; sharp paring knife; 3-quart saucepan; colander or strainer; loaf pan 9¼ × 5¼ inches × 2¼ inches deep (measured inside); heavy-duty aluminum foil; ruler; pastry brush; 12-inch long flat oval or rectangular platter; serrated knife for slicing the loaf.

Baking time: 450°F for 20 minutes; 350°F for 40 minutes. Chill overnight to serve cold.

Quantity: One 9-inch-long loaf; 16 slices, each a generous ½ inch thick, for 16 appetizer portions.

Hot Water Pastry (page 61) prepared
with 2 cups flour and the following
herbs, worked in with the dry
ingredients: ½ teaspoon each dry
thyme leaves, dry dill, and dry
marjoram plus ¼ teaspoon celery
salt. (Note: This amount of pastry
exactly fits the recommended loaf
pan. If your pan is slightly larger,
increase the pastry recipe
proportionally by one half—3 cups
flour.)

Egg glaze: 1 egg beaten with 1
tablespoon water

Filling

3 tablespoons vegetable oil

1 large yellow onion, chopped

1 large clove garlic, minced

1 pound each ground beef and ground
veal plus ⅓ pound ground pork.
(Note: Equivalent amount of
"meatloaf" combination sold in
supermarkets may be used, or all
beef may be substituted.)

½ teaspoon each salt, dried dill, dried
thyme

¼ teaspoon each dry rosemary and
freshly ground black pepper

1½ pounds fresh spinach leaves,
washed, stemmed, and torn into
small pieces, or 2 (10-ounce)
packages frozen leaf spinach

3 tablespoons margarine or butter,
melted

4 eggs

½ cup each grated Parmesan and sharp
cheddar cheese

4 hard-boiled eggs, peeled and chilled

1. Prepare the pastry and set in the refrigerator to chill while the filling is prepared.

2. Measure the oil into a frying pan and set it over medium heat. Add the onion and garlic and sauté until golden. Add the ground meats and cook, stirring with a wooden spoon to break up clumps, until the meat is no longer pink. If more than 3 tablespoons fat and liquid remain in pan after cooking, skim off the excess. Stir in the salt, pepper, and herbs. Set aside to cool.

3. If you are using fresh spinach, place it in a saucepan with about 4 tablespoons water, cover, and steam over medium heat for about 3 minutes. Drain in a colander, pressing out *all* the water. Or cook the frozen spinach as directed on the package, but only for 3 or 4 minutes. Drain well. If the spinach looks as if it is retaining moisture, cool it well, then pick it up in your hand and squeeze out the liquid. Add the melted margarine or butter to the drained spinach, stir, and set aside.

4. Generously butter the loaf pan. After the pastry is well chilled, remove ¾ of the dough from the refrigerator. Roll it out on a lightly floured surface, making a rectangle 13 × 16 inches and about ⅛-inch thick. Drape it over the rolling pin, lift, and center the dough over the pan. Ease the pastry down into pan and press it into the bottom and sides, being careful not to stretch the dough. Prick any bubbles to let the air escape, then press and pinch to mend any tears that occur. Pleat the dough over onto itself at the corners, trim away any excessive folds, and pat smooth.

Trim a ½-inch overhang above the rim of the pan and pinch it up into a neat edging about ¼-inch high. To make the pastry lid, roll out the remaining dough on a lightly floured piece of heavy-duty aluminum foil. Trim it to a rectangle about 6 × 10½ inches (slightly larger than pan). Refrigerate the rolled-out lid and pastry-lined pan for at least 10 minutes, while you complete the filling. For a quicker chill, they can be set in the freezer. Reserve dough scraps for decorative cutouts.

5. Beat the 4 eggs in a mixing bowl with the grated cheese and a dash of salt and pepper. Stir half this egg-cheese mixture into the spinach, and the other half into the meat. Preheat the oven to 450°F if you plan to bake the loaf immediately.

6. Remove the pastry-lined pan from the refrigerator or freezer. Brush the inside surface with moisture-proofing egg glaze. To fill, spread half the meat mixture into the bottom of the pastry-lined pan. Top with half the spinach. Arrange the 6 hard-boiled eggs end to end, pressing them into the bed of spinach. Top the eggs with the remaining spinach, then cover with the rest of the meat. Pat the top gently with your hand to compress the filling.

7. Brush the pastry overhang with egg glaze. Remove the pastry lid from

the refrigerator. Invert it over the loaf pan and peel off the foil backing. Trim an overhang ½-inch larger than the pan and reserve the scraps. Fold the lid overhang over the bottom crust and pinch to seal. Crimp the edges all around with floured fork. With the tip of a paring knife, cut a ½-inch wide, 1-inch long oval steam vent in the top of the pastry lid. Brush the lid with egg glaze.

To decorate the lid, cut 5 or 6 oval leaves from rolled dough scraps. Press a pattern of veins into the dough leaves with the back of a knife (page 47). Apply the leaves or other cutout shapes to the glazed pastry lid, then brush the cutouts with egg glaze.

At this point, the loaf can be refrigerated for several hours, or it can be baked immediately. To bake, set in the lower third of the preheated 450°F oven for 20 minutes. Reduce the heat to 350°F, raise the loaf to the center of the oven, and bake about 40 minutes longer, or until the pastry is a deep golden brown. Check the pastry after half the baking time and cover the top with aluminum foil to protect it from overbrowning if necessary. Cool the loaf on a wire rack. If you are serving it warm, let it stand about 20 to 30 minutes to settle before unmolding (step 8) and slicing. If it is to be served cold, chill at least 6 hours, or overnight.

8. To unmold, run a sharp knife around the inside edge of the pan to release the dough. If the loaf has already been chilled and the butter lining the pan is hardened, dip the bottom of the pan in a small roasting pan of boiling water for about 15 seconds to melt the butter. Then place a flat serving platter on top of the loaf, hold both together, and invert. Lift off the loaf pan. It should come off very easily, sliding on the butter. If it sticks, rap the bottom a few times, or return to the hot water bath for another second or two. Invert again and slice the loaf with a serrated knife.

ENGLISH VEAL AND HAM PIE

This classic English meat pie is versatile and relatively easy to prepare once you have read through the recipe to understand how the parts are put together. The traditional meats are veal and ham, but other leftover cooked meats may be substituted and baked with the hard-boiled eggs in this unusual lemon-herb flavored gravy. The meat filling is formed in a pie plate enclosed in a short or puff pastry crust with a glazed and decorated top that makes an elegant presentation at table. It can be served hot, as an entrée, or filled with aspic and served cold at a picnic or buffet, as is traditionally done in England.

Advance preparation: The pastry can be prepared ahead and frozen; thaw before using. Leftover, cooked meats can be substituted for the veal and ham. Filled with aspic, the pie can be baked and chilled well in advance of serving. If you are serving it hot without aspic, prepare the filling and pastry separately, in advance. Assemble and bake it as close to mealtime as possible; the crust softens on standing.

Special equipment: 3-quart heavy-bottom saucepan or Dutch oven with lid; strainer; 9-inch pie plate; pastry brush; small frying pan; large mixing bowl; small saucepan; sharp knife; aluminum foil; small funnel.

Cooking time for the veal: 45 minutes.

Baking time: 450°F for 30 minutes; 350°F for 60 to 65 minutes.

Quantity: One 9-inch pie, serves 4 to 6.

*Unbaked pastry for a 2-crust, 9- or
10-inch pie (the larger amount
leaves more dough for trimming)
made with Lard Pastry (page 62),
Hot Water Pastry (page 61), or ¾
pound Classic Puff Pastry (page
85), or Quick Puff Pastry (page 82)*
Egg glaze: *1 egg beaten with 1
tablespoon water*

Filling
*1 pound uncooked stewing veal, cubed,
    gristle removed, cooked with
    2 tablespoons oil; 1 small onion
    diced; 2 dried bay leaves;
    ¼ teaspoon each dried thyme, celery
    salt, black pepper. Or, 1 pound
    cooked veal from the shoulder, leg,
    or filet, cut in ½-inch cubes.*
2 tablespoons yellow onion, diced
2 tablespoons vegetable oil
*½ pound cooked ham, cut in ½-inch
    cubes or chopped coarse*
*2 teaspoons minced dried parsley, or 1
    tablespoon fresh*
*½ teaspoon dried rosemary, or 1½
    teaspoons fresh*
1½ teaspoons grated lemon zest
*¼ teaspoon each salt and freshly ground
    black pepper*

1 cup veal or chicken stock or veal
stewing liquid, plus extra ½ cup
stock or stewing liquid for aspic
Optional: *2 to 3 tablespoons cognac or*
port
2 hard-boiled eggs, shelled and sliced

For hot gravy
1½ tablespoons cornstarch dissolved in
2 tablespoons cold water

For cold aspic
2 teaspoons (1 envelope) unflavored
gelatin

1. If you are using raw veal, cook as follows: Heat 2 tablespoons oil in a large saucepan or Dutch oven, add the cubed veal, and sauté about 5 minutes over medium heat, to seal in the juices. Add the diced onion and sauté a few minutes longer, stirring, until the onion is soft. Add 2½ cups water, the bay leaves, thyme, celery salt, and pepper to taste. Cover and simmer about 45 minutes, until the meat is fork-tender. Then strain and reserve the cooking liquid.

2. Prepare the pastry according to recipe directions. Chill as directed, then divide in half. Refrigerate one part while you roll out the other (page 38) on a lightly floured surface to ⅛-inch thickness. Line the pie plate with the pastry (page 39), then brush egg glaze over the pastry and set it in the refrigerator to chill while you prepare the filling.

3. In a small frying pan, sauté the 2 tablespoons diced onion in the oil until golden. In large mixing bowl, lightly toss together the cooked, cubed ham and the prepared veal; then add the sautéed onion, as well as the parsley, rosemary, lemon zest, salt, and pepper.

4. If you are making the pie to serve hot, measure the reserved stewing liquid into a saucepan, add water if necessary to make 1 cup, and bring to a boil; or use 1 cup well-flavored chicken or veal stock. Stir the dissolved cornstarch into the boiling liquid and stir over heat 2 or 3 minutes, until thickened and clear. Taste and correct the seasoning. If the gravy is too thick, add a little more stock. Set it aside.

If you are making the pie to be filled with jelled aspic and served cold, prepare as follows: Measure ¾ cup reserved stewing liquid or stock into a saucepan and sprinkle on the gelatin. Allow this to sit about 3 minutes to soften, then stir in an additional ¾ cup stewing liquid or stock (total is 1½ cups, slightly more than the gravy). If you wish, you can also stir in 2 or 3 tablespoons cognac or port, for flavor. Taste and add a little more salt and pepper if needed. Set the pan over medium heat and stir until the gelatin is dissolved—just before the mixture reaches the boiling point. Remove from the heat and set aside to cool.

Before you use the aspic, you should test its jelling ability. To do this, pour about ½ inch into a small shallow bowl and refrigerate it about 15 minutes. Stir it with a fork and see how it holds its shape. If it is too stiff and rubbery, add a little (⅓ to ½ cup) more stock; if too soft, add another 1 teaspoon gelatin and cook it into the mixture until dissolved. A well-prepared aspic should hold its shape, but should not be too rubbery. Test until the correct consistency is achieved, then set it aside, at room temperature, until ready to use.

5. Arrange half the meat mixture in the bottom of the prepared, pastry-lined pan. Top with sliced eggs, then cover with the remaining meat. Brush egg glaze over the exposed overhanging edge of the pastry. For a pie to be served hot, pour on the thickened gravy mixture.

6. Roll out the remaining pastry on lightly floured surface, fold it in quarters, and lift onto the filled pie. Unfold and position evenly. Trim the edges as follows: If you are using puff pastry, trim both top and bottom overhanging layers at the same time, using a sharp knife. Press them together to seal. Then cut into the edge at ¼-inch intervals to seal all around and help the puffed layers rise together.

If you are using Lard or Hot Water Pastry, trim the edges, then fold the top and bottom over together, making a raised lip around the pie edge; flute to seal, or crimp with fork. With the tip of a sharp knife, cut a ½-inch diameter hole in the center of the top crust for a steam vent. Brush the top crust with egg glaze. If you wish, cut scraps of rolled-out dough into small oval leaves and stems (page 386). Position the cutouts on the glazed pastry, then brush their tops with more glaze.

Chill the pie in the refrigerator at least 30 minutes, or up to several hours. Brush egg glaze over the top once more just before baking.

7. To bake, preheat the oven to 450°F and set the pie in the lower third of oven for 20 minutes. Cover the edges of the pastry with foil strips if necessary to prevent overbrowning. Reduce the heat to 350°F, raise the pie to the center shelf, and continue baking for 30 to 35 minutes longer, until pastry is a rich golden brown. Cool slightly on a wire rack. If you are serving hot, cut into wedges or slices.

8. If you are serving cold, let the pie cool completely on a wire rack. Check your previously prepared aspic; ideally, it should be just beginning to thicken slightly. If it is already solidified, warm it slightly over low heat. If it is too liquid, chill by setting the aspic bowl in a large bowl of ice cubes and stirring until

slightly thickened and syrupy. Set a small funnel into the steam vent in the top crust. Into this, pour the aspic. Lift and tilt the pie gently to distribute the aspic. Repeat, using as much aspic as the pie will hold. Remove the funnel and refrigerate the pie for several hours, or overnight. Slice and serve cold.

VARIATIONS:

Chicken and Ham Pie. Prepare Veal and Ham Pie but substitute 1 pound raw, cubed or leftover cooked chicken for the veal. Sauté raw chicken cubes in diced onion and oil for 3 minutes, until partially cooked through (see step 3). Remove from the heat and complete the recipe as directed.

Turkey and Ham Pie. Prepare as for Chicken and Ham Pie, above, substituting raw or left-over cooked turkey meat for the chicken.

VOL-AU-VENT WITH SEAFOOD FILLING

"Fly-in-the-wind" is the literal translation of "vol-au-vent," a definition whose meaning will be obvious to anyone who has bitten into this superbly puffed up crisp and flaky pastry shell. It is actually a large glazed puff pastry container, in which you traditionally serve creamy blends of savory filling for an entrée. When the same dough is formed in the same manner, but much smaller, it produces *bouchées*, or "mouthfuls," which are filled and served as hors d'oeuvre (page 399).

Before beginning this recipe, read About Classic Puff Pastry (page 83). The whole trick to making a successful Vol-au-Vent is to shape it carefully, according to directions, chill the dough sufficiently where indicated, and bake it in a sufficiently hot, preheated oven. The suggested filling, or any other stew or creamed mixture you may prefer to use (see index), is prepared separately and put hot into the warmed pastry case just before serving. Presenting this dish at table is high drama, for which you will receive well-deserved compliments.

Advance preparation: The pastry may be made ahead and frozen; thaw before shaping. However, the ideal method is to prepare the pastry, shape the Vol-au-Vent, and then freeze it. Alternatively, you can bake it, then wrap it airtight, set it in a protective box and freeze (for no longer than 2 weeks, or the buttery taste will change slightly).

Special equipment: 8-inch and 5-inch round templates (use pie plates or pot lids); sharp paring knife; pastry brush; 2 flat baking sheets or large round pizza pans sprinkled with cold water; toothpick or skewer; aluminum foil; flat serving platter; 12-inch frying pan; slotted spoon.

Baking time: 425°F for 20 minutes; 350°F for 35 to 45 minutes; 200°F for 15 to 20 minutes.

Quantity: One 8-inch case, serves 4 to 6.

> *Classic Puff Pastry (page 85). Give the*
> *dough 6 turns*
> Egg glaze: *1 egg beaten with 1 tablespoon*
> *water and pinch of salt*
>
> **Seafood Filling**
> *1 pound fresh shrimp*
> ¼ *cup unsalted butter*
> *1 large clove garlic, pressed*
> *2 to 3 shallots, minced fine*
> *1 pound bay scallops; or sea scallops,*
> *cut up*
> *10 to 12 fresh mushrooms, washed and*
> *sliced*
> *3 to 4 tablespoons dry white wine*
> *1¼ cups heavy cream*
> *2 egg yolks*
> *Salt, pepper, a pinch of thyme*
> Optional thickener: *1½ tablespoons*
> *cornstarch dissolved in 3 tablespoons*
> *milk or water*
> ¼ *to* ½ *teaspoon lemon juice*
>
> **Garnish**
> *Fresh parsley, minced*

(*Note:* The procedure is to prepare the Vol-au-Vent case and lid, and bake them. After they are baked, you can prepare the filling, which is done very quickly. Place the warm filling in the warm case immediately before serving. The case will soften if left standing too long after filling.)

To Make Vol-au-Vent Shell

1. On a lightly floured surface, roll out the dough into a rectangle ⅜-inch thick and 12 × 20 inches. Note that you always cut puff pastry shapes at least ½-inch apart, and the same distance away from the edges of the dough. Plan the spacing for your shapes as follows. Set an 8-inch template on one half of the dough, at least ½ inch from the edge; press lightly to make the shape. Move the template over and press a second 8-inch shape (a). If the two circles are properly

positioned, replace the template over each one in turn and hold it down while you cut around the edge. Be sure to make clean straight cuts with a sharp blade; do not pull or stretch dough, or it will not rise evenly. Peel up the dough scraps, wrap them in foil and refrigerate to use later for decoration.

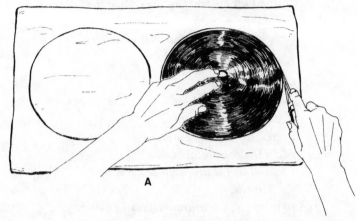

A

2. Set a dampened baking sheet nearby. Gently fold one 8-inch disk lightly into quarters, lift it up, and unfold, setting it upside-down in the center of the baking sheet. Or you can roll it up onto the rolling pin, then lower it into place. Placing the dough upside-down on the baking sheet helps it to rise straight up, instead of slanting in at the top as it might do if positioned right side up. Brush egg glaze over the top of the disk (don't drip glaze onto the sides).

3. Take the 5-inch template and set it in the center of the 8-inch disk remaining on the counter. Cut around the template, leaving a dough ring (b). Working carefully so as not to stretch the dough, fold the ring into quarters, lift it, and position it upside-down over the first disk, pressing the ring onto the dough and lining up the edges. Press the layers together with your fingertips.

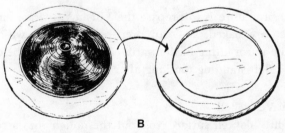

B

4. To make the lid, set the remaining 5-inch dough disk upside-down onto a second dampened baking sheet. Refrigerate until the dough is firm.

5. To make the edges of the dough in the Vol-au-Vent rise evenly together, you must scallop them, or indent them slightly with the back of a knife at

½-inch intervals all around the edge (c). The French call this technique *chiqueter*, "to chew"; the English call it "knocking up the edge."

At this point, you can refrigerate the dough for at least 30 minutes or until firm, or freeze it. Chilling relaxes the dough and helps it rise evenly.

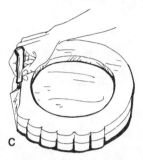

6. To complete the lid, remove it from the refrigerator and roll it out about 2-inches larger than it presently is. Recut it into a neatly edged 5-inch disk. With the back of a knife, scallop the edge as you did the larger case. Then, prick the entire area all over with a fork, to allow steam to escape and prevent excessive rising. Return the lid to the refrigerator.

7. To prepare the Vol-au-Vent for baking, remove it from the refrigerator or freezer. Score decorative crisscross or diagonal lines into the top surface of the dough ring (d). To allow this entire 2-layer ring to rise unimpeded, the center area (which will hold the filling) should be partially cut loose. Score around the inner edge of the ring, cutting into the first few layers of the dough in the center area (arrow, d).

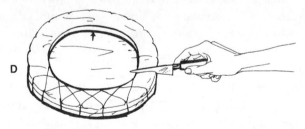

8. Prick the whole inner area (but not on the ring) with the tines of a fork (e), to allow steam to escape and prevent this section from rising as high as the outer ring. Then take a toothpick or skewer and pierce the ring at 6 or 7 equally spaced intervals all around, going through *both* layers, all the way to the bottom. This helps the layers to rise evenly.

9. Preheat the oven to 425°F. Brush egg glaze over the top of the ring. Do not let the glaze drip down the sides, or they will be glued together and will not rise.

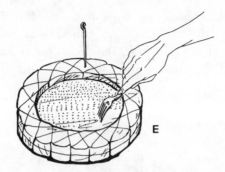

10. Also brush egg glaze over top of the lid. If you want to decorate the lid, you can cut out small oval leaves from the dough scraps. Cut veins into the leaves with a knife blade. Or cut any other geometric shapes, or even thin, rolled ropes you can set in an overlapping crisscross pattern. Set these shapes onto the glazed lid (f), then brush them with egg glaze.

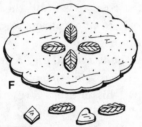

11. To bake, set the Vol-au-Vent and the lid on a baking sheet in the center of the preheated oven and bake 20 minutes, until well risen and lightly golden. Reduce the heat to 350° F and bake an additional 40 minutes, or longer, until the pastry is a rich golden brown. Check the pastry after half the baking time and cover the top with a piece of foil if necessary to protect the crust from overbrowning. Cool on a wire rack.

12. Remove the top layer of the center area from inside the ring: Score around this edge again using a paring knife. Then pick the center out with a fork. It may come out in one solid piece, in which case it could be used as a lid or frozen for another use, or it may break in pieces, in which case you can serve it alongside the filling as a bonus bit of crust.

After removing this top layer, use the fork to pick out the uncooked layers of dough inside. Leave as a base the completely cooked layers below. Finally, turn over the case and check the color of the bottom. If it is burned or over-browned, gently rub it against the side of a box grater to "sand off" the darkest color. Then return the case to the baking sheet and set it in a warm (200° F) oven for another 15 to 20 minutes, just to dry out the interior.

Fill and serve case (g) immediately, or store it overnight in an *unheated* oven (to keep it crisp), or wrap and freeze. If cold or frozen, reheat the case before filling by setting in a preheated 400°F oven for about 10 minutes, or until warmed through.

To Make Seafood Filling

1. Peel and devein the shrimp. Measure the butter into a frying pan, add the pressed garlic and shallots. Sauté, stirring with a spoon, for 2 minutes. Add the shrimp and sauté *just* until they lose their raw texture and turn pink. Using slotted spoon, remove the shrimp to a bowl.

2. Add the scallops and mushrooms to the frying pan with a little more butter if necessary. Sauté 2 minutes, then add the wine and cook, stirring, about 3 minutes, until the scallops are just barely cooked through.

3. Add the cream, bring the mixture almost to a boil, then lower the heat and simmer gently. While the sauce simmers, whisk the yolks together in a small bowl. Add a large spoonful of the hot cream sauce to the yolks, whisking vigorously (so you don't poach the eggs), then add the warmed yolks to the frying pan, stirring constantly. Return the shrimp to the pan and season with salt, pepper, and thyme, to taste. Simmer gently about 3 to 5 minutes, then taste and correct seasoning. If the sauce is not thick enough to coat a spoon, prepare the cornstarch mixture and stir it in, then cook over low heat 2 or 3 minutes, until smooth and thick. If the sauce must wait a while before being served, you can thin it slightly with a little cream and/or wine when reheated. Never let sauce boil; reheat *very* gently over low heat, so the shrimp and scallops are not toughened. Add lemon juice to taste just before serving.

4. Spoon the hot seafood mixture into the prepared, warm pastry case. Garnish with chopped parsley, then add the pastry lid. To serve, scoop out the filling onto each plate, and break off a piece of the lid to go with it. When you no longer need the Vol-au-Vent to contain the filling, serve that as well.

GAME PIES

Hunters have combined their game with dough almost since the beginning of time. The ancient Romans carried the art to great heights, often wrapping the game completely in the pastry. They baked all manner of hunted creatures into pies. For example, they commonly used ostrich, partridge, crane, duck, wood pigeon, turtledove, figpecker (a variety of warbler), peacock, goose, chicken, pheasant, and flamingo, to name but a few favored birds. Their basic cooking technique was recorded in the third century:

> You give a bird a greater flavor and make it more nourishing and keep
> all the fat in, if you wrap it in pastry made of oil and flour and cook it in
> the oven.*

In medieval England, nearly as many birds were served at table: blackbirds, bitterns, cranes, herons, thrushes, larks, ortolans (buntings), sparrows, spoonbills, wheatears, capons, ducks, geese, pigeons, woodcocks, and partridge, among others. Some were roasted on spits, while others were combined into pies topped with pastry. Probably the most famous of these is the pie of "four and twenty blackbirds," served frequently at the court of the Tudor kings in the sixteenth century, though that was an "animated pie,' in which the live birds were temporarily encased in pastry, to be set free when the dough was cut. Blackbirds were frequently cooked into the pies, as well.

* *The Roman Cookery Book*, translated by Barbara Flower and E. Rosenbaum (London: George G. Harrap, 1958).

FOUR-AND-TWENTY BLACKBIRDS PIE

Sing a song of sixpence
A pocket full of rye,
Four and twenty blackbirds,
Baked in a pie;
When the pie was opened,
The birds began to sing;
Was not that a dainty dish
To set before the king?

Tom Thumb's Pretty Songbook, 1744

When I was a child, my fascination with this rhyme was primarily in imagining the gigantic size of the pie needed to contain so vast a number of birds. Now older and slightly wiser, I have learned that European blackbirds are not even related to the black crows I had imagined, and that the pie, though perhaps large, was not abnormally so. The reason they needed four-and-twenty was that after all is said and sung, the birds are so small—the size of an American robin, in fact, to which they *are* related.

Animated pies, or pastry cases full of live birds, were once considered great fun, appearing at banquets throughout the fourteenth, fifteenth, and sixteenth centuries and culminating in the extravagant delights of the Tudor court. The crowning moment, of course, was "when the pie was opened," and the birds flew out at the guests.

Baked blackbird pies were also eaten during this period, and their popularity continues to this day in many parts of the British Isles. Northwestern Connecticut's local meat and game expert Phil Gargan tells me he recalls eating blackbird pie as a boy in Ireland. On dark, windy nights on top of the heath, the birds would hide on the sheltered side of the hedgerows, and Phil and his cronies would "beat the bushes" with sticks to bag their quarry for dinner.

You can make this pie successfully with any small game bird, such as Cornish game hens sold in many supermarkets, or squab or quail. I must confess that when I tested the recipe most recently, I made it with a combination of Cornish hens and ruffed grouse, and was reminded of a marvelous *New Yorker* cartoon by artist Lee Lorenz published in 1981. In the drawing, a pastry chef, carrying an enormous pie through the castle halls en route to the king, says, in response to an inquiring glance by a passing waiter, "Actually, it's *three* and twenty blackbirds and a grackle."

You should be aware that the average blackbird weighs about one-half pound; thus, twenty-four birds would produce 12 pounds of meat. As small birds are so difficult to come by, this recipe is based upon 12 one-pound birds, and thus is accurate at least in spirit and weight if not in actual numbers. Although the recipe takes some time to prepare, chiefly because of the large quantities of ingredients, it can all be done in advance, and is worth the trouble because it is a guaranteed show-stopper and party conversation piece.

Advance preparation: The pastry can be prepared ahead and frozen; thaw before using. The birds can be cooked a day or two ahead, and refrigerated. To prevent the dough from softening on contact with the gravy, roll out the dough and assemble the pie no more than 3 hours before baking; chill in the refrigerator at least 30 minutes (or up to 3 hours) before baking and serving hot.

Special equipment: Cutting board and carving knife; paring knife; optional: food processor fitted with steel blade and slicing disk; pastry brush; 8-quart heavy-bottom pot or extra-large Dutch oven with lid; 2 mixing bowls; slotted spoon; paper towels; wax paper; whisk; one 14- or 15-inch round baking pan about 3 inches deep (such as a paella pan) or three 10-inch pie plates or a 12¼ × 16½ inch × 2½ inch deep roasting pan; optional: ceramic pie bird (page 24).

Cooking time: Braising the birds: 30 minutes; baking complete pie: 400°F for about 60 minutes.

Quantity: One 14- to 15-inch pie 3 inches deep or three 10-inch pies; serves 20 to 24.

> *A* triple *recipe of unbaked pastry for a*
> *1-crust 10-inch pie (3 times 1½*
> *cups flour, or 4½ cups flour, total)*
> *made with Basic All-Purpose Flaky*
> *Pastry, Herb or Sesame Seed Pastry*
> *Variation (page 35), using egg yolk*
> *and lemon juice, or use an*
> *equivalent quantity of Butter-Lard*
> *Pastry (page 63) or Quick Puff*
> *Pastry (page 82). (Note: This is a*
> *single crust pie.)*
> *2 to 3 thick slices of bacon or salt pork*
> *2 large yellow onions, chopped*
> *2 cups fresh mushrooms, sliced*
> *4 to 5 tablespoons butter*
> *Vegetable oil*

All-purpose flour
12 small (1 pound each) game birds such
     as Cornish hens, squab, or quail,
     cut into serving pieces
3 cups chicken broth
4 large carrots, peeled and sliced into
     ⅛-inch rounds
Bouquet garni: ½ teaspoon each dried
     thyme, rosemary, marjoram, 2 bay
     leaves, ½ teaspoon basil, bunch of
     fresh parsley stems, all tied up in a
     cheesecloth bag
1 cup fresh parsley leaves, minced
2 cups dry white wine or dry Vermouth
½ teaspoon ground mace
A dash of ground cloves
¼ teaspoon each salt and freshly
     ground pepper

Gravy
½ cup dry white wine
2 tablespoons all-purpose flour
2 tablespoons butter, softened
1 cup chicken broth
4 generous tablespoons Madeira wine
2 tablespoons cognac or brandy
¾ pound (3 medium-sized) white
     potatoes, cut in ½-inch dice (about
     2 cups), boiled until tender, drained
     and set aside
3 hard-boiled egg yolks, quartered
Egg glaze: 1 egg beaten with 1
     tablespoon water

Relish
Elderberry jelly or mint jelly

1. In an 8-quart pot or a large Dutch oven, sauté the bacon over medium heat until *nearly* crisp. Remove and drain on paper towels. Leave the fat in the pan and sauté the onions until golden. Remove all but 1 tablespoon of the fat and reserve it for later use. Add the mushrooms and sauté them 1 minute. Do

not simmer the mushrooms, or they will soften. Remove the onions and mushrooms from the pan with a slotted spoon, putting them into a mixing bowl. Return 2 or 3 tablespoons bacon fat (if you have enough) to the pot and add 2 or 3 tablespoons butter (or use a combination of oil and butter).

2. Put some flour into a second mixing bowl and, working with a few pieces at a time, dredge (coat) the bird pieces in flour. Set them on wax paper as they are done. Heat the fat in the pot and brown the bird pieces a few at a time, on both sides. Add more fat as needed. Remove the pieces with a slotted spoon and set them aside in the bowl with mushrooms and onions. Remove all the fat from the pot. If the glazed flour on the pot bottom is burned, wash the pot. If not burned, leave as it is, add 1 cup chicken broth, and stir to deglaze the pan, lifting any browned flour from the bottom. To the broth add all the bird pieces plus the mushrooms, onions, and crumbled bacon. Top with carrots, bouquet garni, parsley, wine, and the remaining 2 cups of chicken broth. The liquid should come slightly more than halfway up the sides of the meat. If necessary, add slightly more broth or wine. Stir in the mace, cloves, salt, and pepper. Cover, bring to a boil, then reduce the heat and simmer gently until the birds are fork-tender—about 30 minutes.

3. While the birds are cooking, prepare the pastry and refrigerate it until needed. When the birds are tender, lift out the contents of the pot with a slotted spoon and transfer it to the final pan or pans in which the birds will be covered with pastry and baked. Leave the cooking liquid in the pot; you should have about 6 cups. (*Note:* At this point you can, if you wish, remove the meat from and discard the bones; however, the bones are traditionally left in.)

4. To make the gravy, add about ½ cup white wine to the liquid in the pot and boil it down rapidly to reduce it by about half, to nearly 3 cups. Remove and discard the bouquet garni. In a small bowl, stir the 2 tablespoons flour into the 2 tablespoons softened butter, then whisk this into the reduced pot liquid. Add the 1 cup chicken broth and the tablespoons Maderia. Cook, stirring, for 3 to 4 minutes, until the mixture thickens enough to lightly coat a metal spoon. Stir in the cognac or brandy. Taste and correct the seasoning. You should have nearly 4 cups gravy.

5. To the birds in their baking pan(s), add the diced boiled potatoes and quartered egg yolks, then pour the gravy over all. The gravy should come a little less than halfway up the pan sides. Add a little more chicken broth or a little heavy cream if necessary, but do not water down the gravy too much. If you are using a ceramic bird, set it in the center of the pie with its base resting on the bottom of the pie plate.

6. Be sure the baking pan and ingredients are well-cooled. Wipe the pan rim clean of gravy, then brush it with the egg glaze. On a lightly floured surface, roll

out the pastry ⅛-inch thick and cut it about 1-inch larger around than the diameter of the baking pan(s). Cut a ¾- to 1-inch diameter hole in the center of the rolled dough. Lift the dough and position it over the pie, setting the hole over the pie bird's beak. Or, if you are not using the bird, let the hole form the central steam vent. Pinch the pastry to the glazed rim, then crimp it with a fork to seal. Cut a few extra steam vents in the pie top with a sharp knife. Brush egg glaze over the top of the pastry. With a sharp paring knife, cut several decorative birds, leaves, or geometric shapes from scraps of rolled dough and apply them to the glazed pastry. Brush glaze over the cutouts.

7. Preheat the oven to 400°F. Set the prepared pie in the refrigerator until the pastry feels firm, at least 30 minutes or longer. If you are using a pie bird, hold the pie level so as not to dislodge the device.

To bake, set the pie in the center of the preheated oven and bake 60 minutes, or slightly longer, until the crust is browned and the pie is bubbling hot. Serve immediately, garnished with elderberry or mint jelly.

PHEASANT PIE

First, catch the pheasant. Though if I am given a choice, I readily confess I prefer mine delivered oven-ready in a plain brown wrapper. If you are lucky enough to have a husband like mine who goes pheasant hunting, however, you are likely one day to find yourself the proud possessor of a brace or more of these magnificently plumed birds.

Once you get into the art of game cookery, you can quickly become overwhelmed by the variety of methods for determining the age and sex of your birds, to say nothing of the techniques for bleeding, hanging, drawing, and dressing. Forget all that. This easy-to-prepare recipe braises the meat (cooks it slowly in liquid) and thus is excellent for young or old birds of any sex. Moreover, since it is not roasted, the skin is not needed. Lucky for you. This means you do not have to pluck feathers, but can simply skin the bird. The old adage about hanging pheasant to mature the flavor is rapidly losing popularity, and our advice is this: Eviscerate, chill, and cook the fresh-killed bird as soon as possible. Or prepare the meat and freeze it for later cooking. I guarantee the flavor will be superb.

Advance preparation: The pheasant can be cleaned, cut up, and refrigerated or frozen in advance. The pastry can be prepared ahead and frozen; thaw before using. The prepared pie topped by its pastry can be refrigerated up to 1 hour before baking.

Special equipment: Carving knife; paper towels; optional: heavy-duty aluminum
   foil or freezer wrap; paring knife; large, deep frying pan or electric skillet,
   with lid; 2 to 2½-quart oven-proof casserole; pastry brush; small saucepan.
Cooking time for the stew: 30 to 40 minutes.
Baking time: 425°F for 35 to 45 minutes.
Quantity: 4 to 6 servings.

> *6 shallots, minced*
> *Butter and vegetable oil*
> *1 carrot, diced*
> *1 celery stalk, diced*
> *¾ cup all-purpose flour*
> *1 large pheasant (1¾ pounds, or if*
>   *small, use 1½ to 2 birds),*
>   *prepared as directed below*
> *⅔ cup dry white wine*
> *½ cup water*
> *½ teaspoon each dried thyme, marjoram,*
>   *and rosemary*
> *1 tablespoon fresh parsley leaves, minced,*
>   *or 1 teaspoon dried*
> *1 cup fresh mushrooms, sliced*
> *3 tablespoons cognac*
> *⅔ cup heavy cream (or light cream)*
> *1 tablespoon cornstarch dissolved in 2*
>   *tablespoons milk or water*
> *Salt and pepper to taste*
> *Egg glaze: 1 egg beaten with 1*
>   *tablespoon water*
> *⅓ recipe Quick Puff Pastry (page 82)*
>   *(or scraps of Classic Puff Pastry,*
>   *page 85); or Basic All-Purpose*
>   *Flaky Pastry (page 34) or Potato*
>   *Pastry (page 68)*

Note: To prepare a fresh-killed pheasant for this recipe, ask your hunter to
cut off the bird's head, feet, and wings (at their base). Then insert a sharp carving
knife at the throat, and cut down through the midline just underneath the
skin; peel off the skin and feathers all in one piece. To gut, cut around the inner
cavity and eviscerate. Rinse inside and out with cold running water, wipe with

paper towels, and cut into serving-size pieces, as you would a chicken. As you go along, pick out any visible bird shot with the tip of the knife. Cook immediately, or refrigerate, loosely covered, for a day, or wrap in heavy-duty foil and freeze.

1. Sauté the shallots in 2 tablespoons butter plus 1 tablespoon oil in a frying pan or an electric skillet on medium heat. When the shallots are golden, add the diced carrot and celery and sauté 4 or 5 minutes, stirring, until they begin to get tender. Remove all the vegetables to an ovenproof casserole.

2. Add about ¾ cup all-purpose flour to a mixing bowl, then dredge (coat) the pheasant pieces in the flour. Measure about 1 tablespoon butter plus 2 or 3 tablespoons oil into the frying pan and set over medium heat. Brown the pheasant, a few pieces at a time. Add the pheasant to the casserole as it is done. Pour off any excess fat from the pan. Return all the meat pieces, plus all the vegetables, to the frying pan.

3. Add ½ cup white wine and ½ cup water to the frying pan and sprinkle on the herbs. Cover and simmer over medium-low heat for 30 to 40 minutes until the meat is fork-tender. Add more water or wine if the sauce starts to dry out. Five minutes before the end of the cooking time, add the sliced mushrooms to the pan and stir them into the sauce.

4. When cooked, spoon the meat and vegetables back into the casserole. Warm the cognac over low heat in a small pan; ignite it and pour it, flaming, over the meat in the casserole. Tip the casserole gently to allow the cognac to flow over all the pieces.

5. Deglaze the frying pan by adding 2 or 3 tablespoons white wine and stirring with a wooden spoon to lift any cooked bits from the pan bottom. Then stir in the cream and the dissolved cornstarch mixture. Stir over medium heat until thick enough to coat the spoon. Season to taste with salt and pepper. Pour the sauce over the ingredients in the casserole; it should about half-cover the meat.

6. Preheat the oven to 425°F. Brush egg glaze around the rim of the casserole. On a lightly floured surface, roll out the pastry to ⅛-inch thick, and cut to shape about 1-inch larger around than the casserole. Lift the dough and position it over the casserole. Pinch the dough edge to the glazed casserole rim, or crimp with a fork, to seal. If you want the pastry to puff up into a bubble, do not cut steam vents, but be sure the dough edge is well-attached to the casserole. If you want a flat top, cut steam vents. In either case, brush the top with egg glaze. If you wish, you can decorate the top with cutout bird shapes made from the dough scraps. Set the cutouts on the glazed dough, then glaze the tops of the cutouts. At this point, the pie should be refrigerated at least 1 hour, to chill the dough; or it can be refrigerated several hours, for convenience.

7. Forty-five minutes before serving, set the pie in the center of the preheated oven and bake 35 to 45 minutes, or until the pastry is golden brown. Serve it hot, breaking off a piece of the topping crust to accompany each serving of pheasant and sauce.

VENISON PIE

Pick a crisp day with snow on the ground to drive through a northern Vermont village (or other rural area) during hunting season. (You probably won't even have to write "car" on the side of your vehicle, but I did once see a labeled cow.) Chances are, you will pass a house or two with a deer carcass hanging from the maple tree in the front dooryard. Let me tell you: It's for show —to inform passersby (other pickup truck hunters mostly) that *this* fella *already* got *his!* The truth is, hanging (or aging) deer is less popular than it once was, with more hunters enjoying the flavor of quickly chilled and butchered venison. Our advice is to quick-dress (eviscerate) your deer—should you get one—in the field, and pack the cavity with snow to chill the interior quickly. Then, when you get the deer home, quickly skin, butcher, and freeze all the meat you do not wish to cook right away. It sounds a fierce project to be sure, but ever since our rough and ready Vermont friend Roger Sweatt capably showed us how, my husband and I can cope quite adequately. And fortunately for us "downstate hunters," Roger generously refurbishes our venison supply from time to time when he's had a good year.

The principle of cooking the meat fresh, as opposed to aging it, is that the flavor never becomes gamey. Quick-chilling the deer also prevents "high" flavors from developing. When we are fortunate enough to have rib steaks or other tender cuts, I like to pan-fry them quickly in butter and eat the meat rare, like lamb; the flavor is delightfully sweet. For tough cuts, I braise or stew the meat, exactly as I would beef or any other meat. With this method, the age of the animal doesn't matter—young or old, cooking in liquid tenderizes the meat. Enrich the sauce with herbs and wine, top the stew with a pastry lid, and serve it with a green salad and a hearty red wine—the perfect meal for a winter evening beside the fireplace.

Advance preparation: The pastry can be prepared ahead and frozen; thaw before using. The stew also can be made ahead and frozen. Add the pastry lid and bake shortly before serving.

Special equipment: Dutch oven with lid; paring knife; slotted spoon; food processor fitted with slicing disk or knife and cutting board; 3-quart casserole or ovenproof deep dish.

Cooking time: For the stew: 2½ to 3 hours; for the complete pie: 400°F for 25 to 30 minutes.

Quantity: Serves 4 to 6.

> *Unbaked pastry for a single-crust 9- or*
> *10-inch pie made with Basic*
> *All-Purpose Flaky Pastry, Herb*
> *Pastry Variation (page 35), or*
> *Potato Pastry (page 68)*
> *Egg glaze: 1 egg beaten with 1*
> *tablespoon water*

> **Stew**
> *3 pounds stewing venison, cut into 1-inch*
> *cubes (shoulder, breast, or flank,*
> *for example)*
> *All-purpose flour, for dredging*
> *½ cup margarine*
> *Vegetable oil*
> *1 large onion, sliced*
> *1 clove garlic, pressed*
> *2 large carrots, peeled and cut into*
> *2-inch sections*
> *2 stalks celery, plus tops, cut into*
> *2-inch sections*
> *1 bunch fresh parsley, minced*
> *½ teaspoon each dried thyme and dill*
> *2 bay leaves*
> *Salt and pepper to taste*
> *3 cups dry red wine*
> *3 cups water*
> Optional: *2 tablespoons tomato paste*
> *½ pound fresh mushrooms, sliced*

1. Prepare the venison stew as follows: Dredge the venison cubes by tossing them in mixing bowl with the flour. In a Dutch oven, heat 2 or 3 tablespoons of the margarine with 1 tablespoon oil and add the meat, a few pieces at a time. Sear and brown the meat, stirring with a wooden spoon over medium heat. Remove pieces with a slotted spoon and set them in a bowl as they are done.

2. Add 2 more tablespoons margarine and 1 tablespoon oil (unless sufficient fat remains in the pot) and sauté the onion slices until golden. Add the garlic

and sauté 1 minute. Return the browned meat to the pan and top with the carrots, celery, parsley, herbs, bay leaves, and a generous pinch of salt and pepper. Top with wine and water. If you wish, stir in the tomato paste. Set over medium heat, cover, and cook approximately 2½ hours, until the venison is fork-tender. During the last 5 minutes of stewing time, add the mushrooms to mixture and stir. If you like a thickened gravy, stir 2 tablespoons flour into 2 tablespoons margarine until smooth, then stir this into the stew along with the mushrooms.

3. While the stew cooks. prepare the pastry. When stew has cooked, set it aside to cool, then transfer it to an oven-proof casserole and set aside to cool further, or refrigerate overnight. (It is not possible to seal pastry to the edge of a warm dish.) When you are ready to assemble and bake the pie, roll out the pastry on a lightly floured surface to the thickness of ⅛ inch and 1 inch larger around than the diameter of the casserole. Brush egg glaze around the rim of the casserole. Lift the pastry and position it over the pan. Pinch the pastry to the glazed rim, then crimp with fork to seal. Cut steam vents in the top with a knife. Cut decorative oval leaves or other shapes from the pastry scraps. Brush egg glaze over the top of the pastry, then apply the decorative cutouts and glaze their tops. Or cut the pastry into wide (1½ inch) strips and set them across the top of the stew in a lattice (woven) pattern (page 47), pinching the strip ends to the glazed rim. It is all right if the pastry rests right on top of the stew. Glaze the pastry strips as you would a flat pastry top. Preheat the oven to 400°F. Refrigerate the pie 30 minutes, to firm up the pastry.

4. Set the pie in the center of the preheated oven and bake 25 to 30 minutes, or until the stew is bubbling hot and the pastry is golden. Serve hot. Leftovers can be frozen.

TIMBALES

The word *timbale* was originally applied to drumlike containers of metal or pottery meant to hold beverages or food. The term, by extension, was also applied to edible containers of piecrust, from which various foods were served. The technique is an old and classic one in the French repertoire, but it is making a comeback today, and various small companies in the United States are marketing metal molds upon which to form the pastry lids. There are also ceramic timbales, designed to look like a real piecrust, but in the words of Prosper Montagné, author of *Larousse Gastronomique:*

> . . . the true gourmand is not satisfied with a timbale whose crust is not edible; when served with a real timbale, this gourmand enjoys not only the contents but the container too.*

A beautifully designed, golden-glazed pastry timbale is a work of art and makes as grand a presentation when served at table as, say, a Vol-au-Vent, or other puff pastry creation. However, it is no more difficult to make than any ordinary piecrust. In fact, the bottom half of the case is simply that—an empty, completely prebaked pie shell. The top or lid is the same piecrust dough, pressed over a domed metal mold, decorated with dough, glazed, and baked. The only time-consuming part—and it is up to you how involved you wish to get—is decorating the dome with dough cutouts. After baking, the timbale lifts off the mold to be set upon the filled pastry shell.

* *Larousse Gastronomique,* edited by Charlotte Turgeon (New York: Crown Publishers, Inc., 1961).

After it is brought to the table, the decorated dome, or lid, is removed and the filling is ladled onto individual plates with a broken piece of the lid served alongside. If you have devoted considerable time and effort to decorating your timbale, it may take more willpower than you can muster to break it up and cover it with gravy. If you prefer, you can serve pieces of the bottom pastry shell, and save the lid by returning it to the metal mold, setting it into a protective airtight container, and freezing it for another use.

In this section, I will first give directions for forming a timbale lid, then follow these with several recipes for suggested fillings. For appropriate variations, see the other savory pie fillings in the index. If you wish, instead, to serve a sweet timbale, use a fruit compote, or any of the fillings for fresh fruit pie or chiffon pie, or use scoops of ice cream, previously formed and fast-frozen in a pie shell or bowl.

TIMBALE CASE

Advance preparation: The prepared timbale (both the domed lid and the pie shell bottom) can be completely prebaked and frozen in advance. Thaw before using. For best flavor, warm the bottom shell in the oven before filling. The timbale lid can be preserved for reuse by returning it to the mold and freezing it.

Special equipment: One metal timbale mold: a 10¾-inch dome-shaped form usually sized to fit over a deep-dish 10-inch quiche pan with removable bottom; one deep-dish 10-inch quiche or tart pan with removable bottom (be sure the diameter of the timbale equals that of the tart pan which will form its base); pastry brush; small sharp paring knife; toothpick; flat baking sheet; 12-inch flat serving platter (or larger); tape measure; aluminum foil. *Note:* Two-piece timbale molds are available in specialty cookware shops. Or substitute an upside-down oven-proof dome-shaped bowl that will fit evenly on a pie or tart pan.

Baking time: Completely prebaked bottom shell: 425°F for 10 minutes with pie weights, then 350°F for 15 to 20 minutes empty; timbale lid: 425°F for 20 to 25 minutes.

Quantity: One 10-inch timbale, serves 4 to 6 (or more, depending on the quantity of filling).

To make both bottom shell and lid,
make double the recipe for Basic
All-Purpose Flaky Pastry (page 34)

for a 2-crust 10-inch pie prepared
with 6 cups flour and 2 whole eggs
(1 for each recipe) added as part of
measured liquid; omit the sugar
Egg glaze: *2 eggs beaten with 2*
tablespoons water

1. First make the bottom shell. Preheat the oven to 425°F. Prepare the pastry according to recipe directions. Be sure to use one whole egg as part of the liquid; it moisture-proofs the crust and gives it necessary strength. Chill the pastry as indicated, then remove about ⅓ of the dough and roll it out a generous ⅛-inch thick on a lightly floured surface. Butter the tart mold, running your buttered fingertip into each curve in the fluted edging of the pan. Line the buttered pan with dough as described on page 39. Trim a ¾-inch overhang, fold the edge inward, and press it to the sides of the pan. Run a rolling pin over the top of the pan to trim the excess dough. Prick the pastry bottom with a fork, chill the dough until firm, then completely blind-bake it (page 42). Return any dough scraps to the remaining refrigerated dough. Cool on a wire rack. (*Note:* For safe keeping until ready to fill this shell, it is best to keep it *in* its baking pan.) Unmold (page 43) after rewarming it, just before setting it on a flat serving platter, filling, and serving.

2. To make the timbale lid, first determine the size of the dough circle needed to cover the mold. To do this, take a tape measure and measure across the top of the mold from one edge to the other. This measurement is the diameter of your dough circle. For a 10¾-inch diameter dome-shaped timbale mold 3-inches deep, you need a 12½-inch dough circle.

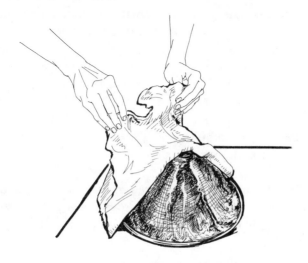

3. On a lightly floured surface, roll out the remaining dough to a generous ⅛-inch thick and the measured diameter of the mold; it should not be *too* thick, but slightly stronger than an ordinary piecrust because it will receive considerable handling and must be free-standing. Generously butter the outside surface of the timbale mold and set it aside.

4. Fold the rolled dough disk into quarters, lift it up, and unfold it, placing the center of the dough on the summit of the dome. Cover the mold with the dough, pressing it flat with the palm of your hand to remove any air pockets. Trim the dough edge flush with the edge of the mold. Save any dough scraps. Set the dough-covered mold flat on a table.

5. Brush the entire surface of the dough with egg glaze. To decorate, cut scraps of dough as directed below and apply them to the timbale with egg glaze, which glues them in place. In preparation for this process, set paring knife, egg glaze, and pastry brush nearby.

6. The basic design for the timbale may be simple—a wavy vine meandering around the dome, with a few leaves projecting from it at evenly spaced intervals, and perhaps 5 or 6 leaves arranged in the center with a cluster of berries. Or you may do a fancy rose surrounded by 3 or 4 leaves at the top, with vines and leaves and other flowers climbing up the sides. To give added strength to the timbale for lifting and handling, *always* cut a ½-inch-wide dough strip and apply it around the bottom edge of the mold; it will look like part of the design.

To make a decorative vine (a), cut narrow (⅛- to ¼-inch) strips of dough, or roll long thin ropes. For leaves, cut 1-inch long ovals, and press naturalistic-looking veins into them with the back of a knife blade. (*Note:* When applying leaves to the timbale, curve them and raise them slightly for a 3-dimensional look instead of pressing them flat; they will bake well this way and will look more natural.) To make a simple flower, cut a 3- × ¾-inch strip of dough and roll it up loosely; then pinch at the base to make the petals open out. To form a rose, mold individual rounded petals and pinch them together over a small, central cone-shaped piece of dough; apply a drop of egg glaze as you add each petal. Cut off the thickest part of the base when the rose is completed. To make berries, roll small dough balls. To anchor the shapes to the timbale, brush the spot where the shape will go with some glaze, then apply. Poke a toothpick through thick shapes to connect them completely to the timbale dough below. Berries look especially realistic with a toothpick hole pressed into the center.

After you have added your decorations (b), brush egg glaze over all the shapes.

7. Set the timbale on a flat tray and refrigerate it at least 30 minutes to an hour, until the dough is firm. Preheat the oven to 425°F. Brush the timbale again with egg glaze. Bake in the center of the preheated oven for 20 to 25

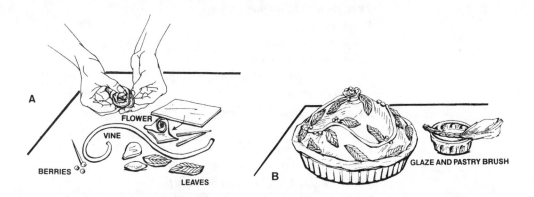

minutes, or until the dough is a rich golden brown. Protect high 3-dimensional shapes such as roses from overbrowning by covering them halfway through the baking with a small folded foil tent.

Cool the timbale on a wire rack. When cold, check the lower edge and cut off any dough that appears to be caught. Then lift the timbale off the mold. It should release easily. Hold it by gripping on opposite sides of the bottom edge. Store the timbale on its metal mold, wrapped and boxed airtight, in the freezer.

ORANGE CHICKEN TIMBALE

A spicy orange-flavored chicken dish that can be prepared in advance and reheated to serve in the timbale pastry shell.

Advance preparation: Prepare this dish ahead, refrigerate it covered for a day, or freeze. Reheat before serving in the timbale. The timbale can be prepared in advance and frozen until needed. Warm shell before filling it with the hot chicken mixture.
Special equipment: Tongs; sharp knife; cutting board; plastic bag; whisk; wax paper; 12-inch frying pan; Dutch oven; slotted spoon; flat serving platter.
Cooking time: Orange chicken: 25 to 30 minutes; timbale, see page 384.
Quantity: Serves 4 to 5.

> *1 completely cooked timbale case (page*
> *384)*
> *1 frying chicken (3 pounds), boned*
> *⅓ cup all-purpose flour*
> *½ teaspoon each salt, pepper, dried*
> *thyme*

1 egg, beaten in a bowl
Vegetable oil for frying
1 cup orange juice
1 clove garlic, pressed
¼ cup raw green bell pepper, chopped
    fine
1 teaspoon prepared regular-style
    mustard
2 tablespoons soy sauce
1 tablespoon molasses or honey
3 tablespoons tomato sauce or catsup
Thickener: *2 tablespoons cornstarch*
    dissolved in ¼ cup orange juice
1 whole orange, sliced into cartwheels
    ⅛-inch thick

1. Prepare timbale lid and shell as described on page 384.

2. Cut up the chicken into bite-size pieces and set them aside. Measure the flour into a plastic bag (or a large bowl). Add salt, pepper, and thyme to the flour and stir. Working with a few pieces at a time, dip the chicken pieces in the egg, stirring to coat. Use tongs to lift the pieces out and drop them into the flour mixture. Toss the chicken to coat, then set the pieces on wax paper and repeat with the remaining chicken.

3. Measure enough oil into a frying pan to coat the bottom generously. Heat until hot enough to brown a piece of bread or a drop of the egg-flour batter in a 15 seconds. Set the chicken pieces into the hot oil and quickly fry them until golden brown. (Be sure the oil is hot enough; cool oil is absorbed and destroys the texture of the coating.) Turn the pieces once. Set the browned chicken directly into a Dutch oven or large pot. Discard oil in the frying pan.

4. Deglaze the frying pan by adding the orange juice and stirring with wooden spoon to lift all the baked bits from the bottom. Pour the mixture over the chicken in the pot.

5. To prepare the sauce, combine the pressed garlic, chopped pepper, mustard, soy sauce, molasses or honey, and tomato sauce. Stir. Pour the sauce over the chicken, cover, and set over low heat. Simmer about 20 minutes, until the chicken is fork-tender and the sauce is well cooked. Occasionally during cooking, ladle the sauce over the chicken. If you wish to thicken the sauce, dissolve the cornstarch in the orange juice and stir it into the chicken shortly before the end of the cooking time. Set over medium heat and cook, stirring, until the sauce is thickened and clear. Taste and correct the seasoning. Stir in the sliced orange cartwheels. Keep warm until ready to fill timbale case and serve. Or

cool, then refrigerate or freeze. (Omit sliced orange cartwheels if freezing dish). Shortly before serving, reheat the chicken while at the same time warming the bottom of the timbale shell in a 350°F oven for about 5 minutes. Unmold the shell (page 43) and set it on a flat serving platter. Ladle as much chicken as will fit into the shell, top with the timbale lid, and serve.

CRABMEAT AND SHRIMP TIMBALE

This rich, creamy seafood filling is prepared by making the Seafood Filling for Vol-au-Vent (page 371) and substituting 1 pound shelled fresh crabmeat (or lobster) pieces for the scallops in the original recipe. Or alternatively, you can simply add the crabmeat to that recipe, thereby enlarging it slightly. To serve 6.

VEAL AND MUSHROOM TIMBALE

This is a rich, creamy filling mellowed with wine, a somewhat heartier dish than the seafood mixture above. The egg yolks in this sauce are optional; corn-starch can be used to thicken the cream instead of (or in addition to) the yolks.

Advance preparation: The timbale can be prepared in advance and frozen until needed. Warm the shell before filling it with the hot veal and mushroom mixture. The filling cooks very quickly. It is best prepared just before serving, though it can be made somewhat ahead and rewarmed.

Special equipment: Sharp knife; cutting board; 12-inch stainless steel or enamel frying pan; slotted spoon; 2 mixing bowls; whisk.

Quantity: Serves 5 to 6.

> *Prebaked timbale lid and shell made as*
> *described on page 384*
> *1 pound (12 large slices) thin veal*
> *scallops*
> *¼ cup unsalted butter or margarine*
> *3 large shallots, minced*
> *1 large clove garlic, pressed*
> *½ pound fresh mushrooms, sliced*
> *¼ cup dry white wine*
> *1½ cups heavy cream*
> Optional: *2 egg yolks*

A pinch of thyme
Salt and pepper to taste
1½ tablespoons cornstarch dissolved in
    3 tablespoons milk or water

Garnish
2 tablespoons fresh parsley, minced

1. Prepare the timbale lid and shell as described on pages 384–87. Cut the veal into ¼-inch wide strips and set aside.

2. Measure 2 tablespoons butter into a frying pan, set over medium high heat, and sauté the veal 2 or 3 minutes, stirring just until the meat loses its pink color. Remove the veal to a bowl.

3. Add I more tablespoon butter to the pan and add the shallots and garlic. Sauté them for a minute or 2 until golden. Add another tablespoon butter, raise the heat slightly, and add the sliced mushrooms. Stir about 2 minutes, until the mushrooms are just cooked through. Remove all ingredients to a bowl.

4. Add the wine to the frying pan and stir with wooden spoon to deglaze the cooked bits from the bottom. Add the cream, bring to a boil, then lower the heat and simmer gently. At this point, the yolks can be added if you wish, to thicken and enrich the sauce, or you can omit the yolks and use the cornstarch thickener. To add yolks, whisk them together in a small bowl. Add a large spoonful of the hot cream sauce to the yolks while whisking vigorously (so you don't poach the eggs), then add the warmed yolks to the frying pan while stirring constantly. Return the veal and the mushroom-shallot mixture to the pan. Add the thyme and season with salt and pepper to taste. Simmer gently about 5 minutes over low heat; taste and correct the seasoning.

If the sauce is not thick enough to coat a spoon, or if you did not use the yolks, prepare the cornstarch mixture and stir it in. Cook on low heat for 2 or 3 minutes, until smooth and thick. If the sauce must wait awhile before serving, you can thin it slightly with a little more cream and/or wine while warming it over low heat just before serving.

5. Spoon the hot veal and mushroom mixture into the prepared, warm pastry shell set on a serving platter. Garnish with minced parsley, then add the pastry lid. To serve, scoop out a portion of filling onto each plate, and break off a piece of the lid to go with it. When you no longer need the pastry shell to hold the filling, serve this as well.

INDIVIDUAL SAVORY
HORS D'OEUVRE

The recipes in this section represent a selection of hors d'oeuvre from England, Argentina, Russia, France, Greece, and China. This small international sampling contains recipes specifically formed into bite-sized portions. However, nearly every savory pie or tart in this book can be prepared in small tartlet shells, to extend endlessly the range of small patties and petit pâtés in your repertoire.

CORNISH PASTIES

The Cornish Pasty is a whole meal turnover traditionally carried for lunch by the miners of Cornwall, England. The Cornish are likely to combine any number of ingredients inside the crisp pastry envelope. In fact, there is an old Cornish saying that "the devil will not come into Cornwall for fear of being put into a pie." Other savory ingredients one might find include eel, chicken, rabbit, and fish, while sweet pasties, served at teatime, can include apples, jam, or blackberries. Our meat-and-potatoes recipe is the one most commonly served.

A fine semantic point to note, should you be in Cornwall: a pasty is a turnover joined at the sides. When the seam is down the center of the top, it becomes a *Cornish hoggin.* My English friend, Thérèse Davies, who generously shared her recipe, also notes that Americans should take care to pronounce "pas" as in "pass" and "ties" as in "golf tees." After that, the making of it is a cinch.

When made bite-sized, pasties are an excellent hors d'oeuvre; traditionally, however, they are made quite large (6 inches or more) and become perfect tailgate or lunch box fare. Whatever their size, we like them best hot from the oven, with brown gravy, though the Cornish prefer them cold. They freeze well, and when reheated make quick and satisfying snacks or suppers, accompanied by a green salad.

Advance preparation: The pastry can be made ahead and frozen; thaw before using. The completely baked pasties can also be frozen, wrapped airtight, then thawed and warmed before serving.

Special equipment: 4-inch round cup or cookie cutter; paring knife; baking sheets; pastry brush.

Baking time: 425°F for 15 minutes; 375°F for 20 to 25 minutes.

Quantity: About 42 bite-sized turnovers or 9 entrée-sized turnovers (6 × 3 inches).

> *Double recipe for Lard Pastry or*
> *Butter-Lard Pastry (page 63)*
> *made with 4 cups flour*
> ½ *pound (8 ounces) lean beef, cut in*
> ¼-*inch cubes, or ground*
> *1 medium potato (about 5 ounces), peeled*
> *and cut in* ¼-*inch dice*
> *1 small (2 ounces) onion, chopped fine*
> *Optional: 3 to 4 tablespoons raw, fresh*
> *(or frozen) peas or 1 medium turnip*
> *or 1 medium carrot, cut in* ¼-*inch*
> *dice*
> ½ *teaspoon salt*
> ¼ *teaspoon black pepper*
> ¼ *teaspoon each dried thyme, oregano,*
> *basil*
> 2½ *tablespoons beef stock or gravy or*
> *water, to moisten the mixture*
> *Egg glaze: 1 whole egg beaten with 1*
> *tablespoon water*

Gravy
Leftover or canned rich brown gravy

1. Prepare the dough and chill it until ready to roll out. Meanwhile, prepare the filling. (*Note:* Pasties are always made with raw, not precooked, potatoes and meat, so they steam in their own juices when baking.) Butter the baking sheets. Preheat the oven to 425°F. Prepare all the filling ingredients and toss them together in a mixing bowl. The vegetables can be used or omitted as you like.

2. Roll out dough on a lightly floured surface to a thickness of about ⅛-inch. Cut into 4-inch rounds. (*Note:* British pasty aficionados favor larger sized turnovers; you can make yours 6 to 10 inches in diameter if you prefer them big.)

3. Place filling in the center of each dough circle. Use about 1 teaspoon for 4 inch hors d'oeuvre. Brush egg glaze around the edge, then fold the dough over the filling. Press the edges to seal, then crimp with floured fork. Or fold the edge back over onto itself, making a narrow double rim, and flute or pinch into evenly spaced ridges as you would for a pie crust. Place the pasties on a greased baking sheet. Brush the tops with egg glaze, and bake at 425°F for 15 minutes; lower the heat to 375°F and bake 20 to 25 minutes longer, or until golden brown. Serve warm, with gravy, or cold. To reheat, warm 15 minutes at 325°F.

SPICY BEEF TURNOVERS (*EMPANADAS*)

Empanadas are Spanish in origin, and are served throughout Central and South America. Nearly every city and certainly every village has its own recipe. Some are made very large and served as luncheon entrées, others, as in this recipe, are shaped into bite-sized turnovers for snacks or hot hors d'oeuvre. Some are deep-fried, others (also as in this recipe) are oven-baked. The fillings can be sweet (jam, preserves, or chopped fresh fruit mixed with sugar, raisins, cinnamon, and nuts) or savory, varying from the fiery chili empanadas served in parts of Mexico to this moderately spicy version containing olives, raisins, and hard-boiled eggs. It was shared with me by an Argentine-born neighbor, Diana de Vries.

Advance preparation: The pastry can be prepared ahead and frozen; thaw before
   shaping. The baked or unbaked empanadas may also be frozen.
Special equipment: Cutting board or food processor fitted with steel blade; garlic
   press; paring knife; 12-inch frying pan; ruler; 4-inch round cookie cutter or
   teacup; pastry brush; buttered, flat, edged baking sheet (jelly roll pan).
Baking time: 400°F for 15 to 20 minutes.
Quantity: 48 empanadas 4 inches wide.

> *Double recipe for Flour Paste Pastry*
>   *(page 61); or Hot Water Pastry*
>   *(page 61); or Butter-Lard Pastry*
>   *(page 63), prepared with 1 teaspoon*
>   *baking powder added along with*
>   *the flour*
> Egg glaze: *1 egg beaten with 1*
>   *tablespoon water*

Filling

2 tablespoons vegetable oil

2 tablespoons yellow onion, chopped

2 cloves garlic, pressed

1 pound lean hamburger (ground
*   chuck)*

¼ cup fresh parsley, chopped; or 1
*   tablespoon dried*

3 tablespoons seedless raisins

1 hard-boiled egg, chopped fine

10 green or black olives, pitted and diced

⅛ teaspoon ground cayenne pepper,
*   or more to taste*

½ teaspoon cumin

2 tablespoons tomato purée or tomato
*   sauce*

4 to 8 tablespoons water, as needed

Salt and pepper

1. Prepare the pastry and refrigerate it while you prepare the filling.

Add the oil to a frying pan and set it over medium heat. Add the chopped onion and pressed garlic and sauté for about 3 minutes, stirring with a wooden spoon.

Crumble in the ground beef, and cook until the meat loses its raw color, about 5 minutes. Stir to break up any clumps. Add all the other filling ingredients and stir well. If the mixture looks too dry, add water, to make it juicy but not runny. Cook together about 1 minute, then remove from the heat and set aside to cool. Add salt and pepper to taste.

2. Preheat oven to 400°F. To form the empanadas, remove about half the dough from the refrigerator. Roll it out on a lightly floured surface to a thickness of ⅛-inch. Cut the dough into 4-inch rounds, using a cookie cutter or an inverted teacup with its rim dipped in flour.

Brush egg glaze around the edge of each dough round, then put a teaspoon of meat filling in the center. Fold the dough over, covering the filling and making a half-moon shape. Dip a table fork in flour and press the tines along the cut edge to seal. Or form the edge into a twisted rope by pinching over and pressing down the cut edge at ½-inch intervals. This is a fancy way of fluting, something like what you would do on a piecrust, to seal 2 edges to contain the juicy filling.

3. Set the completed empanadas on a buttered baking sheet. Brush the tops with egg glaze. Bake in the center of the preheated oven for 15 to 20 minutes, or

until a deep golden brown. Cool slightly on a wire rack; serve warm. To prepare ahead, cool completely, then wrap and freeze. To serve, reheat at 350°F for 15 to 20 minutes.

MEATBALLS IN PASTRY POCKETS (*PIROZHKI*)

A *pirog* is a Russian pie; these little pies are called *pirozhki,* and the diminutive is also affectionate, because they are beloved by everyone.

For easy entertaining, the *pirozhki* can be frozen, before or after baking.

Advance preparation: The pastry can be prepared ahead and frozen; thaw before using. The meat mixture can be prepared and refrigerated a day in advance. Ideally, the *pirozhki* should be formed, baked, and frozen, then warmed through just before serving.

Special equipment: Optional: food processor fitted with steel blade; sharp knife; wax paper; ruler; pastry brush; spatula; edged baking pan (jelly roll pan).

Baking time: 375°F for 20 to 30 minutes.

Quantity: About eighty to one hundred 3-inch bite-sized *pirozhki.*

> *Double recipe for unbaked Cream*
> *Cheese Pastry (page 65)*
> Egg glaze: *1 egg beaten with 1*
> *tablespoon water*

Filling
1 slice whole wheat bread (or ½ cup
  cooked kasha or bulgur)
¼ cup wheat germ
⅓ cup milk
1 egg
1 pound lean hamburger (ground
  chuck)
1 clove garlic, pressed
½ cup fresh mushrooms, chopped fine
2 tablespoons yellow onion, chopped
  fine
2 teaspoons dried dill, or 3 tablespoons
  fresh
¼ teaspoon freshly ground black pepper
½ teaspoon salt

Sour Cream-Horseradish Sauce

1 cup sour cream
1½ tablespoons white horseradish

Garnish

Fresh dill sprigs

1. Prepare the pastry according to recipe directions (remembering to double the quantities). Chill the dough in the refrigerator while preparing the sauce and meat filling. Preheat the oven to 375°F.

2. Prepare the meat filling: In a mixing bowl (or the work bowl of your processor), combine the bread and wheat germ with milk. Blend to soften. Add the egg and stir. Add all the remaining filling ingredients, crumbling in the meat. Stir well to be sure the mixture is thoroughly blended (a vigorous stirring with a fork, or hard squeezing with your hands, or only a few pulses with the processor).

3. Divide the dough in half or in smaller batches; keep the greater amount chilling in the refrigerator while you shape *pirozhki* with the smaller piece of dough. For that matter, you can refrigerate all but a small amount of meat mixture while working.

Roll out the dough between 14-inch lengths of lightly floured wax paper to about ⅛-inch thick.

4. Remove the top piece of wax paper and cut the dough into 3-inch squares. Dip your knife in flour if it sticks. (*Note:* If the dough feels soft, as sometimes happens quickly in hot weather, rechill it as necessary.) Brush the tops of the squares with egg glaze.

Place about 1 teaspoon of meat mixture in center of each square. To form an envelope or pocket, pull up and pinch together 2 opposite corners of dough. Then pinch together the remaining 2 corners. Finally, pinch the side edges closed. Brush the tops with egg glaze.

5. Dip spatula in flour, then slide it under the formed pastry pockets and lift them onto an ungreased edged baking sheet or jelly roll pan. Arrange the pockets about 1 inch apart. (*Note:* You can also set the pastry squares on the baking sheet, then add the meat and do the shaping right in place. Repeat, using up all the pastry and meat.) Make additional egg glaze, if needed.

6. Bake the *pirozhki* in the center of the preheated oven for 20 to 30 minutes, or until golden brown. Be careful when removing the pan from oven as there may be some hot fat in the bottom. Prepare sauce while *pirozhki* bake: Simply stir together the sour cream and horseradish until well blended. Taste and add more horseradish if you prefer a sharper flavor. Spoon the sauce into serving bowl and top with fresh dill sprigs.

7. Serve the *pirozhki* on a warm platter, garnished by the bowl of sour cream horseradish sauce. To eat, dip the *pirozhki* into the sauce.

PUFF PASTRY COCKTAIL SAVORIES
(*CHAUSSONS* AND *SACRISTINS*)

When puff pastry scraps are rerolled, they will never rise quite as high as the original product; for this reason the pastries made from them are called in French *demifeuilletage*. But they are still light, flaky, and delectable to eat. The savory cocktail snacks, *chaussons* (turnovers), and *sacristins* (twisted sticks), utilize this leftover dough. Both are simple to make and can be prepared ahead for easy entertaining.

Advance preparation: Leftover puff pastry scraps can be frozen until ready to use; thaw before shaping. The prepared hors d'oeuvre can be frozen before baking, or they can be fully baked and then frozen.

Special equipment: Paring knife; food processor fitted with steel blade or blender; 3-inch round cookie cutters, pizza-cutting wheel, or sharp knife; 2 flat baking sheets sprinkled with cold water; pastry brush.

Baking time: 425°F for 5 to 10 minutes.

Quantity: Depends upon quantity of dough scraps; filling recipes are sufficient for about 15 to 24 pieces.

> *Leftover Puff Pastry dough (page 85)*
> Egg glaze: *1 egg beaten with 1*
>   *tablespoon water*

CHAUSSONS JAMBON ET FROMAGE
(*HAM AND CHEESE TURNOVERS*)

Filling
(To fill about 15 3-inch turnovers)
2 tablespoons grated Parmesan cheese
A pinch of salt
A pinch of freshly ground pepper
3 tablespoons baked ham or prosciutto,
    chopped
1 teaspoon chives, minced fine
1 tablespoon cream cheese blended with
    1 tablespoon plain yogurt or sour
    cream, or use sour cream plus
    drained ricotta cheese

SACRISTINS *(WALNUT CHEESE STICKS)*

Filling
½ *cup chopped walnuts (or use almonds
     or hickory nuts or other nuts of your
     choice)*
½ *cup grated Gruyère or Swiss or
     cheddar cheese*
½ *cup grated Parmesan cheese*

1. To prepare puff pastry scraps (*rognures*) for reuse, set them flat on a lightly floured surface and arrange them side by side. The object is to reroll them, keeping the layers as horizontal as possible in order to retain the maximum rising power. To this end, cut any very long or awkward pieces, set them together as close as possible, or stack them in a double layer. Roll them out, compressing them into a usable sheet of dough. As an alternative method, you can make the dough sheet described, then spread it with a few tablespoons of butter, fold it in thirds and give it two or three turns (page 88). (*Note also:* To make the following hors d'oeuvre, you can use Quick Puff Pastry (page 82) instead of, or in addition to, Classic Puff Pastry scraps.)

After rolling out the sheet of dough scraps, refrigerate it on a piece of foil or a baking sheet for at least 30 minutes, or until firm.

2. To form *Chaussons,* combine all the filling ingredients and blend well. If the mixture seems too stiff, add a little milk or cream.

Roll the chilled dough ⅛-inch thick. With 3-inch cookie cutters, cut rounds of dough. Peel away any dough scraps to reuse. Brush the edges of the rounds with egg glaze. Add a scant 1 teaspoon ham-cheese filling in the center of each round, fold the rounds in half and press the edges together to seal them. Then recut the half-moon edge using only half the cutting surface of the cookie cutter; or cut with a knife. To make the edges rise together evenly, cut indentations along the edge at ¼-inch intervals with back of a knife blade. Brush egg glaze over the tops. Do not let the glaze drip down onto the cut edge, or the pastry will glue together and will not rise evenly. Refrigerate the *chaussons* 30 minutes. Preheat the oven to 425°F.

Before baking, brush *chaussons* again with egg glaze and score a decorative crisscross pattern in the top with a knife blade. Prick once with a fork to make a steam vent.

Bake in the center of the preheated oven for about 10 minutes, or until well puffed and richly golden. Cool on a wire rack. Serve warm, or hot from the oven. If you freeze the baked *chaussons,* reheat them at 350°F for about 7 to 10 minutes to warm through before serving. (*Note:* For an alternate filling, try the one used for *Spanakopitta* [page 332] or that of *Tiropetes* [page 401].)

3. Preheat oven to 425°F.

To form *Sacristins,* roll the chilled dough into a rectangle ⅛-inch thick. Brush the top of the dough with egg glaze. Sprinkle on a layer of chopped walnuts. Lift the dough and turn it face down on the counter. Brush the top with egg glaze. Sprinkle on a layer of the 2 types of grated cheese. With a pizza cutter or a sharp knife, cut the dough into narrow matchsticks, about ½-inch wide and between 3 inches and 6 inches long. One by one, lift the sticks and twist them along the entire length as you set them down, slightly separated, on a dampened baking sheet. Press on ends slightly to hold.

Bake in the center of the preheated oven for 5 to 7 minutes, or until well puffed and richly golden. Cool on a wire rack set over wax paper to catch the crumbs. Serve warm or hot from the oven. If you freeze baked *sacristins,* reheat them at 400°F for 4 to 5 minutes to warm through before serving.

BITE-SIZED PUFF PASTRY CASES (*BOUCHÉES*)

Bouchées, literally "mouthfuls," are elegant litle puff pastry cases filled with creamy blends of warm savory filling and served as hors d'oeuvre. They are made in the same manner as the larger Vol-au-Vent cases. For illustrations, see pages 368–371. I will give the *bouchée* shaping technique here; for fillings, use any of those suggested for Timbales (page 383) or Vol-au-Vent, or any stew (see index). (*Note: Bouchées* must have a straight-up, high-rising edge in order to be properly formed and hold the filling; for this reason, you must use Classic Puff Pastry, not the quick version. Read About Classic Puff Pastry [page 83] before beginning the recipe.)

Advance preparation: The pastry may be prepared ahead and frozen; thaw before shaping. The ideal method, however, is to prepare the pastry, shape the *bouchées,* and then freeze. Alternatively, you can bake them, then wrap them airtight, and set them in a protective box to freeze (for no longer than 2 weeks, or buttery taste will change slightly).

Special equipment: 3½-inch and 2-inch round or fluted cookie cutters; flat baking sheet sprinkled with cold water; pastry brush; sharp paring knife; skewer or toothpick.

Baking time: 425°F for 15 to 20 minutes.

Quantity: 9 cases 3½-inch diameter (reserve the scraps of dough for other uses).

Classic Puff Pastry (page 85). Give the
dough 6 turns
Egg glaze: *1 egg beaten with 1*
tablespoon water and a pinch of salt

1. Work with half the dough at a time, keeping the remaining piece chilled. On a lightly floured surface, roll the dough to 3/16- to ¼-inch thickness, making as large a rectangle as you can. With a 3½-inch round or fluted round cookie cutter, stamp out as many disks as you can, keeping in mind that you should not cut within ½ inch from the edge or from other shapes or the dough will not rise evenly. Peel away the excess dough and refrigerate or freeze it for other uses (page 85). Carefully lift half the disks and place them, upside down, onto a dampened baking sheet.

Brush egg glaze over the tops of the disks on the sheet. Do not drip glaze onto the sides, or the *bouchées* will not rise evenly.

2. With a 2-inch round cutter, cut a circle from the center of the remaining disks on the counter. To make 9 *bouchées,* you will need 9 rounds and 9 rings of dough. Be sure you cut all the way through the dough layers. For sketches illustrating this procedure, see the similarly assembled *Vol-au-vents*, pages 368–70, steps b, c, d, and e. Lift these rings and set them, upside-down, on top of the glazed disks on the sheet. Press the rings in place with your fingertips, to seal them well. (Add the leftover small center rounds to your scraps, or, on a separate baking sheet, glaze them and sprinkle them with grated cheese, to make small hors d'oeuvre to be baked along with the *bouchées*.)

3. In order for the *bouchées'* double-layer edges to rise together evenly, they must be scalloped, or cut slightly with the back of a knife blade, at ¼-inch intervals all around the edge. Hold the top layer flat with your finger as you make the cuts, so the round shape is not distorted.

At this point, if the dough begins to feel soft to you, refrigerate it for at least 30 minutes, or until very firm. Repeat the above steps with the remaining dough.

4. To complete the *bouchées,* score (lightly cut) a decorative crisscross of lines in the top of the ring. Then prick the entire inner area (not the ring) with a fork, to allow steam to escape and to prevent excessive rising. Finally, to allow the 2-layer ring to rise unimpeded, the pricked center area must be scored around the edge. To do this, cut into the first few layers of the dough around the *inner* edge of the ring. Again, if the dough has softened, refrigerate it until firm. Or freeze the *bouchées* until ready to bake.

5. Preheat the oven to 425°F. Before baking, with a toothpick or skewer pierce the rings at 4 or 5 equally spaced intervals all around, going through *both* layers to the bottom; this helps them rise evenly.

Then brush the tops of the rings with egg glaze. Do not drip glaze down the sides, or the shapes will not rise evenly. Chill the *bouchées* until firm, at least 30 minutes.

6. Bake the *bouchées* in the center of the preheated oven for 15 to 20 minutes, or until golden brown and well risen. Cool on a wire rack. (*Note:* If the *bouchées* are baked frozen, extend the baking time slightly, to be sure the interiors are cooked through.)

7. With the tip of a paring knife, score again around the inner edge of the raised ring. Use a fork or knife tip to pry out this central disk. Lift out the uncooked layers of dough inside. Leave as a base the completely cooked layers below.

Fill and serve the *bouchées* immediately, or store them empty overnight in the *unheated* oven (to keep them crisp), or wrap and freeze them. If cold or frozen, reheat the *bouchées* by setting them into a preheated 400°F oven for about 5 minutes, or until warmed through. Then add the warm filling mixture and serve immediately.

GREEK CHEESE TRIANGLES (*TIROPETES*)

Tiropetes are one of my greatest delights: a warm creamy blend of tangy feta cheese and eggs scented with dill and wrapped in a crisp, flaky envelope of golden phyllo pastry. Form these into bite-sized triangles and serve them as hot hors d'oeuvre. I guarantee you will never have enough to go around. Be sure to read About Phyllo (page 96) before beginning.

I received this recipe by special request just moments after I tasted my first bite, some fifteen years ago, in the Paris home of my good friend, Susan (Charley) Kanas, an American artist married to the Greek painter/writer, Andreas Kanas.

Advance preparation: The phyllo leaves can be purchased frozen; thaw as described on page 98. The shaped, unbaked *tiropetes* can be frozen, then baked unthawed as needed. To freeze, set the *tiropetes* on a cookie sheet and fast-freeze them uncovered. Then transfer them to an airtight box, or a plastic bag set in a protective box, and return them to the freezer. To bake, set the frozen *tiropetes* on a baking sheet in a preheated 350°F oven for 20 to 25 minutes, until golden and hot through.

Special equipment: Small saucepan; 2-quart heavy-bottom enamel or stainless steel saucepan; mixing bowl; whisk; spoon; flat, edged baking sheet; spatula; pastry brush; sharp knife; flat tray; wax paper; dampened tea towel.

Baking time: 350°F for 20 minutes.

Quantity: 56 bite-sized pieces.

½ *pound (½ package) frozen phyllo*
 leaves, thawed as directed (page
 98); or fresh strudel dough (page
 91) cut as directed for tiropetes
 strips
¾ *cup unsalted butter, melted*

Filling

½ *cup plus 2 tablespoons milk*
3 tablespoons unsalted butter
3 tablespoons all-purpose flour
2 eggs plus 1 yolk
¾ *pound feta cheese, drained and*
 crumbled fine
⅛ *teaspoon freshly ground pepper*
2 tablespoons fresh dill, minced, or 1
 teaspoon dried

1. Prepare the filling before setting out the phyllo leaves. First, measure the milk into a small saucepan and set it over low heat to warm. Remove from heat just before it boils, when little bubbles appear all around the edges.

2. In a heavy-bottom saucepan, melt the butter, then add the flour and cook together over medium-low heat, stirring constantly for about 2 or 3 minutes until well blended. Remove from the heat, pour in the hot milk all at once; and whisk vigorously until smooth. Return the mixture to the heat and cook, whisking constantly, 1 or 2 minutes, until the sauce is smooth and thick. Remove from the heat and set aside.

3. In a small bowl, beat together the eggs and yolk. Then whisk in about ¼ cup of hot cream sauce, to warm the eggs. Turn the warmed eggs back into the sauce, whisking constantly (so the eggs do not poach). Cook over low heat, whisking, for 2 minutes. When thick and smooth, remove from the heat. Crumble the feta into the warm sauce, add the pepper and dill and stir well. Set aside, along with the melted butter, baking sheet, and pastry brush.

4. Set the phyllo leaves flat on a tray. (The remaining ½ pound of dough can be refrozen in an airtight plastic bag.) Cover the phyllo leaves with wax paper topped by a dampened tea towel, to prevent them from drying out. Briefly, lift the towel and, with a sharp, pointed knife, cut a 2-inch wide strip lengthwise through the stack of leaves. Preheat oven to 425°F.

5. Remove one 2-inch-wide strip of phyllo from the tray, cover the rest, and set the strip flat in front of you on the counter. Brush the entire length of it with melted butter. Place 1 teaspoon of cheese mixture at one end (a). Now, fold the strip as if it were a flag, in a continuous series of triangles:

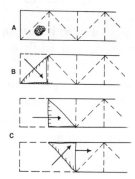

Fold over the end containing the cheese so the short strip end meets the side edge (b). Continue folding into triangles (c), as if folding a flag, to the end of the strip. Tuck under the loose end of the strip and set it, open end down, on a baking sheet. Leave a little space between pieces so they can rise. Brush the top of each triangle with melted butter. Repeat with all the remaining ingredients. (*Note:* You can also cut phyllo strips wider, say 4 or 5 inches, to fill with more cheese for larger, entrée-sized triangles.)

6. At this point the *tiropetes* can be frozen as described in *Advance preparation* above. To bake, set them in the center of the preheated oven for about 20 minutes, or until golden brown. Serve hot.

CHINESE PORK PASTRY TRIANGLES

This spicy stir/fried mixture of pork, water chestnuts, and ginger makes an excellent filling for phyllo pastry envelopes. Formed into bite-sized triangles, the effect is like a unique version of egg roll. At your next party, add this recipe to a selection of hot hors d'oeuvre and serve alongside one or two dipping sauces.

Advance preparation: Filling may be prepared ahead, as it should be refrigerated until cold, or overnight, before using. Phyllo leaves can be purchased frozen; thaw as described on page 98. Shaped triangles may be prepared and frozen; or they may be refrigerated until ready to fry (for no longer than 12 hours, or the pastry gets soggy). After frying, pastries have best texture and flavor if served hot, immediately. However, they can be fried, then reheated at 350°F for about 7 minutes, spread in a single layer on a baking sheet. They can also be fried a short time ahead and kept at room temperature until ready to serve without reheating.

Special equipment: Wok with wok spoon, or electric frying pan; slotted spoon; mixing bowl and spoon; paring knife; flat tray; paper towels; wax paper, one dampened tea towel; flat baking sheet or aluminum foil; sharp knife; pastry brush; optional: chinese strainer-spoon.

Frying time: 4 to 6 minutes, or until golden brown on both sides.
Quantity: 36 triangles, bite-sized; recipe can easily be doubled.

10 leaves phyllo pastry (use frozen phyllo,
thawed as directed or use fresh
strudel dough, page 91, cut as for
phyllo strips, below)
Egg glaze: *1 egg, beaten*
Cornstarch
Peanut oil for frying

Filling
½ *pound ground pork*
½ *cup water chestnuts, diced*
1 tablespoon ginger root, minced
⅓ *cup scallions, minced*
¼ *teaspoon salt*
½ *teaspoon each sugar, sesame oil,*
hot chili sesame oil
1 teaspoon each catsup, dry sherry
1 tablespoon each soy sauce, Hoisin sauce

DIPPING SAUCES

Hot Spicy Sauce
1 tablespoon soy sauce
2 tablespoons vinegar
2 teaspoons hot sesame chili oil

Apricot Sauce
4 tablespoons apricot preserves
¼ *teaspoon minced ginger root*
2 teaspoons soy sauce

1. Prepare filling first. In wok or electric skillet, heat about 2 tablespoons peanut oil. Add ground pork and cook over medium-high heat until color changes and meat is cooked through. Stir meat often as it cooks, to keep it broken into small bits. Add water chestnuts and ginger root and stir/fry (stir, lift and gently toss, keeping it in constant motion) for about 2 minutes. Spoon out excess oil.

Add scallions and all seasonings and sauces. Stir to blend, then place in a bowl, cover, and refrigerate until chilled, or overnight.

2. Set out phyllo leaves flat on a tray. (The remaining package of phyllo can be rewraped and frozen in an airtight plastic bag.) Cover phyllo leaves with wax paper topped by a dampened tea towel, to prevent leaves from drying out. Briefly, lift the towel and, using a sharp knife, cut a 4 inch wide strip lengthwise through the stack of leaves. Re-cover, leaving phyllo in place beneath towel. Cut additional 4-inch-wide strips as needed.

3. Set nearby a flat baking sheet or a sheet of aluminum foil with ½-inch lip folded up all around the edges; sprinkle this tray lightly with cornstarch, to receive the triangles when they are shaped. Also set nearby a small cup of peanut oil to brush on the phyllo, and a pastry brush.

4. Remove one 4-inch strip of phyllo (keeping the others covered), set it flat, and fold it in half lengthwise. Dip the pastry brush in oil, then brush it along the length of the strip. Place about 1 teaspoon of filling at one end of the strip. then fold the end over, so the short strip end meets the side edge, forming a right-angle triangle. Continue folding into triangles, as for a flag, to the end of the strip (see Greek Cheese Triangles illustrations, page 403). Tuck under the loose end of the strip, sealing it in place with a dab of beaten egg. Set the completed triangle on the baking sheet or foil. Keep the pastries from touching one another, so they do not stick together. When one tray is filled, prepare another.

5. To cook, heat a good quantity of peanut oil in a wok or electric skillet, over medium-high heat. The temperature should be about 375°F, or the temperature at which a small crust of bread dropped into the oil will rise surrounded by bubbles and brown crisp in 15 to 20 seconds. You will have to adjust the heat as you go along, because adding new triangles cools it off.

Deep-fry the pastries, about 3 or 4 at a time, until a rich gold color on one side; turn them over with a slotted spoon and fry the other side, then drain them on a double layer of paper towels. Serve warm or hot. To reheat, see *Advance preparation,* above.

6. If you wish dipping sauces, stir together ingredients and serve them in bowls, along with the triangles.

INDEX

ABOUT THE AUTHOR

Former food writer for the Gannett newspapers, Susan G. Purdy is the author of the acclaimed A Piece of Cake, *as well as five other cookbooks and over twenty-five books for young readers. She studied cooking in Paris at the Cordon Bleu and pastry at l'École de Cuisine La Varenne and at the Country Epicure's International Pastry Arts Center under Albert Kumin. A member of the International Association of Culinary Professionals, Mrs. Purdy teaches the art of pastry at cooking schools throughout New England. In addition, she writes on food and travel for a variety of national magazines. She lives with her husband, Geoffrey, and their daughter, Cassandra, in northwestern Connecticut.*

"Herman, dinner's served...
as soon as the smoke clears!"